The Unchanging God of Love

SECOND EDITION

D1523526

Michael J. Dodds, O.P.

The Unchanging God of Love

𝔇

Thomas Aquinas and Contemporary Theology

on Divine Immutability

SECOND EDITION

The Catholic University of America Press
Washington, D.C.

Second edition of Michael J. Dodds, O.P., *The Unchanging God of Love: A Study of the Teaching of St. Thomas Aquinas on Divine Immutability in View of Certain Contemporary Criticism of This Doctrine* (Fribourg: Editions Universitaires, 1986)

Library of Congress Cataloging-in-Publication Data
Dodds, Michael J.
The unchanging God of love : Thomas Aquinas and contemporary theology
on divine immutability / Michael J. Dodds. — 2nd ed.
p. cm.
Includes bibliographical references and index.
ISBN 978-0-8132-1539-6 (pbk.: alk. paper)   1. Thomas, Aquinas, Saint,
1225?–1274.   2. God (Christianity)—Immutability.   I. Title.
BT153.I47D64 2008
231´.4—dc22
2008021198

To My Family

Contents

Abbreviations

Abbreviations for the Works of Thomas Aquinas

Breve principium	*Breve principium de commendatione Sacrae Scripturae*
Cat. aur. in joann.	*Catena aurea in Joannem*
Cat. aur. in matt.	*Catena aurea in Matthaeum*
Comp.	*Compendium theologiae*
Contra doc. retra.	*Contra doctrinam retrahentium a religione*
Contra err. graec.	*Contra errores graecorum*
Contra impug.	*Contra impugnantes Dei cultum et religionem*
De aeter. mundi	*De aeternitate mundi*
De art. fid.	*De articulis fidei et ecclesiae sacramentis*
De car.	*De caritate*
De duobus praec.	*De duobus praeceptis caritatis*
De ente	*De ente at essentia*
De malo	*Quaestiones disputatae de malo*
De pot.	*Quaestiones disputatae de potentia*
De prin. nat.	*De principiis naturae*
De rat. fid.	*De rationibus fidei*
De sp. cr.	*Quaestio disputata de spiritualibus creaturis*
De sub. sep.	*De substantiis separatis*
De un. int.	*De unitate intellectus*
De unione verbi	*Quaestiones disputatae de unione verbi incarnati*

De ver.	*Quaestiones disputatae de veritate*
De virt.	*Quaestiones disputatae de virtutibus in communi*
Epis. ad bern.	*Epistola ad Bernardum abbatem Casinensem*
In de an.	*In Aristotelis librum De anima commentarium*
In de caelo.	*Commentarium in libros Aristotelis De caelo et mundo*
In de div. nom.	*In librum beati Dionysii De divinis nominibus expositio*
In de mem.	*In librum De memoria et reminiscentia commentarium*
In de sensu	*In librum De sensu et sensato commentarium*
In eth.	*Sententia libri Ethicorum*
In jer.	*In Jeremiam prophetam expositio*
In meta.	*In Metaphysicam Aristotelis commentaria*
In peri herm.	*Commentarium in Aristotelis libros Peri hermeneias*
In phys.	*In octo libros Physicorum Aristotelis expositio*
In psalmos	*In psalmos Davidis expositio*
ITOO	*Opera omnia ut sunt in Indice Thomistico*
Prin. biblicum	*Principium de commendatione et partitione Sacrae Scripturae*
Q. de an.	*Quaestio disputata de anima*
Quodl.	*Quaestiones quodlibetales*
Resp. ad venet.	*Responsio ad lectorem Venetum de 36 articulis*
Resp. ad ver.	*Responsio ad magistrum Ioannem de Vercellis de 108 articulis*
SCG	*Summa contra gentiles*
Sent.	*Scriptum super libros Sententiarum*
Sermo	*Sermo de omnibus sanctis*
ST	*Summa theologiae*
Super ad col.	*Super epistolam ad Colossenses lectura*
Super ad eph.	*Super epistolam ad Ephesios lectura*
Super ad gal.	*Super epistolam ad Galatas lectura*
Super ad hebr.	*Super epistolam ad Hebraeos lectura*
Super ad phil.	*Super epistolam ad Philippenses lectura*

Super ad rom.	*Super epistolam ad Romanos lectura*
Super de causis	*Super librum De causis expositio*
Super de trin.	*Expositio super librum Boethii De Trinitate*
Super decret.	*Expositio super primam et secundam decretalem*
Super ev. jo.	*Super evangelium S. Ioannis lectura*
Super ev. matt.	*Super evangelium S. Matthaei lectura*
Super I ad cor.	*Super primam epistolam ad Corinthios lectura*
Super I ad tim.	*Super primam epistolam ad Timotheum lectura*
Super II ad tim.	*Super secundam epistolam ad Timotheum lectura*
Super iob	*Expositio super Iob ad litteram*
Super is.	*Expositio super Isaiam ad litteram*
Super sym apos.	*Expositio super symbolo apostolorum*

Other Abbreviations

Denz.	*Enchiridion Symbolorum,* ed. H. Denzinger and Peter Hünermann
IPQ	*International Philosophical Quarterly*
MS	*Mediaeval Studies*
Meta.	Aristotle, *Metaphysics*
NS	*The New Scholasticism*
PACPA	*Proceedings of the American Catholic Philosophical Association*
PG	*Patrologiae Cursus Completus, series Graeca,* ed. J. P. Migne
Phys.	Aristotle, *Physics*
PL	*Patrologiae Cursus Completus, series Latina,* ed. J. P. Migne

Introduction

⌘

In the theology of St. Thomas Aquinas, the unchanging God revealed in Scripture, attested in the tradition of the Church, and established through philosophical argument is consistently identified as the one who "so loved the world that he gave his only Son" (Jn 3:16). The loving and provident God, the source of "every perfect gift," is also the immutable God "in whom there is no variation or shadow due to change."[1] In affirming divine immutability, Aquinas reflects the constant teaching of the Church, which from its earliest pronouncements always maintained that the God of love is unchanging.[2] He echoes voices of the past, such as St. Augustine, who prayed to the God who is "unchangeable and yet changing all things."[3] He anticipates voices of the future. St. Teresa of Avila, the sixteenth-century Spanish mystic and Doctor of the Church would speak of God as one who "does not change" and

---

1. Jas 1:17. The Revised Standard Version of the Bible (*The Holy Bible* [New York: Collins, 1973]) is used throughout this work, except in translations of passages quoted by Aquinas. Thomas often refers to Jas 1:17, finding in it an affirmation of divine immutability and providence: *Super ev. jo.* XVII, lect. 3 (§2213); *Super I ad tim.* I, lect. 1 (§6); *ST* III, 39, 6, ad 2; *Super ad rom.* I, lect. 4 (§71); *Super I ad cor.* I, lect. 1 (§9); *Super ad phil.* I, lect. 1 (§7); *Super ad hebr.* VI, lect. 1 (§289); *Super ev. jo.* I, lect. 14 (§269); *Super ev. matt.* III, lect. 2 (§300); XXV, lect. 2 (§2059); lect. 3 (§2094).

2. *Denz.* 126 (Nicea, 325); *Denz.* 197 (Toledo, 400); *Denz.* 300 (Chalcedon, 451); *Denz.* 501 (Lateran synod, 649); *Denz.* 683 (Leo IX, 1054); *Denz.* 800 (IV Lateran, 1215); *Denz.* 853 (II Lyons, 1274); *Denz.* 1330 (Florence, 1442); *Denz.* 2901 (Syllabus of modern errors, 1846); *Denz.* 3001, 3024 (Vatican I, 1870); and *Pastoral Constitution on the Church in the Modern World (Gaudium et spes)*, no. 10 in *The Documents of Vatican II*, ed. Austin Flannery (New York: Pillar Books, 1975).

3. Augustine, *The Confessions of St. Augustine*, trans. J. Ryan (Garden City, N.Y.: Doubleday, 1960), bk. I, chap. 4, 45.

"alone suffices."[4] Elizabeth of the Trinity, the French Carmelite contemplative of the last century, would pray to God as "my Unchanging One."[5] And
Sigrid Undset, the twentieth-century Norwegian novelist, would describe
herself as "a pilgrim of the absolute" in search of "that which in no way ever
changes."[6]

Such voices are now challenged by others who question whether an immutable God is truly a God of love. To a number of contemporary theologians and philosophers, it no longer seems the God "in whom there is no
variation or shadow due to change" can really be the "Father of lights," the
providential author of "every perfect gift." They are convinced that an unchanging God must be indifferent, uncaring, and remote from creation. They
therefore propose that the notion of divine immutability be radically modified or quietly abandoned. The theologian they most often single out in their
critique of divine immutability is Thomas Aquinas.[7] As Emilio Brito sums it
up, "Today the immutable God of Thomas Aquinas has bad press."[8]

How are we to respond to this "bad press" and evaluate arguments critical of Aquinas and the tradition he represents? If Aquinas is the theologian
of choice for those who find fault with divine immutability, we should at
least know what he says and, equally important, does not say on the topic.
Our examination of this thirteenth-century theologian may help us see how
a Doctor of the fifth century, a mystic of the sixteenth, and a novelist of the
twentieth can all affirm the Christian God as unchanging. It may also illumi-
nate the sources of difficulties many contemporary theologians encounter in
making a similar affirmation.

Our inquiry will begin on the level of words since problems with divine

4. "Dios no se muda . . . Sólo Dios basta" (St. Teresa of Avila, "Nada te turbe," in *Obras Completas*,
ed. Efren de la Madre de Dios and Otger Steggink [Madrid: Biblioteca de Autores Cristianos, 1967],
511). Translations throughout this work are those of the author unless otherwise indicated.

5. Elizabeth of the Trinity, "O My God, Trinity Whom I Adore," in *The Complete Works*, trans. Aletheia Kane (Washington, D.C.: ICS Publications, 1984), 1:183.

6. Sigrid Undset, *Etapper* (1929), 233, as quoted in Lars Roar Langslet, "La conversion de Sigrid
Undset," *Revue des sciences religieuses* 40 (1966): 240, 247, 249.

7. See, for example, Nicholas Wolterstorff's extensive review and critique of Aquinas's account of divine immutability in his article, "Suffering Love," in *Philosophy and the Christian Faith*, ed. Thomas V. Morris (Notre Dame, Ind.: University of Notre Dame Press, 1988), 196–237.

8. "Le Dieu immuable de Thomas d'Aquin a aujourd'hui mauvaise presse" (Emilio Brito, "Dieu en
mouvement: Thomas d'Aquin et Hegel," *Revue des sciences religieuses* 62 [1988]: 111).

immutability often start with the very word "immutable." Aquinas employs over thirty different words and expressions to signify immutability. He applies these to both God and creatures. Depending on the context, creaturely immutability may be a happy or unhappy condition. Since we know of God from creatures, we will best judge the appropriateness of calling God immutable if we have first seen the positive and negative connotations of creaturely immutability.

The texts of Aquinas provide a kind of laboratory for conducting this investigation. The *Index Thomisticus,* a printed and electronic concordance of all his works, will serve as our "microscope" to expose the ways he uses words for immutability.[9] The results of this research as regards creaturely immutability, presented in chapter 1, provide an overview of the positive and negative connotations of the notion.

Having seen how immutability is said of creatures, we will be ready to consider God's changelessness. Chapter 2 will look at Aquinas's arguments for divine immutability and their biblical, patristic, and philosophical sources, concluding with a reflection on the significance and appropriateness of calling God immutable. Since our investigation will also uncover a number of ways he attributes motion to God, chapter 3 will focus on the "motion of the motionless God."[10] Finally, chapter 4 will show how Aquinas's unchanging God is truly the God of love.

Throughout our discussion, we will address arguments of contemporary theologians who question divine immutability. There were many such thinkers at the time the first edition of this work appeared in 1986, and their number has not diminished. For some, it has become a basic theological as-

9. Robert Busa, ed., *Index Thomisticus: Sancti Thomae Aquinatis Operum Omnium Indices et Concordantiae* (Stuttgart: Frommann-Holzboog, 1975); idem, *Thomae Aquinatis Operum Omnium cum hypertextibus in CD-ROM,* 2nd ed. (Milano: Editoria Elettronica Editel, 1996). The following words were researched throughout Aquinas's works: *figo, firmitas, firma, firmus, fixio, immobilis, immobilitas, immobilitatio, immobilito, immutabilis, immutabilitas, impassibilis, impassibilitas, inalterabilis, incommutabilis, incommutabilitas, inconversibilis, inconvertibilis, indeclinabilis, indeclinabilitas, indefectibilis, indeficiens, indeficientia, indemutabilis, inflexibilis, inflexibilitas, intransmutabilis, intransmutabilitas, invariabilis, invariabilitas.* The following common phrases for the notion of immutability, which are listed separately in the printed edition of the *Index Thomisticus,* were also researched: *"moveo + immobilis,"* and *"moveo + non + moveo," "sine + motu."* The 12,366 references to *"moveo"* and the 13,504 references to *"motus"* were likewise examined in the printed edition. In all, about 3,600 references were individually investigated in the works of Aquinas.

10. *In de div. nom.* IX, lect. 4 (§841).

sumption that the God of Christian faith must be changeable or passible.[11] Not only in process theology, but in such diverse areas of inquiry as liberation theology, Open Theism, feminist theology, and the science-religion dialogue, many scholars have included God's changeableness among the basic tenets of their theology.[12] Followers of Aquinas have also had a good deal to say about divine immutability and related themes in the intervening years.[13] Some evangelical theologians have also taken up the challenge of defending the traditional doctrine of divine immutability.[14] The present edition of this work has profited from the new voices that have emerged both defending and challenging the notion of divine immutability. It is hoped that this study will help us to affirm with Aquinas that the unchanging God is the providential God of love, that "every good endowment and every perfect gift is from above, coming down from the Father of lights in whom there is no variation or shadow due to change" (Jas 1:17).

11. Over twenty years ago, Ronald Goetz observed, "The age-old dogma that God is impassible and immutable, incapable of suffering, is for many no longer tenable. The ancient theopaschite heresy that God suffers has, in fact, become the new orthodoxy" ("The Suffering God: The Rise of a New Orthodoxy," *Christian Century* 103 [1986]: 385). Today, Gloria L. Schaab declares: "I join my voice with those who say that understandings of God as immutable, impassible, and unlimited in power are no longer viable in a cosmos beset by suffering and death" ("The Creative Suffering of the Triune God: An Evolutionary Panentheistic Paradigm," *Theology and Science* 5 [2007]: 290).

12. Among liberation theologians, see Jon Sobrino, *Jesus the Liberator: A Historical-Theological Reading of Jesus of Nazareth* (Maryknoll, N.Y.: Orbis Books, 1993), 240–246, and Leonardo Boff, *Passion of Christ, Passion of the World* (Maryknoll, N.Y.: Orbis Books, 1987), 114–115. Feminist theologian Elizabeth Johnson carefully notes that, although the affirmation of divine suffering is a theologically preferable way of speaking about God, "[i]n no way is this theological speech intended to yield a literal description of God" (*She Who Is: The Mystery of God in a Feminist Theological Discourse* [New York: Crossroad, 1992], 271). At the same time, she seems to endorse the views of other theologians who see divine suffering not only as a linguistic preference but as an ontological truth (246–272). Among proponents of Open Theism, see Clark H. Pinnock, *Most Moved Mover: A Theology of God's Openness* (Grand Rapids, Mich.: Baker Books, 2001). Regarding figures in the science and religion dialogue, see Ian Barbour, *Religion and Science: Historical and Contemporary Issues* (San Francisco: HarperSanFrancisco, 1997), 322–332; Arthur Peacocke, *Theology for a Scientific Age: Being and Becoming— Natural, Divine, and Human* (Minneapolis, Minn.: Fortress Press, 1993), 113–134; and Gloria L. Schaab, *Creative Suffering of the Triune God: An Evolutionary Theology* (New York: Oxford University Press, 2007), 15, 141–168.

13. See, for example, Mario Enrique Sacchi, "El Dios inmutable de la filosofía perenne y de la fe Católica," *Doctor Communis* 42 (1989): 243–273; Brian Davies, "The Action of God," *New Blackfriars* 75 (1994): 76–84; *idem, An Introduction to the Philosophy of Religion*, (Oxford: Oxford University Press, 1993), 141–167; and Thomas G. Weinandy, *Does God Suffer?* (Notre Dame, Ind.: University of Notre Dame Press, 2000).

14. See Douglas S. Huffman and Eric L. Johnson, eds., *God under Fire: Modern Scholarship Reinvents God* (Grand Rapids, Mich.: Zondervan, 2002).

CHAPTER ONE

The Immutability of Creatures

𝕯

In this chapter, we will track down the thirty-some words and expressions Aquinas uses for creaturely immutability and identify their positive and negative connotations. To him the whole spectrum of creation is marked by change and changelessness. In tracing creaturely immutability, we will have to wend our way through technical thickets of Thomas's metaphysics, cosmology, psychology, and even angelology—since all created things, from oysters to angels, get labeled as immutable in some way or other.[1] Our aim is not to explain these subjects in depth, only to see how immutability is involved in each. Once we've waded through these topics, we will be able to give a synthetic account of the positive and negative aspects of creaturely immutability. We will then be ready to look at the plusses and minuses of divine immutability.

THE SPECTRUM OF CREATURELY IMMUTABILITY

Human Beings

Change and changelessness are applied to humans in many ways. Human nature is changeable in some ways and unchangeable in others. "Al-

---

1. See Michael J. Dodds, "Of Angels, Oysters and an Unchanging God: Aquinas on Divine Immutability," *Listening* 30 (1995): 35–49.

though nature, considered independently, is unchangeable (*immobilis*), nevertheless, considered according to its being, it is necessary that it change accidentally as the individual person changes."[2] Humans are both spiritual and physical and are marked by motion and immobility in each aspect. Physically, mobility is a plus and immobility a minus. Being mobile is a sign of life; being "immobile (*immobile*)," a mark of death.[3] In the realm of human emotion, immobility may be good or bad. The immobility of love is a sign of its preeminence. Love is the first, strongest, and most perfect of affections precisely because it is from love as "an immovable first principle (*primo immobili quieto*)" that all other affections proceed.[4] The bodily immutability brought on by excess anger, fear, or sorrow, however, is not desirable and may be fatal, leading to "taciturnity, immobility (*immobilitas*) of the outward members and sometimes even death."[5] If excess emotion is bad, so is deficient passion, since it may signal the indifference or "impassibility (*impassibilitas*)" of the vice of "insensibility (*insensibilitas*)."[6] Spiritually, the soul is "immutable (*immutabile*)" in its being and "unfailing (*indeficientem*)" in its life.[7] As the source of life and motion for the body, it acts as an "unmoved mover (*movens non motum*)."[8]

Human intellectual life is marked by motion and immutability. Our intellect involves mobility since it "reaches to the understanding of truth by arguing, with a certain amount of discourse and movement." It is consequently imperfect since "it does not understand everything," and since "in those things it does understand, it passes from potency to act." Recognizing these limitations, Aquinas argues "there must be a higher intellect by which the soul is helped to understand" since "what is such by participation and what is movable and what is imperfect always requires the pre-existence of something essentially such, immovable (*immobile*), and perfect."[9] This higher in-

---

2. *Sent.* II, 31, 1, 1, ad 1. Cf.: IV, 26, 1, 1, ad 3; *ST* II-II, 57, 2, ad 1; Q.184, 4, ad 1; *In eth.* V, lect. 12 (line 156 c. and line 198 c.).

3. *SCG* III, c.139.17 (§3144).

4. *Sent.* III, 27, 1, 3, co. Cf.: *Sent.* III, 27, 1, 3, ad 1; *ST* I-II, 25, 2.

5. *ST* I-II, 48, 4, ad 3. Cf.: *Super is.* VIII, v.12 (line 368 c.); *ST* I-II, 39, 3, ad 1; Q.37, 2; Q.35, 8, co.; *Sent.* III, 26, 1, 3, co.

6. *ST* II-II, 142, 1.   7. *De ver.* Q.22, 6, ad 1. Cf.: *De sp. cr.* a.2, sc.

8. *SCG* II, c.65.5 (§1430).   9. *ST* I, 79, 4, co. Cf.: *De sp. cr.* a.10, co.

tellect is identified as God. The human intellect, to the extent that it participates that superior intellect, is "impassible (*impassibilis*)."[10]

Our intellectual faculty may be distinguished into the "possible intellect,"
which knows the forms of sensible things immaterially, and the "agent intellect," which makes those forms actually intelligible by abstracting them from
their material conditions in things.[11] The forms or species are abstracted by
the agent intellect and then received by the possible intellect. As a receiver, it
has a kind of "passibility (*passio*)" and so is said "to suffer (*pati*)."[12] In its substance, however, it is "immutable (*immutabilis*)." Since its substance is immutable and since "what is received into something is in it according to the mode
of the receiver," the intelligible species are received into the possible intellect
"immovably (*immobiliter*)."[13] The universal concept that the possible intellect
then produces is also "immobile (*immobile*)," allowing us to "know the truth
about changeable things (*mutabilibus*) unchangingly (*immutabiliter*)."[14]

The characteristic acts of the intellect are understanding, judging, and
reasoning. While understanding happens "without motion (*sine motu*)," reasoning entails movement and is compared to understanding "as movement
is to rest."[15] Still, reasoning begins with first principles that are "immovable
(*immobiles*)" and "unchangeable (*incommutabiles*)," being "a certain likeness of
uncreated truth." So "when we judge about other things through them, we
do this through unchangeable (*incommutabiles*) principles or through uncreated truth."[16]

Aquinas classifies the speculative sciences according to their varying degrees of abstraction from matter and motion.[17] Physics or natural philosophy is an "immovable (*immobilem*)" science of movable things.[18] It gives us
"knowledge of mutable and material things existing outside the soul through
universals which are immobile (*immobiles*) and are considered without par-

---

10. *ST* I, 79, 4, co.; 5, ad 1; *SCG* II, c.78.8 (§1592).

11. *ST* I, 79, 3.

12. *In de an.* III, lect. 7 (§676); *De un. int.* c.1, line 333 c.

13. *Super I ad Cor.* XIII, lect. 3 (§791); *Quodl.* III, Q.9, a.1 (21), co.; *ST* I, 79, 6, co.; *ST* I, 84, 1, co.

14. *ST* I, 84, 6, ad 1; Q.86, 1, co. Cf.: *Super de trin.* Q.5, 2, ad 4; *In eth.* VI, lect. 1 (line 194 c.).

15. *Sent.* II, 12, 1, 5, *div. text.*; *ST* I, 79, 8, co. Cf.: Q.58, 3, co.

16. *De ver.* Q.10, 6, ad 6. Cf.: *In eth.* VI, lect. 9 (line 159 c.); *Quodl.* X, Q.4, a.1 (7), co.

17. *Super de trin.* Q.5, 1, co. Cf.: *In phys.* II, lect. 11.3 (§243).

18. *ST* I, 84, 1, ad 3.

ticular matter."[19] Mathematics yields mathematical objects that are "immobile (*immobilia*)" insofar as they are considered apart from motion, though they really exist only in material or mobile things.[20] Metaphysics allows us to study entities existing without matter and motion. The contemplation of the "immutable (*immutabiles*)" objects of this science is one of the greatest human pleasures.[21]

The human will, like the intellect, is characterized by change and changelessness. As the intellect adheres necessarily to unchangeable first principles, the will adheres "naturally and immovably (*immobiliter*)" to its last end of happiness.[22] The will is directed by a knowledge of the good in general, which it possesses "naturally and invariably (*immutabiliter*) and without error."[23] The natural habit of the first principles of action (synderesis), which warns against evil and inclines to good, is a "permanent principle which has unwavering (*immutabilem*) integrity."[24] In other ways the will is changeable. As an appetitive power, it is moved by the things it apprehends. Each of them, in relation to the will, is called an "unmoved mover (*movens non motum*)," while the will is a "moved mover (*movens motum*)."[25]

As regards free choice, the will is "changeable (*vertibile*) by its very nature."[26] This changeability is good: "Although a creature would be better if it adhered unchangeably (*immobiliter*) to God, nevertheless that one also is good which can adhere to God or not adhere."[27] The foundation of the will's changeable freedom is its unchanging determination to its last end: "Because everything mobile is reduced to what is immobile (*immobile*) as its principle, and everything undetermined to what is determined, that to which the will is determined must be the principle of tending to the things to which it is not determined; and this is the last end."[28] Humans in this life are not

---

19. *Super de trin.* Q.5, 2, co.
20. *In meta.* VI, lect. 1.18 (§1161). Cf.: *Super de trin.* Q.5, a.3, co.; *In phys.* II, lect. 3.7 (§163).
21. *In eth.* X, lect. 10 (line 124 c.). Cf.: *ST* II-II, 180, 8, co.
22. *ST* I, 82, 1, co.
23. *De ver.* Q.24, 8, co. Here the Mandonnet edition (Paris: Lethielleux, 1925) is used. This agrees with the Vivès edition (Paris, 1889), the Marietti edition (Turin, 1953), and ITOO. The Leonine edition (1976) changes "*immutabiliter*" to "*universaliter*" without explanatory note.
24. *De ver.* Q.16, 2, co. Cf.: *ST* I, 79, 12, ad 3.   25. *ST* I, 80, 2, co. Cf.: *De ver.* Q.25, 1, co.
26. *ST* II-II, 137, 4, co.   27. *De ver.* Q.24, 1, ad 16.
28. *De ver.* Q.22, 6, co.

marked by "immutability (*immobilitas*)" of will, but by "mutability (*mutabilitas*) in body and soul."[29] The virtuous person does not necessarily practice virtue "unchangingly (*immobiliter*),"[30] and the vicious one is not "immovable (*immobilem*)" in the tendency to evil.[31]

To remain virtuous, humans must develop good habits and persevere in them "immovably (*immobiliter*)."[32] A habit becomes a virtue only when possessed "firmly (*firme*)" and "immutably (*immutabiliter*)."[33] Aquinas finds Aristotle and St. Paul in agreement on this point: "Among the various conditions of a good will, one is that the will be firm (*firma*) and steadfast (*stabilis*) . . . Whence the Apostle admonishes: 'Be steadfast (*stabiles*) and immovable (*immobiles*).' And according to the Philosopher, it is required for virtue that one act firmly (*firmiter*) and immovably (*immobiliter*)."[34]

The theological virtues provide an example of such immovability. By faith, we embrace the "never-changing truth (*semper eodem modo se habentem veritatem*)" of divine knowledge and so are "freed from the instability and multiplicity of error."[35] We enjoy the "immutability (*immobilitatem*)" of the faith of the elect who stand "immovably (*immobiliter*)" and are "firmly (*firmiter*)" established in the truth.[36] In hope, we find a "most steadfast (*firmissimum*)" consolation, which is associated with two "immutable (*immobiles*)" things: "God, who promises and who does not lie" and "the oath in which the confirmation of the truth is greater."[37] As an anchor "immobilizes (*immobilitat*)" a ship, hope "firmly fastens (*firmat*) the soul to God in this world, which is a kind of sea."[38] Finally, charity unites us with God and "rests immovably (*sistat*)" in him.[39] Charity is the root of all virtues since virtue arises from a desire for the "immutable (*incommutabilis*)" good, and charity is that very desire for or love of God.[40]

---

29. *SCG* IV, c.71.4 (§4058); *Comp.* I, c.145.   30. *ST* II-II, 137, 4, ad 1.

31. *De ver.* Q.24, 12, co.; *SCG* IV, c.71.4 (§4058).

32. *In eth.* II, lect. 4 (line 85 c.); *Super ad col.* I, lect. 3 (§22).

33. *De ver.* Q.27, 5, ad 11. Cf.: *ST* II-II, 137, 1, ad 3.

34. *Contra doc. retra.* c.12 (line 25 c.); *ST* I-II, 100, 9, co. Cf.: II-II, 58, 1, co.; *Sent.* II, 38, 1, 5, ad 5; *In eth.* 11, lect. 4 (line 74 c.).

35. *De ver.* Q.14, 8, co.

36. *Super II ad tim.* II, lect. 3 (§69–70); *In de div. nom.* VII, lect. 5 (§737).

37. *Super ad hebr.* VI, lect. 4 (§324).   38. Ibid. (§325).

39. *ST* II-II, 23, 3, co.; 6, co.   40. *ST* I-II, 84, 1, ad 1.

If virtue consists in being in some way "immutably fastened (*fixus*)" to
God, vice is found in those who, lacking this attachment, seek their happiness in other things.[41] Sin is defined as a turning from the "immutable (*in-
commutabili*) good to some changeable good."[42] It is the mark of Christian
maturity to abandon the instability of the child who "is never fixed (*fixus*) or
determined in anything," and to become firm in faith.[43] Such stability does
not imply apathy or insensitivity. Following Aristotle, Aquinas rejects the
opinion of the Stoics that virtues are "certain apathetic states (*impassibilitates
quasdam*)."[44] Inordinate impassibility, like inordinate passion, is a vice: "As
the intemperate man abounds in his quest for pleasures, so the insensible
(*insensibilis*) man—his counterpart—is deficient in the same affairs. . . . But
one following a middle course in these matters is temperate."[45] The "immobility" of virtue does not denote imprisonment in apathy but the freedom
of the children of God: "Paul induces to good when he says, 'Stand fast.' As
if to say: Since you have been set free from the bondage of the Law through
Christ, stand fast and, with your faith firm (*firma*) and feet planted (*fixo*),
persevere in freedom. When he says, 'Stand fast,' he exhorts them to recti-
tude. . . . Likewise he exhorts them to be firm: 'Therefore, be steadfast and
unmovable (*immobiles*).'"[46]

The virtuous cannot remain unchangeably upright through human power alone. Every creature, since it is made from nothing, is changeable. And
whatever is changeable in itself "needs the help of an immovable mover
(*moventis immobilis*) so that it may be fixed on one objective." The human being who is changeable in the choice of good or evil "needs divine help in order to continue immovably (*immobiliter*) in the good."[47] This aid is found in

41. *Contra impug.* cap.10, ad 4 (line 121 c.); *Super iob* IX, v.31 (line 685 c.).

42. *ST* II-II, 20, 1, ad 1.

43. *Super ad eph.* IV, lect. 5 (§219).

44. *De malo* Q.12, 1, ad 13. Cf.: *In phys.* VII, lect. 6.3 (§921); *ST* I-II, 59, 2, ad 1; *In eth.* II, lect. 3 (line 116 c.); *Sent.* IV, 14, 1, 1, qc.2, ad 3.

45. *In eth.* VII, lect. 7 (line 88 c.). Cf.: *ST* II-II, 142, a.1. The word *"impassibilitas"* has two connotations. One, the freedom from suffering of the saints, is to be desired. The other, the apathy by which the
"insensible" avoid suffering, is to be shunned. Cf.: Ludwig Schütz, *Thomas-Lexikon* (Paderborn: F. Schöningh, 1895), 372.

46. *Super ad gal.* V, lect. 1 (§277).

47. *SCG* III, c.155.2 (§3281). Cf.: 155.4 (§3283); *De ver.* Q.24, 1, ad 16); *De pot.* Q.1, 2, ad 4; *Resp. ad
ver.*, art.18 (line 294 c.).

grace, which "draws free choice to the character (*rationem*) of its own invariability (*immutabilitatis*), joining it to God."[48] Given our changeable human will, however, even one who has received grace does not necessarily abide "unchangeably (*immobiliter*)" in good.[49] Only by a special gift of God is one able to remain steadfast in grace until death.[50]

On the social level, some human institutions are characterized by immutability. Perfect friendship, for instance, is "of itself unchangeable (*intransmutabilis*)."[51] Civil happiness does not possess an unqualified "invariability (*immutabilitatem*)," but is called "unvarying (*immutabilis*)" in that it is not easily changed.[52] In the area of law, Aquinas makes a number of distinctions. The eternal law, which is the design (*ratio*) of divine wisdom as moving all things to their due end, is itself "unchangeable truth (*veritas incommutabilis*)."[53] Natural law, which is the participation of the eternal law in the rational creature, "is altogether immutable (*immutabilis*) in its first principles." This law, however, may be changed by addition (when it is supplemented by divine and human laws), and it may be changed by subtraction in its secondary principles "in some particular cases of rare occurrence."[54] The commandments of the divine law (especially the Decalogue) are "unchangeable (*immutabilia*)" with respect to the principles of justice they embody. As applied to individual actions (in determining for instance, whether or not a particular action should be considered murder), they admit of change, sometimes by divine authority alone, and sometimes also by human authority.[55] Human laws are changeable since human reason is changeable and imperfect.[56]

In their original state of innocence, humans were in some ways "impassible (*impassibilis*)." Aquinas explains that in the proper sense of the word "passion (*passio*)" refers to what a thing is said "to suffer (*pati*)" when it is changed from its natural disposition. In this sense, human beings were "im-

48. *De ver.* Q.24, 8, ad 6.
49. *ST* II-II, 137, 4, co.
50. *ST* I-II, 109, 10, co.; II-II, 137, 4, co.; *Super iob* IV, v.18 (line 456 c.).
51. *In eth.* VIII, lect. 4 (line 86 c.); lect. 6 (line 194 c.).
52. *De ver.* Q.24, 7, ad 10.   53. *ST* I-II, 93, 2, co.; a.1, co.
54. *ST* I-II, 94, 5, co. Cf.: Q.91, 2, co.   55. *ST* I-II, 100, 8, ad 3.
56. *ST* I-II, 97, 1, ad 1. Cf.: ad 2; Q.90, 4, co.; Q.91, 3, co.

passible (*impassibilis*) both in soul and in body" since they could prevent both "suffering (*passionem*)" and death so long as they refrained from sin.[57] In a more general sense, "passion (*passio*)" refers to any sort of change, including those changes that are part of the "perfecting process" of nature, such as understanding and sensation. In this sense, humans were "passible (*passibilis*) both in body and soul."[58] Such possibility, however, might better be called perfectibility since it is not a source of "suffering (*passum*)," but of becoming "perfected (*perfectum*)." All beings are passible in this sense, except the one who is completely perfect or "pure act, namely God."[59]

Aquinas argues that in the life to come humans will enjoy a condition free from change (*statum immutabilem*).[60] They presently experience a natural desire for lasting happiness, which the vicissitudes of this life cannot satisfy: "Unless the human attains unmoving (*immobilem*) stability along with happiness, he is not happy, for his natural desire is not yet at rest."[61] Indeed, the very notion of happiness implies a certain "immovability (*immobilitas*)."[62] In presenting his arguments about the next life, Thomas recognizes that change is often a source of enjoyment for us now. That fact, however, merely indicates the present imperfection of our human nature, which needs change "because it is neither simple nor completely good, for motion is the act of what is imperfect."[63] Our imperfect and changeable nature makes change a source of pleasure for us. We like change because what is suitable to us at one time does not suit us at another, as sitting close by the fire is enjoyable, but only until we feel sufficiently warmed.[64] Similarly we may find joy in contemplation since it delights the intellect, but not an unbroken diet of it since it neglects the imagination.[65] As regards knowledge, change is desirable because we want to know things completely and can sometimes do this only if the thing changes "so that one part may pass and another suc-

57. *ST* I, 97, 2, co. Cf.: II-II, 164, 1, co.; *Sent.* II, 19, 1, 4, co.

58. *ST* I, 97, 2, co. Cf.: ad 4; *De ver.* Q.18, 6, ad 7.

59. *Sent.* II, 19, 1, 3, co.

60. *ST* III, 59, 5, ad 3. Cf.: ad 1; I-II, 102, 4, ad 2; *De ver.* Q.29, 6, ad 5; *In de div. nom.* I, lect. 1 (§39); *Comp.* I, c.150; c.174; *Super ev. Jo.* X, lect. 5 (§1449).

61. *SCG* III, c.48.3 (§2248).

62. *De ver.* Q.24, 8, co.; *Sent.* II, 7, 1, 1, sc 1; IV, 49, 1, 1, qc.4, co.; *Super ad hebr.* VI, lect. 4 (§325).

63. *In eth.* VII, lect. 14 (line 286 c.).   64. *ST* I-II, 32, 2, co.

65. *In eth.* VII, lect. 14 (line 245 c.).

ceed and thus the whole be perceived."[66] Because we are not yet perfect and we achieve perfection through change, we find change itself pleasurable. For although in changing we do not have perfectly what we are seeking, we do have the beginnings of it, "and in this respect motion itself has something of pleasure."[67]

In the next life we will attain our ultimate perfection and find happiness not in change but in a good that is "altogether unchangeable (*omnino intransmutabile*)," the goodness of God.[68] Possessing that good, we will enjoy complete immutability of mind and will. The restless inquiry of our intellect will cease when it attains the first cause in whom all things are known. The will's hunger for the good will be satisfied when it possesses the ultimate good. "Thus it is clear that man's ultimate fulfillment consists in perfect rest (*perfecta quietatione*) or immovability (*immobilitate*) both with respect to his intellect and with respect to his will."[69]

If the eternal reward of the just is marked by immutability, so is the eternal punishment of the wicked. The will is changeable only as long as soul and body are united in this life. Separated from the body at death, the will becomes "immovable (*immobilis*)" with regard to its desire for the ultimate end.[70] Then the just will cleave "unchangeably (*immobiliter*)" to God as the good that they have chosen in this life, and the wicked will cleave "unchangeably (*immobiliter*) to the end they have chosen."[71] The just will enjoy the dynamic changelessness of ultimate fulfillment, but the wicked will suffer the frozen immobility of eternal loss.

When the soul is reunited to the body in the resurrection, the "immutability (*immobilitatem*)" of the will shall remain.[72] The wicked will receive bodies "capable of suffering (*passibilia*)," and the resurrection will play a part in their punishment. The just will receive bodies "incapable of suffering (*impassibilia*)," and the resurrection will be part of their reward.[73] Since the soul is

---

66. Ibid. 67. *ST* I-II, 32, 2, ad 1.
68. *ST* I-II, 31, 2, co.
69. *Comp.* I, c. 149. Cf.: *SCG* III, c.62.10–11 (§2373–74); IV, c.92; *Comp.* c.174.
70. *SCG* IV, c.95.5 (4276). Cf.: *De rat. fid.* c.5 (line 78 c.).
71. *SCG* IV, c.93.5 (4270).
72. *SCG* IV, c.95.9 (§4280).
73. *SCG* IV, c.96.1 (§4281). Cf.: *Comp.* I, c.176; *ST* I, 97, 3, co.; *Sent.* IV, 44, 2, 1, qc.1, sc 1; *De art. fid.* 11 (line 395 c.); *Super sym apos.* ar. 11.

naturally united to the body, it cannot enjoy "perfect rest (*perfecta quietatio voluntatis*)" until it is reunited to the body. Resurrection is therefore necessary for the just if they are to enjoy "complete immovability of will (*omnimoda immobilitas voluntatis*)."[74]

The bodily impassibility of the saints will exclude only what is harmful.[75] The receptivity essential to sense knowledge will not be impeded, and through their senses "their vision will be refreshed by the beauty of God's creation."[76] Since nothing will then be harmful to them, they will experience only the passions that regard the good, such as love and joy, and not those that regard evil, such as sadness, fear, or anger.[77] For the saints, immutability will open a way to joy unattainable in this present life:

Beatitude cannot calm our human longing unless it is stable. For the more we love the good things that we have, the more we suffer at the thought of losing them. Thus the Philosopher says that the chameleon, which changes its color under our glance, is not to be considered happy. Rather beatitude must be immutable (*immutabilem*). But that is not found in this life where both external things and the human body itself are subject to diverse changes of fortune. So we can say from experience that stability is not to be found in this life. "Never does man remain in the same state" (Job 14:2). "He busies himself with the extremes of joy and sorrow" (Prov. 15:13).[78]

For Thomas, as for Augustine, "true immortality is true immutability (*immutabilitas*)."[79] And the promise of such immutability gives rise to reverence and thanks:

[St. Paul] concludes that since unchangeable (*immobilia*) good things are promised to us in the New Testament, we ought to serve Christ who promises them in fear and reverence. . . . Because God promises us an unchangeable (*immobilia*) heaven and earth (through which the unchangeable (*immobilia*) and eternal future good things are represented), "we possess," that is we render "grace," that is, thanksgiving: "I give thanks to God for his inexpressible gift" (2 Cor. 9:15).[80]

---

74. *Comp.* I, c.151.   75. *Sent.* IV, 44, 2, 1, qc.1, co.
76. *SCG* IV, c.86.4 (§4221); *Sent.* IV, 44, 2, 3, qc.2, co. Cf.: ad 3.
77. *De ver.* Q.26, 8, co.
78. *Sermo de omnibus sanctis*, pp. 89–90. Cf.: *Sent.* II, 7, 1, 1, sc 1; *In eth.* I, lect. 15 (line 140 c.).
79. *Q. de an.* a.14, ad 3.   80. *Super ad hebr.* XII, lect. 5 (§722–23).

Inanimate Things

The same word that describes the "unchangeable (*immobilia*)" treasures of heaven also characterizes more humble "immovable (*immobilia*)" things such as "stones and the like."[81] Its connotations are far less positive when applied to the lower reaches of creation.[82] Lacking the perfection of self-motion of living things, inanimate objects "such as stones and wood" are called "dead" or "lacking life." Though some may be called "alive" metaphorically, others are just plain dead: "Waters streaming out of the earth by the force of their motion are called 'living,' while immobile (*immobiles*) waters gathered together in ponds are called 'dead waters.'"[83]

Living Things

The mark of living things is to "move themselves by some kind of motion."[84] If these are ranked by the quality of their motion, plants end up on the lowest rung. Though capable of nourishment, growth, and generation, they remain "immovably (*immobiliter*) fixed to the earth." They lack sensation and local motion "by which the animate and the inanimate are chiefly discernible."[85] On the next rung, we find animals such as oysters that have a form of life "scarcely superior to plants." Though they enjoy the sense of touch, they are locally "immobile (*immobilia*)."[86] Animals that can move from place to place (*animalia progressiva*) are more perfect than these "immovable animals (*animalia immobilia*)."[87] They have not only all five senses and the power of local motion, but also a higher capacity for knowledge. "Imperfect or immovable animals (*animalia imperfecta idest immobilia*)" can recognize what is necessary for them when it is offered and so are better off than plants, which have no knowledge. Perfect animals are better still since by their imagination they can know things not present and by their estimative power they can recognize danger and perform other instinctive tasks. In

81. *SCG* II, c.16.4 (§935).   82. *SCG* IV, c.11.2 (§3462); I, c.97.4 (§814).
83. *Sent.* III, 35, 1, 1, co. Cf.: *SCG* I, c.97.3 (§813); *ST* I, 18, 1, ad 3.
84. *ST* I, 18, 1, co.
85. *ST* I, 69, 2, ad 1. Cf.: Q.18, 2, ad 1.
86. *SCG* II, c.68.6 (§1453). Cf.: *Q. de an.* a.7, co.; *In de mem.* lect. 1.1; *In eth.* I, lect. 20 (line 23 c.).
87. *SCG* II, c.95.2 (§1807).

these ways, their knowledge resembles intellectual cognition, which is not determined to the here and now.[88]

Though "immovable (*immobilia*)" animals are called imperfect in relation to higher animals, in their own species they are not "defective (*orbata*)" but "perfect" since they are capable of proper life functions such as generation and growth. Since their local immobility is in accordance with their nature, they do not seem "monstrosities (*monstra*)."[89] Higher animals, on the other hand, do look like monsters if they lack the freedom of motion that should be theirs. Aquinas gives the example of Behemoth, conceived as an elephant whose "inflexible (*inflexibiles*)" members suggest the "obstinacy and cruelty of the devil."[90]

Living things acquire their perfection through motion and cannot exist "without motion (*sine motu*)." A plant dies without the activity of nourishment, and an animal dies without the movement of the heart.[91] Through motion, they mirror the goodness of the immutable God: "Simply speaking, something is most conformed to God when it has whatever the condition of its nature requires, because it then best imitates the divine perfection. Thus, the animal heart is more conformed to the immovable God (*Deo immobili*) when it is moved than when it ceases from motion, because the perfection of the heart lies in being moved, and its cessation is its destruction."[92]

Cosmological Principles

The most fundamental, intrinsic principles of Aquinas's cosmology are substantial form and primary matter. They explain substantial change or generation, which is the most basic kind of change, the transformation of one substance into another (e.g., of wood into ash). As the primary principles of change, substantial form and primary matter are themselves unchangeable. Primary matter, the subject that endures through any substantial change, is itself nothing more than pure potency, the mere "possibility

---

88. *In de sensu* lect. 2.6 (§23). Cf.: *ST* I, 78, 1, ad 4; a.4, co.; *De ver.* Q.25, 2, co.

89. *In de an.* III, lect. 14 (§811).

90. *Super iob*, XL, v.13 (lines 371–85).

91. *De pot.* Q.5, 9, co. Cf.: *ST* I, 18, 2, co.; *De ver.* Q.15, 1, co. Cf.: Q.8, 3, ad 12; *ST* I, 77, 2, co.; II-II, 2, 3, co.; *SCG* III, c.19.5 (§2008); c.20–21.

92. *Sent.* IV, 43, 1, 1, qc.1, ad 4.

of being." Substantial form is a principle of actuality, which determines the potentiality of primary matter to exist as one kind of substance or another. Aquinas follows Aristotle's arguments to show that these principles are in themselves immutable:

[Aristotle] shows that this conclusion is untenable, namely, that nothing is eternal and immobile (*sempiternum et immobile*). He does this first with respect to matter; and second, with respect to form. Accordingly, he says first that if nothing is eternal, it is impossible for anything to be generated. He proves this as follows. In every instance of generation, there must be something which comes to be and something from which it comes to be. Therefore, if that from which it comes to be is itself generated, it must be generated from something. Hence there must either be an infinite regress in material principles or the process must stop with some first thing which is a first material principle that is ungenerated. . . . Now if the process were to go on to infinity, generation could never be completed, because what is infinite cannot be traversed. Therefore it is necessary to hold either that there is some material principle which is ungenerated, or that it is impossible for any generation to take place.[93]

Primary matter is this "ungenerated and incorruptible (*ingenita et incorruptibilis*)" principle, which in itself is "altogether unchangeable (*omnino intransmutabilis*)."[94] If primary matter, as the subject of substantial change, is ungenerated, so is substantial form, as the terminus of such change, the principle in which the change ceases with the instantiation of the new substance. There cannot be an infinite series of generated forms in any single act of generation. Otherwise the process of generation would never reach its terminus, and nothing would be generated. So there must be some form as the terminus of generation that is not itself as such generated.[95] This is the substantial form. It is not itself generated, but comes to be incidentally (*per accidens*) in the generation of that which is properly speaking generated, namely, the composite.[96]

Though primary matter and substantial form are not in themselves gen-

93. *In meta.* III, lect. 9 (§450). Cf.: *In phys.* I, lect. 15.11.

94. *In phys.* I, lect. 15.11 (§139); *ST* I, 92, 3, ad 1.

95. *In meta.* III, lect. 9 (§451–52). Cf.: Ibid., XII, lect. 3 (§2442–43).

96. *In meta.* VII, lect. 7 (§1417–20). Cf.: *ST* I, 65, 4, co.; *In meta.* VII, lect. 8 (§1458) *De prin. nat.* 2 (line 90–96); *Super de trin.* Q.5, 2, ad 6; *In phys.* VIII, lect. 12.5 (§1073).

erated or changeable, there are some ways they can be said to change accidentally. Matter is said to change incidentally in that it ceases to be characterized by the privation of a certain substantial form once that form is
instantiated (as the matter of the wood no longer "lacks" the form of ash after the wood is burned).[97] It also changes accidentally in that its potentiality for various substantial forms is affected or influenced by the form that it
presently possesses. The primary matter of iron, for instance, will immediately accept the form of rust but not the form of gold, even though primary
matter considered in itself is in potentiality to all substantial forms.[98] Substantial form may be said to change indirectly or accidentally (*per accidens*)
as the substance changes in which it is found. It may, for instance, be said
to change in that it is removed when the substance changes.[99] The form or
life principle of an animal, for instance, changes when the animal dies in the
sense that that form is no longer present. It is also said to change accidentally in that the subject changes with respect to it.[100] When an animal dies,
the matter of the animal changes with respect to its form in that the matter
acquires a new form. Since substantial form is not itself the subject of being,
but rather that through which the composite substance has being, it changes
not as the subject of change, but as that according to which the composite
substance changes.[101]

Besides substantial change, Aquinas's cosmology also recognizes accidental change. Here a substance retains its substantial identity but is modified in some incidental way (as when the sculptor's clay is given a new shape
or accidental form). In such cases, the accidental form is unchangeable in
one sense but changeable in another. It is "unchangeable (*invariabilis*)" in
that it is not the subject of change. For instance, when a clay square is shaped
into a sphere, it is the clay (the subject) that becomes round. The accidental
form (squareness) does not turn into roundness. In this way, the accidental form is understood not as something changeable in itself, but as "something steadfast (*consistens*) in an unchanging (*invariabili*) essence." In another
sense, accidental form is said to change since "something else changes ac-

97. *In phys.* I, lect. 15.11 (§139). Cf.: *Sent.* I, 8, 3, 2, ad 4; *In phys.* V, lect. 2.8 (§656).
98. *In meta.* XII, lect. 2.15 (§2438).   99. *Sent.* I, 8, 3, 2, ad 3.
100. *ST* I, 9, 2, ad 3.   101. Ibid.

cording to it, as when we say that whiteness is changed because a body is changed in its whiteness."[102] The accident is said to change because the subject participates in it more or less (as a T-shirt might have a "whiter white" after washing).[103]

Local motion or change of place is another kind of accidental change with an element of immutability. The accident of "place" does not itself change but "remains immovable (*immobile perseverat*)" when something changes places.[104] Thomas and Aristotle define place as the "immovable (*immobilis*) boundary of the containing thing." The "immobility (*immobilitas*)" of place is illustrated through the example of a ship anchored in a flowing river. The ship's place is determined not in relation to the changing water, but in relation to the whole river. In this sense, the place of the ship is called "immovable (*immobilis*)."[105]

Heavenly Bodies

For Aquinas, the word "heaven" refers properly to "some lofty body which is actually or potentially luminous and incorruptible by nature." His cosmology includes three heavens arranged concentrically around the earth.[106] The first and highest is the "empyrean heaven." The second is the "aqueous or crystalline heaven," and the third is the "starry heaven." Heavenly bodies are called changeable and changeless in many ways. We will look first at their immutability and motion, and then at the earthly effects these properties produce.

The empyrean heaven is uniform, completely luminous, "immovable (*immobile*)," and incorruptible.[107] This is the heaven Scripture sees as the dwelling place of the blessed. Its existence is known not through observation and reason but by the authority of revelation alone.[108]

The aqueous or crystalline heaven is uniform and mobile.[109] Its existence is affirmed by Scripture, but may also be known through observation and

---

102. *De ver.* Q.1, 6, co.
103. *De virt.* Q.1, a.11, ad 2.
104. *De ver.* Q.1, 6, co.
105. Ibid.
106. *ST* I, 68, 4, co.
107. *Sent.* II, 2, 2, 2, co.; d.14, 1, 4, co. Cf.: *ST* I, 68, 4, co.
108. *Sent.* II, 2, 2, 1, co.; *ST* I, 66, 3, co.
109. *Sent.* II, 14, 1, 4, co.; *ST* I, 68, 4, co.

reason. The scriptural evidence is found in Genesis 1:7, which refers to the "waters above the firmament." Aside from the Bible, astronomers were led by their observations to posit a sphere existing beyond the sphere of the fixed stars to account for the diurnal rotation of the heavens. Aristotle had thought that the sphere of the fixed stars itself accounted for that motion. After the discovery of the precession of the equinoxes by Hipparchus around 150 B.C., however, astronomers began to think of the sphere of the fixed stars as causing the precession of the equinoxes by moving extremely slowly in a different direction from the diurnal motion of the heavens. Since the sphere of the fixed stars could not cause both the precession of the equinoxes and the diurnal rotation of the heavens, it was necessary to posit an additional sphere to account for the latter. Both Thomas and Albert the Great agreed in identifying this newly postulated outermost movable sphere (the *primum mobile*) with the crystalline heaven.[110]

The starry heaven is in part transparent and in part actually luminous. It is composed of eight concentric spheres. The outermost sphere is the sphere of the fixed stars (*stellarum fixarum*). The others are the spheres of the seven planets.[111] Each of these eight spheres rotates around the earth according to its own proper pattern of regular circular motion.

Within the motion of the spheres of the starry heaven, the sometimes erratic appearance of the movements of the planets or "wanderers" presented a particular challenge to an astronomy that sought to preserve the regular circular motion of all the heavenly bodies: "It must be noted that certain anomalies, that is, irregularities, appear with respect to the motion of the planets. For the planets seem sometimes faster, sometimes slower, sometimes stationary, and sometimes retrograde in their motion. But this does not seem suitable for the motions of the heavens."[112]

Two explanations for the movements of the planets and the other heav-

---

110. *ST* I, 68, 2, ad 3. Cf.: Albert the Great, *In Sent.* II, d.14, a.2; d.15, a.3; *In Meta.* XI, tr.2, cap.24. All of Thomas's references to the precession of the equinoxes may be found in Thomas Litt, *Les corps célestes dans l'univers de saint Thomas d'Aquin* (Louvain: Publications Universitaires, 1963), 308–19. The question is also discussed in Joseph de Tonquédec, *Questions de cosmologie et de physique chez Aristote et saint Thomas* (Paris: J. Vrin, 1950), 60, and in William A. Wallace, "Appendix 3" and "Appendix 9," in *Summa Theologiae*, ed. Thomas Gilby (London: Eyre and Spottiswoode, 1967), 10:182–87, 219–24.

111. *ST* I, 68, 4, co. Cf.: *Sent.* II, 14, 1, 4, co.

112. *In de caelo* II, lect. 17.2. Cf.: *In de div. nom.* IV, lect. 2 (§302).

enly bodies were available to Aquinas. The explanation of Aristotle and Eudoxus (408–355 B.C.) involved a series of concentric spheres whose center was the earth. That of Ptolemy (d. ca. 170 A.D.) pictured each planet rotating around a circle whose center was on another circle that rotated around the earth. Both explanations were equally able to "save the appearances" by adding more circles in order to account for actual observations. Thomas generally followed the explanation of Aristotle, but realized that both were tentative: "The suppositions which the astronomers devised are not necessarily true. For although the appearances are saved by the suppositions which they have made, it is not necessary to say that these suppositions are true. For the apparent movements of the stars might possibly be explained in some other way not yet known to man."[113]

Thomas sees all heavenly bodies as incorruptible by nature. While earthly substances are corruptible since their matter is always in potency to receiving new forms, heavenly bodies are incorruptible since their matter is completely perfected by its form. In them there is no privation and no potentiality for another form. They are not subject to substantial change, and their being is "unfailing (*indeficiens*)."[114] They are not composed of the same four elements (earth, air, fire, and water) that make up the corruptible things of the sublunar regions, but of a "fifth body" or "fifth essence" characterized by "impassibility (*impassibilitatem*)," and ungenerated, incorruptible, inaugmentable, "inalterable (*inalterabile*)," and "altogether unchangeable (*totaliter intransmutabile*)" in its substance and power.[115]

The heavenly bodies are moved locally with regular circular motion. Because they move only locally, and not through alteration or generation, they resemble the first source of motion, which must be something "immutable (*immobile*)." Local motion is more perfect than other kinds of motion since it involves a less radical form of change. Local motion does not affect the thing moved in any inherent way, but only according to something extrinsic

---

113. *In de caelo* II, lect. 17.2. Cf.: Ibid., I, lect. 3.7; *ST* I, 32, 1, ad 2; *In meta.* XII, lect. 9 (§2566); lect. 10 (§2567–70). William Wallace and Thomas Litt believe that Thomas remained neutral regarding the preferability of one explanation over the other. Pierre Duhem maintains that in his later life Thomas began to prefer the Ptolemeic system over that of Aristotle. See Wallace, "Appendix 9," 220–21; Litt, *Les corps*, 361–65; Pierre Duhem, *Le système du monde* (Paris: Hermann, 1959), 3:354.

114. *Sent.* II, 7, 1, 1, co. Cf.: *ST* I, 9, 2, co.

115. *In de caelo*, I, lect. 6.1; II, lect. 8.7; *Sent.* II, 14, 1, 1, ad 2. Cf.: *In de div. nom.* VIII, lect. 5 (§789).

(place). It may therefore belong to an already perfected thing.[116] The circular-ity of the heavenly body's motion implies a "certain immobility (*quandam im-mobilitatem*)" by reason of the "fixedness (*fixione*)" of its center.[117] The regular-ity of its motion again betokens "a kind of immobility (*quandam immobilitatis speciem*)."[118] The movements of the celestial spheres are therefore called the "changeless changes of the heavenly bodies (*immutabiles immutationes caeles-tium corporum*)."[119]

The earth stands at the center of the rolling heavens. It is a realm of change and corruptibility, distinct from the immutability of the heavenly spheres.[120] In various ways, however, immutability is predicated also of the earth. The fact that it will never cease to exist gives it a certain "immutabil-ity (*immutabilitatem*)." In addition, it "rests (*quiescit*)" in its natural place at the center of the world and "is in no way moved (*nullo modo movetur*)."[121] In this way, the stability of the earth is contrasted to the constant motion of the heavens: "Immobility (*immobilitas*)" and "rest (*quies*)" belong to the nature of the earth, just as "to be always moved" belongs to the nature of the heav-ens.[122]

A number of consequences follow on the unchanging existence and per-petual motion of the heavenly bodies. Since it is subject to local notion, the heavenly body may be measured by time. Because it is "invariable (*invari-abile*)" and "unchangeable (*intransmutabile*)" in its being, it should also be measured by aeviternity.[123] Since the motion of the heavenly body is abso-lutely regular, it serves as the rule and measure for all other motion.[124]

Because of their "impassibility (*impassibilitatem*)," heavenly bodies can-not enter into composition with lower bodies.[125] They do influence them, however, since by reason of their substantial immutability they are the cause of all change in lower bodies:

---

116. *SCG* III, c.82.576 (§2576–7).
117. *In phys.* VIII, lect. 23.6 (§1169).
118. *SCG* III, c.72.4 (§2482).
119. *Super iob* XXXVIII, v. 31 (line 528–31).
120. *Super iob*, XX, v.6 (line 56 c.).
121. *In de caelo* II, lect. 26.7. Cf.: *ST* I, 10, 3, co.
122. *Super iob*, IX, v.7 (line 172 c.).
123. *In de div. nom.* X, lect. 3 (§875); *De pot.* Q.5, 4, ad 1; *ST* I, 10, 5, co. Cf.: *In phys.* VIII, lect. 21.15 (§1155).
124. *In de caelo* II, lect. 8.1; *In de div. nom.* IV, lect. 2 (§303).
125. *ST* I, 91, 1, ad 2. Cf.: Q.76, 7, co.; *Sent.* II, 17, 3, 1, co.

Since every multitude proceeds from unity; and since what is immovable (*immobile*) is always in the same way of being, whereas what is moved has many ways of being: it must be observed that throughout the whole of nature, all movement proceeds from the immovable (*immobili*). Therefore the more immovable (*immobiliora*) certain things are, the more they are the cause of those things which are most movable. Now the heavenly bodies are the most immovable (*immobilia*) of all bodies since they are not moved except by local motion. Therefore the movements of bodies here below, which are various and multiform, must be referred to the movement of the heavenly bodies, as to their cause.[126]

Since the heavenly bodies are subject to local motion, they are not absolutely immovable and cannot be the ultimate source of all motion. Their substantial immutability, however, allows them to be the first principle of a particular order of motion. Such a principle need not be "absolutely immovable (*immobile simpliciter*)," but only "immovable (*immobile*)" according to that same genus of motion. The heavenly body is subject to local motion, but it is "immovable with respect to alteration (*immobile secundum alterationem*)." It can therefore be the "first cause of alteration (*primum alterans; principium omnis alterationis*)." But since alteration is itself the source of all other kinds of motion among lower bodies, the heavenly body, as the source of alteration, is rightly called the cause of all motion among lower bodies.[127]

The heavenly bodies exercise their influence upon the terrestrial world in two ways. They are the source of all change and the ground of all stability. These two modes of influence are ascribed to two distinct celestial motions.

The stability and regularity found in the ordered pattern of days and nights, seasons of the year, and life cycles of plants and animals are due to one heavenly motion. Diversity such as heat and cold, light and darkness, and life and death, derive from another. Stability arises from the regular diurnal motion of the outermost sphere (the *primum mobile*).[128] (This is the sphere Thomas identified as the aqueous or crystalline heaven.) Diversity originates in a heavenly motion that, though regular in itself, is variable in its relation to the earth. This is a more problematic heavenly motion variously

---

126. *ST* I, 115, 3, co. Cf.: *SCG* III, c.82.5 (§2576).

127. *Sent.* III, 3, 5, 3, ad 2; *SCG* III, c.82.7 (§2578). Cf.: c.91.6 (§2666); *De ver.* Q.5, 9, co.; *ST* I-II, 109, 1, co.

128. *In meta.* XII, lect. 6 (§2510); *De pot.* Q.5, 1, ad 7. *ST* I, 104, 2, co.

explained by Ptolemy and Eudoxus. It is most evident in the yearly motion of the sun along the oblique circle called the zodiac. But it is also found in the motion of the planets and, to a lesser extent, in that of the fixed stars. It is a motion common to all bodies in the region Thomas calls the starry heaven, and its effect is attributable in some measure to all of them.[129]

During his career, Aquinas changed his mind about the influence of the empyrean heaven on the lower heavens. In his *Commentary on the Sentences* (1252–56), he argued that since the empyrean heaven is immobile, it cannot exercise a natural influence over other bodies. Although it would be possible for God to give it a special power of influence, that possibility should not be affirmed since it can be established by neither reason nor revelation. All we can know of the empyrean heaven is that it was established as the dwelling place of the blessed.[130] In his *Summa theologiae* (1266–68), he expresses a different opinion: "It is sufficiently probable, as some assert, that the empyrean heaven, having the state of glory for its ordained end, does not influence inferior bodies of another order—those, namely, that are directed only to natural ends. Yet it seems still more probable that it does influence bodies that are moved, although it is not moved itself."[131] The empyrean heaven exercises its influence upon the first heaven, which is moved (the *primum mobile*) by producing in it something "fixed and stable (*fixum et stabile*) such as the power of conservation or causation, or something of the kind pertaining to dignity."[132] This conserving power may in turn be shared with the higher planets such as Saturn, which is said to cause "fixed and permanent things (*res fixas et permanentes*)."[133] In the sixth of his *Quodlibeta* (1270 c.), Thomas notes his changed opinion: "Certain individuals hold that the empyrean heaven has no influence on any bodies since it was not created for the sake of natural effects, but that it might be the dwelling place of the blessed. And so indeed it once seemed to me."[134] He now thinks he can better represent the order of the universe by admitting such influence. This order is found in the way corporeal things are ruled by spiritual things, and lower bodies by higher ones. If the empyrean heaven,

129. *In meta.* XII, lect. 6 (§2511); *ST* I, 68, 2, ad 3; Q.115, 3, ad 2.
130. *Sent.* II, 2, 2, aa.1–3.   131. *ST* I, 66, 3, ad 2.
132. Ibid.   133. *ST* I, 104, 2, co.
134. *Quodl.* VI, Q.11, a.1 (19), co.

the highest corporeal body, were to exercise no influence on lower bodies, it would not be part of the order and unity of the universe.[135]

By including the empyrean heaven in the causality of the heavenly bodies, Thomas can show how the various heavens exercise their influence according to their varying degrees of unity and immutability. The unity of "rest (*quietis*)" precedes the uniformity of motion just as the uniformity of motion precedes the manifoldness of motion. For what is moved is in some way different now from what it was before, but what is at rest is the same now as it was before. What is "at rest (*quies*)" may, in this sense, be said to have pure unity, while what moves has unity along with diversity. Among the three heavens, the empyrean heaven alone may be said to be at rest since it alone is not moved by regular circular motion. Accordingly, it exercises its influence singularly "through its rest (*per suam quietem*)." By its influence, it causes something fixed and stable in the first heaven that is moved, namely the aqueous or crystalline heaven (the *primum mobile*). The aqueous heaven in turn exercises its influence through its uniform diurnal motion. By its influence, it causes the regularity and "continuity (*perpetuitatem*)" that is manifest in the lower heavenly bodies and in terrestrial events. Finally, the starry heaven exercises its influence through the manifoldness of its motion. The motion of the bodies found within this heaven is multiple since they move not only according to the diurnal motion of the aqueous heaven, but also according to their own proper motion along the oblique circle of the zodiac. The motion of an individual planet within this heaven, for instance, is the result of the combined motions of a complex series of spheres as variously explained by Ptolemy or Eudoxus. By its influence, the starry heaven causes the change and diversity that are evident in generation and corruption and in the many other events of the terrestrial world.[136]

Of the three heavens, the empyrean heaven alone exercises its influence "without motion (*absque motu*)." It is the highest of the heavens and the highest corporeal thing. For this reason, it is understood as attaining or "coming into contact (*attingens*)" with that higher order of beings that are known as the spiritual substances or angels.[137]

---

135. Ibid. Cf.: *SCG* III, c.69.17 (§2447). See also Litt, *Les corps*, 260.
136. *Quodl.* VI, Q.11, a.1 (19), co.   137. Ibid.

Angels

Pondering what human intelligence and will might look like apart from bodiliness, Aquinas speculates on the angels. Existing without matter, they are essentially unchanging, free from generation and corruption. Their immutability allows them to play a special role in the motions of the cosmos and gives them distinctive ways of knowing and loving.

The motions of the heavens require an incorporeal mover. No material thing (not even one composed of celestial matter) can move unless moved by another, and there cannot be a progression to infinity among material movers.[138] The source of heavenly motion must therefore be not corporeal but spiritual or intellectual.[139] Philosophers and Doctors of the Church identify this source as the incorporeal substances or angels.[140] They are "unchangeable (*inalterabilia*)" and "wholly impassible (*penitus impassibilia*)," having "unchangeable being (*esse intransmutabile*)" and "invariable life (*vitam invariabilem*)."[141] Though subject to no physical movement, they are said to be in a place or to move from place to place as they exercise their power in one place or another.[142] Thomas follows Aristotle's arguments that there must be as many "everlasting and essentially immovable (*sempiternae et secundum se immobiles*)" substances (angels) as there are motions of the heavens.[143] He does not agree, however, that there are only as many angels as heavenly movements. Rather, just as the number of incorruptible heavenly bodies exceeds the number of corruptible earthly bodies, so the number of angels exceeds the number of heavenly bodies since they stand in relation to bodies as the "immovable (*immobile*)" and immaterial to the mobile and material.[144]

Angels are capable of knowledge and love. If these activities are considered a sort of motion, "there is nothing to prevent movement of this kind

---

138. *SCG* III, c.23.3 (§2036); *ST* I, 110, 1, ad 1. That no body moves unless it is moved by another is "evident from induction" (*ST* I, 3, 1, co.) and may also be shown by argument (*SCG* II, c.20.2 [§963]; *Sent.* II, 2, 2, 3, co.).

139. *SCG* III, c.23.2 (§2035). Cf.: *ST* I, 70, 3; *Sent.* II, 1, 2, 3; d.14, 1, 3, co.

140. *ST* I, 110, 1, co.

141. *In de caelo* I, lect. 21.8; *In de div. nom.* VIII, lect. 2 (§754); VI, lect. 1 (§683).

142. *ST* I, 53, aa.1–3; Q.9, 2; *Super de trin.* Q.5, 4, ad 3.

143. *In meta.* XII, lect. 9.5 (§2557).

144. *SCG* II, c.92.7 (§1789). Cf.: *In meta.* XII, lect. 10 (§2589); *ST* I, 50, 3, ad 3; *De pot.* Q.6, 6, co.

from existing in the angels."[145] In this sense, the "motions of the angelic minds (*motus angelicarum mentium*)" are "unfailing (*indeclinabilem*)" and cannot become false.[146] The knowledge of the angels seems changeable in that they can grow in knowledge, not with respect to things they know naturally, but with respect to things supernaturally revealed to them.[147] In another sense, the knowledge of the angels is called "immutable (*immobilis*)" since they understand the truth of things by a simple intuition and not through the discursive movement that is characteristic of human knowing. Their knowledge is "incapable of defect (*indefectibilis*)" since they directly see the very natures of things regarding which the understanding is incapable of error.[148] By a simple intuition, the angel knows not only unchanging things, but also things that are in motion. It knows composite things simply, movable things "immovably (*immobiliter*)," and material things immaterially.[149] Because the angel is turned "immovably (*immobiliter*)" to what it knows and because it receives knowledge of the truth "without any motion (*sine aliquo motu*)," it is said to have a "godlike understanding (*deiformem intellectum*)."[150]

Since the angelic intellect is immutable in its mode of knowing and since the will is proportionate to the intellect, the angelic will is also naturally "immutable (*immutabilis*)" regarding those things that pertain to the order of nature. Regarding supernatural things, however, "change (*mutatio*)" is possible.[151] Thomas therefore calls angels "immutable (*immutabiles*), excepting only for their act of choice." Through their free act of choice angels merit beatitude.[152]

Once an angel has chosen something, it adheres to it "fixedly (*fixe*)" and "immovably (*immobiliter*)." In this angels are different from human beings, who adhere "movably (*mobiliter*)" to what they have chosen and, during this life, are able to change and choose something else. The human will

145. *ST* I, 59, 1, ad 3. Cf.: Q.50, 1, ad 2; Q.58, 1, ad 1.
146. *In de div. nom.* IV, lect. 7 (§368); VI, lect. 1 (§684).
147. *ST* I, 57, 5, co.; Q.58, 1, co.
148. *SCG* III, c.91.5 (§2665). Cf.: IV, c.55.6 (§3937); *ST* I, 64, 2, co.
149. *ST* I, 58, 4, co.
150. *De ver.* Q.15, 1, co.; *Sent.* II, 3, 1, 6, co.
151. *De malo* Q.16, 5, co.
152. *SCG* III, c.112.7 (§2862). Cf.: *ST* I, 59, 3; Q.62, 4.

is thus "flexible (*flexibile*)" both before and after it chooses, while the angelic will is flexible before choosing, but "inflexible (*inflexibile*)" afterward.[153] For this reason, the angel is said to have an "unchangeable mutability (*vertibilitatem immutabilem*)," while the human has a "changeable mutability (*mutabilem vertibilitatem*)."[154] The immutability of the angelic will after it has once chosen is due to both nature and grace. By nature, the appetitive power is proportioned to the cognitive power. Since the angelic intellect apprehends immovably, the angelic will naturally clings "immovably (*immobiliter*)" to the object it has chosen.[155] This is true for angels who choose good and those who choose evil. Those who choose evil remain in evil "according to the immutability (*immutabilitatem*) of their nature." Having freely chosen evil, they cling "immovably (*immobiliter*)" to that which they have chosen.[156]

Angels who choose good tend to remain in good according to the immutability of their nature. But since grace perfects nature according to the manner of the nature, angels who have chosen good under the influence of grace and who abide by that choice according to the immutability of their nature immediately receive the consummate grace of beatitude.[157] Through this grace, they attain perfect immortality, which includes "absolute immutability (*omnimodam immutabilitatem*)."[158] This absolute immutability of angelic beatitude cannot be attained without grace. For perfect beatitude consists in seeing God through his essence, and this is beyond the nature of every created intellect.[159] It must also be remembered that the angelic will was created "mutable (*mobilis*)" with respect to falling into sin. But mutability and immutability cannot succeed each other in the same subject in such a way that the one condition as well as the other may be reduced to the natural principles of the subject. Therefore the angelic will cannot become absolutely immutable in avoiding sin by nature alone. Rather, it is made "immutable (*immutabile*)" in this respect not by nature but by grace.[160] Finally,

153. *ST* I, 64, 2, co.; *ST* I, 63, 6, ad 3. Cf.: *SCG* IV, c.55.6 (§3937).
154. *Sent.* II, 3, 1, 6, co.
155. *De malo* Q.16, 5, co. Cf.: *ST* I, 64, 2, co.; *SCG* IV, c.55.6 (§3937).
156. *De rat. fid.* c.5 (line 66 c.; *De malo* Q.16, 5, ad 4.
157. *ST* I, 62, 5, co.; a.2, ad 3; a.7.
158. *ST* I, 50, 5, ad 1. Cf.: *ST* I, 64, 2, co.; Q.62, 9, co.; ad 3.
159. *ST* I, 12, 4; Q.62, 1, co.; a.2, co.   160. *Sent.* II, 7, 1, 1, ad 2.

it may be noted that any creature, considered in itself, is subject to failure. For every creature has a certain potency or incompleteness (deriving from its being *ex nihilo*) that may be a source of failure. If the potentiality is completely actualized through the influence of another being, then the creature, under the influence of that being, will have "immutability and completeness (*immobilitatem et indeficientiam*)." So, the will of the angel, in its orientation toward goodness, is completely fulfilled in the Beatific Vision and becomes completely immutable. Considered in itself, however, the angel is still capable of failure since its immutability is not due to its own angelic nature, but to the grace that is given to it by God.[161]

Since angels are moved in some way, they cannot be the ultimate source of motion. The search for the ultimate cause of motion will therefore lead beyond angels to the unchanging principle of all motion, the "first mover put in motion by no other," which Thomas identifies as God.[162] Before examining his arguments for divine immutability, though, we will first look at the nuances of creaturely immutability. This will help us see what the word means and does not mean when said of God.

THE MEANING OF CREATURELY IMMUTABILITY

We have now watched Aquinas label every creature in the universe immutable in one way or another. The sundry uses of the term have various connotations. The immovability of the angelic will, for instance, is quite different from that of the oyster, though both are said to "cling immovably (*immobiliter inhaerere*)."[163] Some types of immutability may seem desirable and others not. It depends on the kind of motion involved and the being to which the motion is attributed or denied.

Aquinas distinguishes two general kinds of motion: motion in the "broad sense" and motion in the "strict sense."[164] Later commentators use the hand-

---

161. *Sent* II, d.7, 1, 1, co. Cf.: *ST* I, 62, 2, ad 3; a.8, co.; ad 1; *De pot.* Q.5, 1, ad 8.
162. *ST* I, 2, 3. Cf.: *In meta.* III, lect. 4 (§385).
163. *ST* I, 69, 2, ad 1; *De malo* Q.16, 5, ad 4.
164. *De ver.* Q.24, 1, ad 14.

ier terms "immanent" and "transient" motion, for this distinction.[165] Immanent motion, as the name suggests, remains in the doer. Examples are the actions or operations of knowing and willing (though the activities of life and sensation in plants and animals may also be included in a qualified sense).[166] Transient motion is understood as "passing" from a doer to a receiver, as the activity of sawing passes from the carpenter to the wood. In reference to the doer, it is called action, and as regards the receiver, passion. We can use these distinctions to sort out the plusses and minuses of immutability.

Immutability and Transient Motion

For Aquinas, transient motion or motion in the strict sense is always (by definition) "the act of the imperfect." It is found in corporeal things in potency to the perfection of a new actuality or form, as water in a teakettle is in potency to a new perfection of heat. It involves a doer (the agent in act) and a receiver (the mobile object that is in potency). Fundamentally, it is the act of the mobile object since it is defined as the "act of that which is in potency."[167] In some ways, however, it belongs to both doer and receiver. For "what the agent causes by acting and what the mobile object receives by being acted upon are the same motion." (The heating on the part of the fire and the being heated on the part of the water are the same motion.) The one motion as proceeding from the mover to the mobile object is the act of the mover. But the same motion as present in the mobile object and coming from the mover is the act of the mobile object.[168] As the act of the agent or mover, it is "the act of the active" and is called "action." As the act of the mobile object, it is the "act of the passive," and is called "passion."[169] It is the act of the agent as "from this," and the act of the mobile object as "in this."[170] Because the act proceeding from the agent and the act received by the mobile object

165. On the origin of these terms, see Yves Simon, *Introduction à l'ontologie du connaître* (Paris: Desclée de Brouwer, 1934), 72n1; Joseph de Finance, *Etre et agir dans la philosophie de saint Thomas*, 3rd ed. (Rome: Université Grégorienne, 1965), 215n3.

166. *In de an.* III, lect. 12.2 (§766). Cf.: *In meta.* IX, lect. 8.10 (§1865); *ST* I, 27, 5, co.

167. *In phys.* III, lect. 2.3 (§285); lect. 4.1 (§297); 4.6–7 (§302–3). Cf.: *SCG* I, c.13.9 (§89–90); III, c.20.4 (§2012); *De ver.* Q.24, 1, ad 14; *De pot.* Q.5, 5, obj.19.

168. *In phys.* III, lect. 4.10–11 (§306–7). Cf.: lect. 5.10–11 (§317–18).

169. Ibid., lect. 5.2 (§309); 5.7 (§314).

170. Ibid., lect. 5.18 (§325). Cf.: *In meta.* XI, lect. 9.23 (§2312).

are the same one motion, this motion is said to "pass (*procedit; transit; egred-itur*)" from the agent to the object moved.[171] By this motion, the perfection or actuality already specifically, or at least virtually, present in the agent comes to be actually present in the mobile object.[172] For example, in boiling an egg, the perfection of heat actually present in the boiling water perfects or actual-izes the potentiality for heat in the egg. The result is not the perfection of the agent (the boiling water), but the perfection of the mobile object (the "per-fect" three-minute egg).

Transient motion is found in two fundamentally different kinds of change.[173] One is substantial change, in which one substance becomes a dif-ferent kind of substance (as when iron turns to rust or a living dog becomes a corpse). The other is accidental change, in which a substance is modified incidentally (in quantity, quality, or place) while remaining the same kind of thing (as when an apple changes in color).[174] In either type, there must be some potency (material cause) in the original object for acquiring a new ac-tuality (formal cause). In substantial change, the potency is actualized by a new substantial form, a principle by which a substance is the kind of thing it is. In accidental change, the potency is actualized by a new accidental form, a principle by which the new accidental property is realized. Both cases also require the influence of some agent (efficient cause) that acts for some end or goal (final cause).[175]

The new condition of the object that is achieved through motion is con-sidered an actuality (act) in relation to which the object was originally in

---

171. *ST* I, 18, 3, ad 1; *De pot.* Q.3, 15, co.

172. *De pot.* Q.3, 15, co.; *SCG* II, c.1.2 (§853); c.23.5 (§993); *ST* I-II, 31, 5, co.

173. In this section we will offer a synthetic account of Aquinas's fundamental teaching on motion, drawing on his various works but following our own order of presentation and offering our own exam-ples to clarify the different concepts.

174. In his commentary on the *Physics*, Thomas points out that Aristotle's original definition of mo-tion (*motus*) includes every sort of mutation (*mutationis*). Aristotle later distinguishes substantial change (generation and corruption) from accidental changes in quantity, quality, and place. He then restricts the term "motion (*motus*)" to accidental change (*In phys.* III, lect. 2.4 [§286]; V, lect. 2.1 [§649]). Cf.: *In de div. nom.* IV, lect. 7 (§369); *De ver.* Q.5, 2, ad 6. In our discussion, we will use the word "motion" in the origi-nal sense of the definition as including all forms of mutation, substantial as well as accidental.

175. *In phys.* II, lect. 10.15 (§240). On the contemporary application of these principles, see Michael J. Dodds, "Top Down, Bottom Up or Inside Out? Retrieving Aristotelian Causality in Contemporary Science," in *Science, Philosophy and Theology*, edited by John O'Callaghan (South Bend, Ind.: St. Augustine's Press, forthcoming).

a state of potency. But the motion itself, the very process of achieving that new condition, is also a kind of act. So, initially the object that is about to be moved has two sorts of potentiality, the potency for full achievement of the new condition and for movement toward that new condition. In Aquinas's example, materials that are going to be made into a house are in potentiality both "to the *process* of being built" and "to the *form* of a house" (the completed structure).[176] We might also think of how a baseball in the pitcher's hand has the potency both for *moving toward* the catcher's mitt and for *being in* the mitt. Motion is the actualization of the first of these potencies and endures only until the second potency is realized. (The motion of the ball stops once the potency for being in the catcher's mitt is achieved.) Motion is therefore a peculiar kind of actuality, which is found in a being that is in a state of potency only so long as that being remains in that state of potency. For this reason, motion always involves a kind of incompleteness. So long as the motion continues, there is always a further actuality to be achieved, for motion is (as the definition says) the act of something existing in potency (only) inasmuch as it is (still) in potency.

Understood in this sense, motion involves both perfection and imperfection. It is a perfection in that it is itself a kind of actuality. But it is a perfection or act that always includes a note of imperfection, of something still to be achieved—the full actualization toward which the motion is proceeding and which remains unachieved so long as the motion continues. Motion is described as an "imperfect act" or the "act of something imperfect."[177] It is "imperfect" since "it is compared to further act as potency," and it is "act" since "it is compared to something less perfect [namely the potency of the object that has not yet begun to move] as act."[178] In this sense, motion may also be called a mean between potency and act (for instance between the mere potency of the baseball about to be thrown and the full actuality of the ball in its new place in the catcher's mitt).[179] Motion is also the act of something imperfect in that only something that is imperfect, that does not yet

---

176. *In meta.* XI, lect. 9.9 (§2297). Cf.: *In phys.* III, lect. 2.3 (§285).

177. *In meta.* XI, lect. 9 (§2305). Cf.: *Sent.* I, 4, 1, 1, ad 1; *De ver.* Q.26, 1, ad 8; *De pot.* Q.8, 1, ad 9; *In phys.* III, lect. 3.6 (§296); *In de an.* III, lect. 12 (§766).

178. *In phys.* III, lect. 2.3 (§285). Cf.: 2.5 (§287); 5.17 (§324).

179. See *In phys.* III, lect. 2.3 (§285); lect. 3.6 (§296).

fully possess a given form or perfection or location, can be moved toward the attainment of that form.[180] For example, only the ball that is not actually in the catcher's mitt can be thrown (moved) toward the catcher, and once it is in the mitt (has achieved the new actuality of place) it can no longer be moved toward it. Similarly, only an untuned (imperfect) string on an instrument can be set in tune. Once in tune (once perfected), it can no longer be set in tune.

Creaturely immovability regarding transient motion can mean quite a number of things, as Aquinas explains in his commentaries on the *Physics* and *Metaphysics* of Aristotle.[181] First, things that are "easily moved" may be called "immovable" when they do not move "when they can and where they can and how they can." This sort of immutability is known as "rest."[182] A billiard ball, for instance, is quite easily moveable, but may be called "immobile" when it is at rest. Rest is the contrary of motion since it is the lack or privation of motion in things that are by nature capable of motion. As a sort of privation, rest has negative connotations. A thing at rest could achieve something if it would move, but it is not doing so. Such lack of accomplishment might connote a sort of stagnation. So Aquinas explains that unmoved waters may be called "dead."[183] But the immobility of rest also has positive connotations. As the completion or perfection of motion, rest is related to motion as the "perfect" to the "imperfect."[184]

Rest is both the perfection of motion, as implying the attainment of a certain perfection, and the privation of motion, as implying a lack of further actualization. The unfinished statues of Michelangelo known as the "slaves," for instance, may be said to rest in the perfection of form that they attained under his artistry, but they lack the further perfection they might have achieved had he completed the work. The dual character of rest may be traced to the inherent limitation of the changeable creature. Each creature possesses a principle

180. *SCG* III, c.20.4 (§2012). Cf.: *Sent.* I, 5, 3, 1, ad 1.
181. *In phys.* V, lect. 4.6 (§683); *In meta.* XI, lect. 12.26–28 (§2401–3). Cf.: *Phys.* V, c.2 (226b 10–15); *Meta.* XI, c.12 (1068b 20–25).
182. *In phys.* V, lect. 4.6 (§683). Cf.: *In meta.* XI, lect. 12.28 (§2403).
183. *Sent.* III, 35, 1, 1, co.
184. *De ver.* Q.15, 1, co. Cf.: *ST* I, 73, 1, ad 2; *SCG* III, c.123.6 (§2039); *Sent.* I, 40, 4, 2, ad 1; *ST* I, 5, 6, co.; I-II, 25, 1, co.

of potency that might be actualized by any number of forms, but can be actualized by only one form of a given sort at any given time. A block of marble
might become a "David," a "Moses," or a "Pietà," but not all three at once. The
fundamental principle of potency in material things is primary matter. Since
the primary matter of any particular thing cannot simultaneously possess all
forms of which it is capable, it achieves its perfection "by receiving in succes-
sion all the forms to which it is in potency, so that its entire potentiality may
be successively reduced to act, which could not be done all at once."[185] So long
as primary matter is actualized by one particular form, it enjoys the perfection
of the form it possesses. At the same time, though, it suffers the privation of
the other forms by which it might also be perfected.

If things easily moved can be called immutable, so can things moved
with difficulty.[186] Sometimes the arduousness occurs in the process of moving. A lame man, for instance, might be called immobile because he can move
only slowly and laboriously. Aquinas thinks elephants and animals that lack
self-motion are in the same predicament.[187] In such cases, immovability is
a negative notion, implying either a defect in a given nature (as in the lame
man) or a nature of a less perfect sort (such as oysters and other imperfect
animals). Other times, the difficulty occurs in setting something in motion.
In this way, large stones are called immovable. Here again, immobility may
be either desirable or undesirable since the boulder in question may resemble either the "rock of refuge" (Ps 31:2) or the stone of Sisyphus. In the first
case, immovability is a desirable condition, denoting the presence of a power
to resist various forms of corruption, destruction, or change for the worse.[188]
In the second case, it betokens an undesirable resistance to motion. Such
unfortunate immutability might manifest itself in the stubbornness of Sisyphean stone or in a paralysis brought on by fear or anger.[189]

If "immobility" can be applied to things moved easily or with difficulty,
it can also be said of those incapable of moving at all.[190] In some cases, such

---

185. *SCG* III, c.22.4 (§2027). Cf.: *ST* I, 7, 2, co.
186. *In Phys.* V, lect. 4.6 (§683). Cf.: *In meta.* XI, lect. 12.27 (§2402).
187. *Super iob*, XL, v.13 (lines 371–85).
188. *In meta.* V, lect. 14.7 (§960). Cf.: IX, lect. 1.11 (§1778).
189. *ST* I-II, 48, 3, ad 3.
190. *In phys.* V, lect. 4.6 (§683). Cf.: *In meta.* XI, lect. 12.26 (§2401).

immobility indicates a lack of perfection; in others, the fullness of perfection. The immobility ascribed to the cosmological principles of primary matter, substantial form, and accidental form betokens a lack of perfection. Primary matter is "altogether unchangeable (*omnino intransmutabilis*)," but is also mere potentiality.[191] As such it has imperfect existence. It cannot exist by itself but only with substantial form through which it receives existence in the composite substance.[192] Norbert Luyten calls it an "intrinsic constitutive inadequacy" or "fundamental deficiency" of a material substance since it explains why the substance can cease to be what it is and become something else.[193] The imperfection of primary matter explains why the immovability associated with it betokens not perfection but lack of perfection.

The immovability predicable of substantial form is likewise associated with imperfection. Substantial form has only imperfect being since it does not exist in itself but only as united with primary matter in a composite substance.[194] The immovability of substantial form is inseparable from its condition of imperfect existence. The same is true of accidental form, which depends completely on the substance in which it is found. As the terminus of accidental change, accidental form is invariable, but its invariability is tied up with the imperfect condition of its existence.

Heavenly bodies and angels are also in some ways incapable of change. Their immutability, however, bespeaks not imperfection but fullness of perfection. The heavenly body enjoys abundant perfection in that the entire potency of its matter is completely fulfilled or perfected by its form. No privation of, or potentiality for, a different substantial form is to be found in it. To the extent that no privation is found in it, it is without evil since "evil is the very privation of the good." Although among lower substances, "the good is mutable and mixed with its contrary evil, this cannot occur in the higher or-

---

191. *ST* I, 92, 3, ad 1; *In meta.* VIII, lect. 1.9 (§1689). Cf.: *In phys.* V, lect. 2.6 (§654).

192. *De prin. nat.* 1 (lines 30–33); 2 (lines 109–19); *De ver.* Q.5, 9, ad 8; *In meta.* XII, lect. 2.14 (§2437).

193. Norbert A. Luyten, "Matter as Potency," in *The Concept of Matter*, ed. Ernan McMullin (Notre Dame, Ind.: University of Notre Dame Press, 1963), 128, 131, 139. See also idem, "Der Begriff der Materia Prima nach Thomas von Aquin," in *La philosophie de la nature de saint Thomas d'Aquin*, Studi Tomistici, no. 18, ed. Léon Elders (Vatican City: Libreria Vaticana, 1982), 41; Antonio Moreno, "Generation and Corruption: Prime Matter and Substantial Form," *Angelicum* 57 (1980): 66.

194. *Sent.* I, 8, 3, 2, ad 3. Cf.: *De ver.* Q.9, 3, ad 6.

36THE IMMUTABILITY OF CREATURES

der of substances." Since no potentiality is found in the heavenly body, it is
not liable to substantial change, for "it is obvious that change cannot take
place where there is no potentiality to something else, for motion is the 'act
of that which exists in potency.'"[195]

The heavenly body is unfailing in action as well as being. Although the
movements of lower bodies may sometimes diverge from their proper order
because of the defect of their nature, no deviation or defect is to be found in
the movements of the heavenly body. The immutability of the heavenly body,
manifested in the incorruptibility of its substance and in the invariability of
its motion, indicates it belongs to a higher order of being and goodness than
the corruptible substances of the sublunar world.[196]

The immutability of the angel, like that of the heavenly body, follows
upon the perfection of its nature. The angel is a subsistent form existing separately from matter. Although the essence of the angel is related to its existence as potency to act, it is not consistent with the nature of the angel that
it be deprived of this act. For existence follows immediately upon form, and
a thing can perish only by losing its form. In the form itself, however, there
is no potentiality for non-existence. As subsisting forms, angels are "immutable and invariable in being."[197]

The immutability both of the angel and of the heavenly body results
from the perfection of their respective natures. The heavenly body is perfect
in that the potentiality of its matter is completely perfected by its form. The
angel is perfect since it is itself a subsisting form. In each case, immutability
indicates not a condition of imperfection, but the highest level of creaturely
perfection.

Immutability and Immanent Motion

Immanent motion, or motion in the broad sense, is the "the act of the
perfect."[198] It bears some affinity to transient motion, considered both as pas-

195. SCG III, c.20.4 (§2012).   196. De ver. Q.5, 4, co.
197. ST I, 9, 2, co.
198. De ver. Q.24, 1, ad 14. Cf.: ST I, 58, 1, ad 1; I-II, 109, 1, co.; Sent. I, 37, 4, 1, ad 1; In de an. III, lect.
12.2 (§766); In meta. XI, lect. 7.6 (§2253). See also Giles Langevin, "L'action immanente d'après saint
Thomas d'Aquin," Laval théologique et philosophique 30 (1974): 253; Francis Nugent, "Immanent Action in
St. Thomas and Aristotle," NS 37 (1963): 172.

sion and action. Both immanent motion and passion are the act of something in motion. Passion is the act of the mobile object (the water being heated), and immanent motion is the act of the operator (the one knowing or willing).[199] But while the first is the "act of the imperfect" (of something in potency), the second is the "act of the perfect" (of a being in act through its form). The first belongs to something in potency to acquiring a new form; the second, to something in act precisely because of the form it already possesses.[200]

Immanent motion is also like transient motion considered as action. Action is defined as the "act of the active," and immanent motion or operation is understood as the "act of something existing in act."[201] Still there are differences. Action proceeds from the agent to the mobile object, but operation remains in the agent. The actions of heating and cutting, for instance, pass into external matter, but the operations of knowing and willing remain in the agent.[202] Action and operation are also distinct in that action is the perfection of the external mobile object while operation is the perfection of the agent itself.[203] For example, when fire heats water, it is not the fire that is perfected but the water. When the intellect knows something, however, the operation of knowing is the perfection of the intellect itself. A final distinction is that operation may be considered as an end while action may not. Since action is essentially directed toward producing a certain perfection in the mobile object, it is fundamentally aimed at some end and so cannot be an end in itself. Operation, however, has the character of an end since it remains in the agent and is itself the perfection of the agent.[204]

Immutability is attributed to creatures that lack immanent motion and those that possess it. Things like "stones and wood" are called "immovable (*immobilia*)" because they lack the perfection of life manifested in self-motion and in the immanent activities of sensation and imagination.[205] This immovability indicates not perfection but the imperfection of lower creatures.

199. *ST* I, 18, 3, ad 1.
200. *In de an.* III, lect. 12.2 (§766); *In meta.* IX, lect. 8.7–10 (§1862–65).
201. *In phys.* III, lect. 5.2 (§309); *ST* I, 18, 3, ad 1.
202. *ST* I, 18, 3, ad 1; 54, 2, co.; I-II, 74, 1, co.; *In de div. nom.* V, lect. 7 (§369); *De ver.* Q.8, 6, co.
203. *ST* I, 18, 3, co; ad 1; I-II, 31, 5, co.; *De pot.* Q.10, 1, co.; *SCG* II, c.1.2 (§853); II, c.23.5 (§993).
204. *De pot.* Q.5, 5, co.; ad 14.
205. *Sent.* III, 35, 1, 1, co.; *SCG* I, 97.3 (§813).

Things that manifest immanent motion may also be called immovable. The rational mind, for instance, is mobile as regards immanent action but "not mobile" regarding transient motion "since such motion belongs only to bodies."[206] Similarly, delight is a "movement of the soul" that consists in immanent but not transient motion.[207] Here immovability suggests not imperfection, but freedom from the imperfection of transient motion.

In itself, immanent action implies no imperfection since it involves no potency. It is not the "act of a being in potency," but the "act of a being in act." As found in creatures, however, it is subject to the potentiality and limitation inherent in the nature of the creature. In them it varies in its perfection according to the kind of immanent action and the sort of creature of which it is predicated. In perfect animals, for instance, one finds the immanent activity of sensation. This is the act of a being in act since it is the activity of an animal already in act through its form.[208] But it still implies a certain passivity or potency on the part of the animal since sensation can occur only in the presence of the sensible object by which the power of sense is activated. (The eye can see something blue only if there is something blue to be seen). Because the power of sensation depends upon its object for its actualization, it is called a passive power.[209]

Similarly, the immanent actions of human knowing and willing, though more perfect than the activity of sensation, also involve a certain potency. The possible intellect is in potency to the impressed species, and reasoning involves a sort of movement from potential to actual knowledge.[210] Because of its characteristic potency, the passive intellect holds a place among intellectual beings analogous to that of primary matter among material beings. As primary matter is a mere potentiality or capacity for being and has no actuality until perfected by form, the passive intellect has a mere potentiality for knowledge and can understand nothing until it is perfected by the intelligible species.[211] In a similar way, the immanent activity of the will depends

---

206. *De ver.* Q.24, 1, ad 14.   207. *ST* I-II, 31, 1, co.; a.2, co.; ad 1.
208. *In de an.* III, lect. 12.2 (§766).
209. *De ver.* Q.26, 3, ad 4. Cf.: *ST* I, 27, 5, co.; Q.78, 3, co.; *Sent.* III, 14, 1, 1, qc.2, co.
210. *ST* I, 14, 2, ad 2.
211. *De ver.* Q.8, 6, co. Cf.: *ST* I, 14, 2, ad 3. See also Richard Lambert, "A Textual Study of Aquinas's Comparison of the Intellect to Primary Matter," *NS* 56 (1982): 80–99.

on the object presented to it. The will stands in relation to the apprehended appetible as a "moved mover" to a "mover which is not moved."[212] Through its choices, the will is able to actualize its potentiality for virtue but in this life remains changeable in its choice of good and evil.[213]

Even in the angelic nature, the immanent activities of knowing and willing are not without some potency. For, though the angel has its natural knowledge through a single and unchanging intuition, its intellect may be in potency since it does not always consider everything it knows. It is also in potency to further knowledge through revelation.[214] The angelic will is originally changeable with respect to supernatural things, but becomes fixed in the choice it makes. The angel is also in potency regarding place as it wills to apply its power in one place or another.[215] Finally, in the immanent activity of delight, the angel is said to be able to grow in happiness accidentally.[216]

IMMUTABILITY AND CREATURELY PERFECTION

Seeing the positive and negative implications of immovability among creatures, we can understand how change and changelessness are related to creaturely perfection. Motion among creatures always implies potency and imperfection. Transient motion (the act of a being in potency) implies imperfection in its very definition. Immanent motion (the act of a being in act) does not imply imperfection in its definition, but as found in creatures, it is always associated with potency and imperfection. Both sorts of creaturely motion entail the incompleteness of the creature and suggest a perfection yet to be attained.[217]

Though motion itself implies imperfection, it is paradoxically through motion that the creature attains perfection. Through transient motion, the perfection of a new form is achieved. Through immanent action, the creature's potentiality for knowledge and love is actualized. To the extent that a creature is in potency with respect to a perfection yet to be attained, change

212. ST I, 80, 2, co.   213. ST I-II, 2, 7, co.
214. ST I, 58, 1, co.; Sent. I, 37, 4, 1, co.   215. ST I, 53, aa.1–3.
216. ST I, 64, 2, co. Q.62, 9, co.; ad 3.
217. De pot. Q.6, 6, co. Cf.: ST I, 9, 2; Q.65, 1, ad 1; Sent. I, 8, 3, 2.

is not only good but necessary. In this way, immovability looks like stagnation, a lack of progress toward perfection. To the extent that a creature has attained some perfection, however, immovability seems desirable (at least with respect to the perfection already achieved) since change suggests the possibility of losing that perfection.[218] Since motion and immovability are so closely related to the perfection of the creature, we can describe the relative perfection of various creatures in terms of their motion and immovability. We can do in two ways: first by considering the perfectible creature, which attains its perfection through motion, and then by considering the perfected creature, which preserves its perfection through immovability.

The Perfectible Creature

The creature achieves its perfection through transient and immanent motion.[219] By transient motion, it attains the perfection of a certain form. But motion does not stop there since a new form implies new activity.[220] Creatures find their perfection not in rest but in the actions that follow on their forms or natures: "Indeed all things created would seem in a way to be purposeless if they lacked an operation proper to them; since the purpose of everything is its operation. For the less perfect is always for the sake of the more perfect: and so, as matter is for the sake of form, form (which is the first act) is for the sake of operation (which is the second act); and thus operation is the end of the creature."[221] The creature's action may be either transient (passing into external matter) or immanent (remaining in the creature itself). In both cases, action is perfective of the creature. It constitutes a "second" perfection, following on the creature's form or "first" perfection:

The perfection of a thing is twofold, the first perfection and the second perfection. The first perfection is that according to which a thing is substantially perfect, and this perfection is the form of the whole, which form results from the whole having its parts complete. But the second perfection is the end, which is either an operation (as the end of the harpist is to play the harp) or something that is attained by an operation (as the end of the builder is the house that he makes by building). But the

---

218. *In de div. nom.* VIII, lect. 3 (§769).   219. *SCG* III, c.22.7 (§2030).
220. *ST* I, 5, 4, co.; a.5, co.
221. *ST* I, 105, 5, co. Cf.: *Sent* IV, 49, 1, 2, qc.4, ad 4; *SCG* III, c.25.3 (§2057).

first perfection is the cause of the second, because the form is the principle of opera-tion.[222]

Creatures seek their perfection in all that they do.[223] In immanent mo-tion, the action itself is the end or perfection of the creature.[224] In transient motion, it is not the action itself, but the end of the action (i.e., the perfec-tion of the external object) that is the end of the creature.[225] This is seen most readily in the action of generation, where the end of the action (the production of a new animal) is also the end of the agent (the perpetuation of the species).[226]

Since all perfection is attained through motion, immovability may seem utterly undesirable. Changelessness looks like stagnation when a creature in potency to a new form fails to actualize it. Inactivity looks like inertness if a creature in possession of a certain form fails to act in accordance with it.[227] Motion, on the other hand, may allow the creature to attain "some per-fect participation in divine good." In this sense, the motion of the heavenly body, which participates divine causality by moving, is "more excellent (no-bilior)" than the motionlessness of the earth at the center of the heavens.[228] Similarly, the multiple motions of the rational mind in thinking and judging are more excellent than the uniform motion of the highest heavenly sphere, since by its motions the mind achieves a more perfect end:

It is not always necessary that a thing which can attain its end with fewer motions or operations be nobler, because sometimes one thing attains a more perfect end with many operations than another can attain with a single operation. . . . In this way, ra-tional minds are found to be more perfect than the highest heaven, which has only one motion, because they attain a more perfect end, although they do it with many operations.[229]

---

222. *ST* I, 73, 1, co. Cf.: I, 105, 5, co.; I-II, 3, 2, co.; *SCG* II, c.46.3 (§1231).

223. *ST* I, 44, 4, co.

224. *De pot.* Q.3, 15, co.

225. *SCG* III, c.16.1 (§1985). Cf.: I, c.100.3 (§830). On the relation of transient and immanent ac-tion to the perfection of the creature, see Jean-Marie Henri-Rousseau, "L'être et l'agir," *Revue thomiste* 53 (1953): 491; 55 (1955): 86–89; Finance, *Etre*, 257–61; Simon, *Introduction*, 82n1.

226. *SCG* III, c.24.7 (§2052). Cf.: c.22.5 (§2028).

227. *De pot.* Q.3, 7, co.   228. *Sent.* IV, 48, 2, 2, ad sed contra 5.

229. *De ver.* Q.24, 1, ad 15.

The superior perfection of motion is also seen in that changeable creatures best imitate their Creator not by resting but by exercising their proper motions. The animal's heart participates divine perfection not by stopping but by beating.[230] The temperate person reflects the goodness of God through the movements of pleasure more than the insensitive person does by the stoical suppression of all emotion.[231] Every creature capable of action best imitates divine being not by inactivity but by the exercise of its proper causality.[232] Active creatures seek the "divine peace" not by resting but by pursuing their proper activities.[233] The very order of the universe, which "declares the glory of God" (Ps 19:2), is achieved not through inactivity but by the action of creatures: "If actions be taken away from things, the mutual order among things is removed, for, in regard to things that are different in their natures, there can be no gathering together in unity of order unless by the fact that some of them act and others undergo action."[234]

The Perfected Creature

Though motion is necessary for creatures in attaining their perfection, once they achieve some degree of perfection immutability becomes desirable for its preservation. The beatified angel, for example, since it has attained the highest perfection "proper to itself in accordance with divine predestination," cannot increase or decrease in beatitude. Its changelessness, however, does not imply imperfection, but the achievement of the highest possible degree of perfection.[235] On a less exalted level, medieval cosmology teaches that fire remains at rest once it has attained its proper place in the universe (which is basically "up"). Its motionlessness does not imply lack of perfection, but the attainment of its proper perfection of place.[236]

Motion is good for the creature with respect to any further perfection it may attain, but immovability is good regarding the perfection already achieved. The relationship between motion, immovability, and creaturely perfection may be illustrated using the medieval comparison between the

230. *Sent.* IV, 43, 1, 1, qc.1, ad 4.   231. *In eth.* VII, lect. 7 (line 88 c.).
232. *SCG* III, c.21.8 (§2023); 21.2 (§2018); 21.7 (§2022); c.69.14 (§2444).
233. *In de div. nom.* XI, lect. 3 (§919).   234. *SCG* III, c.69.17 (§2447).
235. See *ST* I, 62, 9, esp. obj.3 and ad 3.   236. *ST* I, 6, 3, co.

perfection of the heavenly body and that of fire as an element of the sublunar world. Below the sphere of the moon, creatures achieve their perfection through motion. Primary matter is perfected when it attains the form of fire, which in turn is perfected when it achieves its proper place in the universe. The substance of fire, however, is still in potency to becoming a mixed body, and the mixed body to the vegetative soul, the vegetative soul to the sensitive soul, and the sensitive soul to the human soul.[237] So the substantial immovability of fire has positive connotations insofar as it indicates primary matter's attainment of a certain form and fire's attainment of its proper place. But it has negative connotations in that it suggests the lack of motion toward the further substantial perfection of which fire is capable. The substantial immovability of the heavenly bodies, in contrast, has only positive connotations since they already possess the highest substantial perfection proper to them, and no further perfection is possible.[238]

The attainment of one's proper perfection does not imply inertness. Since "each thing acts according as it is in act," the more a creature's perfection is actualized, the more it is able to act in sharing its perfection with others.[239] So the more a creature is immutable in the possession of its own perfection, the more it can be the dynamic source of perfection in others. In this way, the heavenly bodies in Aquinas's cosmology, which are completely immovable as regards alteration, may be the dynamic source of all change occurring in lower bodies.[240]

The Degrees of Creaturely Perfection

Since immutability is associated with creaturely perfection, we can rank the ontological perfection of creatures in terms of their changelessness. On the top rung we find the angels or separated substances, which are in no way subject to transient motion since they have no matter. Next come the heavenly bodies, which manifest uniform local motion, but are not subject to generation and corruption. Among themselves, these can be ranked accord-

---

237. *SCG* III, c.22.7 (§2030).
238. *ST* I, 58, 3, co. Cf.: *De ver.* Q.15, 1, co.; *Comp.* 1, c.216.
239. *SCG* III, c.69.26 (§2456).
240. *ST* I, 115, 3, co.; *SCG* III, c.82.7 (§2578).

ing to the multiplicity of their motions.[241] Finally, there are the lower bodies, which hold the "lowest rank in goodness and the lowest grade in being" since they are subject not only to local motion but also to generation and corruption.[242]

Since creatures attain their perfection through motion, we can also determine the ranks of creaturely perfection by considering how much motion each requires to attain its perfection and what level of perfection it achieves.[243] At the bottom of the heap is that creature which can acquire no perfection at all and has no motion toward perfection. The situation of this creature is compared to the condition of a person with an incurable disease who takes no medicine since no improvement is possible. Though Thomas does not mention what creature he has in mind here, it may be supposed that he intends primary matter, which of itself can acquire no goodness and has no motion toward goodness since it has no actuality.[244] Next come those things that can acquire imperfect goodness through a small number of motions and those things that can acquire imperfect goodness through many motions. These are like a person who may attain imperfect health through a small number of remedies or through many remedies. Here Aquinas places irrational creatures, which can attain a certain imperfect goodness. Inanimate creatures, plants, and imperfect animals can attain imperfect goodness through few motions. Perfect animals can achieve a higher but still imperfect perfection through many motions. These are followed by those entities that can acquire perfect goodness by many motions. They are compared to the person who can attain perfect health by much exercise or many remedies. Here Thomas is thinking of the human being that attains the perfection of beatitude through many operations. Above humans are things that acquire perfect goodness through a few operations. They are comparable to a per-

---

241. *In de caelo* II, lect. 18.6.

242. *SCG* III, c. 20.4 (§2012); c.72.4 (§2482). Cf.: *De ver.* Q.9, 2, co.; *Super de causis*, prop. 30, page 138 (line 30ff.); *SCG* III, c.62.11 (§2374); c.94.11 (§2695); *Comp.* I, c.74.

243. The discussion presented here is a synthesis of Thomas's treatment of the topic in *ST* I, 77, 2, co., and *De ver.* Q.8, 3, ad 12.

244. The question of whether goodness may be attributed to primary matter is discussed in *De ver.* Q.21, 2, ad 3; *SCG* III, c.20.5 (§2013); *ST* I, 4, 1, co.; and Q.5, 3, ad 3. The variations in Thomas's teaching on the subject are noted by Vernon J. Bourke in the English translation of *SCG* III, c.20.5, p. 79, n. 5.

son who acquires perfect health by a little exercise or a few remedies. In this category, Thomas places the angels, who attain the perfect goodness of beatitude by a simple movement of will. Finally, above all creatures, is the one who possesses perfect goodness with no motion at all. This is like the person who enjoys perfect health without the help of any remedies or medicine. This is God, who possesses his goodness with no motion whatsoever.

From our analysis of the relation between motion, immovability, and the perfection of the creature, two general conclusions become evident. First, motion is positive and desirable for the creature to the extent that it is in potency to further perfection to be attained through motion. Second, immutability is positive and desirable for the creature to the extent that it has already attained its proper perfection. These conclusions imply that, at one extreme, motion would be unconditionally desirable only to an entity for which any change whatever would be an improvement. This would be the case only for an entity that possesses absolutely no perfection or actuality at all in itself. Such an entity would be a mere capacity for perfection, a mere potentiality toward actualization, a pure potency. No such entity can be found since any existing thing, to the extent that it exists, possesses at least the perfection of its own being. In material things, however, one may distinguish a principle of pure potentiality, which is called primary matter. Although this principle never exists in itself, it may be considered in itself.[245] When so considered, apart from any form by which it is presently actualized, it is a principle to which any change whatsoever is desirable. At the other extreme, immutability would be unconditionally good and desirable only for an entity that has absolutely no potentiality for further perfection because it is itself pure actuality. This is precisely the entity, according to Thomas, that "everyone understands to be God."[246] Now that we have seen the positive and negative implications of the notion of immutability with respect to creatures, we are ready to consider Thomas's arguments for predicating immutability of God.

245. *De ver.* Q.3, 5, co.; ad 3.
246. *ST* I, 2, 3, co. Cf.: *ST* I, 115, 1, ad 2; *In meta.* XI, lect. 9.1 (§2289); *SCG* I, c.17.7 (§139–40); c.43.6 (§361).

CHAPTER TWO

The Immutability of God

☞

AQUINAS'S ARGUMENTS FOR
DIVINE IMMUTABILITY

Thomas refers to the immutability of God in almost all his major works. In the *Summa contra gentiles* he even makes it a "principle of procedure" for discovering other divine attributes.[1] In this chapter, we will examine his arguments for divine immutability first in his commentaries and then in his independent works, following the chronological order of his writings as much as possible.

Theological Commentaries

Commentary on the Sentences

Book I, d.3, Q.1, a.1, *div. text*. Aquinas first discusses divine immutability in his *Commentary on the Sentences* of Peter Lombard, one of his earliest works written while he was a bachelor of the Sentences at the University of Paris between 1252 and 1256.[2] God's changelessness surfaces in his examination of Peter Lombard's four arguments for "the unity of the divine essence." He explains them using the three ways of Dionysius for knowing God from

---

1. *SCG* I, c.14.4 (§119).
2. Regarding the dating of this work, see Jean-Pierre Torrell, *Saint Thomas Aquinas,* trans. Robert Royal (Washington, D.C.: The Catholic University of America Press, 1996), 1:39–45; James A. Weisheipl, *Friar Thomas D'Aquino: His Life, Thought, and Works* (Oxford: Blackwell, 1975), 67–80, 358–59.

creatures: causality, remotion (or negation), and eminence.[3] The second argument follows the way of remotion and is taken from Augustine: beyond all imperfect beings there must be some perfect entity having no admixture of imperfection.[4] Aquinas explains that since both corporeal and incorporeal creatures are changeable and imperfect, there must exist beyond them "some incorporeal, immovable (*immobile*), and completely perfect being, and this is God."[5]

Sent. I, 8, 3, 1, *exp. text* Divine immutability is treated more extensively in Distinction VIII. There Peter Lombard uses Jerome and Augustine to show that God alone may truly be said to exist since only he exists immutably.[6] Aquinas frames his discussion of divine immutability in terms of God's perfection in being, arguing that Lombard wished to deal especially with what pertains "to the perfection of the divine being insofar as it is perfect being." Since perfection in being excludes potentiality, "immutability (*immutabilitas*)" must be affirmed of it. Unlike the being of creatures that is caused by another and characterized by potentiality and "mutability (*mutabilitatem*)," God is the cause of all being who abides "unchangingly (*immutabiliter*)."[7]

Sent. I, 8, 3, 1 In the *sed contra* of this article, Thomas provides biblical and philosophical arguments for divine immutability. The scriptural passages are also found in Peter Lombard's text: "I am God and I am not changed" (Mal 3:6), and "With whom there is no change nor shadow of alteration" (Jas 1:17). The philosophical argument, based on Aristotle, has been called a "first sketch" of the first way of showing God's existence in Aquinas's later *Summa theologiae:* "Besides, as the Philosopher proves in the *Physics*, everything which

3. Dionysius, *De div. nom.* VII, 3 (*PG* 3, 879). It is now recognized the author of this work is really the late fifth-century "Pseudo-Dionysius" and not the "Dionysius" of Acts 17:34. We will refer to the author simply as "Dionysius," however, following Aquinas's usage.

4. Augustine, *De civ. Dei* VIII, 6 (*PL* 41, 231).

5. "Ergo ultra omnes species mutabiles, sicut sunt animae et angeli, oportet esse aliquod ens incorporeum et immobile et omnino perfectum, et hoc est Deus" (*Sent.* I, 3, 1, 1, *div. text*).

6. Jerome, *Epist.* XV, 4 (*PL* 22, 357); Augustine, *De trin.* V, 2 (*PL* 42, 912).

7. "[E]xcluditur potentialitas; et quantum ad hoc ponitur immutabilitas. . . . Esse creaturae est causatum ab alio, et habet, quantum in se est, potentialitatem et mutabilitatem; sed esse divinum est causa omnis esse, immutabiliter permanens" (*Sent.* I, 8, 3, 1, *exp. text*).

is moved is moved by another. If therefore that by which the mobile thing itself is moved is also moved, it is necessary that it be moved by another. But it is impossible to proceed to infinity. Therefore it is necessary to come to a first mover which moves and is in no way moved. And this is God. Therefore he is altogether immutable (*immutabilis*)."[8] In the corpus, Aquinas argues for divine immutability from God's nature as pure act: "All motion or mutation, in whatever way it is predicated, results from some potentiality since motion is the act of something existing in potency. Therefore, since God is pure act, having no admixture of potency, there cannot be any change in him."[9] Transient motion as "the act of a being in potency (*actus existentis in potentia*)" must therefore be denied, but transient motion as related to the agent (the act of the active) and immanent motion (the "act of a being in act") do not imply potency and so may be affirmed. Aquinas illustrates this in his replies to the objections.

The second objection used Augustine's assertion that "the Creator Spirit moves itself" to affirm divine mutability.[10] Aquinas explains that Augustine is referring either to the immanent actions of knowing and willing or to the act of creating. In both ways, motion may be predicated of God: "Augustine takes 'to be moved' in the broad sense, according to which even 'to understand' and 'to will' are in a way 'to be moved,' although properly speaking these are not motions except by comparison. . . . Or, it may be said that God moves himself in the production of creatures."[11]

In his replies to the first and fourth objections, he shows how motion may be attributed to God in the act of creation. The first objection was that since divine wisdom is changeable (Wis 7:24) and is identified with God

8. "Praeterea, sicut probat Philosophus, omne quod movetur, ab alio movetur. Si igitur illud a quo movetur mobile ipsum, etiam movetur, oportet quod ab aliquo motore moveatur. Sed impossibile est ire in infinitum. Ergo oportet devenire ad primum motorem, qui movet et nullo modo movetur; et hic est Deus. Ergo omnino est immutabilis" (*Sent.* I, 8, 3, 1, sc 2). "One can see here the first sketch of the first way" (Fernand Van Steenberghen, *Le problème de l'existence de Dieu dans les écrits de s. Thomas d'Aquin* [Louvain: Editions de l'Institut Supérieur de Philosophie, 1980], 29).

9. "Respondeo dicendum, quod omnis motus vel mutatio, quocumque modo dicatur, consequitur aliquam possibilitatem, cum motus sit actus existentis in potentia. Cum igitur Deus sit actus purus, nihil habens de potentia admixtum, non potest in eo esse aliqua mutatio" (*Sent.* I, 8, 3, 1, co.).

10. St. Augustine, *Super gen. ad litt.* VIII, 20 (*PL* 34, 388). Thomas points out (ad 2) that motion is similarly attributed to God by Plato and Averroes. See Plato, *Laws* X (896); XII (966 E); *Phaedrus* (245 C); Averroes, *Metaphysica* XII. cap. 2. Cf.: Aristotle, *Meta.* XI, 6 (1071b 37).

11. *Sent.* I, 8, 3, 1, ad 2.

himself, God must be mutable. The fourth was that since everything that passes from inactivity to activity must be moved in some way and since God sometimes creates in act or infuses grace that he had not done previously, there must be "at least a change in him from habit to act."

In response to the first objection, Thomas shows how divine wisdom both resembles and differs from motion in producing its effects. There is a similitude between divine causality and motion that allows Dionysius to say divine goodness or wisdom proceeds into creatures.[12] As a locally moved object proceeds from one place to the next according to a certain order, divine wisdom may be said to proceed to its effect as it imprints its similitude in creatures according to a certain order, from superior to lesser creatures. This procession of divine wisdom, however, is not properly motion since it is not divine wisdom as such that proceeds into creatures, but a similitude or participation of it.

In response to the fourth objection, Thomas shows how God's "transient action" in the production of creatures is directed by his immanent activity of knowing and willing. God's operation is unlike that of creatures since it is his very substance. Things whose operation is different from their substance must be moved to action since in acting they acquire a new actuality they cannot give themselves. Since God's operation is his substance, he does not need to be moved by another to operate. As his substance is eternal, so is his operation. The effect of his operation, however, need not be eternal. It proceeds from him not eternally, but according to the order of wisdom in God's immanent activity of knowing and loving.

Sent. I, 8, 3, 2 To determine "whether every creature is mutable," Aquinas again uses both Scripture and reason. The biblical evidence is from Psalm 101:28: "You will change them and they will be changed." The philosophical argument belongs to John of Damascus: "Each thing which is from nothing is capable of being turned into nothing. For that which began to be by change is necessarily subject to change. But all creatures are of this sort, so all creatures are changeable."[13]

---

12. Dionysius, *Cael. Hier.* I, 1 (*PG* 3, 119).
13. John of Damascus, *Fidei orth.* I, cap. 3 (*PG* 94, 795).

As in the previous article, Thomas formulates his own response in terms of potency and act: "Since every creature has something of potency, in that God alone is pure act, it is necessary that all creatures be mutable, and God alone immutable (*immutabilem*)." The potentiality of the creature is then considered in two ways, regarding what the creature possesses and what it is natural for it to possess.

The first way concerns the being (*esse*) of the creature, which it possesses not of itself, but from another. Since its being is from another, the creature is not "necessary (*necesse*)" but "possible (*possibile*)," and depends on another either for its whole existence or for some aspect of its being. Since it depends on God for its whole being, it is "changeable" in the sense that it could cease to be altogether. For two reasons, however, such "changeability into nothing (*vertibilitas in nihil*)" is not change in the proper sense of the term. First, change always involves an enduring substratum, and complete annihilation would exclude this. Secondly, nothing is called possible if its instantiation would require something impossible. The annihilation of the creature, however, presupposes something impossible. For the creature could only cease to be if the influx of divine goodness were withdrawn. This, however, is impossible because of the "immutability (*immutabilitate*)" of the divine will.[14] The whole being of the creature is changeable, therefore, only on the presupposition that it be abandoned to itself. As regards some aspect of its being, the creature is again changeable and dependent on another. It can lose what it has from another if some unchanging cause does not prevent this. The saints, for instance, are immutable in glory only on account of the "immutability (*immutabilitatem*)" of the divine will.[15]

When the potency of the creature is considered in the second way (according to what it is natural for it to possess), the creature is again mutable. By nature the creature is not absolutely perfect, but can always receive additional perfection. In this way, every creature is changeable if change is taken in a broad sense in which any act of receiving is considered a change. Here, we find the radical distinction between God and creatures spelled out in terms of changeability. For God, who is completely perfect (pure act), change

14. *Sent.* I, 8, 3, 2, co.
15. Ibid.

is neither possible nor desirable. For the creature, which remains always in some sense in potency and perfectible, change, in the sense of some growth in knowledge or goodness, is always both possible and desirable.

Commentary on Boethius's On the Trinity, Q.5, a.4

The theme of divine immutability is also found in the *Commentary on Boethius's On the Trinity*. This work, which belongs to the same genre as the *Commentary on the Sentences*, was written relatively early in Thomas's career, sometime between 1256 and 1260.[16]

Divine immutability is discussed in the article on "whether divine science treats of what exists without matter and motion." To resolve the question, Thomas explains the sort of perfection proper to the principles of divine science (which include both God and angels). These are complete natures in themselves and principles of all other beings. Since they are most perfect in being, they are characterized by immutability:

Since that which is the principle of being for all things must be supremely being, as the *Metaphysics* says, such principles [of divine science] must be most perfect and therefore supremely in act, so that they have no potency whatsoever or the least possible, because actuality is prior to and more excellent than potency, as the *Metaphysics* says. For this reason, they must be without matter, which is in potentiality, and without motion, which is the actuality of the potential. And of this sort are divine beings, because if the divine exists anywhere it exists especially in such an immaterial and immobile (*immobili*) nature, as is said in the *Metaphysics*.[17]

After establishing the immutability of divine beings in the corpus of the article, Thomas explains in his responses to the objections how it is also possible to predicate motion of them. The second objection employs argu-

---

16. M.-D. Chenu favors the earlier date in his *Toward Understanding St. Thomas* (Chicago: Regnery, 1964), 277. Weisheipl allows for a later date: "completed by 1258 or 1260 at the latest" (Weisheipl, *Friar*, 137). Torrell suggests 1257–58 or the beginning of 1259. Torrell, *Thomas*,.1:68, 345.

17. "Et quia id, quod est principium essendi omnibus, oportet esse maxime ens, ut dicitur in II *Metaphysicae*, ideo huiusmodi principia oportet esse completissima, et propter hoc oportet ea esse maxime actu, ut nihil vel minimum habeant de potentia, quia actus est prior et potior potentia, ut dicitur in IX *Metaphysicae*. Et propter hoc oportet ea esse absque materia, quae est in potentia, et absque motu, qui est actus exsistentis in potentia. Et huiusmodi sunt res divinae; 'quia si divinum alicubi exsistit, in tali natura,' immateriali scilicet et immobili, maxime 'exsistit,' ut dicitur in VI *Metaphysicae*" (*Super de trin.* Q.5, 4, co.).

ments from Scripture, Augustine, and Plato to show that God is "mobile" and "moves himself."[18] In his response Aquinas explains that both immanent and transient action may be predicated in certain ways of God without implying any change in him. It is reminiscent of his account in the *Commentary on the Sentences:*

We do not attribute motion to God properly, but by a kind of metaphor, and this in two ways: first, according as the operation of the intellect or will is improperly called motion; and in this way a person is said to move himself when he knows or loves himself. In this sense, as the Commentator says, the statement of Plato is true, that the First Mover moves himself in that he knows and loves himself. Secondly, according as the flowing forth of effects from their causes can be called a procession or motion of cause to effect insofar as the likeness of the cause is left in the effect itself; and so the cause, which previously existed in itself, afterward comes to be in the effect through its likeness. And in this way God, who has communicated his likeness to all creatures, in a certain respect is said to be moved by them all or to go forward to all things. Dionysius frequently uses this manner of speaking. And this also seems to be the meaning of the statement in Wisdom that "Wisdom is more mobile than all mobile things," and that "It reaches from end to end mightily." However, this is not motion in the proper sense of the term, and so the argument does not follow.[19]

An Exposition on the First and Second Decretals I (lines 178–87, 208–12)

Thomas's *Exposition on the First and Second Decretals* includes a brief affirmation of divine immutability. The work is a summary explanation of the first and second canons of the Twelfth Ecumenical Council (Lateran IV, 1215),[20] which were integrated into the Decretals of Gregory IX as part of medieval canon law. The date of the work is uncertain, but most authorities believe it to have been written while Aquinas was in Italy between 1261 and 1269.[21] Though short, the passage is of interest as a rare instance where Aquinas affirms divine immutability with reference to a council of the Church.

18. Wis 8:22, 24. St. Augustine, *Super gen. ad litt.* VIII, 20 (*PL* 34, 388). Plato, *Laws* X (896); XII (966 E); *Phaedrus* (245 C).

19. *Super de trin.* Q.5, 4, ad 2.

20. Denz. no. 800.

21. H.-F. Dondaine, "Préface," in *Super decret.* (Leonine edition), E-6; Weisheipl, *Friar*, 393–94. Torrell specifies 1261–65, the Orvieto period (*Thomas*, 1:125, 352).

It occurs in his exposition of the first decretal. By declaring that God is "eternal" and "unchangeable (*incommutabilis*)," the council "shows the excellence of the divine nature or essence." Commenting on the term "eternal," Aquinas explains that the divine essence "is not changed through past and future, for nothing is taken from it nor is anything able to come to it anew." Eternity is signified in the name by which God reveals himself to Moses: "Whence he says to Moses, 'I am who I am' [*Ex* 3:14], because his to-be (*esse*) admits of neither past nor future, but always possesses to-be (*esse*) presently." In a brief comment on the term "unchangeable (*incommutabilis*)," Thomas shows that the statement of the council is confirmed by Scripture: "Third, it is shown that the divine nature surpasses all mutability when it is called 'unchangeable (*incommutabilis*)' because with him there is no variation according to James: 'With whom there is no change or shadow of vicissitude.'"[22]

The *Commentary on Dionysius's On the Divine Names*

In de div. nom. Book IX, lect. 2 The *Commentary on Dionysius's On the Divine Names* provides a detailed discussion of divine immutability. Thomas seems to have written this commentary during the years 1265–67, while he was at the convent of Santa Sabina in Rome.[23] *On the Divine Names* itself was probably written in the late fifth century and came to be attributed to Dionysius, the disciple of St. Paul who is mentioned in Acts 17:34. Aquinas wrestles with its vagaries of Neoplatonic thought, remarking at one point that "the Blessed Dionysius uses an obscure style in all of his books," and noting that "very often he employs the style and way of speaking that was in use among the Platonists but uncommon among the moderns."[24]

---

22. "Deinde ostendit excellentiam divinae naturae sive essentiae. Et primo quantum ad hoc quod non comprehenditur tempore: quod significatur cum dicitur, *aeternus*. Dicitur enim aeternus, quia caret principio et fine, et quia eius esse non variatur per praeteritum et futurum. Nihil enim ei subtrahitur, nec aliquid ei de novo advenire potest. Unde dicit ad Moysem *Exod.* III, 14: 'Ego sum qui sum,' quia scilicet eius esse non novit praeteritum nec futurum, sed semper praesentialiter esse habet. . . . Tertio ostenditur quod excedit omnem mutabilitatem, cum dicitur, *incommutabilis*, quia scilicet nulla est apud ipsum variatio, secundum illud *Iacob.* I, 17: 'apud quem non est transmutatio, nec vicissitudinis obumbratio'" (*Super decret.* I, lines 178–87, 208–12).

23. Petros Caramello, "Introduction," in *In de div. nom.* (Turin: Marietti, 1950), xxi; Weisheipl, *Friar*, 382. Jean-Pierre Torrell sees the date as uncertain, sometime between 1261 and 1268; *Thomas*, 1:127.

24. *In de div. nom.*, Prooemium. The translation is from Chenu, *Toward*, 288nn49–50.

Dionysius allows names normally used of creatures to be applied to God through the ways of causality, remotion, and eminence. We have already seen this in the *Commentary on the Sentences*.[25] Thomas believes that *On the Divine Names* is especially concerned with the way of causality. Names applied to God in sacred Scripture are derived from "intelligible perfections, such as being, life and so forth, which proceed from God into creatures."[26] Names signifying such creaturely perfections may be applied to God, but the qualities they represent exist more perfectly in God than in creatures. In predicating such perfections of God, therefore, the limitations of their creaturely manifestations must be denied (the way of remotion), and their positive signification must be affirmed in a surpassing way (the way of eminence).

The discussion of immutability in the ninth chapter shows its positive implications. The chapter is concerned with names implying relation to another. In the discussion of the terms "same and other" (lect. 2) and "standing, sitting, and motion" (lect. 4), divine immutability is considered. Various scriptural passages are cited where God is said to be "the same," "to stand," "to sit," to be "immovable (*immobilis*)," and to "move."[27]

Inquiring how "same" and "other" are applied to God, Aquinas points out that "sameness" is attributed to God "in terms of his immutability (*secundum immutabilitatem*)." Immutability is then considered in four respects: (1) being, (2) local motion, (3) alteration, augmentation, and diminution, and (4) relationship to other things.[28]

Divine immutability implies first of all perfection in being. Unlike other things, God is "not changed as regards being and non-being." Neither generated nor corrupted, God is eternally the same or "supersubstantially eternal" and "inalterable (*inconversibile*)." Unlike generated things he does not change from one thing into another, but is always "the same existing being" and so is called "ungenerated (*ingenitum*)."[29] Since the term "ungenerated" has both

25. *Sent.* I, 3, 1, 1, *div. text.*

26. *In de div. nom. Prooemium* I, lect. 3 (§104).

27. See Ps 101:28; Amos 7:7; Is 9:7; Mal 3:6; Gen 3:8; Wis 7:24.

28. *In de div. nom.* IX, lect. 2 (§815–21).

29. "Attribuitur autem idem Deo secundum eius immutabilitatem, prout in Psalm. 101 legitur: 'Tu autem idem ipse es.' Immutabilitas autem Dei, primo quidem attenditur quantum ad hoc quod non transmutatur secundum esse et non esse, sicut generabilia et corruptibilia et ideo dicit quod Deus 'est idem aeternum,' inquantum est 'supersubstantialiter' aeternus; sed quia quaedam habent quamdam

positive and negative connotations, the negative must be denied and the positive affirmed in a supereminent way. It has negative overtones when applied to something not yet generated and to be generated in the future, since it indicates that the thing has not yet received the perfection of being (*esse*). This negative understanding must denied of God and the respective positive quality affirmed. So God is ungenerated "not as something not yet generated" but as "always existing." The term "ungenerated" is also negative when applied to something whose generation has begun but is not yet completed, since it implies the thing has only imperfect being. God in contrast is called ungenerated "not as imperfect" but as "existing perfectly through himself."[30]

Local motion must be denied of God since it implies imperfection. God is not moved from place to place, nor is he contained in any place. Rather, he is "contained in himself as in a place without place." The exclusion of alteration, augmentation, and diminution indicates God's perfection in form. God is not changed from one form to another, losing one and acquiring another, but "stands always immovably according to the same form."[31] Two reasons are given for God's immutability regarding alteration. First Dionysius uses the term "strong" to signify that God possesses a perfection of power for resisting change. Second, he uses the word "invariable (*invariabile*)" to show that God has in himself no principle of mutability. This lack of an inner principle of change, however, implies no imperfection. For, as Thomas goes on to explain, an inner principle of mutability indicates not perfection but imperfection. This is shown in four ways. First, the principle of variation may indicate the admixture of something extraneous. This is excluded from God, who is called "pure" or unmixed with any "extraneous blemish." Second, the potency of matter might be a principle of variation, but matter is an inherently imperfect principle. It is therefore excluded from God by the term "immaterial." Third, variability may arise from the fact that a given thing is composed of diverse things. In this way, mixed bodies are variable both because they are material and because they are composed of contraries. In con-

---

aeternitatem, inquantum non deficiunt penitus in non esse, in aliqua alia convertibilia, ad hoc excludendum consequenter dicit: 'inconversibile'" (*In de div. nom.* IX, lect. 2 [§815]). "[A]d excludendum vero transmutationem generationis, subiungit: 'ingenitum,' idest non-generatum" (§818); cf.: §821.

30. Ibid. (§819–20).

31. Ibid. (§815; cf.: §819–20).

trast to such things, God has the perfection of simplicity. Finally, variation may be due to the indigent condition of that which is changed. For anything imperfect naturally seeks its own perfection. In God, however, such an imperfect condition is to be excluded, and therefore he is called "not indigent." For these reasons, divine immutability with respect to alteration implies not imperfection but the highest perfection of form.[32]

Finally, motion implied by relationship to other things is excluded from God, who is always "in the same way present to all things (*eodem modo omnibus praesens*)." Those things, however, are not always related in the same way to God. The relationship of things to God may change because of variations in things.[33]

Once the meaning and perfection of God's immutability have been established, it is then shown that "otherness" may also be attributed to God "insofar as he is present to all things as they participate him through a certain similitude according to the perfections which they receive through his providence."[34] Since creatures participate God's perfection, God can "always be designated through the participation of his similitude," that is, through the perfections found in creatures. This creaturely participation also allows Dionysius to speak of the procession of divine goodness into creatures. As Aquinas interprets Dionysius's text, he is careful to exclude all suggestion of imperfection in God. God is not changed through this procession of his goodness into all things, but "remains in himself." His procession into things may be compared to the way a form such as fire, in generating a form like itself, is said to come to be in the generated fire. Yet the divine procession into things, unlike the procession of fire, implies no imperfection. For, unlike the generating fire, God neither changes, nor proceeds forth from himself, nor acts by diverse operations, nor acts intermittently, nor suffers, nor grows weary.[35] Once such imperfections have been excluded, "otherness" may be predicated of God through the "processions of divine abundance to all things."[36]

---

32. Ibid. (§817).
34. Ibid. (§823).
36. Ibid. (§827).

33. Ibid. (§815).
35. Ibid. (§824).

In de div. nom. **Book IX, lect. 4** In the fourth lecture, divine immutability is involved in the discussion of Dionysius's musings on scriptural references to God's "standing, sitting, and moving." The basic insight is that "they are attributed to God supersubstantially" since God is "above all sitting and standing."[37] When said of God, sitting and standing denote "a certain immovability (*immobilitas quaedam*)" which may be discussed in terms of being, operation, and passivity. As regards being, God "exists in himself" and "remains in himself . . . according to immovable identity (*secundum immobilem identitatem*)." God "depends on no other thing and is immovable (*fixus*) and placed above all other things."[38] Regarding operation, God "always acts according to the same wisdom, power and goodness" since it is "by knowing and loving himself that he does all things." Also, his mode of operation is always the same, "for in acting he grows neither weaker nor stronger."[39] Finally, passivity is removed from God since "he has no cause of his motion (*transmutationis*) outside of himself" and since he "cannot be moved into a contrary condition by anything external." He is therefore "totally immovable (*totaliter immobilis*)."[40]

After explaining how "standing" and "sitting" imply immutability, Aquinas then follows Dionysius in determining how "motion" may be said of God. Here, proper nuance is essential: "When the doctors of Sacred Scripture say that God who is immovable (*immobilis*) is moved (*moveri*) and proceeds towards all things, this must be understood in a way that is fitting for God." God is not moved in the way of creatures. Subject to no imperfect and limiting creaturely motion, he is said to be moved in that he brings all things into existence, contains them in his being, and "universally provides for all

---

37. Ibid. (§838).

38. "Attribuit autem Deo stationem et sessionem, tripliciter: primo quidem, quantum ad hoc quod ipse in se existit; et hoc est quod dicit quod 'de divina statione' et 'sessione,' per quae immobilitas quaedam designatur, nihil aliud dicere possumus, praeter hoc quod ipse non stat aut sedet tamquam sustentatus in aliquo altero sicut nos, sed in seipso manet . . . secundum immobilem identitatem. . . . Sic enim sibi ipsi innititur quod a nullo alio dependet et est 'fixus et' omnibus 'supercollocatus'" (ibid. [§837]).

39. Ibid.

40. "Tertio, attribuit Deo stationem et sessionem per remotionem omnis passionis vel transmutationis ab ipso; et dicit quod statio aut 'sessio' attribuitur Deo, 'et secundum quod non habet ex seipso' aliquam causam suae transmutationis 'et secundum quod non potest' ab aliquo exteriori 'moveri in contrarium,' sed 'totaliter est immobilis'" (ibid.).

things, giving them life, wisdom, power, and so on, and conserving [these gifts] in them."[41]

God's creative activity resembles motion in two ways. First, his universal presence in all things as creator has a similitude of motion since "we [limited creatures] are not able to be present to diverse things unless we are moved." Second, the procession of divine goodness in the act of creation can be viewed as a kind of motion since the gifts God confers on creatures "are first considered in God as in the highest source and thence are imparted, as through a certain effusion, into other things."[42]

Since motion and immutability may both be attributed to God, the attempt to reconcile these mutually incompatible notions soon runs up against the limitations of human thought and language. Dionysius seems eager to break those limits when in a mystical hymn of praise he attempts to show how "rectilinear, spiral, and circular motions" are attributable to God. Aquinas follows him in the adventure.

The explanation of rectilinear motion is fairly straightforward. God's action is rectilinear since it extends "straight" through all intermediaries to its ultimate effect and is not diverted from its intended course. It proceeds "unfailingly (indeclinabiliter)" and "unchangingly (inflexibiliter)." The explanations of spiral and circular motion are somewhat more tortuous. God's action is "spiral" since, just as spiral motion is composed of the other two kinds of motion (rectilinear and circular), so God's operation simultaneously involves both "motion (processus)" and "rest (statio)." It includes motion or procession "with respect to the production of things," and rest or standing still "with respect to the invariability (invariabilitatem) of the divine operation." Dionysius expresses this dual character of divine activity with the oxymora "stable procession (processus stabilis)" and "productive stillness (statum generativum)." Finally, God's activity is called circular since he contains, in the identity of his own existence, both principles and ends, "things contain-

41. "Dicit ergo primo quod quando sacrae Scripturae doctores 'dicunt' Deum, qui est immobilis, moveri 'et ad omnia' procedere, 'intelligendum est' sicut 'decet Deum. Religiose enim' et secundum rectam fidem 'aestimandum est' quod Deus moveatur. . . . [D]icitur Deus moveri, inquantum omnia ducit ad hoc quod sint 'et' inquantum continet 'omnia' in suo esse; et non solum agit ad 'substantiam' et in ea continet res, sed inquantum universaliter 'omnia' providet, dans rebus et vitam et sapientiam et virtutem et alia huiusmodi et in eis conservat" (ibid. [§840]).

42. Ibid. (§841).

ing and things contained," and "the turning to himself of those things which proceed from him as from a principle."[43] Here, the limits of human thought have surely been reached, if not already breached. Those, however, who are able to grasp in some measure the profound but elusive content of this text might affirm with Aquinas that "not only do theologians attribute motion to God, but it is also granted us that we may fittingly praise the motion of the immovable God (*motum Dei immobilis*)."[44]

Philosophical Commentaries

The *Commentary on Aristotle's Physics*

Book VII, lect. 2 The *Commentary on Aristotle's Physics*, written about 1268,[45] contains two arguments for an immovable first mover. The first occurs in Book VII after six books establishing the nature and divisions of motion. There, the principles are established that "whatever is moved is moved by another," and that "movers and mobile objects cannot proceed to infinity." From these principles the existence of a first unmoved mover is demonstrated. The intricacies of the argument have provided a rich source of philosophical discussion ever since Aristotle. Thomas himself notes the comments and arguments of Galen (d. 201 A.D.), Avicenna (d. 1037), and Averroes (d. 1198). In our time, the discussion is still very much alive.[46] Here, we are concerned not

43. Ibid. (§842).

44. "Et non solum theologi motum Deo attribuunt, 'sed' et nobis 'permittitur' ut decenter laudemus motum 'Dei immobilis'" (ibid. [§841]).

45. Fernand Van Steenberghen suggests the year 1268; *Problème*, 249. Weisheipl proposes 1269–70, but certainly "after the *prima pars*" (1266) and "prior to the beginning of 1271"; *Friar*, 282, 376. Torrell favors the academic year 1268–69; *Thomas*, 1:231.

46. See, for example, Simon Oliver, *Philosophy, God and Motion* (New York: Routledge, 2005); Lloyd P. Gerson, "Aristotle's God of Motion," in *God and Greek Philosophy: Studies in the Early History of Natural Theology* (New York: Routledge, 1990), 82–141; Eric A. Reitan, "Aquinas and Weisheipl: Aristotle's Physics and the Existence of God," and David Twetten, "Why Motion Requires a Cause: The Foundation for a Prime Mover in Aristotle and Aquinas," in *Philosophy and the God of Abraham: Essays in Memory of James A. Weisheipl, O.P.*, ed. R. James Long (Toronto: Pontifical Institute of Mediaeval Studies, 1991), 179–90, 235–54; David Twetten, "Clearing a 'Way' for Aquinas: How the Proof from Motion Concludes to God," *PACPA* 70 (1996): 259–78; James F. McNiff, "Aristotle's Argument from Motion," *IPQ* 32 (1992): 313–23; J. William Forgie, "The Cosmological and Ontological Arguments: How Saint Thomas Solved the Kantian Problem," *Religious Studies* 31 (1995): 89–100; John F. X. Knasas, "Ad mentem Thomae: Does Natural Philosophy Prove God?" *PACPA* 61 (1987): 209–20; Robert Fogelin, "A Reading of Aquinas's Five Ways," *American Philosphical Quarterly* 27 (1990): 305–14; William Wallace, "The Cosmological

so much with establishing the validity of the argument as with examining its implications for divine immutability.

It is important to notice the word *immobile* does not occur at all in the Aristotelian text upon which Aquinas is commenting.[47] When Aristotle concludes his argument by affirming a first cause of motion, he is probably thinking of a first self-mover in which one part moves another.[48] Aquinas goes beyond this notion to affirm an immovable first cause:

> After the Philosopher has shown that whatever is moved is moved by another, here he proceeds to prove the principal proposition; namely, that there is a first motion and a first mover. . . . Let us accept something which is moved with respect to place. This is moved by another. This other is either moved or is not moved. If it is not moved, the proposition is established, namely, that there is an immovable mover (*movens immobile*). This [immobility] is a characteristic feature of the first mover. If however this mover is itself moved, then it must be moved by another. Now this cannot continue to infinity, but must stop with something. There will be, therefore, some first mover which will be the first cause of motion, such that it is not moved itself but moves others.[49]

Argument: A Reappraisal," PACPA 46 (1972): 43–57; Antonio Moreno, "The Law of Inertia and the Principle 'Quidquid movetur ab alio movetur,'" *Thomist* 38 (1974): 306–31; Norbert Luyten, "Der erste Weg: Ex parte motus," in *Quinque sunt viae,* Studi Tomistici, no. 9, ed. Léon Elders (Vatican City: Libreria Vaticana, 1980), 29–41.

47. "Quoniam autem omne quod movetur ab aliquo movetur, necesse est et omne quod movetur in loco, moveri ab altero. Et movens igitur ab altero, quoniam et ipsum movetur; et iterum hoc ab altero. Non autem in infinitum abibit, sed stabit alicubi, et erit aliquid quod primo causa erit motus" (Aristotle, *Libri physicorum textus Aristotelis* VII, c.1, no. 3, in *In phys.,* 454).

48. See J. Paulus, "La theorie du premier moteur chez Aristote," *Revue de philosophie* 33 (1933): 282.

49. "Postquam ostendit Philosophus quod omne quod movetur, movetur ab alio, hic accedit ad principale propositum ostendendum, scilicet quod sit primus motus et primus motor. . . . Dicit ergo primo, quod cum ostensum sit universaliter, quod omne quod movetur ab aliquo alio movetur, necesse est hoc etiam verum esse in motu locali, scilicet ut omne quod movetur in loco, ab altero moveatur. Applicat autem specialiter ad motum localem quod supra universaliter demonstratum est, quia motus localis est primus motuum, ut in octavo ostendetur; et ideo secundum hunc motum procedit hic ad demonstrandum primum motorem. Accipiatur igitur aliquid quod movetur secundum locum; hoc movetur ab altero; aut ergo illud alterum movetur, aut non. Si non movetur, habetur propositum, scilicet quod aliquid sit movens immobile; quod est proprietas primi moventis. Si autem et ipsum movens movetur, oportet quod moveatur ab altero movente; et hoc iterum movens, si et ipsum movetur, movetur ab altero. Sed hoc non potest procedere in infinitum, sed oportet in aliquo stare. Erit ergo aliquid primum movens, quod erit prima causa motus: ita scilicet quod ipsum non movetur, sed movet alia" (*In phys.* VII, lect. 2.1 [§891]).

For Aquinas, a "first mover" must be an "immovable mover" since immovability is its "characteristic feature."[50] This implies that Aquinas is affirming a far more transcendent mover than what Aristotle probably has in mind.

In phys. VIII, lect. 9–13, 23 At the conclusion of the eleventh lecture of Book VIII, Thomas summarizes a more nuanced version of the argument for the existence of a first immovable mover:

[Aristotle] says that it is clear from the above that there must be a first immovable mover (*primum movens immobile*). For since movers and things moved by another do not go on to infinity, it is necessary to stop at some first which is either immovable (*immobile*) or a self-mover. It makes no difference whether movers and things moved stop at a first immovable [mover] (*aliquod primum immobile*) or at some first thing which moves itself. In either case, the first mover will be immovable (*immobile*), for in a self-mover one part is an immovable mover (*movens immobile*), as has now been shown.[51]

This is the conclusion of a long process of argumentation that began in the seventh lecture: "After the Philosopher has explained his intention, he here begins to develop it; namely, not everything is sometimes moved and sometimes at rest. Rather there is something which is absolutely immovable (*omnino immobile*) and something which is always moved."[52] In the course of this argument, the premises for establishing the existence of the immovable mover are more elaborately explained than they were in Book VII. The premise that "whatever is moved is moved by another," which was originally

50. Compare also Aristotle's text in VII, 1 (242b 30–35) with Thomas's commentary (VII, lect. 2.4 [§894]). While Aristotle concludes that "there will be something which will be moved first (*quod primum movebitur*)," Thomas asserts that "there will be some first mobile object which is moved by another immovable thing (*quod scilicet moveatur ab altero immobili*)." Léon Elders notes a similar modification of Aristotle by Thomas in *In meta.* XII, 9 (§2555). Where Aristotle mentions a mover that is "immovable according to itself" (1073a 27), Thomas speaks of one that is "altogether immovable (*omnino immobile*)." See Elders, "St. Thomas Aquinas's Commentary on the 'Metaphysics' of Aristotle," *Divus Thomas* (Piacenza) 86 (1983): 319.

51. "Et dicit [Philosophus] manifestum esse ex praemissis, quod necesse est ponere primum movens immobile. Cum enim non procedatur in infinitum in moventibus et motis ab alio, sed necesse sit stare ad aliquod primum, quod est immobile vel movens seipsum; sive moventia et mota stent ad aliquod primum immobile, sive ad aliquod primum quod movet seipsum, utrobique accidit quod primum movens sit immobile; propter hoc quod moventis etiam seipsum una pars est movens immobile, ut nunc ostensum est" (*In phys.* VIII, lect. 11.7 [1068]).

52. Ibid., lect. 7 (§1021).

proved in Book VII, is here "verified for all movers and mobile objects."[53] The premise that it is impossible "to proceed to infinity with respect to movers and things moved," which was also established in Book VII, is here demonstrated "in a more certain way."[54]

From these premises, Thomas does not here conclude directly to the existence of a first unmoved mover (as he did in Book VII), but follows Aristotle in concluding to the existence of a first mover that is "either immovable (*immobile*) or moves itself."[55] As Thomas explains the argument, Aristotle has here assumed initially "in accordance with the common opinion of the Platonists" that "every mover is moved." He has then argued that since there is no process to infinity, and since the first mover is not moved by another, "it must be moved by itself."[56]

Next, it is shown that the assumption "every mover is moved" is not universally true. For if every mover is moved, it must be moved either *per se* or *per accidens*. But if all movers were moved *per accidens*, it would also be possible that they not be moved. And if they were not moved, then nothing would be moved. But this is not possible since Aristotle has already shown that motion is eternal.[57] Therefore, it is impossible that all movers be moved *per accidens*. But if a mover is moved *per se*, it will be moved either with respect to the same species of motion or with respect to some other species of motion. Yet it cannot be moved with respect to the same species of motion, for then the mover would also be moved in the same way that it moves. Thus, someone who is teaching would simultaneously be taught the same thing that he is teaching. Similarly, the one throwing would also be thrown, and the one

53. See *In phys.* lect. 1 (§885–90); lect. 7–8.

54. *In phys.* VII lect. 2 (§892–96); VIII lect. 9 (§1040). On the relation of these arguments to the first and second ways of *ST* I, 2, 3, co., see Michael Buckley, *Motion and Motion's God* (Princeton, N.J.: Princeton University Press, 1971), 61–62.

55. See all of Book VIII, lect. 9, esp. §1049. Cf.: *Phys.* Book VIII, 5 (257a 25–35).

56. *In phys.* VIII, lect. 9 (§1040–41).

57. *Phys.* VIII, 1 (252b 5). As a Catholic theologian, of course, Thomas does not hold that either the world or its motion is eternal, and he is careful to explain his position (*In phys.* VIII, lect. 2 [§986–87]). In the *Commentary on the Metaphysics*, Thomas shows first that Aristotle's arguments for the eternity of motion "are neither demonstrative nor necessarily conclusive" (*In meta.* XII, lect. 5 [§2496–98]), and then that the conclusions regarding the eternity and immateriality of the first substance, which are drawn from the assumption that motion is eternal, are not thereby invalidated (§2499). See also *SCG* I, c.13.29–30 (§109–10). Cf.: James Doig, *Aquinas on Metaphysics* (The Hague: M. Nijhoff, 1972), 328.

building would also be built. But all of these are clearly impossible. But if the mover is moved according to some other species of motion, this cannot proceed to infinity since the species of motion are not infinite. Therefore, either there will be "some first immovable mover (*aliquod primum movens immobile*)" or the species of motion will be repeated. If the species of motion are repeated, then that which is moved with respect to place, for instance, will be moved by the nearest mover that is increased, and that again will be moved by something that is altered, and that in turn will be moved by something that is moved with respect to place. But since "whatever is moved is moved more by a higher mover than by a lower one, and consequently much more by the first mover," that which is moved with respect to place will be moved more by the first mover, which is also moved with respect to place, than by the second mover, which is altered, or the third mover, which is increased. This means that what moves with respect to place will be moved with respect to place. But that involves the same impossible situation that was just rejected. For the mover will itself be moved with respect to the same species of motion as the object moved. So, the teacher will be taught, the builder will be built, and so on. It therefore becomes clear that not every mover is moved.[58]

If the assumption that "every mover is moved" is eliminated from the original argument, the argument will no longer conclude to a first mover that moves itself, but to a first mover that either moves itself or is "unmoved (*immobile*)."[59] This dichotomy is then resolved by examining what it means for something to move itself. Since a self-mover is mobile, it is also divisible into parts. In moving itself, the whole thing cannot move the whole thing, for then it would be both in act and in potency at the same time and in the same respect. Rather, there must be one part that is moved and another that moves while remaining itself "absolutely immovable (*omnino immobilis*)." So a self-mover must be distinguished into two parts, one of which is moved but does not move, and the other of which moves, but is itself not moved. We therefore arrive at the conclusion quoted at the beginning of the discussion, that "there must be a first immovable mover (*necesse est primum movens immobile*)."[60]

58. *In phys.* VIII (§1043, 1046–48).

59. "Hoc autem primum oportet quod vel sit immobile, vel sit movens seipsum" (*In phys.* VIII, lect. 9.12 [§1049]).

60. *In phys.* VIII, §1051–53, 1068.

Once the existence of this immovable first mover has been established, the precise nature of its immovability remains to be considered. For "immovability" might be taken either too extensively or too restrictively. Immovability would be understood too extensively if it were taken to refer to immanent as well as transient motion. To avoid such an interpretation, Thomas explains that when Aristotle says "exempt from all extrinsic change" he "does not intend to exclude that motion or operation which is in that which acts insofar as understanding is called a motion and insofar as appetite is moved by that which is desirable. For such motion is not excluded from the first mover which he intends."[61]

Immovability would be taken too restrictively if it did not exclude all possibility of the first mover's ceasing to exist. For there are certain things that sometimes exist and sometimes do not, but may still be called unchangeable in the sense that they are not as such generated or corrupted. We have already seen an example of this in the form or soul of the animal. Lest it be thought, therefore, that what moves the first self-mover is, like the soul of an animal, immovable *per se* but movable *per accidens*, it is necessary to show "that the first mover is incorruptible and that it is moved neither *per se* nor *per accidens*." But because that which is moved *per se* or *per accidens* is able at times to be and at other times not to be, showing that the first mover is moved neither *per se* nor *per accidens* amounts to the same thing as showing that the first mover always exists or is eternal: "It is clear that if a thing is not moved either *per se* or *per accidens*, it is eternal (*perpetuum*). And if it is eternal, it is moved neither *per se* nor *per accidens* because it is eternal."[62]

Accordingly, two arguments are given to show that the first mover is eternal and is therefore moved neither *per se* nor *per accidens*. The first is derived "from the eternity of the generation and corruption of animals which move themselves." Because the pattern of generation and corruption continues eternally, and because the first mover is the cause of generation, the first mover must also be eternal. From the eternity of the first mover, its oneness and absolute immutability may be established:

61. Ibid. (§1071).
62. Ibid. (§1069; 1073).

For if motion is eternal, . . . the motion of the first self-mover which is given as the cause of the whole eternity of motion must be eternal and continuous. For if it were not continuous, it would not be eternal. And that which is consecutive is not continuous. In order for motion to be continuous it must be one, and in order for it to be one, it must be the motion of one mobile object and must be from one mover. If, then, there are different movers, the whole motion will not be continuous, but consecutive. It is absolutely necessary, therefore, that the first mover is one and eternal. But an immovable mover (*ens immobile*) which is moved *per accidens* is not eternal. . . . Hence it follows that the first mover is absolutely immovable (*omnino immobile*), both per se and per accidens.[63]

The second argument is "derived from moving principles." It is shown first that if the moving principle of a self-mover (such as the soul of an animal) is moved *per accidens*, it is not always in the same disposition for moving. Thomas explains that the soul of an animal is here understood to be moved *per accidens* both in that it sometimes causes local motion in the animal and sometimes does not, and in that it is itself moved accidentally from place to place when the animal is moved locally. That such a principle cannot be the first moving cause of the universe is then demonstrated:

If some principle is an immovable mover (*ens immobile*) which nevertheless is moved incidentally (*secundum accidens*), it cannot cause continuous and eternal motion. The reason why the souls of animals do not always move is that they are moved *per accidens*. But it was shown above that the motion of the universe must be continuous and eternal. Therefore, the first moving cause in the whole universe must be immovable (*immobilem*), such that it is not even moved *per accidens*.[64]

Thomas then explains why the first immovable mover is not itself moved accidentally when it causes motion in the first mobile object, unlike the soul of an animal, which is moved accidentally when it causes the animal to move from place to place. His explanation affirms the perfection in *being* of the first immovable mover and of the movers of the various other heavenly spheres:

The reason for this diversity is that the movers of the higher orbs are not constituted in their being (*esse*) by a union to bodies, and their connection is invariable (*invariabi-*

---

63. Ibid. (§1076, 1074, 1077). Cf.: (§1166).
64. Ibid. (§1080, 1081).

lis). Therefore, although the bodies of the orbs are moved, their movers are not moved *per accidens*. But the souls which move animals are constituted in their being (*esse*) by a union to bodies, and they are connected with them in an inconstant manner (*variabiliter*). Therefore, according to the mutations of bodies, these souls are also said to be changed *per accidens*.[65]

At this point in the text, the arguments regarding the immovable mover are suspended and the discussion turns to the eternity of the first motion. It is by no means clear, however, that the arguments thus far presented in the commentary on Book VIII have reached an immovable mover that might be identified as God. It is clear, for instance, that when Thomas explained that immanent motion is not excluded from the first mover, he was referring not to God, but either to Aristotle's "soul of the first sphere," or to some other intelligible substance that moves the first sphere. For he allowed that the appetite of this mover might be "moved" by that which it desires. And even after Thomas has indicated that a certain transcendence is proper to the first mover, there is still no solid textual evidence to show that this first mover is anything more than the immovable moving part of the first self-mover (the soul of the outermost sphere). The fact that the discussion has not progressed beyond the first self-mover should not, however, be too surprising. For Thomas is here following the text of Aristotle, and Aristotle, for his part, once he has identified the first self-mover as the most likely cause of motion, concerns himself solely with discovering the nature this mover.[66]

The discussion of the immovable mover is taken up again in lecture 23, where the "unity of the first mover" is considered. First, certain arguments are summarized, showing that there is a motion that is eternal, continuous, and caused by one mover. Then, the existence and nature of this mover are discussed. In the summary of the arguments establishing the existence of this mover, however, no mention of any self-mover is made. In this respect,

65. Ibid. (§1082).

66. Ibid. (§1061, 1068, 1071). "The first moved, [Aristotle] continues, is either put in operation by an exterior and immobile being or moves itself. Aristotle thinks the second hypothesis more probable and, for his part, adopts it. And Book VIII will do nothing else but develop this idea of a first cause of movement which moves itself" (J. Paulus, "Théorie," 267). Cf.: Joseph Owens, "Aquinas and the Proof from the *Physics*," *MS* 28 (1966): 122–27. Aristotle explains his preference for a first self-mover in *Phys.* VIII, 5 (257a 25–30).

the summary resembles the arguments presented in Book VII more than those presented in Book VIII:

[Aristotle] says, therefore, first that one motion which is from one mover is from either a moved or an unmoved mover (*motore non moto*). If it is a moved mover, it follows that it is moved by another, according to what has been proved above. But this cannot proceed to infinity, as was established above, for this order of movers and mobile objects will end and will arrive at some first mobile object which is moved by an immovable mover (*immobili motore*).[67]

Because this mover is moved by no other, no necessity of moving is placed upon it by another mover. Because it is totally unchangeable, it does not tire in its moving. For both of these reasons, it can move with an "eternally continuous motion."[68]

Thomas notes that Aristotle identifies this mover as the mover of the outermost sphere. It is present "in the circumference" of that sphere, "preferably in the east where it begins to move." Yet Thomas is again careful to maintain the transcendence of the first mover in explaining the mode of its presence in the outermost sphere:

But it must be stated that the first mover is not said to be in some part of its mobile object through a determination of its own substance, but through its power of motion. For it begins to move from some part of its mobile object, and therefore it is said to be in the heavens rather than in the earth, and preferably in the east where it begins to move. This cannot be understood in the sense that the first mover is fixed to some determinate part of its mobile object. For no determinate part of the mobile object is always in the east. Rather that part which is now in the east is later in the west. And so it is clear that its motive power is said to be in the east because of the influence of its motion, and not because of a determination of its substance.[69]

Through this argument, Aquinas appears to leave some room for his own interpretation or understanding of the nature of the first immovable mov-

___

67. "Dicit ergo primo, quod motus unus, qui est ab uno motore, sicut dictum est, aut est a motore moto, aut a motore non moto. Si quidem igitur sit movens motum, sequitur quod movetur ab aliquo, secundum ea quae supra probata sunt. Sed hoc non potest procedere in infinitum, ut supra probatum est: quare stabit iste processus motorum et mobilium, et pervenietur ad aliquod primum mobile, quod movetur ab immobili motore" (ibid. [§1166]).

68. Ibid. (§1166–67).   69. Ibid. (§1168–69).

er. For he here employs a mode of expression that, it has been noted, might "apply equally to the soul of the outermost sphere or to the transcendent God."[70] There are certain other indications as well that, as Thomas reaches the conclusion of his commentary, the first mover that he has in mind is not simply the immovable part of the first self-mover (the soul of the outermost sphere) with which Aristotle had occupied himself in Book VIII. We have already noted that Thomas (and Aristotle also, as it happens) makes no mention of a self-mover in his review of the arguments establishing the existence of the immovable mover. Here again, the way to a more transcendent understanding of the immovable mover is left open. Thomas also makes reference to the numerous immovable movers that Aristotle will posit in the *Metaphysics*.[71] Again, the statement is somewhat ambiguous. For it may refer either to the separate and transcendent intelligible substances that are the final causes of the motion of the heavens (and among whom the highest will be explicitly identified as God)[72] or to the souls of the various heavenly spheres that are the immanent efficient causes of the motion of the heavens. Following Aristotle, Thomas then reviews certain qualities of the first mover. The "first immovable mover (*primum movens immobile*)" must be infinite in power, indivisible, and, "in a way, outside the genus of magnitude." It will be noticed that these qualities are also applicable in some way either to the soul of the outermost sphere or to the separate and transcendent first cause of motion. Regardless of what Aristotle may intend, it is clear that Thomas means the latter. The first immovable mover is not just the immovable part (or soul) of the outermost sphere, but God himself: "And thus the Philosopher ends his general discussion of natural things with the first principle of the whole of nature, who is over all things, God, blessed forever, Amen."[73]

Commentary on the Metaphysics of Aristotle, Book XII, lect. 5–12

The discussion of the immovable first mover is found in the concluding book of the *Commentary on the Metaphysics of Aristotle*. This work, like the *Commentary on Aristotle's Physics*, is usually thought to have been written later in Thomas's career during his second sojourn in Paris, around the year 1270.[74]

70. Owens, "Proof," 143.
71. *In phys.* (§1166, 1171); *Meta.* XII, 8.
72. *In meta.* XII, lect. 8 (§2544).
73. *In phys.* VIII, lect. 23.9 (§1172).
74. Torrell, *Thomas*, 1:232, 344; Weisheipl, *Friar*, 379; Chenu, *Toward*, 224.

The final book of the commentary begins with an examination of Aristotle's argument that the science of metaphysics is concerned primarily with substances (lect. 1). It then goes on to examine the various types of substances (lect. 2), and finally considers the existence and nature of the first immovable substance (lect. 5–12).

Substances are divided into the three classes of eternal (*sempiternae*) sensible substances (the heavenly bodies), perishable (*corruptibiles*) sensible substances (the substances of the sublunar world), and "immovable substance that is not sensible (*substantiae immobilis quae non est sensibilis*)."[75] The third class includes all separated substances—both God and angels. These are spoken of collectively at first. For example, in listing the properties of eternal substance, Thomas follows Aristotle in referring to the substance sometimes in the singular form and sometimes in the plural.[76] Later, the "first immovable substance (*prima substantia immobilis*)" will be distinguished from the other immovable substances in that it produces the first motion, the motion of the outermost sphere.[77]

Once sensible substances have been discussed (lect. 2–4), immovable substance is treated (lect. 5). Because the existence of such a substance "is not evident to all," before its nature can be discussed, "it must first be shown that it is necessary that there be an eternal immovable substance (*aliquam substantiam sempiternam immobilem*)."[78] Accordingly, it is first shown that an eternal substance exists, and then that the eternal substance is immovable.

The existence of an eternal substance is readily shown. The eternity of motion and time have already been established in the *Physics*. Since something is eternal, there must be an eternal substance. If no substance were eternal, nothing would be eternal since substances are the primary kind of being.[79]

---

75. *In meta.* XII, lect. 2.1, 3 (§2424, 2426).

76. See, for example, *In meta.* XII, lect. 5 (§2492, 2494, 2495). Fernand Van Steenberghen notes the same use of the plural form in Books II and V. As he explains, "Without doubt, it is Aristotle's text that explains the plural" (*Problème*, 268).

77. *In meta.* XII, lect. 9 (§2555–56). The relationship between the first immovable substance and the other immovable substances, however, remains ambiguous in Aristotle. See Van Steenberghen, *Problème*, 264. For Thomas, as we have seen (*Sent.* I, 8, 3, 2; *Super de trin.* Q.5, 4, ad 4), it is clear that God alone is pure act and that the separate substances have some potency not because they are material, but because their essence is distinct from their act of being (*esse*).

78. *In meta.* XII (§2426, 2488).

79. *Phys.* VIII, 1 (251b 10–252b 5); *In meta.* (§2417–23, 2489).

In determining the nature of this eternal substance, the eternity of motion plays a major role. Since motion is eternal, the substance in question must be not only eternal, but also constantly moving or acting. If the substance had only the power of acting but were not actually exercising that power, motion would cease. If the substance is to be always acting, however, "its essence (*substantia ejus*) must be act." No potentiality may be admitted "for if a mover is such that it contains potentiality, it can possibly not be, because whatever is in potentiality may possibly not be." But if this substance could cease to be, motion could also cease, and so would not be necessary and eternal. "Thus there must be some first principle of motion of such a sort that its essence is not in potentiality but is act only." From this it follows also that "such a substance must be immaterial . . . since matter is always in potency."[80]

Once the existence and nature of the eternal substance have been established, its immovability is demonstrated. Even though the third class of substances has already been called "immovable," and even though their eternity and lack of all potentiality necessarily imply immovability, the actual argument given for their immovability does not proceed directly from these attributes. It emerges rather from a consideration of the process or cycle of generation.

Once it has been established that generation is eternal, it is then shown that the eternal process or cycle of generation requires both a cause of its permanence (since the cycle itself is unending) and a cause of its variety (since first one thing and then another is generated and corrupted). The cause of the permanence or "eternity (*perpetuitatis*)" of generation is attributed to the invariable movement of the outermost sphere. The cause of variety is found in the motion of the sun and the other planets along the oblique circle called the zodiac.[81]

From the eternal, invariable motion of the outermost sphere, the existence of an eternal unmoved mover is then demonstrated. The argument depends on two premises originally established in the *Physics:* "whatever is moved is moved by another" and "there is no procession to infinity in mov-

80. *In meta.* (§2492, 2494–95).
81. Ibid. (§2508–13).

ers and things moved."[82] Given the eternal motion of the outermost sphere, the first premise demands that "there must be an eternal mover." Given the three classes that are found among movers and things moved ("the lowest of which is something that is merely moved; the highest, a mover which is not moved; and the intermediate, something that both moves and is moved"), one may then use the second premise to conclude that "there must be an eternal mover that is not moved":

From what has been said above, he [Aristotle] infers the eternity of the unmoved mover. For since everything which is being moved is being moved by something else, as has been proved in the *Physics*, if both the heavens and their motion are eternal, there must be an eternal mover. But since three classes are found among movers and things moved: the lowest of which is something that is merely moved, the highest a mover which is not moved, and the intermediate something that both moves and is moved, we must maintain that there is some eternal mover which is not moved (*aliquid sempiternum movens quod non movetur*). For it has been proved in Book VIII of the *Physics* that since there is no procession to infinity in movers and things moved, it is necessary to come to some first immovable mover (*aliquod primum movens immobile*). For even if one might come to something that moves itself, it would again be necessary for the above reason to come to some immovable mover (*aliquod movens immobile*) as has been proved in that work.[83]

Once the immovability of the eternal substance has been demonstrated, attributes deducible from its immovability are established.[84] In this discussion, it becomes clear that this first mover is considerably more transcendent than the one in Aristotle's *Physics*. That mover is now identified as the "proximate mover of the outermost sphere," which is itself moved by the absolutely

---

82. *Phys.* VIII, 4 (254b 6–256a 4); 5 (256a 4–256a 20).

83. "Concludit ex praedictis perpetuitatem motoris immobilis. Cum enim omne quod movetur, ab alio moveatur, ut in physicis probatum est; si caelum est perpetuum, et motus est perpetuus, necesse est aliquod esse movens perpetuum. Sed quia in ordine mobilium et moventium inveniuntur tria, quorum ultimum est quod movetur tantum, supremum autem est movens quod non movetur, medium autem est quod movetur et movet; necesse est, quod ponatur aliquod sempiternum movens quod non movetur. Probatum est enim in octavo *Physicorum*, quod cum non sit abire in infinitum in moventibus et motis, oportet devenire in aliquod primum movens immobile: quia et si deveniatur in aliquod movens seipsum, iterum ex hoc oportet devenire in aliquid movens immobile, ut ibi probatum est" (*In meta*. XII, lect. 6 [2517]). Cf.: lect. 7 (§2531).

84. Ibid., lect. 7–8.

immovable mover that has now been discovered. This mover, as absolutely immovable, does not cause motion as a "natural mover," but as a "desirable and intelligible object." As such it is separate from the first mobile object (the outermost sphere). It is not the soul of that sphere, but the end or goal in view of which some proximate mover moves that sphere.[85]

From the fact that the first unmoved mover moves as a desirable and intelligible object, further perfections are deduced. As the first cause of motion, it is the first intelligible and appetible good. Since it causes the knowledge and love that are the source of pleasure in the soul of the first sphere, it must itself be able to know and love and must draw a "wondrous happiness" from these activities. Since intellectual activity is a most perfect kind of life, this mover, now identified as God, not only possesses life, but "his very substance is life." He is also shown to be incorporeal, infinite in power, and (again) in no way movable. He is "eternal and unchangeable (*immobilis*) and separate from sensible things."[86]

As this "first immovable substance (*prima substantia immobilis*)" accounts for the motion of the outermost sphere, other immovable movers explain the motions of the other spheres. Aristotle saw these unmoved substances as related to one another according to the same hierarchical order as the motions that they cause in the heavens. Accordingly, he limited their number to that of the heavenly spheres whose motion requires them. Here Aquinas does not consider Aristotle's argument to be conclusive and allows that there may be more separated substances than motions of the heavens.[87]

Thomas agrees with Aristotle, however, that the first immovable substance, rather than some intermediary intelligence, may be considered the immediate final cause of the motion of the outermost sphere (in that it is the immediate cause moving that intelligible substance by which the outermost sphere is moved). In this, Thomas disagrees with Avicenna, who had argued

85. Ibid. (§2519–21). This proximate mover is later identified as the soul of the first heavenly sphere. In so identifying it, however, Thomas is careful to note that it is "an opinion of Aristotle" that each heavenly sphere is "animated by a soul which understands and desires" (§2536). He does not seem to share this opinion, although he does believe the spheres are moved by separate intelligible substances. See *De ver.* Q.5, 9, ad 14; *ST* I, 70, 3; *De sp. cr.* a.6; *De pot.* Q.6, 6, co.

86. *In meta.* (§2547, 2523–27, 2536–44, 2548–51).

87. *Meta.* XII, 8 (1073a 35–39; 1074a 15); *In meta.* XII, lect. 10 (§2556, 2589).

that since the first mover is absolutely one, it can cause only one thing. It causes only the first intelligence, which in turn, because it is not absolutely simple but has potency and act, can cause many things. Among these are the outermost sphere itself, the intelligible substance moving it, and the motion it exhibits.[88] In Thomas's reply to Avicenna, it is evident he considers the first immovable substance not only the ultimate final cause of the motion of the outermost sphere (as did Aristotle), but also its ultimate efficient cause:

But this [conclusion of Avicenna] is not necessary. For an efficient cause in the realm of superior substances does not act like an efficient cause in the realm of material things, in the sense that a single effect is produced by a single cause. For in higher substances, cause and thing caused exist according to intelligible being. Hence, just as many things can be understood by a single superior substance, so many effects can be produced by a single superior substance. And it seems fitting enough that the first motion of corporeal things, on which all other motions depend, should have as its cause the principle of immaterial substances, so that there should be some connection and order between sensible and intelligible things.[89]

It is to this immutable cause of the motion of the outermost sphere—a final cause only in the *Metaphysics* of Aristotle, but both a final cause and an efficient cause in the commentary of Aquinas—that both thinkers give the name "God": "Aristotle's conclusion is that there is one ruler of the whole universe, the first mover, [who is] both the first intelligible object and the first good, whom above he called God, who is blessed for ever and ever. Amen."[90]

Commentary on Aristotle's *On the Heavens*, Book I, lect. 21, nos. 7–13

The theme of divine immutability also appears in the *Commentary on Aristotle's On the Heavens*. This work is believed to have been written dur-

88. *In meta.* XII, lect. 9 (§2559). Avicenna, *Metaphysics* IX, 3 (104rb); 4 (104vab).
89. *In meta.* XII, lect. 9 (§2560). Thomas's choice of words here is a clue to his own opinion on the matter. He does not want to exclude Aristotle's view (as Avicenna did) since Aristotle's opinion is "fitting enough (*satis conveniens*)" and since Avicenna's position implies that a creature is capable of an act of creation. But when Avicenna's opinion that there are intermediary intelligible substances is divorced from the rest of his argument, his opinion is both more fitting and "more probable (*magis probabile*)," and seems to be the opinion Thomas makes his own. See his remarks in *De sub. sep.* c. 2 (line 165ff.), a work contemporary with *In meta.*
90. *In meta.* XII, lect. 12 (§2663).

ing the last years of St. Thomas's life (1271–74), and was left unfinished at his death.[91] The immovability of the heavenly movers is often referred to in the work, but the unchangeable first mover is formally discussed in Book I, lect. 21. Thomas has followed Aristotle in showing that sensible bodies and their properties, such as place and time, cannot exist outside the heavens. He now considers those beings that do exist beyond the heavens. These include God and the separated substances. The *Physics* showed that these beings are "separate from all magnitude and motion."[92] Their immovability is fitting since they "surpass the ultimate movement" in that they are beyond the outermost sphere, the first movable thing and source of all other motion in the universe.[93]

Beyond place and time, beyond the movement of the outermost sphere, these beings are "inalterable and completely impassible (*inalterabilia et penitus impassibilia*)." Their life is most perfect since they are totally separate from matter and self-sufficient, having all they need for their eternal activity and preservation. They are for others the source of life and being in virtue of their perfect life and "eternal being (*esse sempiternum*)."[94]

Thomas explains Aristotle's two arguments why God, as the highest of these beings, is absolutely immutable. First, there can be nothing "better" by which God might be acted upon or "moved" since God is the highest being. Because there is no being by which God can be moved and because whatever is moved must be moved by another, God must be completely immovable.[95] Second, whatever is moved "is either moved so that it may escape some evil or so that it may acquire some good." Since God is completely perfect, there is no evil that he needs to avoid and no further good for him to attain. Since

91. J. Weisheipl, "The Commentary of St. Thomas on the *De Caelo* of Aristotle," *Sapientia* 29 (1974): 15; *Friar*, 376. Torrell suggests 1272–73 (*Thomas*, 1:344).

92. *Phys.* VII, c.4–7, 10.

93. "Et his convenit quod dicitur, quod eorum nulla sit transmutatio: quia superexcedunt supremam lationem, scilicet ultimae sphaerae, quae ordinatur sicut extrinseca et contentiva omnis mutationis" (*In de caelo* I, lect. 21.7).

94. *In de caelo* I, lect. 21.8, 10.

95. "Deinde . . . ponit rationes ad ostendendum quod dixerat, scilicet quod primum et supremum sit intransmutabile. . . . [P]onit duas rationes: quarum prima talis est. Semper movens et agens est melius moto et passo; sed non est aliquid melius primo et summo divino, quod possit ipsum movere, quia illud esset adhuc divinius; primum ergo divinum non movetur, quia omne quod movetur necesse est ab alio moveri, ut probatur in VII et VIII *Physic.*" (*In de caelo* I, lect. 21.12).

he can be moved neither to something better nor to something worse, "he is in no way moved (*nullo modo movetur*)."[96]

Scriptural Commentaries

Commentary on the Book of Job, Chapter IV, vv. 17–18, (lines 408–40)

The *Commentary on the Book of Job* contains a brief reference to divine immutability that outlines the relationship between being, actuality, and changelessness. The commentary was written between 1261 and 1264, and stems from a series of lectures given at the Priory of San Domenico in Orvieto, Italy.[97] The reference to divine immutability occurs in the fourth chapter, where Thomas is defending Eliphaz's contention that no man may ever justify himself before God (Job 4:17–18).

One argument uses the example of the angels, who, though closer to God and more firmly established in goodness than humans, were still capable of sin. In showing how their proximity to God is related to enduring goodness, Aquinas notes that potency is the cause of mutability, while "act is the cause of immutability (*causa immutabilitatis est actus*)." Potency is naturally related to being and non-being. The more perfectly potency is actualized, however, the more firmly it remains in being through the particular form that is actualizing it. Since actuality is the cause of immutability, that being which "according to its very nature (*secundum se*)" is pure act must be "totally immovable (*omnino immobile*)."[98]

The argument is then transferred from the ontological to the moral order. The will is compared to the good as potency to act or matter to form. Just as God, understood as pure act, is "totally immovable (*omnino immobile*)," so God as goodness itself is "totally immutable (*omnino immutabile*)."[99] All other

---

96. "Omne quod movetur, aut movetur ad hoc quod evadat aliquod malum, aut ad hoc quod acquirat aliquod bonum; sed primum non habet aliquod malum quod possit evadere, neque indiget aliquo bono quod possit acquirere, quia est perfectissimum; ergo primum non movetur" (*In de caelo* I, lect. 21.13).

97. Weisheipl, *Friar*, 153, 368; Torrell, *Thomas*, 1:338; A. Dondaine, "Prefatio," in *Super iob* (Rome: Typographia polyglotta, 1965), 17*–18*.

98. "Manifestum est enim quod causa mutabilitatis est potentia, causa immutabilitatis est actus: est enim de ratione potentiae quod se habeat ad esse et non esse, sed secundum quod magis perficitur ab actu firmius stat in uno, id vero quod secundum se actus est omnino immobile est" (*Super iob* IV, v.18, lines 420–26).

99. "Sciendum est autem quod sicut materia comparatur ad formam ut potentia ad actum, ita

things are compared to him as potency to act. Just as that potency or matter which was more perfectly actualized by a particular form remained more firmly in being under that form, so the creature that adheres more perfectly to God as its good remains more firmly in good. Since the angels cling to God most closely, they are more firmly established in good than any other creatures. Yet they were capable of sin. How much greater, then, is the human capacity for evil.

Our interest here is not the validity of Eliphaz's statement or the stability of the angelic will but the relationships between actuality and immutability and between perfection in act and perfection in being. These relationships make it clear the immutability Aquinas is predicating of God is the unchangeability of ultimate perfection.

Commentary on the Letter to the Hebrews, Chapter I, lect. 5 (§71–78)

In the *Commentary on the Letter to the Hebrews,* Aquinas explains how divine eternity and immutability show the difference between God and creatures. Like the *Commentary on Job,* it was probably written during his sojourn in the Roman province (1259–65).[100] The discussion of divine eternity and immutability begins with a statement of St. Paul: "You, O Lord, did found the earth in the beginning, and the heavens are the work of your hands; they will perish but you remain. They will all grow old like a garment, like a mantle you will roll them up, and they will be changed. But you are the same, and your years will never end" (Heb 1:10–12).

Whether addressed to the Father or the Son, Paul's words establish Christ's superiority over the angels by pointing out the difference between creator and creature. The creator is eternal and unchangeable. The creature is temporal and mutable. The specific creature in question here is the heavens. Although the heavens will never "perish" by entirely ceasing to exist, they will "pass away" in a sense when their motion ceases at the last judgment. For "according to Augustine and the Philosopher, in any change there is generation and corruption," since whatever changes "passes away" from the con-

---

voluntas ad bonum; id igitur quod est ipsum bonum, scilicet Deus, omnino immutabile est" (ibid., lines 427–30).

100. Weisheipl, *Friar,* 248–49, 372–73. Torrell suggests 1265–68 (*Thomas,* 1:340).

dition in which it was previously. In contrast to such things, Scripture testifies that the Creator and Christ remain eternally the same: "But you yourself are the same."[101]

Commentary on the First Letter to Timothy, Chapter VI, lect. 3, (§268–69)

The discussion of divine immutability in the *Commentary on the First Letter to Timothy* also involves God's transcendence. This commentary was probably produced in Italy between 1259 and 1265.[102] The discussion begins with St. Paul's assertion that the second coming of Christ "will be made manifest at the proper time by the blessed and only Sovereign, the King of kings and Lord of lords, who alone has immortality and dwells in unapproachable light" (1 Tim 6:15–16). Aquinas argues these words identify the Triune God as the author of the second coming in three ways: according to the perfection of God's beatitude, the uniqueness of his power, and the incomprehensibility of his nature.

The third way involves divine immutability. Since each thing is comprehensible insofar as it is actual and since God transcends all created nature, he transcends all that is actual in creatures and so transcends all that is comprehensible in them. God's transcendence of all created being is implied in Paul's assertion that God "alone has immortality." All things other than God are subject to change, and change implies a "certain corruption (*quaedam corruptio*)" since "whatever is changed, insofar as it is changed, ceases to be such a thing." Only that which is "completely immutable (*penitus immutabile*)" is truly incorruptible. Since God alone is "completely immutable (*omnino immutabilis*)," he transcends all creation.[103]

101. "Dicendum est, quod secundum Augustinum et Philosophum, in qualibet mutatione est generatio et corruptio. unde quicquid mutatur, perit a statu in quo erat. . . . Omnes peribunt a statu in quo nunc sunt, et sic quodammodo peribunt, sed tu, Domine, permanebis. . . . Hic ostendit permanentiam creatoris, quasi dicat: 'In te nulla est transmutatio nec vicissitudinis obumbratio,' ut *Iac.* 1:17 dicitur, et *Thren.* 5:19: 'Tu autem, Domine, in aeternum permanebis, solium tuum in generatione et generationem,' quod potest etiam intelligi de Christo homine. . . . 'Jesus Christus heri et hodie ipse et in saecula.' . . . Deinde subiungit immutabilitatem Dei, cum dicit 'Tu autem idem ipse es'" (*Super ad hebr.* I, lect. 5 [§72–73, 77]).

102. Weisheipl, *Friar,* 372–73. Torrell suggests 1259–68 (*Thomas,* 1:250, 340).

103. "In qualibet enim mutatione est quaedam corruptio, quia omne quod mutatur, inquantum huiusmodi, desinit esse tale. Illud ergo proprie et vere est incorruptibile, quod penitus est immutabile. Quaelibet autem creatura in se considerata, habet aliquam mutationem, vel mutabilitatem: Deus autem

Commentary on the Letter to the Romans, Chapter I, lect. 6 (§114–15)

In his *Commentary on the Letter to the Romans,* Thomas mentions the immutability of God in discussing the kinds of knowledge humans have of God through natural reason. Unlike the New Testament commentaries considered thus far, this work comprises not just a *reportatio* of lecture notes taken down by Reginald during Thomas's time in Italy (1259–65), but an *expositio* edited by Thomas himself during his second sojourn at Paris (1270–72) or perhaps at Naples (1272–73).[104] The brief discussion of divine immutability is of interest since it explains what sort of knowledge of God is implied in predicating immutability of him.

The discussion arises from Paul's statement that "what can be known about God is plain to them because God has shown it to them" (Rom 1:19). To explain it, Aquinas again employs Dionysius's three ways of causality, eminence, and negation.[105] In the way of causality human reason reduces movable and imperfect things to an "immovable (*immobile*)" and perfect principle that it recognizes as God. In the way of eminence, it sees that God is not a univocal cause, but a surpassing cause who is "above all things." In the way of negation, it realizes that, because God is a surpassing cause, no creaturely quality may be predicated of him since all limitation must be denied. For this reason, God is called "immovable (*immobilem*) and infinite and other things of this sort." In predicating "immovability" and other such qualities of God we cannot claim any positive knowledge of the divine nature ("what God is"), since this remains "totally unknown (*omnino ignotum*) to us in this life."[106] Such terms imply only a negative knowledge of God, showing merely that God is not like creatures. They do not tell us what God is, but only what he is not—that he does not resemble the limited and imperfect things that are objects of our knowledge.

---

est omnino immutabilis. . . . Et ex hoc ostendit, quod natura Dei transcendit omne quod est in natura creata" (*Super I ad tim.* VI, lect. 3 [§268]).

104. Weisheipl, *Friar,* 247–49, 372–73; Torrell, *Thomas,* 1:250, 340.

105. Dionysius, *Div. nom.* VII, 3 (*PG* 3, 870). Cf.: *In de div. nom.* VII, lect. 4.

106. "Sciendum est ergo quod aliquid circa Deum est omnino ignotum homini in hac vita, scilicet quid est Deus. . . . Potest tamen homo, ex huiusmodi creaturis, Deum tripliciter cognoscere, ut Dionysius dicit in libro *De divinis nominibus.* . . . Tertio per viam negationis. Quia si est causa excedens, nihil eorum quae sunt in creaturis potest ei competere. . . . Et secundum hoc dicimus Deum immobilem et infinitum et si quid aliud huiusmodi dicitur" (*Super ad rom.* I, lect. 6 [§114–15]).

Commentary on the Gospel of John, Prologue of St. Thomas (§1–6)

Divine immutability is also mentioned in the prologue of Aquinas's *Commentary on the Gospel of John*. This work was produced during Thomas's second sojourn at Paris (1269–72).[107] He prefaces his commentary with a text from *Isaiah* that he finds appropriate since it contains the "words of one who is contemplating (*verba contemplantis*)" and so evokes the contemplative spirit of the Gospel: "I saw the Lord sitting upon a high and lofty throne, and the whole earth was filled with his majesty, and those things which were under him filled the temple" (Is 6:1).

The text, like the Gospel, involves the highest sort of contemplation since its object is God himself. Isaiah's words indicate the "loftiness (*altitudo*)" of this object in four ways: "authority," "eternity," "dignity or excellence of nature," and "incomprehensible truth." It was through the same fourfold contemplation philosophers of old came to a knowledge of God. In the first way, some noted the order of the world and came to know God in his authority as the governor or ruler of all things.[108] In the second way, they saw the mutability of things and found God as their "immutable and eternal principle (*principium immobile et aeternum*)." Thirdly, by reasoning that finite things are beings through participation, they recognized there must be some most excellent being that "through its very essence is being itself (*ipsum esse*), i.e., whose being (*esse*) is its essence." Finally, seeing that each truth known to them was finite and limited, they asserted that there must be a first and highest truth, infinite and incomprehensible, surpassing every intellect, and thus "dwelling in inaccessible light."[109]

---

107. Weisheipl, *Friar,* 246–47, 372; Torrell, *Thomas,* 1:339.

108. *Super ev. jo., prologus* (§3). Here Thomas calls this argument the "most effective way (*via efficacissima*)" of coming to know God. Earlier in his career, he had said the argument from motion was "more evident (*manifestior*)" (*ST* I, 2, 3, co.). Fernand Van Steenberghen believes this indicates a change in Aquinas's thinking in his later life about the efficacy of the various proofs (*Problème,* 148). Etienne Gilson, however, explains Thomas's remarks in terms of the respective purpose of his argument in each work. While the argument from motion might be a "more evident" way to prove God's existence, the argument from governance is "most effective" for his present purpose, which is "not to demonstrate the existence of God, but to show how understanding can come by some knowledge of God's nature" (Gilson, *Elements,* 327n2.).

109. *Super ev. jo., prologus* (§2, 4–6). Cf.: 1 Tim 6:16.

The second of these ways involves divine immutability. It resembles the argument from motion for the existence of God since it begins with mobile things. But instead of proceeding by way of efficient or final causality, it considers the degrees of excellence among creatures and comes to realize that greater immutability is a sign of greater excellence. The first principle of all things, if it is "supreme and most excellent," must be "immovable and eternal (*immobile et aeternum*)." This conclusion of the ancient philosophers is confirmed by the testimony of Scripture (Ps 44:6; Heb 13:8).[110]

Commentary on the Psalms, Psalm 43, no. 2

The *Commentary on the Psalms* provides a rather different reason for predicating immutability of God from those we have seen thus far. It was begun at Naples in the last years of Thomas's life (1272–74) and, like the *Commentary on Aristotle's On the Heavens*, was never finished.[111] The notion of divine immutability arises in the discussion of Psalm 43. Aquinas contrasts the "lesser goods" God provided his people in the Old Testament (such as the temporal benefits of the Promised Land) with the "greater benefits" or spiritual goods afforded in the New Testament. The promise of such greater benefits is the source of a "greater hope." The psalm therefore seeks to "draw the people of the New Covenant away from the desire for earthly prosperity, which was promised in the Old Testament," and to strengthen their hope in the greater promises that God has given to them.

The psalmist recounts the wonders God worked for his people in the past and expresses his confidence in God: "You are yourself my King and my God." In this confession of confidence, Thomas finds an affirmation of the "immutability of God (*immutabilitatem Dei*)." For by asserting that the God

---

110. "Alii vero venerunt in cognitionem Dei ex eius aeternitate. Viderunt enim quod quicquid est in rebus, est mutabile; et quanto aliquid est nobilius in gradibus rerum, tanto minus habet de mutabilitate: puta, inferiora corpora sunt secundum substantiam et secundum locum mutabilia; corpora vero caelestia, quae nobiliora sunt, secundum substantiam immutabilia sunt; secundum autem locum tantum moventur. Secundum hoc ergo evidenter colligi potest, quod primum principium omnium rerum, et supremum et nobilius, sit immobile et aeternum. Et hanc aeternitatem verbi propheta insinuat, cum dicit 'sedentem,' idest absque omni mutabilitate et aeternitate praesidentem; Ps. c. XLIV, 7: 'Sedes tua, Deus, in saeculum saeculi;' Hebr. ult., 8: 'Iesus Christus heri et hodie, ipse et in saecula.' Hanc aeternitatem Ioannes ostendit dicens: 'In principio erat verbum'" (*Super ev. jo., prologus S. Thomae* [§4]).

111. Weisheipl, *Friar*, 302–4, 368; Torrell, *Thomas*, 1:340–41.

of his ancestors is also "his King and his God," the psalmist proclaims that God's power is not diminished and that God is presently able to do "even greater things" for his people than those done in the past.[112] In contrast to other arguments for divine immutability, this one involves no philosophical reasoning but springs spontaneously from a trust in God awakened by a reflection on the covenant experience of God's continuous care for his people. Aquinas finds this way of coming to the truth about God appropriate to this psalm since, like the *Gospel of John*, it is contemplative in character: from its opening word (*"Deus"*), the psalm is addressed to God and so "proceeds according to the mode of prayer, which is an ascent of the mind into God."[113]

Independent Works

On Truth Q. 5, a. 9, co.

In his first year as a master in theology at Paris (1256), Aquinas held the first seven of his academic disputations *On Truth*.[114] In the fifth question of these disputations, he considers divine providence and examines the role of the heavenly bodies in its workings. In refuting astrologers who would make the heavenly bodies themselves the ultimate first principles, he offers a concise summary of the argument for the unmoved mover. We have already seen an early instance of it in the *Commentary on the Sentences* and have explored it in greater detail in the *Commentary on the Physics*.[115] Here again he emphasizes the transcendence of the unchanging first principle:

Some have reduced the bodies here below to heavenly bodies, as though the latter were the absolutely first causes. For they believed [there were] no immaterial substances. Consequently, they said that what is prior among bodies is first among beings. This, however, is clearly false. For whatever is moved must be reduced to an immovable principle (*principium immobile*), since nothing is moved by itself, and one cannot keep going back into infinity. Now, even though a heavenly body does not un-

---

112. "Dei immutabilitatem ostendit, quia Deus fecit hoc patribus; et iterum, quia virtus ejus non est diminuta, et ideo sibi facere etiam majora potest; unde dicit, 'Tu es ipse rex meus et Deus meus, qui non es diminutus.' Item ad te etiam pertinet cura hominis sicut tunc: unde dicit: 'Rex meus,' qui defendis et gubernas: 'et Deus meus,' qui provides mihi" (*In psalmos* XLIII.2).

113. *In psalmos* XLIII.1.

114. Weisheipl, *Friar*, 362–63; Torrell, *Thomas*, 1:334.

115. *Sent.* I, 8, 3, 1, sc.2; *In phys.* VII, lect. 2 (§891); VIII, lect. 11 (§1068).

dergo change by generation or corruption or by a motion which would alter what belongs to its substance, it is nevertheless moved locally. Consequently, the reduction
must be made to some prior principle so that things undergoing qualitative change
are traced back by a definite order to that which causes this change in other things
but is not so changed itself, although it is moved locally; and then further back to that
which does not change in any way at all (*nullo modo movetur*).[116]

On the Power of God

The discussion of divine immutability in the academic disputations *On
the Power of God* again evidences the influence of Aristotle. Like the *Commentary on the Divine Names,* this work was written while Aquinas was teaching at
the Dominican studium of Santa Sabina in Rome (1265–67).[117] The subject
of divine immutability is touched upon in discussing "whether there may be
something which is not created by God" (Q.3, a.5), and "whether angels and
demons have bodies naturally united to themselves" (Q.6, a. 6). In the first
instance, immutability is related to perfection in being; in the second, to perfection in act.

De pot. Q.3, a.5, co. Thomas answers the question, "whether there may be
something which is not created by God," by tracing the historical development of philosophy from the first philosophers, who knew only the material
cause, through those who also recognized the efficient cause, and finally to
those who, like Plato and Aristotle, "affirmed some universal cause of things
from which all other things proceed into being." Noting that this conclusion
is in agreement with the Catholic faith, he demonstrates it with three philosophical arguments taken from Plato, Aristotle, and Avicenna.

The second involves divine immutability. It begins by noting that any

---

116. "Quidam enim haec inferiora in corpora caelestia reduxerunt sicut in causas simpliciter pri-
mas, eo quod nullas substantias incorporeas arbitrabantur; unde priora in corporibus dixerunt esse prima inter entia. Sed hoc manifeste apparet esse falsum. Omne quod enim movetur, oportet in principium immobile reduci, cum nihil a seipso moveatur, et non sit abire in infinitum. Corpus autem caeleste,
quamvis non varietur secundum generationem et corruptionem, aut secundum aliquem motum qui va-
riet aliquid quod insit substantiae eius, movetur tamen secundum locum: unde oportet in aliquod prius
principium reductionem fieri, ut sic ea quae alterantur, quodam ordine reducantur in alterans non alter-
atum, motum tamen secundum locum; et ulterius in id quod nullo modo movetur" (*De ver.* Q.5, 9, co.).

117. Weisheipl, *Friar,* 363; Van Steenberghen, *Problème,* 135; Torrell, *Thomas,* 1:335.

quality that is participated by a number of beings is attributed to each in view of some first being that possesses the quality most perfectly. Fire, for example, possesses heat most perfectly and is consequently the principle of heat in all hot things. As fire is the cause of all heat, there must be a being that is the cause of all being because of its absolute perfection in being. The existence of this being "has been proved by philosophers," who have shown that "there is some mover which is completely immovable (*omnino immobile*) and most perfect." Thomas understands this as the conclusion of the arguments in the *Physics* and *Metaphysics* of Aristotle. By establishing the immovability of the first mover, these arguments are also able to show that the first mover is "the most perfect and most true being (*perfectissimum et verissimum ens*)." Since the first mover is most perfect, "it is necessary that all other less perfect beings receive their being (*esse*) from it."[118] Here the relationship between divine immutability and divine perfection in being, which we have already noted in the *Commentary on the Sentences* and in the *Commentary on the Book of Job*, is again confirmed.[119]

De pot. Q.6, a.6, co. Thomas's answer to the question, "whether angels and demons have bodies naturally united to them," is twofold. He responds both to thinkers, such as the early Greek philosophers, who denied the very existence of immaterial substances, and to those, such as Varro, who affirmed the existence of immaterial substances but insisted that such substances (including God) are always united to bodies.

In answering the first group, he employs an argument from Aristotle's *Metaphysics*, showing act is prior to potency both in nature and in time. All material things are in potency, as their mutability demonstrates. Therefore,

---

118. "Secunda ratio est, quia, cum aliquid invenitur a pluribus diversimode participatum oportet quod ab eo in quo perfectissime invenitur, attribuatur omnibus illis in quibus imperfectius invenitur. Nam ea quae positive secundum magis et minus dicuntur, hoc habent ex accessu remotiori vel propinquiori ad aliquid unum: si enim unicuique eorum ex se ipso illud conveniret, non esset ratio cur perfectius in uno quam in alio inveniretur; sicut videmus quod ignis, qui est in fine caliditatis, est caloris principium in omnibus calidis. Est autem ponere unum ens, quod est perfectissimum et verissimum ens: quod ex hoc probatur, quia est aliquid movens omnino immobile et perfectissimum, ut a philosophis est probatum. Oportet ergo quod omnia alia minus perfecta ab ipso esse recipiant. Et haec est probatio Philosophi" (*De pot.* Q.3, 5, co.).

119. *Sent.* I, 8, 3, 1, *exp. text; Super iob* IV, vv.17–18 (lines 408–40).

prior to all material things, there must be some "immovable eternal substance (*substantiam immobilem sempiternam*)."[120] It is noteworthy that Thomas
does not conclude explicitly either to an immaterial substance (which would
speak directly to the particular question at hand) or to a substance that is
pure act (which would follow directly from his premise). Rather, he concludes to an eternal immovable substance that may be understood, in virtue
of its immovability, to be both immaterial and pure act.[121]

In reply to the second group, he notes that some philosophers who insist
that every immaterial substance be united to a body have understood God
as the soul of the outermost sphere. To answer them he borrows an argument from Aristotle's *Physics*. Since any self-mover is capable of moving and
not moving, it can move continuously and stably only if it is stabilized by
something external that is "completely immovable (*omnino immobile*)."[122] The
outermost sphere of the heavens, if considered as an animated self-mover,
must (because its motion is continuous) be moved by something external
and completely immovable. It therefore cannot be the first mover. Beyond
that soul, there must be a completely immovable mover, joined to no body,
and "subsisting through itself (*per se ipsam subsistens*)." In this way Aquinas
explains Aristotle's argument from the self-mover to the immovable mover. In his reply to the eleventh objection, he notes that Aristotle's reasoning
also allows one to conclude to the existence of an immovable mover without
considering the self-mover. In the corpus of the article, he does not immediately identify the immovable mover as God. For his purpose here is not to
establish the existence of God as such, but to demonstrate the existence of
immaterial substances that are not joined to bodies. According to Aristotle,
a number of such immovable immaterial substances are needed to account

120. "Actus est prius potentia, et natura et tempore, simpliciter loquendo; . . . Unde cum omne corpus sit in potentia, quod ipsius mobilitas ostendit, oportet ante omnia corpora esse substantiam immobilem sempiternam" (*De pot.* Q.6, 6, co.). Cf.: *Meta.* XII, 6.

121. It will be noticed here that Thomas, unlike Aristotle, concludes directly from the priority of act
over potency to an immovable substance. Aristotle concluded from the priority of act over potency to the
eternity of the cycle of generation, then to an eternal cause of that cycle, which was in turn found to be
immutable. See *Meta.* XII, 6–7 (1071b 22–1072a 26); *In meta.* XII, lect. 6.

122. "Tertio, quia cum movens seipsum possit moveri et non moveri, ut dicitur in VII *Phys.*, si aliquid motum ex se continue movetur, oportet quod stabiliatur in movendo ab aliquo exteriori, quod est
omnino immobile" (*De pot.* Q.6, 6, co.). Cf.: *Phys.* VII, 4 (255a 5–20).

for the motions of the various heavenly spheres. Thomas agrees with Aristotle in this but does not limit the number of such substances to the number of heavenly motions. He notes also that both Plato and Aristotle agree that there is one highest substance among these immaterial beings, and that this substance is called God.

On the Separated Substances, **Chapter 2 (lines 10–26)**

In his treatise *On the Separated Substances,* Aquinas again makes use of Aristotle's argument for the existence of substances separated from matter. This work was written in Thomas's later years (1270–73) and left unfinished at his death.[123] Thomas finds Aristotle's argument for separated substances "more manifest and certain" than Plato's. The argument proceeds from the familiar premises that "whatever is moved is moved by another" and "one cannot proceed to infinity in movers and things moved." It concludes, however, not only to "some first immovable mover (*aliquod primum movens immobile*)," but also to "some first mobile thing which is moved by itself."[124] In this, it follows Aristotle's reasoning more closely but remains essentially the same argument we have found even in Aquinas's earliest works.[125]

Summa contra gentiles, **Book I, chapter 13.**

The *Summa contra gentiles* considers divine immutability in its arguments for God's existence. The work was written between 1259 and 1265. The first fifty-three chapters of Book I were written while Thomas was in Paris, and the rest after his arrival in Italy.[126] In the thirteenth chapter of Book I, Aquinas gives four arguments "by which both philosophers and Catholic teachers

---

123. Weisheipl, *Friar,* 388; Torrell, *Thomas,* 350.

124. "Et ideo Aristoteles manifestiori et certiori via processit ad investigandum substantias a materia separatas, scilicet per viam motus. Primo quidem constituens et ratione et exemplis, omne quod movetur ab alio moveri; et si aliquid a se ipso moveri dicatur, hoc non est secundum idem, sed secundum diversas sui partes, ita scilicet quod una pars eius sit movens, et alia mota. Et cum non sit procedere in infinitum in moventibus et motis, quia remoto primo movente, esset consequens etiam alia removeri; oportet devenire ad aliquod primum movens immobile et ad aliquod primum mobile, quod movetur a se ipso eo modo quo dictum est: semper enim quod per se ipsum est, est prius et causa eius quod per aliud est" (*De sub. sep.* c.2, lines 10–26).

125. See *Phys.* VII, 1 (242b 35). Cf.: *Sent.* I, 8, 3, 1, sc.; *De ver.* Q.5, 9, co.

126. J. Weisheipl (*Friar,* 359–60) and F. Van Steenberghen (*Problème,* 104) believe the work was completed in 1263. Torrell (*Thomas,* 1:101–4) argues for 1265.

have proved that God exists." Taken from Aristotle and John of Damascus, they proceed from motion, efficient causality, perfection in being and truth, and the government of the world.[127]

The argument from motion establishes both God's existence and immutability. Two versions are given.[128] The first concludes directly to a first unmoved mover. The second considers the possibility of a first self-mover before concluding to a first unmoved mover. Since we have already given a detailed analysis of the first version in our discussion of Aquinas's *Commentary on the Physics*, we will do no more than state it here:

Everything that is moved is moved by another. That some thing is moved—for example, the sun—is evident from sense. Therefore, it is moved by something else that moves it. This mover is itself either moved or not moved. If it is not, we have reached our conclusion—namely, that we must posit some immovable mover (*movens immobile*). This we call God. If it is moved, it is moved by another mover. We must consequently either proceed to infinity or we must arrive at some immovable mover (*movens immobile*). Now, it is not possible to proceed to infinity. Hence, we must posit some first immovable mover (*primum movens immobile*).[129]

The second version begins with the assumption that every mover is moved, but soon finds there must be "some mover not moved by any exterior cause." This, however, is not necessarily a first unmoved mover. In fact, it seems preferable to see it as a self-mover:

127. For the sources of these arguments, see *Phys.* VII, 1; VIII, 4–6 (motion); *Meta.* II, 2 (efficient cause); *Meta.* II, 1 (perfection in being); John of Damascus, *De fide orth.* I, 3 (*PG* 94, 796) (government of the world).

128. For a detailed analysis of the argument, see Rolf Schönberger, *Thomas von Aquins Summa Contra Gentiles* (Darmstadt: Wissenschaftliche Buchgessellschaft, 2001), 28–35; Norman Kretzmann, *The Metaphysics of Theism: Aquinas's Natural Theology in Summa contra gentiles I* (Oxford: Clarendon Press, 1997), 60–83; Scott MacDonald, "Aquinas's Parasitic Cosmological Argument," *Medieval Philosophy and Theology* 1 (1991): 119–55; Gilson, *Christian*, 59–66; James A. Weisheipl, "Thomas's Evaluation of Plato and Aristotle," *NS* 48 (1974): 121–22.

129. "Omne quod movetur, ab alio movetur. Patet autem sensu aliquid moveri, utputa solem. Ergo alio movente movetur. Aut ergo illud movens movetur, aut non. Si non movetur, ergo habemus propositum, quod necesse est ponere aliquod movens immobile. Et hoc dicimus Deum. Si autem movetur, ergo ab alio movente movetur. Aut ergo est procedere in infinitum: aut est devenire ad aliquod movens immobile. Sed non est procedere in infinitum. Ergo necesse est ponere aliquod primum movens immobile" (*SCG* I, c.13.3 [§83]).

Granted this conclusion—namely, that there is a first mover that is not moved by something external—it yet does not follow that this mover is absolutely immovable (*penitus immobile*). That is why Aristotle goes on to say that the condition of the first mover may be twofold. The first mover may be absolutely immovable (*penitus immobile*). If so, we have the conclusion we are seeking: there is a first immovable mover (*primum movens immobile*). On the other hand, the first mover may be moved by itself. And this seems probable, because that which is through itself is always prior to that which is through another. Hence, among things moved as well, it seems reasonable that the first moved is moved through itself and not by another.[130]

A self-mover, however, must have one part that is only moving and another that is solely moved. Otherwise it will be both in act and in potency at the same time with respect to the same motion, which is impossible. So, within the self-mover there must be an "immovable mover (*movens immobile*)," namely the unmoved part that moves the rest.[131]

There is still the possibility, however, that this mover, through immovable in itself (*per se*), is movable incidentally (*per accidens*). In self-movers such as animals, for instance, the part of the self-mover that does the moving (the soul) is immovable *per se*, but movable *per accidens*. Since the animal is composed of primary matter and substantial form (the soul), it is corruptible or changeable in itself (*per se*). It can therefore cease to be (in the substantial change known as death). When it ceases to be, however, its soul also ceases to be. Its soul, however, is in itself a simple principle that is not as such (*per se*) corruptible or changeable. The soul is therefore said to be changed not in itself (*per se*), but *per accidens* when the animal is changed or corrupted. So something can be corruptible or changeable *per accidens* (since it can in fact cease to be) even though it is not corruptible in itself (*per se*).[132]

The first immovable mover cannot be of this type since it must, in Aris-

---

130. "Quia vero, hoc habito quod sit primum movens quod non movetur ab alio exteriori, non sequitur quod sit penitus immobile, ideo ulterius procedit Aristoteles, dicendo quod hoc potest esse dupliciter. Uno modo, ita quod illud primum sit penitus immobile. Quo posito, habetur propositum: scilicet, quod sit aliquod primum movens immobile. Alio modo, quod illud primum moveatur a seipso. Et hoc videtur probabile: quia quod est per se, semper est prius eo quod est per aliud; unde et in motis primum motum rationabile est per seipsum moveri, non ab alio" (*SCG* I, 13.21 [§101]).

131. Ibid., 13.22–23 (§102–3).

132. Ibid., 13.24 (§104).

totle's argument, be able to account for the eternity of motion. A mover that is moved *per accidens* cannot do this since it would not be eternal itself in its being or motion. So the conclusion is reached that "the first self-mover is moved by a mover [i.e., a moving part] which is moved neither *per se* nor *per accidens.*"[133]

This moving part, however, is not the first unmoved mover. It is only the immovable part of the first self-mover. The first self-mover in Aristotle's cosmology is the outermost sphere of the universe. The soul of that sphere is the unchanging, intrinsic source of its motion (its unchangeable or incorruptible moving part). To get to the first unmoved mover, Aquinas goes beyond Aristotle's *Physics* and incorporates an argument from the *Metaphysics* that shows the relationship between the moving part of the first self-mover and the first immovable mover, who is God:

But because God is not a part of any self-mover, Aristotle continues the investigation in his *Metaphysics* [going on] from this mover which is a part of the self-mover to another absolutely separate mover who is God. For, since everything moving itself is moved through appetite, the mover who is part of the self-moving being must move because of the appetite of some appetible object. This object is higher, in the order of motion, than the mover desiring it, for the one desiring is in a manner a moved mover, whereas an appetible object is an absolutely unmoved mover (*movens omnino non motum*). There must, therefore, be an absolutely immovable separate first mover (*primum motorem separatum omnino immobilem*) which is God.[134]

This ultimate mover might, of course, be reached more easily if one were to begin with the revealed doctrine that the world and its motion have their origin in God's creative act. But such an approach would not be as efficacious in arguing against non-believers. For such an audience—the audience Thomas has in mind in writing the *Summa contra gentiles*—it is better to begin with

---

133. Ibid., 13.25–26 (§105–6).

134. "Sed quia Deus non est pars alicuius moventis seipsum, ulterius Aristoteles, in sua Metaphysica, investigat ex hoc motore qui est pars moventis seipsum, alium motorem separatum omnino, qui est Deus. Cum enim omne movens seipsum moveatur per appetitum, oportet quod motor qui est pars moventis seipsum, moveat propter appetitum alicuius appetibilis. Quod est eo superius in movendo: nam appetens est quodammodo movens motum; appetibile autem est movens omnino non motum. Oportet igitur esse primum motorem separatum omnino immobilem, qui Deus est" (ibid., 13.28 [§108]). Cf.: *Meta.* XII, 7 (1072a 23); Owens, "Proof," 134.

the assumption that the world and its motion are eternal and to argue from that assumption to the existence of the immovable first mover.[135] Either version of the argument from motion might be used. Those who assume with Aristotle that the heavenly spheres are animated will prefer the second and come to the first immovable mover through a first self-mover. Those who reject this assumption may prefer the first, which gets to the first mover in a more direct way. Either version will eventually lead to the discovery of a first cause of motion, which may be called God: "Even Aristotle himself proposed this conclusion as a disjunction: it is necessary either to arrive immediately at an immovable separate first mover (*primum movens immobile separatum*) or to arrive at a self-moved mover from whom, in turn, an immovable separate first mover (*movens primum immobile separatum*) is reached."[136]

Aquinas sees these arguments as establishing both God's existence and his immutability. He therefore feels free in the next chapter to use divine immutability as a principle, confirmed by both reason and Scripture, for determining other divine attributes.

As a principle of procedure in knowing God by way of remotion, therefore, let us adopt the proposition which, from what we have said, is now manifest, namely, that God is absolutely immovable (*omnino immobilis*). The authority of Sacred Scripture also confirms this. For it is written: "I am God and I am not changed" (Mal 3:6). "With whom there is no change" (Jas 1:17). Again: "God is not as man that he should be changed" (Num 23:19).[137]

By looking at these arguments more explicitly as demonstrations of divine immutability, we may get a better picture of their structure and progression. The first version concludes immediately to an immovable being, which is identified as God. The second establishes the property of absolute immovability only gradually. First, universal motion is posited in the assumption that every mover is moved. This is then disproved, and it is established that

---

135. *SCG* I, c.13.29–30 (§109–10).

136. "Et ad hoc dicendum est quod, si primum movens non ponitur motum ex se, oportet quod moveatur immediate a penitus immobili. Unde etiam Aristoteles sub disiunctione hanc conclusionem inducit: quod scilicet oporteat vel statim devenire ad primum movens immobile separatum, vel ad movens seipsum, ex quo iterum devenitur ad movens primum immobile separatum" (ibid., 13.32 [§112]).

137. *SCG* I, c.14.4 (§119).

there is a first mover that is not moved by any exterior cause. It is still possible, however, that this first mover move itself. Further analysis shows, however, that such a self-mover may not move itself as a whole (for then it would be in act and potency at the same time in the same respect). So one part of it must be "immovable and moving the other." Yet it is still possible that this immovable part is immovable only *per se* and movable *per accidens*. When that possibility is disproved, the conclusion is reached that there is a mover that is moved neither *per se* nor *per accidens*. Yet this mover, though not moved in the physical order, may yet be moved in the order of will by the object of its love and desire. The object desired by this mover is therefore "higher in the order of motion" and is "an entirely unmoved mover." So an absolutely immovable being is discovered that is identified as God.

Aquinas is careful to point out that this being, though changeless, is not lifeless. He does this through a brief comparison of how Plato and Aristotle understand motion.

It is to be noted, however, that Plato, who held that every mover is moved, understood the name "motion" in a wider sense than did Aristotle. For Aristotle understood motion strictly, according as it is the act of what exists in potency inasmuch as it is such. So understood, motion belongs only to divisible bodies, as is proved in the *Physics*. According to Plato, however, that which moves itself is not a body. Plato understood by motion any given operation, so that "to understand" and "to judge" are a kind of motion. Aristotle likewise touches upon this manner of speaking in the *De anima*. Plato accordingly said that the first mover moves itself because it knows itself and wills or loves itself. In a way, this is not opposed to the reasons of Aristotle. There is no difference between reaching a first being that moves itself, as understood by Plato, and reaching a first being that is absolutely immovable (*quod omnino sit immobile*) as understood by Aristotle.[138]

Compendium of Theology, Book I, chapters 3–4

The discussion of divine immutability in the *Compendium of Theology* is preceded by three brief chapters containing a general introduction to the

---

138. *SCG* I, 13.10 (§90). See Plato, *Timaeus* 30 a; 34 b; *Phaedrus* 245 c. Cf.: *Sent.* I, 8, 3, 1, ad 2; *SCG* I, 13.10 (§90); II, c.82; *ST* I, 18, 3, ad 1; Q.19, 1, ad 3; *De ver.* Q.24, 1, ad 14; *De pot.* Q.10, 1, co.; *Super de trin.* Q.5, 4, ad 2.

work, a preface to the section on faith, and a demonstration of the existence of God. Conceived as a "brief instruction concerning the Christian religion" intended for Aquinas's secretary, Reginald, the work was probably begun between 1265 and 1267 and was never finished.[139] God's existence is established by the demonstration from motion only. The elaborate arguments for establishing the premises of the demonstration as found in the *Summa contra gentiles* are not mentioned. Thomas simply asserts "we see that all things which are moved are moved by others." Various examples are given. The premise that there is no progression to infinity among movers and things moved is also established by a simplified argument regarding instrumental causality, thought to be understandable "even to the uneducated (*etiam apud indoctos*)." In the *Compendium*, these two premises lead not to an immovable mover, but to a "first mover" who is "highest of all" and who is called God.[140]

God's immovability is then established first from the fact that God is the first mover and secondly from a consideration of the causal relation between motion and immutability. As first mover, God can be moved neither by himself nor by another. If he were moved by another, he would not be the first mover. If he moved himself, he would either be mover and moved with respect to the same thing, or mover with respect to one part of himself and moved with respect to another. God cannot himself be both mover and moved with respect to the same thing, for he would then be both in act and in potency with respect to the same thing, which is impossible. Nor can he be the mover with respect to one part of himself and moved with respect to another, for then he would not be the first mover as such (*secundum se*), but only by reason of some part of himself. That part would then be in some sense prior to him, and he would not be the first mover. Therefore God must be "altogether immovable (*omnino immobile*)."[141]

139. *Comp.* I, c.1. Weisheipl, *Friar*, 387; Torrell, *Thomas*, 1:349.

140. *Comp.* I, c.3.

141. "Ex hoc apparet quod necesse est Deum moventem omnia, immobilem esse. Cum enim sit primum movens, si moveretur, necesse esset se ipsum vel a se ipso, vel ab alio moveri. Ab alio quidem moveri non potest: oporteret enim esse aliquid movens prius eo; quod est contra rationem primi moventis. A se ipso autem si movetur, hoc potest esse dupliciter. Vel quod secundum idem sit movens et motum; aut ita quod secundum aliquid sui sit movens, et secundum aliquid motum. Horum quidem primum esse non potest. Cum enim omne quod movetur, inquantum huiusmodi, sit in potentia; quod autem movet,

The second argument asserts that, since the source of any motion is not moved with respect to the particular kind of motion it initiates, every source of motion must be in some way "immovable (*immobili*)." The heavenly bodies, for instance, are the cause of alteration in all lower substances, but are not themselves subject to alteration. If the source of any motion is in some way immovable, the source of all motion must be completely "immovable (*immobile*)."[142]

Regarding these texts, it might be asked why Thomas here chooses to conclude first to a "first highest mover" and only then to show that this mover is immovable instead of concluding immediately to an immovable mover as he does in the other works that we have examined. A possible answer may be found by considering the intended audience. It is not meant for the theologically "studious (*studiosos*)" but for those otherwise "occupied (*occupatos*)." As a good teacher with apparently some insight into student-centered learning, Aquinas recognizes how important it is to order his arguments carefully for his readers.[143] So it is that in his commentaries on Aristotle he follows the order imposed by those texts in arguing for the existence of God, but reorganizes the material somewhat in his *Summa contra gentiles* for the educated non-Christian audience he is addressing there, and simplifies it into yet another order in the *Compendium* for a less educated audience. He finds the resulting simplification in keeping with the simplicity by which the Word himself "brought the doctrine of human salvation together under a short summary."[144]

---

sit in actu; si secundum idem esset movens et motum, oporteret quod secundum idem esset in potentia et in actu; quod est impossibile. Secundum etiam esse non potest. Si enim esset aliquod movens, et alterum motum, non esset ipsum secundum se primum movens, sed ratione suae partis quae movet. Quod autem est per se, prius est eo quod non est per se. Non potest igitur primum movens esse, si ratione suae partis hoc ei conveniat. Oportet igitur primum movens omnino immobile esse" (ibid., c.4).

142. "Ex iis etiam quae moventur et movent, hoc ipsum considerari potest. Omnis enim motus videtur ab aliquo immobili procedere, quod scilicet non movetur secundum illam speciem motus; sicut videmus quod alterationes et generationes et corruptiones quae sunt in istis inferioribus, reducuntur sicut in primum movens in corpus caeleste, quod secundum hanc speciem motus non movetur, cum sit ingenerabile et incorruptibile et inalterabile. Illud ergo quod est primum principium omnis motus, oportet esse immobile" (ibid.).

143. See *ST, prologus*, and Josef Pieper, *Guide to Thomas Aquinas* (New York: Mentor Books, 1962), 85–89.

144. *Comp*. I, c.1.

In his commentary on Book VIII of the *Physics* and Book XII of the *Metaphysics*, Thomas follows Aristotle's order of discovery regarding God's existence and attributes. From the fact of motion he shows there must be a first mover. Then, on the hypothesis that motion is eternal, he explains this mover must also be eternal. Because it is eternal, it must be immovable. And since it is immovable, it is seen as the supreme substance, enjoying most wondrous life and happiness.

In the *Summa contra gentiles* he presents two arguments from motion for a first immovable mover. In the first he immediately comes to the conclusion that there is an immovable mover, just as he did in commenting on Book VII of the *Physics*. In the second he follows a more complex line of reasoning, drawing on Aristotle's *Physics* and *Metaphysics*, but arrives at the same conclusion, which he then uses as a principle for discovering other divine attributes.

In the *Compendium*, a simpler order is followed. Here, his initial conclusion is less complex than that of the *Summa contra gentiles* and is similar to Aristotle's initial conclusion in Book VII of the *Physics* in that no mention of immovability is made. But unlike Aristotle, who concluded only to "some first mover" and did not rule out the possibility that there may be many such "first movers" to account for the various heavenly motions, Thomas concludes to a "first highest mover." He does this by utilizing a simplified version of the argument from instrumental causality from Book VIII of the *Physics*.[145] Through this argument, he is able to establish the existence of "a certain first mover" that is the "principal agent" from which all motion proceeds. As the principal agent of the whole series of instrumental causes of motion, this mover is "highest with respect to all the others (*omnibus supremum*)." Once the existence of this highest cause has been established, its various attributes may be discussed in a didactically convenient way. So it is that in the *Compendium*, Thomas does not conclude from the fact of motion to "some first mover," and then in turn discover its eternity, immovability, and supremacy (as Aristotle did). Nor does he immediately include the property of immovability in his conclusion regarding the existence of this first mover (as he did in the *Summa contra gentiles*). Instead, he argues from

---

145. *Phys.* VIII, 5 (256a 21–256b 3). Cf.: *In phys.* VIII, lect. 9 (§1041).

the fact of motion to "a first highest mover" and then explains the various properties of this first mover, proceeding simply from immovability to eternity and the other divine attributes.

Summa Theologiae

The topic of divine immutability is again in evidence in the *Summa theologiae*. Thomas began this work while in Italy in 1266 or 1267, but never finished it. Since the discussion of divine immutability occurs early in the work, it was certainly written at that time.[146] The immutability of God is initially established in the first way of showing God's existence and then discussed in more detail later.[147] The work provides a synthesis of Aquinas's mature thought presented in an order of his own design rather than one imposed by the text of someone else, as in the commentaries. For this reason, it is appropriate to conclude our investigation of his arguments on divine immutability with this work, even though it is not chronologically the last one he wrote.

ST I, Q.2, a.3, co.   Thomas begins the *Summa theologiae* with a consideration of the nature of sacred doctrine and, after explaining the general outline of the work, takes up the question of whether God exists. Having established that God's existence is demonstrable and not self-evident to us, he offers five ways it can be shown (*probari*) that God exists. Each proceeds from an observable fact or event: (1) motion; (2) efficient causality; (3) contingency and necessity in beings; (4) grades of perfection in beings; and (5) finality in nature. Each concludes to the existence of a first principle without which the various observed phenomena could not exist: (1) a first unmoved mover; (2) a first efficient cause; (3) a necessary being whose necessity is not from another; (4) a being in the highest degree (*maxime ens*); and (5) an intelligence directing all natural things to their ends. In each case, the ultimate principle is identified as God.

The first way, which he calls the "more manifest," involves divine immutability. It is an adaptation of the Aristotelian argument we have seen

---

146. Torrell, *Thomas*, 1:333; Weisheipl, *Friar*, 360–62; Van Steenberghen, *Problème*, 155. See also Jean-Pierre Torrell, *Aquinas's Summa: Background, Structure and Reception*, trans. Benedict M. Guevin (Washington, D.C.: The Catholic University of America Press, 2005).

147. See *ST* I, 2, 3, co.; Q.9.

many times.[148] Beginning with a fact "certain and evident to the senses," that "some things in this world are moved," it uses two premises (that "everything moved is moved by another" and that there can be no "procession to infinity" among movers and things moved) to show that there must be a "first mover moved by no other (*aliquod primum movens quod a nullo movetur*)."

The first premise is established by analyzing how potency and act are involved in motion: "Nothing is moved except as it is in potency to that toward which it is moved. But a thing moves as it is in act. For to move is nothing else than to reduce something from potency to act. But a thing cannot be reduced from potency to act except by some being in act." From this same reasoning, it follows that a thing cannot "move itself" or be "both mover and moved in the same respect and same way." For then the thing would be both in act and in potency at the same time and in the same respect. Therefore, "everything which is moved must be moved by another."

The second premise is that there is no procession to infinity in movers and things moved. If the procession of movers goes on to infinity, there will be no first mover, and so nothing will be moved since secondary movers do not move unless moved by a first.

The conclusion asserts the existence not just of a first mover (as in the *Compendium*), but of "a first mover which is moved by no other," which is identified as God.[149] So the immovability of God is established, together with his existence. Although the term "immovable" is not found in the conclusion itself, it is used in the reply to the second objection, where the conclusions of the first and third "ways" are used to show why it is necessary that "all things which are changeable and capable of defect be reduced to some first principle which is immovable (*immobile*) and necessary through itself."[150] This first principle is God.

---

148. *Sent.* I, 8, 3, 1, sc.2; *De ver.* Q.5, 9, co.; *SCG* I, c.13; *Comp.* I, c.3; *In phys.* VII, lect. 2; VIII, lect. 7–13, 23; *In meta.* XII, lect. 6. For a summary of contemporary discussions on the validity of the first way, see John F. Wippel, *The Metaphysical Thought of Thomas Aquinas: From Finite Being to Uncreated Being* (Washington, D.C.: The Catholic University of America Press, 2000), 444–59.

149. "Ergo necesse est devenire ad aliquod primum movens, quod a nullo movetur, et hoc omnes intelligunt Deum" (*ST* I, 2, 3, co.).

150. "[O]portet autem omnia mobilia et deficere possibilia reduci in aliquod primum principium immobile et per se necessarium, sicut ostensum est" (*ST* I, 2, 3, ad 2).

ST I, Q.3, *prologus* Having a special article on divine immutability in the *Summa theologiae* might seem superfluous since this attribute was already established in the first way of showing God's existence. In the *Compendium,* a specific chapter on immutability was needed since the argument for God's existence concluded only to a "first highest mover (*primum movens . . . supremum*)," not explicitly to an immovable mover.[151] In the *Summa contra gentiles,* however, no particular chapter on immutability was required since God's changelessness was so thoroughly established in the first demonstration of his existence that it could immediately be employed in succeeding chapters as a "principle of procedure" to explain other divine attributes.[152] Why is it, then, that in the *Summa theologiae* a separate article is dedicated to the subject of divine immutability, even though here, as in the *Summa contra gentiles,* divine immutability is already established through the first demonstration of God's existence? If we look at Thomas's prologue to the discussion of the divine attributes, we may discover not only his purpose in writing a separate article on immutability, but also his object in offering five demonstrations of God's existence.

Immediately after showing God exists, Aquinas introduces the next questions as an attempt to gain a deeper understanding of God. Usually when we investigate things, we try to find out "in what way they exist" (their manner of existing) to better know "what they are" (their essence). We cannot do that here, however, since we are unable to know what God is, but only what he is not. So we have to investigate not "in what way he is" but rather "in what way he is not."[153]

This negative way of knowing God is called the "way of remotion" or the "way of negation." We are already familiar with it as one of the three ways of Dionysius (causality, negation, and eminence) by which we know God from creatures.[154] The way of causality establishes God as the source of creatures. We discover more about him by discerning the modes of his causality. This is the task of theology: "Sacred doctrine most properly treats of God according as he is the highest cause." Unlike philosophy, which can know only what reason discovers about God from creatures, theology is in touch with "that

151. *Comp.* I, c.3–4.   152. *SCG* I, c.13–14.
153. *ST* I, Q.3, *prologus.*
154. *Sent.* I, 3, 1, 1, *div. text; In de div. nom.* VII, lect. 4.

which is known to him alone concerning himself and communicated to others through revelation."[155] Revelation tells us more of God than reason alone could discover but does not let us comprehend God as he is in himself.[156] Theology employs both revelation and reason to seek a deeper (but always inadequate) understanding of God.[157]

Since reason and revelation both tell us God is the cause of creatures, we can know more about him by exploring the ways of his causality. Here we find the theological purpose behind the five demonstrations of God's existence in the *Summa theologiae*, which reveal God as the ultimate efficient, exemplar, and final cause of all things.[158] Since God is the first efficient cause and since "every agent effects something similar to itself insofar as it is an agent," all things, insofar as they have being, "are like God as the first and universal principle of all being."[159] By way of causality, we may come to know something about God through the things he has made. In pursuing this knowledge, however, we must remember that though the creature is like God "it may in no way be admitted that God is like the creature" since mutual resemblance is found only among beings of the same order.[160]

The way of negation is therefore necessary as a corrective to deny that

155. *ST* I, 1, 6, co. Cf.: *Super de trin.* Q.5, 4.   156. *ST* I, 12, 13, ad 1; *Super de trin.* Q.6, 3, co.
157. See *Super de trin.* Q.5, 4.

158. On the significance of the five ways for the study of theology, see Fergus Kerr, "Theology in Philosophy: Revisiting the Five Ways," *International Journal for Philosophy of Religion* 50 (2001): 115–30; William W. Young, "From Describing to Naming God: Correlating the Five Ways with Aquinas's Doctrine of the Trinity," *New Blackfriars* 85 (2004): 527–41; Thomas F. O'Meara, *Thomas Aquinas: Theologian* (Notre Dame, Ind.: University of Notre Dame Press, 1997), 90–95; Oliver, *Philosophy*, 105–7; Wayne Hankey, *God in Himself: Aquinas's Doctrine of God as Expounded in the Summa Theologiae* (New York: Oxford University Press, 1987); idem, "The Place of the Proof of God's Existence in the *Summa Theologiae* of Thomas Aquinas," *Thomist* 46 (1982): 393; Colman O'Neill, *Sacramental Realism: A General Theory of the Sacraments* (Wilmington, Del.: Michael Glazier, 1983), 158–59; "La prédication analogique: l'élément négatif," in *Analogie et dialectique: Essais de théologie fondamentale*, ed. J. L. Marion et al. (Geneva: Labor et Fides, 1982), 85–86; Léon Elders, "Les cinq voies et leur place dans la philosophie de saint Thomas," in *Quinque Sunt Viae*, Studi Tomistici, no. 9, ed. León Elders (Vatican City: Libreria Vaticana, 1980), 143–45. Such theological usage does not diminish the philosophical validity of the five ways. See Denys Turner, "On Denying the Right God: Aquinas on Atheism and Idolatry," *Modern Theology* 20 (2004): 141–61.

159. *ST* I, 4, 3, co. See John F. Wippel, "Thomas Aquinas on our Knowledge of God and the Axiom that Every Agent Produces Something Like Itself," in *Metaphysical Themes in Thomas Aquinas II* (Washington, D.C.: The Catholic University of America Press, 2007); Rudi A. Te Velde, *Participation and Substantiality in Thomas Aquinas* (New York: Brill, 1995), 98; Aidan Nichols, *Discovering Aquinas: An Introduction to His Life, Work and Influence* (Grand Rapids, Mich.: Eerdmans, 2002), 156–57.

160. *ST* I, 4, 3, ad 4.

the limited and imperfect qualities of creatures exist in God. Divine causality also demands, however, that even qualities present imperfectly in creatures must somehow exist in a surpassing way in God since he is the exemplar cause of all things. For this reason, creaturely qualities, to the extent they can be considered without imperfection, must be predicated of God superabundantly by way of eminence.

In the *Summa theologiae*, the argument from motion (the "first way") demonstrates the existence of God as the immovable mover, the first cause of motion. Its purpose, however, is not simply to establish God's existence, but to show he exists precisely *as immovable mover*, as a particular kind of cause. As such, it forms part of the effort of all five ways to discover how God is the highest cause of all things, so that (by the way of causality) the modes of his causation may then be used to attain a deeper understanding of his nature, to the extent that such knowledge is possible in this life.

Since we cannot know what God is (his essence), but only what he is not, we begin not by considering "in what way God is, but in what way he is not." Here, we employ the way of negation to "remove those things from God which are not appropriate to him, such as composition, motion, and so forth." The way of negation is then balanced by the way of eminence. By the way of negation, for instance, "composition" is denied of God by the predication of "simplicity." But because simplicity may also have negative connotations in that "whatever is simple in material things is imperfect and a part of something else," perfection must then be attributed to God by the way of eminence. As Aquinas presents this dialectic, it seems that the predication of "immutability" involves both the way of negation (as a denial of "motion") and the way of eminence as he groups it with the predication of divine perfection:

Now it can be shown how God is not, by denying of him whatever is opposed to the idea of him, viz. composition, motion, and the like. Therefore (1) we must discuss his simplicity, whereby we deny composition in him; and because whatever is simple in material things is imperfect and a part of something else, we shall discuss (2) his perfection; (3) his infinity; (4) his immutability (*immutabilitate*); (5) his unity.[161]

161. *ST* I, Q.3, *prologus*.

In the next questions of the *Summa theologiae*, various divine attributes are discussed through the ways of negation and eminence in light of the modes of divine causality established in the "five ways." The purpose of having a special article on divine immutability may become clearer if we look at it in terms of this method.

ST I, Q.9, a.1 In this article the immutability of God is affirmed through the authority of Scripture in the *sed contra* (Mal 3:6) and by three arguments in the response. The first explains that God, as first being, is pure act and therefore cannot be moved since motion implies potency. To show that God is the first being, Aquinas refers to the conclusions of the five ways: "It has been shown above that there is some first being." The primacy of this being was established in the first and second ways: "a first mover;" "a first efficient cause." The surpassing perfection of this being was established in the fourth way: "being in the highest degree (*maxime ens*), . . . the cause of to-be (*esse*) in all other beings (*aliquid quod omnibus entibus est causa esse*)." That the fourth way is the point of departure for the argument is also indicated in the way Thomas establishes that God is pure act. He does not argue (as he might have) from the analysis of motion as act and potency in the first way to the conclusion that the first mover, in order to be totally unmoved, must be pure act.[162] Rather, he argues from the fact that since God is the "first being" and since potency is, absolutely speaking, posterior to act, God must be "pure act without admixture of any potency." Similarly, in *ST* I, 3, 1, co., he argued that God is pure act not because he is the first mover (established in the first way), but because he is the "first being (*primum ens*)" (established in the fourth way). The fourth way (which established God as the most perfect being and as the source of to-be [*esse*] and of every other perfection in other things) therefore serves as the basis for his first argument for divine immutability.[163]

162. Such an argument, beginning from motion to show God has no potency, may be found in *SCG* I, c.16.6–7 (§132–33), and in *In meta.* XII, lect. 6 (§2518).

163. "Respondeo dicendum quod ex praemissis ostenditur Deum esse omnino immutabilem. Primo quidem, quia supra ostensum est esse aliquod primum ens, quod Deum dicimus, et quod huiusmodi primum ens oportet esse purum actum absque permixtione alicuius potentiae, eo quod potentia simpliciter est posterior actu. Omne autem quod quocumque modo mutatur, est aliquo modo in potentia. Ex quo patet quod impossibile est Deum aliquo modo mutari" (*ST* I, 9, 1, co.).

The second argument begins with the assertion that in anything moved there is some sort of composition. This is evident from the nature of change, which always requires a substrate that persists through the change, an initial privation of some form or quality, and a subsequent possession of that form. Since God is absolutely simple, there can be no composition in him and consequently no motion. God's absolute simplicity was established earlier through five arguments, one of which refers to the conclusion of the fourth way, that God is "the first being (*primum ens*)," and another, to the fact that God is "to-be itself (*ipsum esse*)."[164]

The third argument contends that everything moved acquires something by its motion and achieves something not previously attained. Since God is infinite, he eternally contains in himself "the entire plenitude of the perfection of all to-be (*omnem plenitudinem perfectionis totius esse*)." There is nothing for God to acquire or attain that he does not already possess. Motion can therefore in no way be attributed to him. Here again implicit reference is made to the fourth way, where God's perfection in being was established.[165]

The direct or indirect reference to the fourth way in all these arguments tells us something about their purpose. The discussion of divine immutability is part of a quest for a deeper understanding of God. The search begins with the "five ways," which discover God as the source of created reality. It proceeds by using the ways of negation and eminence to deny any imperfection and attribute all perfection to God in a surpassing way. The use of the fourth way shows these arguments are concerned with God's surpassing perfection in being, since the fourth way began with the grades of perfection in beings and concluded to God as the most perfect being, the ultimate source of being in all other things. Thomas's purpose in the present discussion is therefore something more than simply establishing the attribute of divine

164. "Secundo, quia omne quod movetur, quantum ad aliquid manet, et quantum ad aliquid transit, sicut quod movetur de albedine in nigredinem, manet secundum substantiam. Et sic in omni eo quod movetur, attenditur aliqua compositio. Ostensum est autem supra quod in Deo nulla est compositio, sed est omnino simplex. Unde manifestum est quod Deus moveri non potest" (*ST* I, 9, 1, co.). Cf.: *ST* I, 3, 7.

165. "Tertio, quia omne quod movetur, motu suo aliquid acquirit, et pertingit ad illud ad quod prius non pertingebat. Deus autem, cum sit infinitus, comprehendens in se omnem plenitudinem perfectionis totius esse, non potest aliquid acquirere, nec extendere se in aliquid ad quod prius non pertingebat. Unde nullo modo sibi competit motus" (*ST* I, 9, 1, co.).

immutability. Were that his only objective, he might have achieved it more economically by referring to the conclusion of the first way: God is the immovable mover and is therefore immovable. But that is not the argument he gives.

His arguments show that this discussion of divine immutability does not comprise superfluous musings about a divine attribute already established in the first demonstration of God's existence, but rather proclaims God's perfection in being. As the discussion of divine perfection in Question 4 prevented us from thinking of simplicity as an imperfection, so the discussion of divine immutability in Question 9 ensures that we understand this divine attribute not as an imperfection, but as a sign of the highest possible perfection. Perhaps the intimate relation between immutability and perfection is implied in the small "thus" with which Aquinas ends his arguments: "Thus, certain of the ancient philosophers, as if compelled by truth itself, affirmed the first principle to be immovable (*immobile*)."[166]

We can confirm that the purpose of this discussion of divine immutability is the affirmation of God's perfection in being if we look at the replies to the objections. Exhibiting the same concern for divine perfection, they result not in a confession of divine immutability, but an affirmation of three ways motion may also be attributed to God to the extent that it implies no imperfection.

We are already familiar with the first objection from the *Commentary on the Sentences*.[167] Since Augustine says, "the Creator Spirit moves himself,"[168] and since anything that moves itself must be movable, his words seem to imply that God is movable. Thomas explains that Augustine is using the word "motion" in the broad sense to refer to the acts of understanding, willing, and loving. Such acts, as we have seen, do not imply imperfection since they are not the act of something existing in potency, but the act of something existing in act.[169] Motion of this sort may be affirmed of God, since he is said

---

166. "Et inde est quod quidam antiquorum, quasi ab ipsa veritate coacti, posuerunt primum principium esse immobile" (*ST* I, 9, 1, co.).

167. *Sent.* I, 8, 3, 1, obj. 2.

168. Augustine, *Super gen. ad litt.* VIII, 20 (*PL* 34, 388).

169. See *Sent.* I, 8, 3, 1, ad 2; *Super de trin.* Q.5, 4, ad 2; *In phys.* VIII, lect. 12 (§1071); *SCG* I, c.13.10 (§90).

to "know himself and love himself." Only motion that implies potency and imperfection must be denied.[170]

The second objection is also familiar.[171] Since God is wisdom itself and since Scripture teaches that "wisdom is more movable than all movable things" (Wis 7.24), God must be movable. In his response, Thomas refers to the conclusions of the second and fourth ways by mentioning a "first efficient and formal principle." The second and fourth ways established the existence of a first efficient and exemplar principle of all things, who is called God. That creative principle is more precisely identified now as "divine wisdom." Since divine wisdom is the efficient cause of all things and since "every agent effects something similar to itself to the extent that it is an agent," divine wisdom is understood to produce creatures like itself, "diffusing its similitude even to the most remote things."[172] Because divine wisdom is the exemplar cause of all things, what it creates participates its being and goodness in varying degrees. For this reason, there is said to be a sort of procession or motion of divine wisdom into all things.

Here, we find another kind of divine motion that implies no imperfection. Divine wisdom is called movable "by way of similitude (*similitudinarie*)" as it diffuses "its similitude even to the most remote things." God's creative activity is viewed as a sort of transient motion. It is not like transient motion conceived as passion, which always implies potentiality and imperfection (as the act of a being in potency). It is rather like transient motion understood as action, which implies no imperfection (as the act of the agent or the act of a being in act).[173] Through motion of this sort God manifests himself in creation: "Thus does Dionysius expound the matter, saying that 'every procession of the divine manifestation comes to us by motion from the Father of lights.'"[174]

The third objection argues that since things that imply motion, such as "approaching" and "receding," are said of God in Scripture (e.g., Jas 4:8),

---

170. *ST* I, 9, 1, ad 1.

171. *Sent.* I, 8, 3, 1, obj.1; *In de trin.* Q.5, 4, obj.2.

172. *ST* I, 4, 3, co.; Q.9, 1, ad 2.

173. Despite this likeness, there are still fundamental differences between the transient motion of creatures and the divine activity of creation. See *Sent.* I, 8, 3, 1, ad 1; *In de div. nom.* IX, lect. 2 (§822–24); *In de caelo* I, lect. 21.10.

174. *ST* I, 9, 1, ad 2.

God must be movable. In his response, Aquinas explains that these things are said of God "metaphorically (*metaphorice*)." This term might also be translated as "figuratively" or "by transference." It is different from the predication of motion "by way of similitude (*similitudinarie*)" in the response to the second objection. That referred to the creative act of God as a kind of motion. Here the "motion" in question refers not to something of God, but something in us that is predicated of God "figuratively" or "by transference." It refers specifically to our relationship with God, as we either "receive the influx of his goodness or fall away from him." Such motion really involves only a change in us, but it can be described (and possibly perceived) as a change in God. Such metaphorical usage is the language of religious experience. It describes our changing relationship with God as a motion of God toward or away from us: "Just as the sun is said to enter a house, or to go out, according as its rays reach the house, so God is said to approach us, or to recede from us, according as we receive the influx of his goodness or fall away from him." Since this language is metaphorical, it does not imply any imperfection in God.[175]

ST 1, 9, 2 After explaining God's immutability as a sign of his perfection in being, Aquinas argues that this attribute is proper to God alone and that all creatures are in some way changeable. A thing can be changed either because of a potency (*potentiam*) in it or a power (*potentiam*) in another. In the second way, all creatures are mutable by the power of God, who created them and can reduce them to nothing. In the first way, every creature is changeable through an inherent potency, which may be active (a power) or passive (a potentiality). The passive potency of the creature refers to its capacity for perfection in being and for attaining its end.

Aquinas orders his inventory of changeable creatures according to the medieval cosmological scheme of sublunar bodies, heavenly bodies, and incorporeal substances (angels). Regarding perfection in being, sublunar bodies can change substantially and accidentally. They are subject to substantial change since "their matter can exist with the privation of their substantial form." In such change, primary matter (inherent passive potency) ceases to

---

175. *ST* I, 9, 1, ad 3.

exist through one substantial form and begins to exist through another. (The primary matter of a steer, for instance, may cease to exist under the form of that animal and begin to exist under the "form" of prime rib.) They are liable to accidental change since they can cease to have one accident and acquire another, as an apple might lose its green color and become red. In these ways, everything below the sphere of the moon is somehow changeable.

Beyond the lunar sphere, the heavenly body cannot undergo substantial change since its matter is so perfected by its present form that it cannot exist with any other. It may, however, change place since its nature is compatible with the privation of one place and the achievement of another. Incorporeal substances (angels) are also not subject to substantial change. Each is a subsistent form related to its existence (*esse*) as potency to act, but not "compatible with the privation of that act." The angel cannot lose its form since it is simply a form. Since "existence (*esse*) follows upon form" and since the angels cannot lose their form, they are "immutable and invariable with respect to existence (*immutabiles et invariabiles secundum esse*)." Regarding its inherent passive power to attain its end, the angel is initially mutable with respect to its choice of good or evil. After choosing, however, it cannot change its mind. It remains changeable, however, regarding its inherent active power since it can exercise its power in new places and so attain places it had not attained before. In this it is unlike God, who because of his creative power is always present everywhere.

In this way all creatures are shown to have a potentiality for change, whether in being (as lower substances) or in place (as the heavenly bodies) or with regard to attaining their end and applying their power to diverse things (as the angels). Finally, all creatures are changeable in that it is always in the power of the creator to reduce them to non-being. It is therefore proper to God alone to be "altogether immutable (*omnino immutabilem*)."[176]

---

176. "Respondeo dicendum quod solus Deus est omnino immutabilis, omnis autem creatura aliquo modo est mutabilis. . . . Unde, cum Deus nullo istorum modorum sit mutabilis, proprium eius est omnino immutabilem esse" (*ST* I, 9, 2, co.).

THE SOURCES OF THE ARGUMENTS

Aquinas employs scriptural, patristic, and philosophical sources in his arguments for divine immutability.[177] If we study how he uses them and how he understands the authority of each, we may gain a greater appreciation for the originality of his teaching and a deeper sense of its significance for contemporary theology.

Scripture

In his inaugural lecture as a master of theology at the University of Paris in the spring of 1256, Thomas praised the sublime truth of sacred Scripture as the source of theological wisdom and outlined the role of the theologian in its transmission. On the first day of lectures after his inception, in his comments on Baruch 4:1, he proclaimed that the unchanging truth of Scripture is founded on the immutable nature of God:

The truth of the teaching of this Scripture is immutable (*immutabilis*) and eternal. Whence it follows: "And the law which is eternal" (Bar 4:1). "Heaven and earth will pass away, but my words will not pass away" (Lk 21:33). But this law remains forever on account of three things. First, on account of the power of the legislator: "The Lord of Hosts has determined and who will be able to render it doubtful?" (Is 14:27). Second, on account of his immutability (*immutabilitatem*): "I am God and I am not changed" (Mal 3:6); "The Lord is not like man that he should lie, nor as a son of man that he should be changed" (Num 23:19). Third, on account of the truth of the law: "All your commands are true" (Ps 118:86); "Truthful lips will endure forever" (Prov 12:19); "Truth endures and is strong forever" (1 Esd 4:38).[178]

For Aquinas, the immutable truth of Scripture is the foundation of our faith and the whole theological enterprise proceeding from faith: "If the authority of Scripture be disparaged even in a slight way, there will no longer be anything fixed in our faith which depends on Sacred Scripture."[179]

---

177. On the complexity of tracing and interpreting Aquinas's sources see Mark D. Jordan, "The Competition of Authoritative Languages," in *Rewritten Theology: Aquinas after His Readers* (Oxford: Blackwell, 2006), 18–32.

178. *Prin. biblicum* I (Mandonnet, 4:483; ITOO: line 77 c.). See Weisheipl, *Friar*, 93–104.

179. *SCG* IV, c.29.2 (§3647). Cf.: *ST* I, 1, 8, ad 2; *Super ev. jo.* XXI, lect. 6 (§2656); *ST* III, 1, 3, co.;

If the Bible is the foundation of all theology, it is also the primary source and basis of Aquinas's teaching on divine immutability. Scripture affirms the immutability of God directly, indirectly, and metaphorically. Aquinas cites a number of direct affirmations: "I am God and I am not changed";[180] "God is not as man that he should lie, nor as a son of man that he should be changed";[181] "You will change them and they will be changed, but you are always yourself the same";[182] "Every good endowment and every perfect gift is from above, coming down from the Father of lights with whom there is no change nor shadow of vicissitude";[183] "So when God desired to show more convincingly to the heirs of the promise the immutability (*immobilitatem*) of his counsel, he interposed with an oath, so that through two unchangeable things (*immobiles*) . . . we might have strong encouragement to seize the hope set before us."[184] There are also indirect affirmations of God's immutability, some of which we have already seen in our review of his arguments in the previous section: "You are yourself my king and my God"; "In the beginning was the Word."[185] Immutability is also indicated in scriptural affirmations of

---

Quodl. XII, Q.17, a.1 [26], ad 1. Regarding the scriptural foundations of Thomas's theological work, see Wilhelmus Valkenberg, *Words of the Living God: Place and Function of Holy Scripture in the Theology of St. Thomas Aquinas* (Leuven: Peeters, 2000); Matthew Levering, *Scripture and Metaphysics: Aquinas and the Renewal of Trinitarian Theology* (Oxford: Blackwell, 2004); Chenu, *Toward,* 68, 308–9, 316–18; Maximo Arias Reyero, *Thomas von Aquin als Exeget: Die Prinzipien seiner Schriftdeutung und seine Lehre von den Schriftsinnen* (Einsiedeln: Johannes, 1971), 259–60; Ceslas Spicq, "Saint Thomas d'Aquin, exégète," *Dictionnaire de théologie catholique,* ed. A. Vacant et al. (Paris: Librairie Letouzey et Ané, 1946), vol. 15/ 1, cols. 694–38.

180. Mal 3:6. For references see: *Sent.* I, 8, 3, 1, sc.1; *SCG* I, c.14.4 (§119); III, c.96.13 (§2720); *ST* I, 9, 1, sc; *ST* III, Q.16, a.6, obj. 2; Q.57, 1, ad 1; *Epis. ad bernardum* (line 93); *Prin. biblicum* I (Mandonnet, 483; ITOO: line 77c.); *In de div. nom.* IX, lect. 1 (§800), *Super ad rom.* I, lect. 2 (§37); lect. 7 (§129); *Super ev. jo.* I, lect. 7 (§166); *Super ad hebr.* I, lect. 5 (§77).

181. Num 23:19. For references see: *SCG* I, c.14.4 (§119); III, c.96.13 (§2720); c.98.5 (§2745); *ST* I, 19, 7, sc; *Comp.* II, c.2; *Prin. biblicum,* I (Mandonnet, 483; ITOO: line 77c.); *Super iob* II, v.3, line 54c; *Super is.* I, v.20 (line 688c.); VIII, v.11 (line 346c); XXXI, v.2 (line 16c); *In jer.* (ITOO), XVIII, lect. 2, line 3c.; *Super ev. jo.* VII, lect. 2 (§1025); VIII, lect. 1 (§1134).

182. Ps 101:28. For references see: *Sent.* I, 8, 3, 2, sc.1; *SCG* I, c.15.7 (§126); *De pot.* Q.3, 17, obj.6; *In de div. nom.* IX, lect. 1 (§800); lect. 2 (§815); X, lect. 3 (§874); *Super is.* LX, v.20 (line 202c.); *Super ev. jo.* XX, lect. 1 (§2483); *Super ad hebr.* XIII, lect. 1 (§739). This same verse, as referred to in Heb1:11–12, is cited by Thomas in *In de div. nom.* II, lect. 1 (§119), and *Super ad hebr.* I, lect. 5 (§77).

183. Jas 1:17. For references see: *Sent.* I, 3, 2, 1, obj.2; d.4, 1, 1, obj.1; d.8, 3, 1, sc.1; II, 3, 3, 4, obj.1; d.15, 3, 2, obj.1; *SCG* I, c.14.4 (§119); c.55.10 (§464); *ST* I, 14, 15, sc; III, 61, 4, obj.3; *De ver.* Q.2, 13, sc.1; *Super decret.* I, line 211; *Super ad hebr.* I, lect. 5 (§73 and 77).

184. Heb 6:18. For references see: *ST* II-II; 89, 10, ad 4; *Super ad hebr.* VI, lect. 4 (§322–23).

185. Ps 43:6; Jn 1:1. See our discussion of *In psalmos* XLIII.2, and *Super ev. jo., prologus* (§4), above.

God's eternity,[186] constancy,[187] immortality, and incorruptibility.[188] A "certain immutability (*immobilitas quaedam*)" is likewise implied in some anthropomorphic usages such as divine "standing" and "sitting."[189]

Other scriptural passages seems to imply that God changes. Some are clearly anthropomorphic: "He heard the voice of the Lord God walking in paradise."[190] Others suggest that God changes in response to human actions: "Draw near to God and he will draw near to you"; "If that nation repents of its evil, I will also repent."[191] Scripture even says flatly that God, as Divine Wisdom, is "more changeable than all changeable things."[192]

It looks like Scripture contradicts itself, asserting in one place that God is absolutely immutable and in another that he is most changeable of all things.[193] We have already seen how Thomas resolves these apparent contradictions by distinguishing between the different senses and usages of Scripture.[194] The truth of Scripture is found first in what he calls the "literal sense" and then in various "spiritual senses." In the literal sense, the words of Scripture are understood to signify certain things. The literal sense is the foundation for the spiritual senses, and it alone may be used to ground theological arguments.[195] It comprises not only the meaning intended by the limited

186. See Heb 13:8, cited in *Super ev. jo., prologus* (§4) and *Super ad hebr.* I, lect. 5 (§73); Lam. 5:19, cited in *Super ad hebr.* I, lect. 5 (§73); Ps 30:1, cited in *In psalmos* (ITOO), XXX.1, line 63 c.; Ps 101:12, cited *Super ad hebr.* I, lect. 5 (§72).

187. See Is 46:10, cited in *Contra doc. retra.* c. 10 (line 144 c.).

188. See Rom 1:23 and 1 Tim 6:16, cited in *Super ad rom.* I, lect. 7 (§134).

189. See Amos 7:7 and Is 9:7, cited in *In de div. nom.* IX, lect. 1 (§800); lect. 4 (§837. Cf.: *Super ev. jo., prologus* (§4), *Super is.* c.1, v.20, line 688 c.; *Super ev matt.* IV, lect. 2 (§364); *Super ad hebr.* I, lect. 2 (§42); *ST* I, 3, 1, ad 4.

190. See Gen 3:8, cited in *SCG* IV, c.23.7 (§3597); *In de div. nom.* IX, lect. 1 (§800).

191. See Jas 4:8 and Jer 18:8, cited in *ST* I, 9, 1, obj.3; Q.19, 7, obj.2; *SCG* I, c.91.16 (§766); III, c.96.11 (§2718); 96.15 (§2722); IV, c.23.7 (§3597); 23.9 (§3599); *In psalmos* XXVI.9.

192. See Wis 7:24, cited in *ST* I, 9, 1, obj.2; *Sent.* I, 8, 3, 1, obj.1; *Super de trin.* Q.5, 4, obj.2; *In de div. nom.* IX, lect. 1 (§800); *In psalmos* XVII.8.

193. Scripture affirms divine repentance, for instance in Gen 6:6; 2 Sam 24:16; and Jer 18:8–9. Aquinas notes this usage in *ST* I, 9, 1, obj.3; Q.19, 7, obj.2; *SCG* I, c.91.16 (§766); III, c.96.11 (§2718); 96.15 (§2722); IV, c.23.7 (§3597); 23.9 (§3599); and *In psalmos* XXVI.9. Scripture denies divine repentance in 1 Sam 15:29; Ps 110:4; and Rom 11:29. Aquinas notes this usage in *SCG* I, c.91.16 (§766); III, c.96.13 (§2720); *Super ad hebr.* III, lect. 2 (§184); VI, lect. 4 (§322); and *Super ad rom.* XI, lect. 4 (§924–26).

194. See our discussion of *ST* I, 9, 1, ad 2 and ad 3, above. Cf.: *SCG* III, c.96.11–13 (§2718–20).

195. *ST* I, 1, 10, ad 1. Cf.: Nicholas M. Healy, "Introduction," in *Aquinas on Scripture: An Introduction to His Biblical Commentaries*, ed. Thomas G. Weinandy et al. (London: T and T Clark, 2005), 1–20; Chenu, *Toward*, 254, 257 note 45.

human authors of Scripture but also all that may be intended by the Divine Author, including "all truth which, respecting the terms of the letter, can be fitted to Sacred Scripture."[196] In the various spiritual senses, things signified by the words of Scripture are in turn understood to indicate other things. The words of the Old Testament, for instance, refer to events of the Old Law, but those events in turn point to realities of the New Law. Such deeper spiritual senses are possible because of Scripture's divine authorship.[197]

All of Aquinas's scriptural arguments for divine immutability, including those founded on scriptural metaphors, belong to the literal sense since they are all based on the words of Scripture as they indicate a certain reality, the truth of God's changelessness. Sometimes they indicate this directly. Other times (as in metaphorical usage), they do so indirectly by referring to some figure or image that in turn suggests divine immutability. In these cases, the literal sense is itself "not the figure but that which is figured."[198] So when Scripture speaks of God as sitting or repenting, the literal sense is not that God actually "sits" or "repents," but that God "does" (or "is") what these images signify. So "sitting" indicates God's unchanging being, and "repentance" his causing of one course of action (deliverance) rather than another (destruction).[199]

Though apparent scriptural contradictions can be resolved by referring to its various senses, one still needs to decide what sense to apply to what passage. Which should be taken directly and which indirectly or metaphorically? Aquinas thinks passages referring to God's immutability should be taken directly, while those referring to divine repentance or emotion are metaphorical.[200] Yet he knows other authors do the opposite and take statements about God's "anger" or "sadness" directly rather than metaphorically.[201]

---

196. *De pot.* Q.4, 1, co.

197. *ST* I, 1, 10; *Quodl.* VII, Q.6, aa.1–3 [14–16].

198. *ST* I, 1, 10, ad 3.

199. *In de div. nom.* IX, lect. 4 (§9397); *ST* I, 19, 7, ad 1.

200. On the metaphorical interpretation of divine repentence, see: *SCG* I, c.91.16 (§766); *SCG* I, c.89.12 (§745); II, c.25.9 (§1017); *ST* I, 19, 7, ad 1; *Super iob* II, v.3, lines 49–66; X, v.8, lines 188–94; *In jer.* XVIII, lect. 2; *Super ad rom.* XI, lect. 4 (§924–26); *Super ad hebr.* VI, lect. 4 (§322). Thomas often cites St. Gregory's teaching that "God changes his sentence, but does not change his counsel" (Gregory, *Moral* XVI, 10 [*PL* 75, 1127b]). See *SCG* III, c.96.15 (§2722); *ST* I, 19, 7, ad 2; *De ver.* Q.12, 11, ad 3; *In psalmos* XXXII.10; *Super ad rom.* XIV, lect. 1 (§1109); *Contra doc. retra.* c.10, line 144 c.; *Super is.* I, v. 20, line 688 c.

201. *SCG* I, c.91.18 (§767).

Today's theologians face similar dilemmas. Some agree implicitly with Aquinas's approach. Martin McNamara, for instance, believes that references to divine repentance should not be seen as affirmations of change in God.[202] Paul Helm argues similarly that "metaphysical or ontological or strictly literal data must control the anthropomorphic and anthropopathic data, and not vice-versa."[203] For some contemporary theologians, as for Aquinas himself, God's unchanging faithfulness directly implies his unchanging being.[204]

Other theologians take affirmations of divine immutability metaphorically (as similitudes for God's abiding faithfulness) and references to divine repentance directly (as signifying that God does in fact "change his mind" with respect to some intended action). Wilhelm Maas, for instance, sees divine immutability as a metaphor for "the immutability of God's faithfulness to his covenant." He notes, however, that within that faithfulness God may sometimes "change his mind" as he reacts to "the momentary behavior of his covenant partner."[205] Robert Chisholm also thinks that "the human response to His announcement determines what He will do."[206] A. van de Beek

202. Martin McNamara, "Process Thought and Some Biblical Evidence," in *Charles Hartshorne's Concept of God: Philosophical and Theological Responses*, ed. Santiago Sia (Dordrecht: Kluwer, 1990), 208.

203. Paul Helm, "The Impossibility of Divine Passibility," in *The Power and Weakness of God: Impassibility and Orthodoxy*, ed. Nigel M. de S. Cameron (Edinburgh: Rutherford House Books, 1990), 128–29. Cf.: Millard Erickson, "God and Change," *Southern Baptist Journal of Theology* 1, no. 2 (1997): 43–47; Sacchi, "El Dios," 256–57.

204. See *In psalmos* XLIII.2. Cf.: Jean Galot, "La réalité de la souffrance de Dieu: Actualité du problème théologique," *Nouvelle revue théologique* 101 (1979): 230; Raphael Schulte, "Unveränderlichkeit Gottes," in *Lexikon für Theologie und Kirche*, ed. J. Höfer and K. Rahner (Freiburg: Herder, 1965), vol. 10, col. 536; Hans Pfeil, "Die Frage nach der Veränderlichkeit und Geschichtlichkeit Gottes," *Münchener theologische Zeitschrift* 31 (1980): 3; Louis-B. Gillon, OP, "Dieu immobile et Dieu en mouvement," *Doctor communis* 23 (1976): 145; Michel Gervais, "Incarnation et immuabilité divine," *Revue des sciences religieuses* 50 (1976): 232.

205. Wilhelm Maas, *Unveränderlichkeit Gottes: Zum Verhältnis von griechisch-philosophischer und christlicher Gotteslehre* (München: F. Schöningh, 1974), 25. A number of theologians, agreeing that the affirmation of divine immutability in the Scriptures refers only to the immutability of God's faithfulness, allow that some sort of change may (or must) be predicated of God. See Richard Rice, "Biblical Support for a New Perspective," in *The Openness of God: A Biblical Challenge to the Traditional Understanding of God*, ed. Clark Pinnock et al. (Downers Grove, Ill.: InterVarsity Press, 1999), 11–58; N. Wolterstorff, "Suffering Love," 227; Warren McWilliams, "Divine Suffering in Contemporary Theology," *Scottish Journal of Theology* 33 (1980): 35–53; Joseph Hallman, "The Mutability of God: Tertullian to Lactantius," *Theological Studies* 42 (1981): 373.

206. Robert Chisholm, "Does God 'Change His Mind'?" *Bibliotheca Sacra* 152 (1995): 399. See also R. W. L. Moberly, "'God Is Not a Human That He Should Repent' (Numbers 23:19 and 1 Samuel 15:29)," in *God in the Fray: A Tribute to Walter Brueggemann*, ed. Tod Linafelt and Timothy K. Beal (Minneapolis: Fortress, 1998), 121.

maintains that divine repentance implies "constant change in God's plans, feelings, and actions."[207] Walter C. Kaiser sees Malachi 3:6 as "the doctrine of the immutability or the unchangeableness of the living God" whose "nature, attributes, qualities, being and person . . . may be counted on as a fixed point of reference and as one in whom there is no variableness," but who "can change in his actions toward us as much as any other living person can change."[208]

In deciding when to interpret Scripture directly or metaphorically, Aquinas suggests we pay attention to evidence internal to Scripture and to an external authority. Scripture itself provides evidence for its proper interpretation in various ways. Sometimes the nature of a passage is indicated by the very "manner of the narration." In this way, for instance, Scripture indicates the visionary character of Isaiah's statement, "I saw the Lord sitting."[209] At other times, a given passage may be recognized as metaphorical because the truth it signifies "is expressly clarified" elsewhere in Scripture.[210]

Besides such internal evidence, an external authority is also essential for correct interpretation. Thomas believes this resides in the Church and "chiefly in the supreme pontiff."[211] This authority guides the interpretation of Scripture and specifies the formal object of faith that is "First Truth as manifested in Sacred Scripture and the teaching of the Church."[212] As G. Geenen describes Aquinas's position, the authority of the Church is not in itself a source of revelation but "intimately and indissolubly linked to the sources of revelation" in such a way that it is "indispensable, because it alone has the exclusive right to give us an exact and authentic knowledge of what is taught by Scripture and tradition."[213] Under this guidance, theologians may hold

207. A. van de Beek, *Why? On Suffering Guilt and God* (Grand Rapids: Eerdmans, 1990), 273.

208. Walter C. Kaiser Jr., *Malachi: God's Unchanging Love* (Grand Rapids, Mich.: Baker Book House, 1984), 77, 87–88, 93.

209. Is 6:1, cited in *SCG* IV; c.29.5 (§3650).

210. *SCG* IV, c.29.4–5 (§3649–50); *ST* I, 1, 9, ad 2.

211. *ST* II-II, 11, 2, ad 3; *Super ev. matt.* IV, 2 (§349); *Quodl.* IX, a.1 [16], co. Cf.: Arias Reyero, *Thomas,* 174, n.72.

212. *ST* II-II, Q.5, a.3, co.

213. G. Geenen, "The Place of Tradition in the Theology of St. Thomas," *Thomist* 15 (1952): 119. Cf.: Nicholas M. Healy, *Thomas Aquinas: Theologian of the Christian Life* (Burlington, Vt.: Ashgate, 2003), 157–58; Yves Congar, *The Meaning of Tradition* (New York: Hawthorn Books, 1964; reprint, San Francisco: Ignatius, 2004), 64–72, 152 (page citations are to the reprint edition).

varying opinions on theological questions: "Disciples can take either side when Doctors of Scripture differ—provided their opinions are not at odds with the faith or sound morals. . . . Whoever assents to the opinions of any teacher when these conflict with the evident testimony of Scripture or with what is commonly held on the Church's authority, cannot be excused from a vicious error."²¹⁴ Only through their life in the Church do theologians come to understand the meaning of the Scriptures and share in the wisdom of Christ:

Since the Church was instituted on account of Christ, it is called the fullness of Christ. All things which are of excellence in Christ are, in some way fulfilled in the members of the Church in that all spiritual understanding, gifts, and whatever can be present in the Church—which all superabound in Christ—flow from him into the members of the Church and are perfected in them. So he [St. Paul] adds, "who fills all things in all ways," in that he makes this one, who is a member of the Church, wise according to perfect wisdom which is in himself; and that one just with perfect justice, and so on with others.²¹⁵

In this way, the Church implicitly informs and influences all Aquinas's theological and exegetical work.²¹⁶ Though he rarely mentions the Church or Church councils in his arguments for divine immutability, it is clearly his intention always to follow its mind and teaching.²¹⁷

Fathers of the Church

Aquinas frequently refers to patristic writers in his arguments that God does not change. Here we will consider his views on their authority in relation to contemporary opinions on the Christian authenticity of their teaching on divine immutability.²¹⁸ We will then look more particularly at his use

---

214. *Quodl.* III, Q.4, a.2 [10], co.   215. *Super ad eph.* I, lect. 8 (§71).
216. Arias Reyero, *Thomas,* 255.
217. Divine immutability is related directly to the teaching of the Fourth Lateran Council [Lateran IV, 1215 (Denz. 800)] in *Super decret.* I, lines 208–12.
218. On the notions of passibility and impassibility in Greek antiquity and patristic thought, see Paul L. Gavrilyuk, *The Suffering of the Impassible God: The Dialectics of Patristic Thought* (Oxford: Oxford University Press, 2004); Amuluche Gregory Nnamani, *The Paradox of a Suffering God: On the Classical, Modern-Western and Third World Struggles to Harmonize the Incompatible Attributes of the Trinitarian God* (New York: Peter Lang, 1995); Joseph Hallman, *The Descent of God: Divine Suffering in History and Theology* (Minneapolis: Fortress Press, 1991); Herbert Frohnhofen, *Apatheia tou Theou: Über die Affektlosigkeit Gottes in der*

of Dionysius and Augustine, the Fathers he cites most often in discussing God's changelessness.[219]

Early in his *Summa theologiae,* Thomas makes it clear that the authority of the Fathers does not equal that of Scripture: "Sacred doctrine . . . properly uses the authority of the canonical Scriptures as an incontrovertible proof, and the authority of the doctors of the Church as an argument that is proper to its method, but merely probable. For our faith rests upon the revelation made to the apostles and prophets, who wrote the canonical books, and not on the revelations (if any such there are) made to other doctors."[220] The writings of the Fathers are to be respected since the same Spirit who spoke in the Scriptures also speaks through them.[221] Their authority is honored, but "only insofar as they tell us those things which the apostles and prophets have left in their writings."[222] When controversies arise regarding the doctrinal validity of particular teachings of the Fathers, the authority of the Church is to be consulted since "the teaching of the catholic doctors itself has its authority from the Church."[223]

Unlike Scripture and the doctrinal pronouncements of the Church, patristic authors are not infallible. They are sometimes mistaken in their opinions and can be led astray by philosophers.[224] The differences among them often spring from the particular philosophers they have chosen to follow: "The expositors of Holy Scripture differed from one another according as they followed the different philosophers who taught them their philosophy. Basil, for instance, and Augustine, and many more of the saints follow

griechischen Antike und bei den griechischsprachigen Kirchenväter bis zu Gregorios Thaumaturgos (Frankfurt am Main: Peter Lang, 1987); Henri Crouzel, "La passion de l'impassible: un essai apologétique et polémique du IIIe siècle," in *L'homme devant Dieu. Mélanges offerts au Père Henri de Lubac* (Paris: Aubier, 1963), 1:269–79; Sacchi, "El Dios inmutable," 257–61.

219. Other Church Fathers cited in reference to divine immutability include Jerome, Gregory, and John of Damascus. Jerome (*Epist.* XV, 4 [*PL* 22, 357]) is cited in *Sent.* I, 8, 1, 1, co. Gregory (*Moral* XVI, 10 [*PL* 75, 1127]) is cited in *ST* I, 19, 7, ad 2. John of Damascus (*De fide orth.* I, 3 [*PG* 94, 795]) is cited in *Sent.* I, 5, 2, 2, sc.2; d.8, 3, 2, sc.2; and II, 23, 1, 1, obj.3. His *De fide orth.* II, 3 (*PG* 94, 868) is cited in *ST* I, 9, 2, co.

220. *ST* I, 1, 8, ad 2. Cf.: Godefroid Geenen, "Saint Thomas et les pères," *Dictionnaire de théologie catholique,* ed. A. Vacant et al. (Paris: Librairie Letouzey et Ané, 1946), vol. 15, col.738–39; Geenen, "Place," 117.

221. *Quodl.* XII, Q.17, a.1 [26], co.; *In de div. nom.* II, lect. 2 (§125).

222. *De ver.* Q.14, 10, ad 11.

223. *Quodl.* II, Q.4, a.2 [7], co. Cf.: *Quodl.* IX, q.7, a.1 [16], co.; *ST* II-II, 10, 12.

224. Origen, for instance, was "deceived in many things" by "following the opinions of the ancient philosophers" (*ST* I, 51, 1, ad 1). Cf.: *ST* I, 84, 5; *Quodl.* XII, Q.17 a.1 [26].

the opinions of Plato in those philosophical matters that do not regard the faith. . . . Dionysius, on the other hand, follows Aristotle in almost everything as becomes evident to anyone looking into his books."[225]

Aquinas's awareness of the influence of Greek philosophy on the Fathers of the Church brings us to a complex subject in contemporary theology. An increasing awareness of Greek philosophical influences on the Fathers and on the dogmatic formulations of the councils has led a number of theologians to see much of patristic thought as a "hellenization" of authentic Christianity and to call for a "dehellenization" of Christian theology.

From the earliest centuries of the Church, theologians have accused their opponents of being "led astray by the mentality of the Greeks."[226] The notion of a full-scale hellenization of Christian thought, however, is a more recent development, dating from the sixteenth century.[227] In the twentieth century, Adolf von Harnack wrote that by erecting "a work of the Greek spirit on the soil of the Gospel," the apologists changed Christianity into a "deistic religion."[228] Alfred North Whitehead wryly asserts that "the church gave unto God the attributes which belonged exclusively to Caesar."[229] Jürgen Moltmann echoes this opinion: "[W]hile the Church gained the ancient world with its proclamation of God, the Caesars conquered in the Church. We can see this in the concept of God in the fact that God was now understood in terms of the image of the Egyptian pharaohs, Persian kings, and Roman emperors. . . . This theism is tantamount to idolatry."[230]

225. *Sent.* II, 14, 1, 2, co. Translation from Chenu, *Toward,* 143. Thomas soon modified his opinion regarding Aristotle's influence on Dionysius. See *In de div. nom., prooem.; De malo* Q.16, 1, ad 3.

226. Jaroslav Pelikan, *The Christian Tradition,* vol. 1, *The Emergence of the Catholic Tradition (100–600)* (Chicago: University of Chicago Press, 1971), 45.

227. For a historical account of the development of the notion of hellenization, see Alois Grillmeier, "Hellenisierung-Judaisierung des Christentums als Deuteprinzipien der Geschichte des kirchlichen Dogmas," *Scholastik* 33 (1958): 321–55, 528–58; Leo Scheffczyk, *Tendenzen und Brennpunkte der neueren Problematik um die Hellenisierung des Christentums* (München: Bayerische Akademie der Wissenschaften, 1982); idem, "Die Frage nach der Hellenisierung des Christentums unter modernem Problemaspekt," *Münchener theologische Zeitschrift* 33 (1982): 195–205; Wolfhart Pannenberg, "Die Aufnahme des philosophischen Gottesbegriffs als dogmatischer Problem der frühchristlichen Theologie," in *Grundfragen systematischer Theologie* (Göttingen: Vandenhoeck and Ruprecht, 1967), 296–97.

228. Adolf von Harnack, *Lehrbuch der Dogmengeschichte* (Tübingen: Mohr, 1931), 1:20.

229. Alfred North Whitehead, *Process and Reality,* corrected edition, ed. D. Griffen and D. Sherburne (New York: Free Press, 1978), 342.

230. Jürgen Moltmann, *The Crucified God,* trans. R. Wilson and J. Bowden (New York: Harper and

More recently the notion of a wholesale hellenization of Christian thought has come under increasing criticism. Paul L. Gavrilyuk expresses the critique most succinctly: "The 'Theory of Theology's Fall into Hellenistic Philosophy' must be once and for all buried with honors, as one of the most enduring and illuminating mistakes among the interpretations of the development of Christian doctrine."[231] Jaroslov Pelikan responds specifically to Harnack's argument: "It is even more a distortion when the dogma formulated by the catholic tradition is described as 'in its conception and development a work of the Greek spirit on the soil of the gospel.' Indeed, in some ways it is more accurate to speak of dogma as the 'dehellenization' of the theology that had preceded it and to argue that 'by its dogma the church threw up a wall against an alien metaphysic.'"[232] There is now a greater appreciation of the critical judgment exercised by the Church Fathers in their employment of Greek ideas and of how the historical process of hellenization itself may be seen as not only unavoidable but uniquely valuable.[233]

The continued presence of certain allegedly hellenistic elements in Christian thought, however, is still seen by some as a hindrance to its authentic development. At the forefront of such unwanted elements is the notion of divine immutability. Karl Barth, for instance, believes the "pagan notion" of the

---

Row, 1974), 250. Cf.: Richard Bauckham, "Only the Suffering God Can Help: Divine Passibility in Modern Theology," *Themelios* 9 (1984): 6–12.

231. Gavrilyuk, *The Suffering*, 46. For other examples of such criticism, see Robert Louis Wilken, *The Spirit of Early Christian Thought: Seeking the Face of God* (New Haven: Yale University Press, 2003), 59–61; William V. Rowe, "Adolf von Harnack and the Concept of Hellenization," in *Hellenization Revisited: Shaping a Christian Response within the Greco-Roman World*, ed. Wendy E. Helleman (Lanham, Md.: University Press of America, 1994), 69–98; Richard A. Muller, "Incarnation, Mutability, and the Case for Classical Theism," *Westminster Theological Journal* 45 (1983): 36; Hallman, "Mutability," 373; Scheffczyk, *Tendenzen*, 17–22; "Frage," 203–5; Pelikan, *Emergence*, 55; Edward Schillebeeckx, *Jesus: An Experiment in Christology*, trans. H. Hoskins (New York: Seabury, 1979), 561; Reinhard M. Hübner, *Der Gott der Kirchenväter und der Gott der Bibel: Zur Frage der Hellenisierung des Christentums* (München: Minerva Publikation, 1979), 6–7.

232. Pelikan, *Emergence*, 55, quoting Harnack, *Lehrbuch der Dogmengeschichte*, 1:20; and Werner Elert, *Der Ausgang der altkirchlichen Christologie* (Berlin: Lutherisches Verlagshaus, 1957), 14.

233. On the critical judgment of the Fathers in adapting the Greek notion of divine immutability, see Joseph Ratzinger, *Introduction to Christianity*, trans. Michael J. Miller (San Francisco: Ignatius Press, 2004), 137–48; idem, *Truth and Tolerance: Christian Belief and World Religions* (San Francisco: Ignatius Press, 2004), 90–95; Schillebeeckx, *Jesus*, 60; Pannenberg, "Aufnahme," 341–42; Andrea Milano, "Il 'divenire di Dio' in Hegel, Kierkegaard, e san Tommaso d'Aquino," in *San Tommaso e il pensiero moderno*, Studi Tomistici no. 3 (Vatican City: Libreria Vaticana, 1976), 289; John K. Mozley, *The Impassibility of God: A Survey of Christian Thought* (New York: Macmillan, 1927).

immobile God "can only be a euphemistic description of death" and thinks that in theology "the remembrance of the *immutabilitas Dei* acted . . . like a Soviet Russian veto and hindered any further thinking."[234] Heribert Mühlen maintains "it is scarcely possible" for the faithful to discover "the face of God himself in a new way . . . within the traditional horizon of the all-cosmic understanding of being in which only the omnipotent but apathetic face of the Platonic God gazes at us."[235] Others, however, deny that divine immutability as understood in Christian theology is merely a Greek philosophical notion. They point out that efforts at "dehellenization" have sometimes led theology not closer to the "biblical" God but farther away, toward some other "philosophical" god, far more divorced from the Christian tradition than the God of the patristic writers.[236]

We may find some advice from Aquinas on these issues. First, he respects the authority of the Fathers but does not consider them infallible. Since they might have been led astray by the philosophers they chose to follow, he teaches they should be followed only as they reflect the truth of Scripture interpreted by the Church. When their opinions vary without contradicting that truth, theologians are free to accept, revise, or reject them. Following his own advice, he accepts the teaching of the Fathers on divine immutability but does not hesitate to modify it when he sees a deeper truth. His notion of divine immutability, therefore, though often expressed in the very words of the Fathers, is profoundly different in its significance, as we may see in his use of Dionysius and Augustine.

234. Karl Barth, *Die Kirchliche Dogmatik* (Zollikon: Evangelischer Verlag, 1957–67), II/1, 557; IV/2, 93.

235. H. Mühlen, *Die Veränderlichkeit Gottes als Horizont einer zukünftigen Christologie* (Münster: A. Schendorff, 1969), 9. Theologians who agree that the concept of divine immutability is of Greek origin and hindersome to a proper understanding of Christian faith include Richard Swinburne, *The Coherence of Theism* (Oxford: Clarendon Press, 1986), 215; Chester Paul Michael, *A Comparison of the God-Talk of Thomas Aquinas and Charles Hartshorne* (Ann Arbor, Mich.: University Microfilms, 1975), 74; Pannenberg, "Aufnahme," 327–32; Rem B. Edwards, "The Pagan Dogma of the Absolute Unchangeableness of God," *Religious Studies* 14 (1978): 305–14; Francis House, "The Barrier of Impassibility," *Theology* 83 (1980): 413; Chung Young Lee, *The Suffering God* (Ann Arbor, Mich.: University Microfilms, 1968), 88, 95, 117; Johannes B. Brantschen, "Die Macht und Ohnmacht der Liebe," *Freiburger Zeitschrift für Philosophie und Theologie* 27 (1980): 234; Ludger Oeing-Hanhoff, "Die Krise des Gottesbegriffs," *Theologische Quartalschrift* 159 (1979): 291.

236. See, for example, Scheffczyk, "Frage," 204; *Tendenzen*, 25.

Dionysius

In his very first discussion of divine immutability, Aquinas uses Dionysius to explicate the meaning of the term.[237] In subsequent writings, he frequently invokes Dionysius's three ways of causality, negation, and eminence, finding in them the foundation for all human knowing and naming of God from creatures.[238] His most extensive discussion of divine immutability occurs in the plainly Dionysian context of the *Commentary on Dionysius's On the Divine Names*. He carefully follows Dionysius's exposition of the different senses of the term "immutable," explaining how they may or may not be predicated of God as they imply perfection or imperfection.[239]

Both Aquinas and Dionysius believe God should be called "immutable," but neither thinks the term implies God is "static" or "inert." Quite to the contrary, they see the immutable God as an eminently active reality who, in virtue of his creative and providential causality, may be said to "be moved and to proceed toward all things (*moveri et ad omnia procedere*)."[240] Just as other philosophers were "compelled, as it were, by truth itself" to affirm that God, as the first principle of all things, is immutable, so Thomas and Dionysius "make bold to say on behalf of the truth that he himself, the cause of all things, by his abounding love and goodness is placed outside of himself by his providence for all existing things."[241] God's motion is the movement of love, and his loving activity is described as "stable procession (*processus stabilis*)" and "productive stillness (*statum generativum*)."[242] In view of God's activity, Aquinas asserts, in a phrase stronger than the text of Dionysius, that theologians may "not only attribute motion to God, but it is

---

237. *Sent.* I, 3, 1, 1, *div. text.*

238. *Sent.* I, 2, 1, 3, co.; d.3, 1, 1, *div. text;* a.3, co.; d.22, 1, 2, obj.2; d.35, 1, 1, co.; *ST* I, 12, 12, co.; Q.13, 1, co.; a.8, ad 2; a.10, ad 5; Q.84, 7, ad 3; II-II, 27, 4, co.; *De pot.* Q.9, 7, obj.2; co.; *De malo* Q.16, 8, ad 3; *In de div. nom.* I, lect. 3 (§83, 85, 102, 104); VII, lect. 4 (§729, 731); *Super de trin.* Q.1, 2, co.; Q.6, 2, co.; a.3, co.; *Super ad rom.* I, lect. 6 (§115). On Aquinas's appropriation of the three ways, see Fran O'Rourke, *Pseudo-Dionysius and the Metaphysics of Aquinas* (Leiden: E. J. Brill, 1992), 31–41; Michael B. Ewbank, "Diverse Orderings of Dionysius's triplex via by St. Thomas Aquinas," *Mediaeval Studies* 52 (1990): 82–109.

239. *In de div. nom.* IX, lect. 2; lect. 4.

240. Dionysius, *Cael. Hier.* I, 1 (*PG* 3, 120); *De div. nom.* V, 9–10; IX, 1, 3, 8–10 (*PG* 3: 325, 909, 912, 916–17). *In de div. nom.* IX, lect. 4 (§840); *Sent.* I, 8, 3, 1, ad 1; *ST* I, 9, 1, ad 2; *Super de trin.* Q.5, 4, ad 2.

241. *ST* I, 9, 1, co; *ST* I, 20, 2, ad 1.

242. Dionysius, *De div. nom* IX, 9 (*PG* 916). *In de div. nom.* IX, lect. 4 (§842).

also granted us that we may fittingly praise the motion of the immovable God."[243]

Though both Aquinas and Dionysius attribute motion and immutability to God, their understanding of God is profoundly different. Dionysius understands God in terms of Neoplatonic philosophy.[244] He attributes motion to God in view of the immanence of divine causality in the world, but denies it since God is beyond the motion and rest of creatures.[245] The God of Dionysius, however, is not only beyond creaturely motion and rest, but somehow beyond being itself. For, in his theology, God is to some extent identified with the "One" of Neoplatonic thought, which is the supreme cause of all and the source of all being precisely because it is beyond being. Although Dionysius predicates "being" of God, he intends this predication to mean only that God is the cause of being in creatures.[246] He cannot properly predicate "being" of the One, for that would jeopardize its absolute unity. Although Dionysius does not employ Neoplatonic philosophy uncritically in his theology, his liaison with that system of thought does limit his ability to speak of the God of revelation. For it is difficult to speak of a God who calls himself "He who is" (Ex 3:14) if one is tied to a philosophy that does not allow being to be predicated properly of God.[247]

Thomas agrees with Dionysius that God is above both motion and rest

243. Where Dionysius speaks impersonally, Thomas speaks for theologians in the first person plural. In Dionysius, the Greek text reads: "Alla kai kinēseis theou tou akinētou theoprepōs tō logō synchōrēteon hymēsai [But one must also concede to praise with a word, in a way befitting divinity, the motions of the unmoved God]" (De div. nom. IX, 9 [PG 3, 916]). The Latin text reads: "Sed et motus Dei immobilis, ut decet Deum, laudari sermone permittitur [But it is also allowed that the motions of the immovable God may be praised with a word, as befits God]." Thomas comments: "Et non solum theologi motum Deo attribuunt, sed et nobis pemittitur ut decenter laudemus motum Dei immobilis [And not only do theologians attribute motion to God, but it is also granted us that we may fittingly praise the motion of the immovable God.]" (In de div. nom. IX, lect. 4 [§841]). See Michael J. Dodds, "St. Thomas Aquinas and the Motion of the Motionless God," New Blackfriars 68 (1987): 233–42.

244. Regarding Dionysius's adaptation of Neoplatonic philosophy, see Stephen Gersh, From Iamblichus to Eriugena: An Investigation of the Prehistory and Evolution of the Pseudo-Dionysian Tradition (Leiden: E. J. Brill, 1978), 155, 227–29.

245. Dionysius, De div. nom. IV, 7 (PG 3, 703).

246. See Gilson, Christian, 137–39; The Spirit of Medieval Philosophy (New York: Charles Scribner's Sons, 1940), 430n6; James F. Anderson, St. Augustine and Being (The Hague: Martinus Nijhoff, 1965), 7, 27, 35.

247. Gilson, Christian, 140–41; Being and Some Philosophers (Toronto: Pontifical Institute of Mediaeval Studies, 1952), 39–40.

as found in creatures.[248] He also asserts that God is not "something exist-ing." But he immediately qualifies this: "God is not something existing of the number of existing creatures (*de numero existentium creatorum*)."[249] The meaning and implications of these statements are profoundly different in Aquinas's theology. Even when he uses the very words of Dionysius, their significance is changed because of his radically different understanding of the nature of God. So it may be said that Thomas "never took over a formu-la from Dionysius without altering its content."[250] Aquinas also thinks that God is "above being," but his reason for so thinking is by no means the Neo-platonic teaching that the One must be above being. For him, the fact that God is above being (*ens*) does not imply that being (*esse*) must be denied of God. Rather, God is seen as above the limited being of creatures precisely be-cause he is subsisting being itself: "But according to the truth of the matter, the first cause is above being (*ens*) inasmuch as it is itself infinite 'to be' (*ip-sum esse infinitum*)."[251] As *ipsum esse*, God is radically unknown and unknow-able to us. But the reason for this is again not because God is beyond being, but because he is "is" (*esse*) itself: "'Being (*ens*),' however, is called that which finitely participates 'to be (*esse*)' and it is this which is proportioned to our intellect, whose object is some 'that which is,' as it is said in Book 3 of *On the Soul*. Hence our intellect can grasp only that which has a quiddity participat-ing 'to be (*esse*).' But the quiddity of God is 'to be' itself (*ipsum esse*). Thus it is above the intellect."[252] Even though "what God is" remains unknown to us, we know it is true to say that God is and that he is the cause of being in creatures.[253] In Aquinas's theology, therefore, we can more adequately speak of the God who says of himself, "I am" (Ex 3:14). We can also better represent the transcendent and immanent causality of the God who "proceeds towards

248. *In de div. nom.* IV, lect. 6 (§367). See David B. Burrell, "Distinguishing God from the World," in *Language, Meaning and God: Essays in Honour of Herbert McCabe, O.P.*, ed. Brian Davies (London: Geoffrey Chapman, 1987), 79.

249. *In de div. nom.* V, lect. 3 (§673); *In peri herm.* I, lect. 14.22 (§197).

250. Gilson, *Christian*, 136.

251. *Super de causis* Prop. 6 (Saffrey, p. 47, lines 8–12).

252. *Super de causis* Prop. 6 (Saffrey, p. 47, lines 11–18). Cf.: *Super I ad tim.* VI, lect. 3 (§269); *SCG* I, c.22; *ST* I, 3, 4; Q.13, 11; *De pot.* Q.2, 1. See also Anton Pegis, *St. Thomas and the Greeks* (Milwaukee: Marquette Uni-versity Press, 1951); Cornelio Fabro, "Platonism, Neoplatonism, Thomism," *NS* 44 (1970): 80.

253. *ST* I, 3, 4, ad 2.

all things" and is "in all things innermostly."[254] Finally, we can more reverently approach in love and worship this immutable God "in whom we live and move and have our being" (Acts 17:28).

Augustine

Aquinas refers to Augustine more than any other Church Father in arguing that God is immutable[255] and the first source of motion in all things.[256] Augustine is also employed in showing how divine knowing and loving are ways in which God "moves himself."[257] As Dionysius's thought did not remain unchanged when Thomas used it, so Augustine's ideas receive new meaning in his theology. Augustine speaks from the Platonic background of a philosophy of essence. Thomas speaks from an Aristotelian framework in terms of a philosophy of existence.[258] For Augustine, as for Plato, true being is unchanging. It is distinguished from "becoming," which is understood as a sort of "non-being."[259] So understood, "being is a variable value measured by the stability of the essence." Since God alone is "supremely immutable," he alone is "supremely being."[260]

254. *ST* I, 8, 1, co.

255. The texts of Augustine cited by Aquinas for establishing the immutability of God include the following. *Contra Max. Haeret.* II, 12 (*PL* 42, 768), cited in *Sent.* I, d.8 (text of P. Lombard); I, 8, 2, 1, ad 2; *ST* I, 50, 5, ad 1. *De civ. Dei* VIII, 6 (*PL* 41: 231), cited in *Sent.* I, d.3 (text of P. Lombard); I, 3, 1, 1, *div. text. De civ. Dei* XII, 15 (*PL* 41, 364), cited in *De aeter. mundi,* line 282 (Leonine). *De gen. ad litt.* VIII, 14 (*PL* 34, 384), cited in *ST* III, 57, 1, ad 1. *De gen. ad litt.* VIII, 23 (*PL* 34, 389), cited in *De aeter. mundi,* line 293 (Leonine). *De natura boni* cap.1 (*PL* 42, 551), cited in *Sent.* I, 19, 5, 3, sc.1; *ST* I, 9, 2, sc.; III, 57, 1, ad 1; *Super de trin.* Q.5, 2, obj.7. *De trin.* I, 1 (*PL* 42, 821), cited in *Sent.* I, d.8 (text of P. Lombard). *De trin.* V, 2 (*PL* 42, 912), cited in *Sent.* I, d.8 (text of P. Lombard). On Augustine's arguments for the absolute immutability of divine being, see Robert Teske, "Divine Immutability in Saint Augustine," *Modern Schoolman* 63 (1986): 233–50.

256. References to St. Augustine showing that God is the ultimate cause of motion include the following: *De civ. Dei* VIII, 6 (*PL* 41, 231), cited in *Sent.* I, d.3 (text of P. Lombard); I, 3, 1, 1, *div. text. De gen. ad litt.* VIII, 20 (*PL* 34, 388), cited in *Sent.* II, 39, 3, 2, obj.3; *De ver.* Q.15, 1, co. *De gen. ad litt.* VIII, 26 (*PL* 34, 391), cited in *Sent.* II, 24, 2, 3, co.

257. St. Augustine, *De gen. ad litt.* VIII, 20 (*PL* 34, 388), cited in *Sent.* I, d. 8 (text of P. Lombard); I, 8, 3, 1, obj.2; ad 2; *ST* I, 9, 1, obj.1; ad 1; *Super de trin.* Q.5, 4, obj.2.

258. Gilson, *Christian,* 48–54, 84–95, 130–36.

259. Plato, *Timaeus* 27 D; *Republic* 381 C; *Sophist* 248 D–249 A. Augustine, *In iohannis ev.* XXVIII, 8, 8–10 (*PL* 35, 1678–80); *De trin.* V, 2 (*PL* 42, 912). Cf.: Gilson, *Christian,* 48–49, 86, 102; *Being,* 13ff.; *L'être et l'essence* (Paris: J. Vrin, 1948), 25, 33; Émilie zum Brunn, "L'immutabilité de Dieu selon saint Augustin," *Nova et vetera* 41 (1966): 224; Hallman, *The Descent of God,* 105–23; "The Emotions of God in the Theology of St. Augustine," *Recherches de théologie ancienne et médiévale* 51 (1984): 6–7.

260. Gilson, *Christian,* 49–50; *Being,* 17.

Symptomatic of Augustine's Platonic orientation is his interpretation of the divine name of Exodus 3:14. God uses a form of the word "to be" to proclaims his name to Moses: "I am who I am."[261] Augustine consistently interprets this name as a declaration of divine immutability:

For the angel—and in the angel, the Lord—said to Moses who was asking his name, "I am who am. Say to the children of Israel: He who is sent me to you." The word "Being" means "to be immutable" (*Esse, nomen est incommutabilitatis*). For all changing things cease being what they were and begin being what they were not. Nothing has true being, pure being, authentic being save what does not change. . . . What is meant by "I am who am" unless "I am not able to be changed"?[262]

Through the influence of Augustine and other Church Fathers, this text became a sort of "proof-text" for divine immutability in the Middle Ages.[263]

In the theology of Aquinas, God is just as truly immutable as in Augustine. Yet divine immutability implies something quite different for Thomas because he understands God as *ipsum esse subsistens*, the pure act of existing. The distinction can be illustrated by comparing his explanation of the divine name in Exodus 3:14 with that of Augustine. Thomas discusses the name in many places and suggests various reasons for its appropriateness.[264] On no occasion, however, does he argue that the name is fitting because it indicates the immutability of the divine essence—the most evident (if not the only

261. The meaning of this divine name is still a matter of dispute. See Gerard Hertog, "The Prophetic Dimension of the Divine Name: On Exodus 3:14a and Its Context," *Catholic Biblical Quarterly* 64 (2002): 213–28; Anthony Phillips and Lucy Phillips, "The Origin of 'I Am' in Exodus 3:14," *Journal for the Study of the Old Testament* 78 (1998): 81–84; Jung Young Lee, "Can God be Change Itself?" *Journal of Ecumenical Studies* 10 (1973): 755. For a summary and evaluation of exegetical opinions on the significance of the name, see Roland de Vaux, *Histoire ancienne d'Israel* (Paris: Librairie Lecoffre, 1971), 331–37.

262. St. Augustine, *Sermo.* VII, 7 (*PL* 38, 66). Translation from Gilson, *Christian*, 134. Cf.: Mary T. Clark, "Augustine on Immutability and Mutability," *American Catholic Philosohical Quarterly* 74 (2000): 7–27; Bernard Cooke, "The Mutability-Immutability Principle in St. Augustine's Metaphysics," *Modern Schoolman* 24 (1946): 39–40.

263. Jaroslav Pelikan, *The Christian Tradition*, vol. 3, *The Growth of Medieval Theology* (Chicago: University of Chicago Press, 1978), 20, 111, 146; *Emergence*, 54.

264. *Sent.* I, 8, 1, 1; a.3; Q.3, 3, *exp. text;* d.22, 1, 1, ad 3; a.4, ad 4; *SCG* I, c.22.10 (§211); *ST* I, 2, 3, sc; Q.13, 11; Q.39, 8, obj.5; *De pot.* Q.2, 1; Q.7, 5; Q.10, 1, ad 9; *De sub sep.* XVIII, line 65 (Leonine); *Super decret.* I, line 185 (Leonine); *Epis. ad bern.*, line 98 (Leonine); *In de div. nom.* I, lect. 3 (§97); II, lect. 1 (§119); V, lect. 1 (§632); *Cat. aur. in matt.* XXII, 3, line 297 (ITOO); XXV, 4, line 36 (ITOO); *Cat. aur. in joann.* VI, 2, line 101 (ITOO); VIII, 5, line 225 (ITOO); 7, line 9 (ITOO); 14, line 32 (ITOO); XVII, 1, line 196 (ITOO); *Super ev. jo.* I, lect. 1 (§39); VIII, lect. 3 (§1179); lect. 8 (§1290).

possible) explanation according to Augustine.[265] Both Thomas and Augustine believe this name signifies the nature of God in the most appropriate way possible for human language. For Thomas, however, its fittingness does not lie in the fact that the name signifies divine immutability—true as that signification may be. It is found rather in that the name "does not signify any form, but simply to-be itself (*ipsum esse*)," since it is true of God alone that "his to-be (*esse*) is his very essence."[266] The divine name, "I am," means not simply that God does not change, but that God is dynamic, unlimited to-be (*esse*). For Augustine, divine perfection is seen most clearly in the fact of divine immutability. For Thomas, divine immutability itself points to a deeper level of perfection, the perfection of pure actuality, of pure *esse*:

We come now to that divine attribute which St. Augustine so rightly emphasized but which no one before St. Thomas really grasped—the divine immutability. To say that God is immovable was, for St. Augustine, to have reached the ultimate hidden depths of the divine nature. For St. Thomas there is something still more ultimate, the very reason for this immutability. To change is to pass from potency to act: now God is pure act. He can, accordingly, in no way change.[267]

The dynamic but unchanging perfection of God as pure *esse* will become clearer through our reflection on the philosophical sources Aquinas employs in developing his notion of God's changelessness. We may also gain a greater appreciation of the novelty, depth, and uniqueness of his doctrine of divine immutability.

Philosophical Sources

Aquinas cites Aristotle more than any other philosopher in his discussions of divine immutability. Even in employing Aristotle's arguments, how-

---

265. The name given in Ex 3:14 is associated with divine eternity, and thus indirectly, with divine immutability in *Super decret.* I, lines 178–87; *Epis. ad bern.*, lines 93–98, and in *ST* I, 13, 11, co. Such indirect association, however, is quite different from Augustine's affirmation of immutability as the central meaning of this divine name. See Gilson, *Christian*, 455, n.7.

266. *ST* I, 13, 11, co. Cf.: I, 3, 4; *Super ev. jo.* VIII, lect. 3 (§1179). Etienne Gilson sums up the contrasting opinions of Thomas and Augustine on the significance of the divine name quite concisely: "When St. Augustine read the name of God, he understood 'I am he who never changes.' St. Thomas, reading the same words, understood them to mean 'I am the pure act-of-being'" (*Christian*, 93).

267. Gilson, *Christian*, 102. Cf.: Cooke, "Mutability," 40, 42.

ever, he transforms them in view of his own understanding of God.[268] We
have already seen that the God he affirms at the conclusion of his commentaries on Aristotle is quite different, infinitely more transcendent, than the
entity Aristotle had in mind. His God is not just a first unmoved mover, but
subsistent being itself (*ipsum esse subsistens*). We have also seen how this same
insight into divine *esse* informs his understanding of divine immutability.[269]
We will better appreciate the profound difference between the immovability
of Aristotle's first mover and the unchangeableness of Thomas's Christian
God if we discover how Aquinas's teaching on divine immutability is tied to
his notion of God as *esse subsistens*. That investigation will also help us recognize certain other philosophical influences that shape his theology. First,
however, we need to review his account of how any philosophical argument
is related to theology.

In the first question of the *Summa theologiae*, Thomas reviews the authority of philosophical arguments in theology in relation to scriptural and patristic arguments. Scriptural arguments are proper to the discipline of theology, and their conclusions are necessary since Scripture has the certitude of
faith. Arguments from the Fathers are proper to theology, but merely probable since they lack the certitude of faith. Philosophical arguments, since they
proceed from reason alone, are extrinsic to the principles of theology (the
articles of faith). They are only probable since they do not contain the certitude of faith.[270]

Though human reason can neither prove nor disprove the truths of faith,
its arguments are useful to the theologian in clarifying certain issues, avoiding various possible errors, and refuting the errors of others.[271] The truth of
reason cannot oppose that of faith since there is ultimately only one Truth,
who reveals himself through the world he has created and the word he speaks
in Scripture.[272] Philosophy knows this Truth as discovered by human reason.

---

268. On Aquinas's retrieval and modification of Aristotle into "a new hierarchy of sciences," see Mark
D. Jordan, "Thomas's Alleged Aristotelianism or Aristotle among the Authorities," in *Rewritten Theology*, 88.

269. *ST* I, 9, 1; *Sent.* I, 8, 3, 1, *exp. text; Super I ad tim.* VI, lect. 3. (§269).

270. *ST* I, 1, 8, ad 2.

271. *SCG* I, c.8; II, c.3; *ST* I, 1, 5, ad 2; a.8, co.; ad 2.

272. "[V]erba fidei etsi sint supra rationem . . . non tamen sunt contra rationem, quia veritas non
potest esse veritati contraria" (*Super ad rom.* X, lect. 1 [§828]). Cf.: *SCG* I, c.7; *ST* I, 1, 8, co.; *De un. int.* V, line
415; *In de div. nom.* IV, lect. 4 (§332); VII, lect. 1 (§705); lect. 5 (§737–49).

Theology knows it as revealed by God.[273] The two are not opposed. Rather, one serves the other: "reason should serve faith."[274]

Aquinas's ideas on the relation between faith and reason failed to find universal acceptance in the thirteenth century and have fared little better in ours. The opposition, then as now, to the use of philosophy (especially Aristotelian philosophy) in theological arguments may be illustrated with two quotations: "The spirit of Christ does not reign where the spirit of Aristotle dominates"; "Aristotle's apathetic God was enthroned in men's minds, and no idol has been found so hard to destroy." The first is Absolon of St. Victor, an early-thirteenth-century theologian. The second is William Temple, a twentieth-century Anglican bishop and theologian.[275] Their similarity shows that the relation between faith and reason is as much an issue now as in the thirteenth century.[276] Now as then, philosophical arguments (especially those for divine immutability) are often seen as a contamination of theology. Despite such controversies, Aquinas did not hesitate to use philosophical arguments in his theology when he considered them true. And he did not scruple to engage even Aristotle, that most suspect of philosophers, in his arguments for the immutability of God.[277] In using this Greek philosopher, however, Aquinas transformed his thought in accordance with his own understanding of God and creation.

273. *ST* I, 1, a.5; a.6; Q.12, 13, co.; II-II, 1, 8, ad 1; *SCG* II, c.4; *Super de trin.* Q.5, 4, co.; *Super ad hebr.* XI, lect. 2 (§577).

274. *ST* I, 1, 8, ad 2; a.5, ad 2.

275. Absolon of Saint Victor, *Sermo* 4 (*PL* 211, 37), quoted in Chenu, *Toward*, 35n25. William Temple, *Christus Veritas* (London: Macmillan, 1924), 269.

276. See Pope John Paul II, *Fides et Ratio: On the Relationship between Faith and Reason*, encyclical letter (Washington, D.C.: U.S. Catholic Conference, 1998); Joseph Ratzinger, *The Nature and Mission of Theology: Essays to Orient Theology in Today's Debates*, trans. Adrian Walker (San Francisco: Ignatius, 1995); idem, "Foi, philosophie et théologie," in *Eglise et théologie* (Paris: Editions Mame, 1992), 15–36; Denys Turner, *Faith, Reason, and the Existence of God* (Oxford: Cambridge University Press, 2004); John Jenkins, *Knowledge and Faith in Thomas Aquinas* (Cambridge: Cambridge University Press, 1997); Mark Jordan, "Theology and Philosophy," in *The Cambridge Companion to Aquinas*, ed. N. Kretzmann and E. Stump (Cambridge: Cambridge University Press, 1993), 232–51; Richard C. Taylor, "Faith and Reason, Religion and Philosophy: Four Views from Medieval Islam and Christianity," in *Philosophy and the God of Abraham*, ed. R. James Long (Toronto: Pontifical Institute of Mediaeval Studies, 1991), 217–33.

277. On Aristotle's place in the controversy over faith and reason in the Middle Ages, see Fernand Van Steenberghen, *Thomas Aquinas and Radical Aristotelianism* (Washington, D.C.: The Catholic University of America Press, 1980), 51–52; Pegis, *Greeks*, 78, 88n2; Etienne Gilson, *Reason and Revelation in the Middle Ages* (New York: Charles Scribner's Sons, 1938).

Thomas sees divine immutability as an essential tenet of Christian faith and Greek philosophy.[278] Augustine and Aristotle both espouse the principle that all motion originates from something immovable.[279] Scripture affirms the immutability of God, and Aristotle demonstrates that the first cause of motion is unchanging. We have already seen how Aquinas employs and modifies Aristotle's arguments for an immovable first mover[280] that is the source of all motion[281] and moves all things as final cause.[282] Yet his God is quite different from Aristotle's unmoved mover, since he affirms the tri-une God of Christian revelation, the unchanging and transcendent source of all being, who, as creator of all things, is their efficient, exemplar, and final cause. There is a similarity, however, between Aquinas's God and the first principle of Aristotle that appears most clearly in the attribute of immutability. Noticing this likeness, some theologians accuse Aquinas and his followers of embracing a God that looks too much like a Greek philosophical principle.[283] Others, however, recognize Aquinas's God as the God of Abraham, Isaac, and Jacob, the Trinity of persons revealed in Jesus Christ.[284]

Were Thomas's God identical with Aristotle's first principle, we would do well to reject it. For although Aristotle's immovable mover shares some characteristics of the Christian God such as knowledge, life, and happiness,[285] it remains an inadequate object for worship. Aristotle himself was the first to

278. Gilson, *Elements*, 122–23.

279. St. Thomas notes the agreement of Aristotle and Augustine on this principle in *Sent.* II, 24, 2, 3, co.; *De ver.* Q.15, 1, co. He makes continual use of the principle, often citing either Augustine or Aristotle: *Sent.* II, 39, 3, 2, obj.3; III, 27, 1, 3, co.; *SCG* III, c.91.3 (§2663); c.155.2 (§3281); *ST* I, 75, 1, ad 1; Q.79, 4, co.; Q.82, 1, co.; Q.84, 1, ad 3; Q.113, 1, co.; Q.115, 3, co.; III, 4, 6, ad 2; *De ver.* Q.5, 10, co.; Q.15, 1, co.; Q.16, 2, co.; Q.22, 6, co.; a.12, sc.; Q.25, 4, co.; *De sp. cr.* a.10, co.; *In de caelo*, I, lect. 4.4; *In de an.* III, lect. 14.16 (§833); *Super de trin.* Q.6, 1, co.; *In de div. nom.* IV, lect. 8 (§381); XI, lect. 3; (§919); *Super ad rom.* III, lect. 1 (§266).

280. *Phys.* VIII, 6 (259a 20); *Meta.* XII, 7 (1972a 24).

281. *Phys.* VIII, 6 (258b 10).

282. *Meta.* XII, 7 (1072a 24–1072b 4).

283. Claude Geffré, "Sens et non-sens d'une théologie non métaphysique," *Concilium* 76 (1972): 94; Walter Stokes, "Whitehead's Challenge to Theistic Realism," *NS* 38 (1964): 7; Brantschen, "Die Macht," 234.

284. "[T]he treatise on God as One has as its object, not the God of the *Physics*, but the God of *Genesis*, the God of Abraham, of Isaac, and of Jacob, who will send us Christ" (Chenu, *Toward*, 321). Cf.: Gilson, *Elements*, 58.

285. *Meta.* XII, 7 (1072b 14–29). Cf.: Georges Ducoin, "St. Thomas: commentateur d'Aristote," *Archives de Philosophie* 20 (1957): 395.

recognize this. Though he identified his immovable mover as the truth behind the popular religion of his time, he apparently did not pray to the unmoved mover, but to the gods of the Greek religion.[286] It is misleading even
to say Aristotle identified his first principle as "God" since that term always
carries overtones for us of the Christian monotheistic idea of God. It is more
accurate to say he understood it as a divine principle, perhaps the chief divine principle, but never more than one such principle among others, one
"god" among other "gods."[287]

If the similarity between Aristotle's first principle and Aquinas's God
seems strongest in their common affirmation of divine immutability, the
profound difference between them becomes evident when we consider how
unlike they are in their understanding of that attribute. We will better understand the character and significance of Aquinas's notion of divine immutability by examining the premises of his arguments. If these are radically different from Aristotle's, his conclusions may be correspondingly distinct.

Our review of all Aquinas's arguments for divine immutability reveals
the following premises: divine simplicity,[288] potency and act,[289] divine
perfection,[290] the need for a first immovable mover,[291] God's dwelling beyond the heavens,[292] and God's abiding power and will to save his people.[293]
To establish the uniqueness of God's immutability, he argues from the premises of the composite nature of all created things,[294] potency and act,[295] crea-

286. Aristotle identifies the unmoved mover as the truth behind popular religion in *Meta.* XII, 8
(1074b 1–10). On Aristotle's personal habits of worship, see Gilson, *Medieval,* 44–46; "L'être et Dieu,"
Revue thomiste 62 (1962): 191.

287. J. Owens, *The Doctrine of Being in the Aristotelian Metaphysics* (Toronto: Pontifical Institute of Mediaeval Studies, 1951), 171n47; Philip Merlan, "Aristotle's Unmoved Movers," *Traditio* 4 (1946): 28.

288. *Sent.* I, 8, 3, 1, ad 3; ad 4; *In de div. nom.* IX, lect. 2 (§816–17); *ST* I, 9, 1, co.

289. *Sent.* I, 8, 3, 1, *exp. text;* a.1, co.; *Super de trin.* Q.5, 4, co.; *In de div. nom.* IX, lect. 2 (§817); *Super iob*
IV, lines 408–40; *De pot.* Q.6, a.6, co.; *ST* I, 9, 1, co.

290. *Sent.* I, 3, 1, 1, *div. text;* I, 8, 3, 1, *exp. text; Super de trin.* Q.5, 4, co.; *In de div. nom.* IX, lect. 2 (§816–17);
In de caelo, I, lect. 21.12–13; *Super ev. jo., prologus* (§4); *De pot.* Q.3, 5, co.; *ST* I, 9, 1, co.

291. *Sent.* I, 8, 3, 1, sc.; *In phys.* VII, lect. 2 (§891); VIII, passim, esp., lect. 11 (§1068); lect. 12 (§1076);
lect. 13 (§1078–79); lect. 23 (§1166); *In meta.* XII, passim, esp., lect. 7 (§2517); *Super ad rom.* I, lect. 6
(§115); *De ver.* Q.5, 9, co.; *De pot.* Q.3, 5, co.; Q.6, 6, co.; ad 11; *De sub. sep.* c.2, lines 10–26; *SCG* I, c.13;
Comp. I, c.3–4; *ST* I, 2, 3, co.

292. *In de caelo* I, lect. 21.7.   293. *In psalmos* XLIII.2.

294. *Super de trin.* Q.5, 4, ad 4.

295. *ST* I, 9, 2, co.; *Sent.* I, 8, 3, 2, co.; *Super de trin.* Q.5, 4, ad 4.

turely imperfection,[296] and the dependency of creatures on another for their existence.[297] His premises for predicating motion of God are God's immanent activities of knowing and willing,[298] God's causality when viewed as a sort of motion,[299] and various metaphorical usages.[300] Based upon our research, this classification provides a complete account of the ways Aquinas argues for divine immutability and allows motion to be predicated of God.

The central insight behind all Aquinas's arguments for divine immutability is his understanding of the divine nature as *esse subsistens*. In developing this understanding of God, he is indebted not to Aristotle but to Avicenna, who teaches that essence and existence are identical in God but distinct in creatures.[301] Thomas adopts and develops Avicenna's insight, modifying it according to his own understanding of divine and created reality.[302] To see what Aquinas means by divine immutability, we must understand the premises of his arguments, especially those of divine simplicity, pure actuality, perfection, and causality. But we will comprehend those premises only if we understand his idea of God as *ipsum esse subsistens*. We will therefore consider what the divine attributes mean that serve as the premises of his arguments when they are predicated of God as subsistent being (*esse subsistens*).

God as pure *esse* is absolutely simple. In him even essence and existence (*esse*) are one. Since God is absolutely simple and since motion always implies composition, God must be absolutely immovable. In the creature existence is always distinct from essence. Its essence (what it is) does not explain its existence (the fact that it is). Since its essence does not account for its existence, it must depend on another for existence. Considered in itself, it could cease to exist. In this sense, all creatures are mutable, and God alone (upon whom all creatures depend and who is dependent on no other) is immutable.

---

296. *Sent.* I, 8, 3, 2, co.; *Super ad hebr.* I, lect. 5 (§71–78); *Super I ad tim.* VI, lect. 3 (§268–69).

297. *Sent.* I, 8, 3, 2, co.; *ST* I, 9, 2, co.

298. *Sent.* I, 8, 3, 1, ad 2; *Super de trin.* Q.5, 4, ad 2; *ST* I, 9, 1, ad 1.

299. *Sent.* I, 8, 3, 1, ad 1; *Super de trin.* Q.5, 4, ad 2; *In de div. nom.* IX, lect. 2 (§823–24); lect. 4 (§840–42); *ST* I, 9, 1, ad 2.

300. *ST* I, 9, 1, ad 3.   301. Avicenna, *Metaphysics*, VIII, c.4.

302. *ST* I, 3, 4, co. Cf.: *Sent.* I, 2, 1, 3, co:, d.8, 3, 2, co.; *De ver.* Q.10, a.12, co; *De ente* c.5, line 5 (Leonine). On the resemblance of Thomas's texts at certain points to those of Avicenna, see Weisheipl, *Friar*, 133; Etienne Gilson, "Avicenne en occident au moyen age," *Archives d'histoire doctrinale et littéraire du moyen âge* 36 (1969): 109; Albert Judy, "Avicenna's *Metaphysics* in the *Summa Contra Gentiles*," *Angelicum* 52 (1975): 209–11.

Aquinas's distinction between mutable and immutable being is based on an order of being unknown to Aristotle. Aristotle distinguished mutable from immutable being in terms of form and matter in his analysis of substantial and accidental change, and in terms of motion in his demonstration of the existence of a being (the immovable mover) that, as the source of all such change, is itself free from any potentiality for change. Thomas distinguishes between changeable and unchangeable being in terms of existence (*esse*). In this order, it is not just a distinction between beings that have potency for some sort of change and those that do not. Rather, as L.-B. Geiger points out, it is the difference between "the being to whom the act of existence is attributed by essence (the uniqueness of whom may be shown), and the beings to which it may be attributed only by participation."[303]

Aquinas's deeper understanding of being allows him to uncover the most profound instance of act and potency. Aristotle recognized these principles only according to the order of form in his analysis of change, where the most profound instances of act and potency are the principles of substantial form and primary matter.[304] Thomas understands act and potency not only according to the order of form, but according to the vastly more profound order of existence (*esse*). In this order, he finds the ultimate instance of potency and act in the principles of essence and existence (*esse*).[305] The discovery that essence is related to existence (*esse*) as potency to act is an insight belonging properly to Aquinas and found in neither Aristotle nor Avicenna.[306]

For Aristotle, substantial form is the most fundamental instance of act. It is both a principle of dynamic activity in substances, which causes them to act or behave in certain ways, and a principle of limitation, which determines the unlimited (but at the same time undetermined and thus, in Aristotle's philosophy, imperfect) potency of primary matter.[307] Thomas agrees with this analysis, but sees a deeper level: the order of existence where the potency of essence is related to the act of existing (*esse*), the act "by which" it is.[308]

303. L.-B. Geiger, "Saint Thomas et la métaphysique d'Aristote," in *Aristote et saint Thomas d'Aquin*, ed. P. Moraux et al. (Louvain: Université de Louvain, 1957), 206.

304. Gilson, *Being*, 47; Finance, *Etre*, 80–81.   305. *SCG* II, c.54.

306. Judy, "Avicenna's," 210; Finance, *Etre*, 110.

307. *Phys.* III,6 (207a 8–37). Cf.: W. Norris Clarke, S.J., "The Limitation of Act by Potency: Aristotelianism or Neoplatonism," *NS* 26 (1952): 179.

308. *SCG* II, c.54; *Quodl.* III, Q.2, a.1 [3]; *ST* I, 7, 1; III, 10, 3, ad 1. See Clarke, "Limitation," 180.

Every creature, material and spiritual, possesses an act of existing (*esse*) by which it is. In material things, *esse* is that by which the material substance exists. The material substance itself, however, is made of primary matter and substantial form, resulting in a twofold composition. There is the composition of substantial form and primary matter, which Aristotle recognized. But there is also the composition of the substance itself (essentially considered as the composition of matter and form) and the act of existing (*esse*).[309] In created spiritual substances, the act of existing is again that by which the substance is. In this case, however, there is, in the ontological structure of the creature, but a single composition of act and potency: the potency of the spiritual form or essence and the act of existing (*esse*) by which that form exists.[310] In both spiritual and material creatures, form or essence is therefore a principle of potency with respect to the act of existing, which is "compared even to the form itself as act."[311] It is the act by which the form (in immaterial things) or the composite substance (in material things) exists—"the act of all acts and the perfection of all perfections."[312]

Although the form is in potency to the act of existing, it is still, in its own order, a principle of being. The relationship between the form and the act of existing may be illustrated by an analogy. Form is a principle of being in a substance in the same way transparency is a principle of illumination in the air. As the transparency of the air makes the air a suitable subject for receiving and transmitting light, so the form of a substance makes the substance a suitable subject for receiving the act of existing (*esse*). And as the transparency of the air, apart from the act of the sun's illumination, is darkness, so the form of a substance, apart from the act of existing (*esse*), is non-being.[313]

It is difficult to grasp the nature of the act of existing since it is not a "thing" or an "essence" of which we can properly form a concept. It is precisely not an essence, but that which actualizes an essence. It is not a thing,

309. *SCG* II, c.54.9 (§1295).
310. *SCG* II, c.54.7–8 (§1293–94).
311. *SCG* II, c.54.5 (§1291).
312. "Unde patet quod hoc quod dico *esse* est actualitas omnium actuum, et propter hoc est perfectio omnium perfectionum" (*De pot.* Q.7, 2, ad 9).
313. *SCG* II, c.54.5 (§1291). See Lawrence Dewan, "St. Thomas and the Distinction between Form and Esse in Caused Things," *Gregorianum* 80 (1999): 353–70.

but a dynamic activity, an "energizing" or an "actualizing."[314] It is not "what something is," but the act "by which" something is. As such it is grasped not through abstraction in the static framework of a concept but in the dynamic activity of judgment, when we say of something, "it is." In thinking and speaking of this act, we must of course refer to it through words and concepts. In using such concepts, however, we should remember we are always one step removed from the act itself. The act is not an "it" to be grasped in a concept, but an "is" known through a judgment—the "is" that causes the creature to be.

Because Thomas means something quite other than Aristotle does when he refers to the most profound instance of potency and act, he also intends something fundamentally different when he speaks of God as "pure act." In Aristotle's philosophy, the most profound instance of potency (primary matter) is, considered in itself, undetermined and so in a sense unlimited. In actual substances, however, it is always determined by the principle of act (substantial form). In Thomas's theology, on the contrary, the principle of act (*esse*) is, considered in itself, unlimited. In actual creatures, however, it is always determined or limited according to the principle of potency (the essence of the particular creature that it causes to exist). According to Aristotle, potency (primary matter) is specified or determined by act (substantial form). For Thomas, act (*esse*) is specified and limited by potency (essence).[315] To Aristotle, act (substantial form) is a determining principle. For Thomas, act (*esse*) is, in itself, an unlimited or boundless principle. In creatures, of course, neither substantial form nor *esse* exists apart from its corresponding principle of potency. Both Thomas and Aristotle recognize, however, that there is a being that is "pure act" apart from all potency. The "pure act" Aristotle attributes to this being, however, is the determinate perfection of pure

314. "Things which 'have being' are not 'just there' (*Dasein*) like lumps of static essence, inert, immovable, unprogressive, and unchanging. The act of existence (*esse*) is not a state, it is an act, the act of all acts, and, therefore, must be understood as act and not as any static and definable object of conception. *Esse* is dynamic impulse, energy, act—the first, the most persistent and enduring of all dynamisms, all energies, all acts" (Gerald Bernard Phelan, *Selected Papers* [Toronto: Pontifical Institute of Mediaeval Studies, 1967], 77). Cf.: Etienne Gilson, *God and Philosophy* (New Haven: Yale University Press, 1946), 63–64; Finance, *Etre*, 111–14.

315. *SCG* II, c.54; *De sp. cr.* a.1, co. See Cornelio Fabro, *Participation et causalité selon s. Thomas d'Aquin* (Louvain: Université de Louvain, 1961), 65; Geiger, "Saint," 206, 208–9; Clarke, "Limitation," 167–94.

substantial form. The "pure act" Aquinas envisions is the boundless perfection of pure *esse*.

For Thomas, as for Aristotle, pure act is the immovable summit of all perfection.[316] In Aristotle, this is the immovable mover. For Aquinas, it is the God of revelation. In neither case can this perfect, divine being admit of change. For if the divine being changed, either it would acquire some new perfection (and so would be less than perfect originally), or it would lose some present perfection (and so would cease to be perfect).[317] For Aristotle, however, this perfect divine being, as pure act, is the most determined of all things. It is the finite form most removed from the, in some sense, infinite (but at the same time undetermined and so imperfect) potency of matter.[318] For Thomas, God, as pure act, is infinite unbounded to-be (*esse*)—unlimited by any sort of potency.[319] Pure act is no longer just "the Being which excludes all potency for change, all becoming, all mutability (as in Aristotle)," but "the Being which excludes all limitation, all finitude—the Being which is infinite and for that reason unique."[320] The name "I am," which God speaks to Moses (Ex 3:14), is the most appropriate name for God precisely because it expresses this unbounded and unlimited perfection in being (*esse*).[321]

Though Thomas frequently uses the very words of Aristotle regarding potency, act, and the Being who is pure act, their significance is changed because he understands them in terms of essence and existence (*esse*) rather than matter and form.[322] Among the various influences that led Aquinas to

316. *Meta.* XII, 6 (1071b 20); *SCG* I, c.16; *De pot.* Q.7, 2, ad 9; *ST* I, 3, 1, co.; a.4, co.

317. *Meta.* XII, 9 (1074b 26–28); *ST* I, 9, 1, co.

318. See Clarke, "Limitation," 181; Owens, *Doctrine*, 468; "Immobility and Existence for Aquinas," in *St. Thomas Aquinas on the Existence of God: The Collected Papers of Joseph Owens*, ed. John Catan (Albany: State University of New York Press, 1980), 209, 221.

319. *ST* I, 7, 1, co.; Q.3, 4, co.

320. F. Van Steenberghen, *La philosophie au XIIIe siècle* (Louvain: Publications Universitaires, 1966), 340. Cf.: Van Steenberghen, *Problème*, 322n68; José Maria Laso Gonzales, "La idea del motor inmovil a partir de las doctrinas fundamentales de Aristóteles," *Salmanticensis* 15 (1968): 369–70; Geiger, "Saint," 208.

321. *ST* I, 13, 11, co. See Fergus Kerr, *After Aquinas: Versions of Thomism* (Oxford: Blackwell, 2002), 80–96; Annie Noblesse-Rocher, "Le nom et l'être de Dieu (Exode 3, 14) selon Thomas d'Aquin et Martin Bucer," *Revue d'histoire et de philosophie religieuses* 81 (2001): 425–47; Armand Maurer, "St. Thomas on the Sacred Name 'Tetragrammaton' (Yahweh)," *MS* 34 (1972): 275–86; Luis Clavell, "El nombre mas propio de Dios y el acto de ser," in *Tommaso d'Aquino nel suo settimo centenario* (Napoli: Edizione Domenicane Italiane, 1976), 3:269–74.

322. For examples and analyses of Thomas's usage of Aristotelian terminology, see Joseph Owens,

this transformation and deepening of Aristotle's notions of act and potency are certainly the Christian doctrine of creation,[323] the Platonic notion of
participation,[324] and the insights of the Islamic philosopher Avicenna.[325]

Aristotle and Aquinas both see the "immovable mover" as the first cause of
the motion of the universe. But here again, Thomas's understanding of the causality of this being is quite different from Aristotle's. Thomas sees God as the
efficient, exemplar, and final cause of creatures.[326] Aristotle thinks of God only
as a final cause, and a final cause only of motion.[327] He cannot conceive of God
as an efficient cause since such causes in his philosophy produce only motion
and cannot move without being moved. Aquinas sees that as there is an efficient cause of motion, there must also be an efficient cause of being (esse).[328]
The latter produces its effect without being moved. We might say Aristotle admits only the natural or physical efficient cause while Thomas recognizes also
the divine or metaphysical efficient cause.[329] Thomas inherited the notion of
the metaphysical efficient cause from Avicenna.[330] Employing this distinction,
he shows both why Aristotle admitted only the final causality of the divine being and why it is necessary to predicate efficient causality of God as well.[331]

There is a profound difference between an immovable mover that is only
a final cause of motion and one who is also the efficient cause of existence
(esse). The former moves only the outermost sphere of the universe as an object desired by the soul of that sphere. The latter is the creator of all that exists, expressing his love in each thing he makes and immediately present to
all through his creative power:

"Aquinas as Aristotelian Commentator," in *St. Thomas Aquinas 1274–1974: Commemorative Studies*, ed. A.
Maurer et al. (Toronto: Pontifical Institute of Mediaeval Studies, 1974), 1:213–38; Martin Grabmann,
"Esencia y significacion del aristotelismo de santo Tomás de Aquino," *Ciencia Tomista* 67 (1944): 336;
Ducoin, "Saint," 108–9; Chenu, *Toward,* 197.

323. Owens, "Immobility," 222–24; Grabmann, "Esencia," 334.

324. Van Steenberghen, *Problème,* 312, 319; Grabmann, "Esencia," 333.

325. Avicenna, *Metaphysics,* VIII, c.4.   326. *ST* I, 6, 4, co.

327. *Meta.* XII, 6 (1072a 25–26). Cf.: Gilson, "Prolégomènes," 56; Owens, *Doctrine,* 442, 443.

328. *In meta.* VII, lect. 17 (§1661).

329. Marcia L. Colish, "Avicenna's Theory of Efficient Causation and Its Influence on St. Thomas Aquinas," in *Tommaso d'Aquino nel suo settimo centenario* (Napoli: Edizione Domenicane Italiane, 1975),
1:299–300.

330. *Sent.* I, 7, 1, 1, ad 3; II, 1, 1, 2, ad 1. Cf.: Gilson, "Avicenne," 109.

331. *In meta.* VII, lect. 17 (§1660–61); XII, lect. 7 (§2520); lect. 9 (§2560); *De pot.* Q.6, a.6.

It [the immovable mover of Aristotle] moves only by the love it excites—which it excites, observe, but does not breathe in. When we read in the commentaries on the *Divina Commedia* that the last verse of the great poem merely echoes a thought of Aristotle's, we are very wide of the mark: *l'amor che muove il Sole e l'altre stelle* has nothing but the name in common with the first unmoved mover. The God of St. Thomas and Dante is a God who loves, the god of Aristotle is a god who does not refuse to be loved; the love that moves the heavens and the stars in Aristotle is the love of the heavens and the stars for god, but the love that moves them in St. Thomas and Dante is the love of God for the world; between these two motive causes there is all the difference between an efficient cause on the one hand and a final cause on the other.[332]

Through his creative causality, Aquinas's God "is in all things and innermostly."[333] Because of this causality, he is said "to be moved and to proceed toward all things" as he brings them into being, is present to them, and provides for them, "giving them life and power and other such things, and conserving them in them."[334] This is the transcendent yet present and provident God of revelation, who freely chooses to share his goodness with his creatures and who draws them all, each according to its capacity, to himself in love.[335]

The fact that God is the creator of all things also explains, in a more profound way than was possible in Aristotle's philosophy, why he is their final cause or ultimate good, the ultimate object of their love and desire. For any efficient cause is always somehow desirable and good with respect to its effect:

Anything is good according as it is desirable. What every single thing desires, however, is its own perfection. But the perfection and form of an effect consists in a certain likeness to the agent, for every agent makes something like itself. Hence, the agent itself is desirable and has the notion of good. For the very thing which is desirable in it is that its likeness might be participated.[336]

---

332. Gilson, *Medieval*, 75. Cf.: Eric L. Mascall, *He Who Is: A Study in Traditional Theism* (London: Longmans, Green, 1945), 7.

333. *ST* I, 8, 1, co.

334. *In de div. nom.* IX, lect. 4 (§840).

335. *ST* I, 6, 1, ad 2; I-II, 26, 1, co. See Endre von Ivanka, "S. Thomas platonisant," in *Tommaso d'Aquino nel suo settimo centenario* (Napoli: Edizione Domenicane Italiane, 1975), 1:257.

336. *ST* I, 6, 1, co.

Since God is the first efficient cause of all things, he is also their ultimate good. And since goodness has the aspect of an end, God, as ultimate good, is the ultimate end or final cause of creatures. All things desire God in desiring their own proper perfections, for these perfections are themselves certain likenesses to the being (*esse*) of their creator.[337] The notion of God's goodness (as final cause) therefore presupposes the notion of his efficient causality (insofar as he is the creator of all things) and of his exemplar causality (insofar as what he creates is in some way like himself).[338] As final cause, therefore, God moves the universe not simply as the object desired by the soul of the outermost sphere, but as the Being universally desired or loved by all creatures, each according to its own capacity of nature and grace.[339]

Through his concept of *ipsum esse subsistens*, Thomas attains a radically new and distinctive understanding of the nature of God. The notions of divine simplicity, perfection, actuality, and causality all receive a new and deeper significance in the light of that understanding. Consequently, the attribute of divine immutability that is derived from those notions in Aquinas's arguments for God's changelessness is also transformed. Through this new understanding of God, elements of Platonic and Neoplatonic thought are united with elements of Aristotelian and Islamic thought in a new and deeper synthesis.[340] The God whom human reason discovers as *esse subsistens* is found to be one with the God who reveals himself as "I am." Human reason, far from contradicting the truth of revelation, illuminates it for us.[341] Though "neither Catholic nor pagan knows the very nature of God as he is in himself," both philosopher and theologian may join together in pondering the mystery of God, each admitting the limits of our human thought and

---

337. *ST* I, 5, 4, co.; Q.6, 1, ad 2.

338. *ST* I, 5, 4, co. Cf.: Lawrence Dewan, "St. Thomas and the Causality of God's Goodness," *Laval théologique et philosophique* 34 (1973): 298–99.

339. *ST* I, 6, 1, ad 2; Q.44, 4, ad 3; *In de div. nom.* I, lect. 3 (§95). Cf.: Ivanka, "Thomas," 257.

340. See Seymour Feldman, "Philosophy: Averroes, Maimonides, and Aquinas," in *Religious Foundations of Western Civilization: Judaism, Christianity, and Islam*, ed. Jacob Neusner (Nashville: Abingdon, 2006), 209–44; David B. Burrell, "Thomas Aquinas and Islam," *Modern Theology* 20 (2004): 71–89; Georges Anawati, "Théologie musulmane et théologie de S. Thomas d'Aquin: quelques thèmes comparés," in *Fides quaerens intellectum: Beiträge zur Fundamentaltheologie*, ed. Michael Kessler, Wolfhart Pannenberg, and Hermann Josef Pottmeyer (Tübingen: Francke, 1992), 557–67; Van Steenberghen, *Probléme*, 313; *Philosophie*, 338–39; Gilson, *Christian*, 92; Fabro, "Platonism," 94, 99.

341. *Quodl.* IV, Q.9, a.3 [18].

speech, but realizing also that "to be able to see something of the loftiest realities, however thin and weak the sight may be, is . . . a cause of the greatest joy."[342]

THE MEANING OF DIVINE IMMUTABILITY

The Nature of Theological Discourse

Now that we have reviewed Aquinas's arguments for divine immutability and seen the originality of his thought in relation to his sources, we are
ready to employ his analysis to determine the meaning and appropriateness
of God's changelessness for contemporary theology. We will understand
what immutability means when said of God, however, only if we know how
any human word can be predicated of God. Starting with the metaphysical
grounding of all language about God, therefore, we will first review the various ways we can speak of God and then see what immutability means in
each of those contexts.

The metaphysical ground for all theological discourse is the doctrine of
creation. Because God is the creator, all things are in some way like him.
Scripture tells us that creatures, especially human beings, are like their creator and that this likeness will reach its perfection eschatologically: "When
he appears, we shall be like him."[343] Philosophy teaches us that since "every
agent effects something similar to itself" we can reasonably expect effects or
creatures to resemble their cause or creator. Since God is "the first and universal principle of all being (esse)," all things, "insofar as they are beings (entia), in some way resemble him."[344]

Because creatures are like the creator, we can know something about the
creator through them.[345] Realizing that they cannot explain their own being and action, we discover God as the cause of all things. As we unpack
the modes of divine causality (as efficient, exemplar, and final cause), we see
"those things that necessarily belong to him as the first cause of all things,

---

342. ST I, 13, 10, ad 5; SCG I, c.8.1 (§49).
343. Jn 3:2. This biblical reference, along with Gen 1:26, cited by Thomas in ST I, 4, 3, sc, and Q.12, 1,
sc, provide the theological framework for his discussion of the creature's likeness to God.
344. ST I, 4, 3, co.
345. In de div. nom. VII, lect. 4 (§729); SCG I, c.8.

exceeding all things caused by him."³⁴⁶ In this life, our understanding of God remains imperfect, but will be perfected eschatologically when "we shall be like him for we shall see him as he is" (1 Jn 3:2). The deficiency of our present knowledge is supplied in some measure by love. When the Son, as the "Word who breathes forth Love," is sent to us, we enjoy an intellectual illumination "which breaks forth into the affection of love."³⁴⁷

Presently, we know and speak of God through our knowledge of creatures, using the ways of causality, negation, and eminence.³⁴⁸ Through causality, we know "whether he is" and recognize "his relationship (*habitudinem ipsius*) to creatures as the cause of them all." By negation, we see "the difference of creatures from him inasmuch as he is not any of those things which are caused by him." Through eminence, we find that creatures "are not removed from him by reason of any defect on his part, but because he superexceeds them all."³⁴⁹ All three ways are involved in any knowledge we have of God, but they may be distinguished from one another, and aspects of our knowledge of God may be more related to one than another: "The invisible things of God are known through the way of negation; eternal power, through the way of causality; and divinity, through the way of excellence."³⁵⁰

Through the way of causality we discover God as the source of the very "is" (*esse*) of creatures. God can cause the existence of creatures since he is "is" (*esse*) itself—dynamic unlimited to-be, *ipsum esse subsistens*.³⁵¹ God alone is and can know subsistent being itself. We can know "that God is," but not "what God is."³⁵² Even the finite "is" (*esse*) of creatures lies beyond the limits of our conceptual knowledge. Our concepts bring us only to the essence or "what" of creatures, not to their existence or "is."³⁵³ Though we approach the finite "is" of creatures in our act of judging, God's infinite "is" exceeds all

346. *ST* I, 12, 12, co.

347. *ST* I, 43, 5, ad 2. On the eschatological dimension of our knowledge of God and how knowledge is assisted by love in this life, see O'Neill, "Prédication," 84–85; "Analogy, Dialectic, and Inter-confessional Theology," *Thomist* 47 (1983): 51–53.

348. *ST* I, 13, 1, co.; *In de div. nom.* I, lect. 3 (§89).

349. *ST* I, 12, 12, co. Cf.: *Super ad rom.* I, lect. 6 (§115).

350. *Super ad rom.* I, lect. 6 (§117). Cf.: *De pot.* Q.9, 7, ad 2.

351. *Sent.* II, 15, 1, 2, co.; *ST* I, 8, 1, co.; *De pot.* Q.7, 2.

352. *ST* I, 12, 4, co.

353. *Super I ad tim.* VI, lect. 3 (§269).

our capabilities, and so to us "what [God] is remains utterly unknown."[354] It is unknowable not only "by way of natural knowledge, but also by way of revelation, since the light of revelation comes to us adapted to our own condition."[355]

If the way of causality teaches us we cannot know what God is, the way of negation invites us to discover more about God precisely by knowing "what he is not (*quid non est*)."[356] Since the cause exceeds the perfection of the effect, we can know God by denying of him all the imperfections of the creaturely mode of existing and of our human mode of knowing.[357] In this way, we safeguard his transcendence and refuse to reduce him to the level of human concepts.[358] Because it accents the limits of human knowledge, the way of negation is in some respects the most appropriate way for us to know God in this life.[359] In the way of negation we acknowledge that God is above all we can think since we deny of him all the limited creaturely modes of existence known to us: "To reach him by unsaying progressively all the things in the universe that the human mind can know and to know also that they are not God."[360]

If we acknowledge God's surpassing perfection in the *via negationis* by denying of him the imperfections of creatures, we do the same in the *via eminentiae* by affirming of him the perfections of creatures in a supereminent

354. "[Q]uid vero sit penitus manet ignotum" (*SCG* III, c.49.9 [§2270]). Cf.: *ST* I, 12, 13, ad 1; *Super de trin.* Q.6, 4, co. See also Brian J. Shanley, *The Thomist Tradition* (Dordrecht: Kluwer Academic Publishers, 2002), 48–49; Anton Pegis, "Penitus manet ignotum," *MS* 27 (1965): 212–26; Gilson, *Christian*, 107; James B. Reichmann, "Immanently Transcendent and Subsistent Esse: A Comparison," *Thomist* 38 (1974): 367.

355. *Super de trin.* Q.6, 3, co. Cf.: *ST* I, 13, 10, ad 5.

356. *SCG* I, c.14.2 (§117). Cf.: *In meta.* X, lect. 4 (§1990).

357. *De ver.* Q.5, 2, ad 11; *De pot.* Q.1, 1, co.; *Super de trin.* Q.6, 4, co.; *ST* I, 14, 1, ad 1; *In meta.* II, lect. 1 (§282); lect. 5 (§336).

358. *SCG* I, c.14; c.30.4 (§278); III, c.39.1 (§2167); *ST* I, Q.3, *prologus; Q.*14, 1, ad 1; *Super de trin.* Q.6, 4, co.

359. "Hoc enim est ultimum ad quod pertingere possumus circa cognitionem divinam in hac vita, quod Deus est supra omne id quod a nobis cogitari potest et ideo nominatio Dei quae est per remotionem est maxime propria" (*In de div. nom.* I, lect. 3 [§83]). Cf.: *SCG* I, c.5.3 (§30); *Sent.* I, 8, 1, 1, ad 4; Q.2, 1, ad 1; *De pot.* Q.7, 5, ad 14.

360. A. Pegis, *St. Thomas and Philosophy* (Milwaukee, Wisc.: Marquette University Press, 1964), 72. Cf.: Simon Tugwell, "Spirituality and Negative Theology," *New Blackfriars* 68 (1987): 257–63; Gilson, *Elements*, 146–47; James B. Reichmann, "Aquinas, God, and Historical Process," in *Tommaso d'Aquino nel suo settimo centenario* (Napoli: Edizioni Domenicane Italiane, 1978), 9:430–31.

way. As the first cause, God must exceed all created things in being and perfection.[361] He is the "excelling principle (*excellens principium*) of whose form the effects fall short, but of whom the effects attain a certain similitude."[362] Through the way of eminence, we do not know God as he is in himself; nor do we remain completely ignorant of him. We know him as truly possessing all the perfections of creatures in a way that surpasses our understanding.[363]

The three ways of causality, negation, and eminence are involved in anything we know of God, and none may be omitted without jeopardizing our knowledge.[364] If the way of causality were omitted, for instance, the metaphysical foundation of the other ways would be lacking, and they would be unable to answer the arguments of those who claim our knowledge of God is nothing more than a projection of ourselves. Without the *via negationis*, which underlines the radical difference between God and creatures, the God affirmed in the *via eminentiae* would become nothing more than a beneficent creature "writ large." Without the *via eminentiae*, we would know none of the attributes that may properly be predicated of God. God would remain a faceless enigma beyond the created world.

As we know God from creatures, we also "name him" or speak of God in accordance with our knowledge.[365] Our words do not mean exactly the same thing when said of God as they do when said of creatures. Nor do they mean something entirely different. They are neither univocal nor equivocal, but analogous. The ground for this analogous usage is the resemblance of creatures to God as effects of God's creative action.[366] By analogy, human language is used to speak of God in philosophy, theology, and Scripture itself.

As our knowledge of God involves the ways of causality, negation, and

---

361. *Super ad rom.* I, lect. 6 (§115); *Comp.* I, c.21; *In meta.* XII, lect. 8 (§2543).

362. *ST* I, 13, 2, co.

363. *Sent.* I, 2, 1, 3, ad 2.

364. See Jean-Hervé Nicolas, "Aimante et bienheureuse Trinité," *Revue thomiste* 78 (1978): 277; Geiger, "Saint," 207.

365. *ST* I, 13, 1, co. Cf.: *ST* I, 13, 5, co.; *In de div. nom.* I, lect. 3 (§83, 85, 102).

366. *ST* I, 13, 5; *SCG* I, c.32–34. See Gregory Rocca, *Speaking the Incomprehensible God: Thomas Aquinas on the Interplay of Positive and Negative Theology* (Washington, D.C.: The Catholic University of America Press, 2004); Ralph McInerny, *Aquinas and Analogy* (Washington, D.C.: The Catholic University of America Press, 1996); Brian Shanley, "Commentary," in Thomas Aquinas, *The Treatise on the Divine Nature: Summa Theologiae I, 1–13*, trans. Brian Shanley (Indianapolis: Hackett Publishing, 2006), 333–38; Wippel, *Metaphysical*, 543–72; William Hill, *Knowing the Unknown God* (New York: Philosophical Library, 1971).

eminence, so do the names we apply to God. All three ways are at work in any statement we make. All we say of God is grounded in divine causality, seeks to remove creaturely imperfection from him, and intends to eminently affirm unlimited perfection. When we call God "good," for instance, we recognize (by way of causality) that he is the ultimate cause of goodness in creatures, and (by way of negation) that he is not good in the limited mode of creatures, and (by way of eminence) that he is good in a surpassing way.

While all three ways are involved in whatever we say of God, some of our statements are tied more closely to one way than another. Predicates or names like "creator" are bound to the way of causality. Names like "immaterial" that deny creaturely limitations are related to the way of negation. Names predicated of God in these two ways "in no way signify his substance." Those said of God by way of causality signify God's "relation to something else or rather the relation of creatures to him." Those said by way of negation signify the "removal (*remotionem*) of something from him." Names predicated in the third way, however, assert something about the divine substance itself. Such names (like "good" or "wise") are said of God "substantially (*substantialiter*)." Though the reality signified by such names (*res significata*) exceeds our human mode of understanding (*modus significandi*), we can still be sure that our predication is true when we attribute to God in a surpassing mode by the way of eminence qualities known to us only in a limited way.[367]

Of names said of God substantially, some are predicated properly and others metaphorically.[368] In metaphorical usage, the name of some created thing is applied to God because some aspect of that thing resembles a characteristic feature of God's activity.[369] So God is called a lion "because of his noble spirit or strength."[370] In proper discourse, a name is applied to God because what it signifies is recognized as belonging properly to God (although this signification is known to us only from creatures and according to our limited human mode of understanding). So when we say, "God is good," what is signified by the name "good" is said properly of God even as our lim-

367. *ST* I, 13, 2, co.; a.3, co.; 4, co. See Shanley, *Thomist*, 51.
368. *De ver.* Q.23, 3, co.; Q.7, 2, co.; *Sent.* I, 45, 1, 4, co.; *ST* I, 13, 3, ad 1; Q.19, 11, co.; Q.20, 1, ad 2.
369. *Sent.* I, 34, 3, 2, ad 4; *De ver.* Q.7, 2, co.; ad 5; Q.10, 10, ad 6; *ST* I, 13, 9, co.; III, 8, 2, ad 2; *SCG* IV, c.37.11 (§3759).
370. *Sent.* I, 34, 3, 2, ad 4. Cf.: *ST* I, 13, 6, co.

ited human mode of signifying is denied of God.[371] As goodness and other perfections belong properly to God (and only by participation and similitude to creatures), so the name "good" and other such names (in regard to what they signify) are applied primarily to God and only secondarily to creatures. In human usage, however, such names are subject to the human mode of signifying, and so refer primarily to creatures and only in a secondary way to God. Though they refer to divine perfection, they signify it only according to the human way of knowing. As regards their mode of signification, therefore, they refer primarily to creatures that are known to us first.[372]

Modes of Predicating Divine Immutability

Immutability is predicated of God in all of the ways discussed in the previous section. It is evoked through metaphorical usages and explicitly affirmed through the ways of causality, negation, and eminence. To see the appropriateness of predicating immutability of God, we must understand its significance in each of these contexts.

Metaphor

Metaphorical language for God is especially well suited to our human condition. Since our knowledge is grounded in sensation and metaphors employ sense imagery, they are very effective in communicating divine truth.[373] Using the imagery of lesser creatures such as a rock or a lion to refer to God reminds us that God is beyond all we can say or think and ensures we do not mistake the image for a literal account of the divine nature.[374] Metaphors are also useful vehicles for inspiring devotion and expressing religious experience. We can describe our relationship to God more vividly, for instance, by speaking of God's relationship to us: "Draw near to God and he will draw near to you" (Jas 4:8). By stretching the ordinary meaning of words, images, and concepts, metaphorical language points to the transcendent reality of God with a vitality our more technical theological language often fails to express. As Sallie McFague points out, "Increasingly . . . the idea of metaphor

371. *ST* I, 13, 3; a.12, ad 3; *Sent.* I, 22, 1, 1; *SCG* I, c.30.3 (§277); c.36.2 (§302); *In de div. nom.* V, lect. 3 (§673); *De pot.* Q.7, 2, ad 7; a.5, ad 2.
372. *ST* I, 13, 3, co.; a.6, co.   373. *ST* I, 1, 9, co.; ad 1; *Sent.* I, 34, 3, 1, co.
374. *ST* I, 1, 9, co.; ad 2; ad 3; *Sent.* I, 34, 3, 2, co.

as unsubstitutable is winning acceptance: what a metaphor expresses cannot be said directly or apart from it, for if it could be, one would have said it directly."[375]

Aquinas sees metaphors functioning in various ways. Sometimes the name of a certain creature is predicated of God because some aspect of the creature resembles a divine characteristic, as when God is called a "rock of refuge" (Ps 18:3). In interpreting this type of metaphor, it is important to determine what aspect of the creature is intended. When God is called a "rock," for instance, we should not think of immobile rigidity or "stony" inertness, but rather of strength, stability, and unchanging "granite" steadfastness. Sometimes an activity proper to the creature is predicated of God by transference. So as we "draw near to God" through grace, we may say God "draws near to us" (Jas 4:8). We can appreciate how the metaphor captures the feel of our religious experience, even as we remember that the one changing here is not God but the creature. While some metaphors imply divine movement, others suggest immutability. Anthropomorphic usages such as God's "anger" (Ps 105:40–41), "hatred" (Ps 5:7), and "repentance" (Jer 18:7–8), as well as "hiding his face" (Ps 26:9) and "walking in the garden in the cool of the day" (Gen 3:8), suggest motion. Those such as "standing" (Amos 7:7) or "sitting" (Is 9:7) imply immutability. We have already seen how Aquinas resolves such apparently contradictory scriptural predications.[376]

Some contemporary theologians, recognizing the vitality and appropriateness of metaphorical language, have argued that theology should remain simply on the metaphorical level.[377] They find the imaginative language of metaphor preferable to more technical theological discourse. The "suffering God" of biblical imagery is favored over the "impassible God" of systematic theology. Comparisons of this sort rightly suggest that in certain contexts (such as preaching) the language of metaphor may be preferable to more technical terminology. It is important to remember, however, that metaphorical and proper language about God are two different procedures, each with

375. Sally McFague, *Models of God: Theology for an Ecological, Nuclear Age* (Philadelphia: Fortress, 1987), 33.
376. See *ST* I, 1, 9, ad 2; *SCG* III, c.96.11–13 (§2718–20); IV, c.29.4–5 (§3649–50).
377. For example, François Varillon, *La souffrance de Dieu* (Paris: Seuil, 1975), 18.

its own particular role to play in our human endeavor to speak about God. While metaphorical language is well suited to expressing religious feeling and evoking a sense of the divine mystery, a more technical language is essential to our human understanding, expression, and discussion of the very truth toward which such metaphorical language points. By juxtaposing specific phrases taken from both types of language, one tends to blur the distinction between these languages and so introduces the false dilemma of whether one language is absolutely preferable to the other. Within either sort of language, comparisons of various formulations may fruitfully be made. One may, for instance, compare various statements in systematic theology with regard to their ability to express the truth, and one may compare different kinds of religious imagery in terms of their significance and effectiveness. In the second case, the comparison of the immovable God (Ps 62:3) to the movable God (Hos 11:8) will not lead to the rejection of one image in favor of the other, but to a deeper appreciation of the value and significance of both sorts of imagery.

Other theologians argue that theology must remain on the metaphorical level since all theological language is merely metaphorical. Sallie McFague, for instance, contends that "no language about God is adequate and all of it is improper" and that "no authority—not scriptural status, liturgical longevity, nor ecclesiastical fiat—can decree that some types of language, or some images, refer literally to God while others do not. None do."[378] Jean Galot maintains: "All of our representations of God are in a sense anthropomorphic since they consist in a human thought which is tied to images of the sensible world, and since they are expressed necessarily in human language."[379]

Aquinas also asks whether all speech about God is metaphorical since every name we predicate of God is taken from creatures.[380] He answers that some names, even though they belong to human language and are subject to all the limitations of human thought, can be applied properly (*proprie*) to God.[381] He points out that Scripture itself, though speaking of divine truth metaphorically in some places, teaches that same truth more openly (*expres-*

378. McFague, *Models*, 35.
380. *ST* I, 13, 3, obj.1.

379. Galot, "Réalité," 231.
381. *ST* I, 13, 3, co.; ad 1.

sius) in others.[382] And even when Scripture teaches us about God through metaphors, its intention is not for us to remain on that level but to know the truth.[383]

If all our statements about God were simply anthropomorphic or metaphorical, we could (without further qualifications or distinctions) compare technical theological formulations (e.g., the "impassible God") directly with imaginative metaphorical notions (e.g., the "suffering God"). In fact, it would be the very business of theology to make such comparisons. If all statements about God were simply metaphorical, then theology would be merely a matter of comparing different metaphors and choosing those more pleasing or suitable for any particular occasion or audience. But if theology is reduced to purely metaphorical discourse, it will cease to be a search for understanding (*fides quaerens intellectum*).[384] As James Reichmann points out: "If there were no names which truly indicated something to us of the divine nature, however imperfectly since they derive totally from human experience, then it would not be possible to speak of God in any but a most ambiguous and near meaningless sense."[385]

As we search for the meaning of divine immutability, we must recognize the value of scriptural metaphors both for God's changelessness and for God's motion. But we must never mistake metaphors of either sort for literal descriptions of divine truth.[386] To name the truth contained in these metaphors, we must go beyond metaphor and find a language that, while recognizing all our human limitations, can properly refer to God in both creation and revelation as the cause of all things, who remains distinct from them, but whose supereminent goodness and perfection is somehow reflected in each.[387]

---

382. *ST* I, 1, 9, ad 2.

383. "[S]acra scriptura non proponit nobis divina sub figuris sensibilibus, ut ibi intellectus noster remaneat, sed ut ab his ad immaterialia ascendat" (*Super de trin.* Q.6, 2, ad 1). Cf.: *ST* I, 1, 9, ad 2; III, 48, 3, ad 1; *In de div. nom.* I, lect. 2 (§69).

384. Though Aquinas never uses this phrase of Anselm, he does embrace the concept in quoting John Chrysostom: "Ergo noli quaerere intelligere ut credas, sed crede ut intelligas: quia nisi credideritis, non intelligetis" (*Cat. aur. in joann.* VII, 3, lines 108–10).

385. Reichmann, "Immanently," 358. Cf.: William Hill, "Two Gods of Love: Aquinas and Whitehead," *Listening* 14 (1979): 249; Shanley, *Thomist*, 57–58.

386. *ST* I, 1, 9, ad 3.

387. *ST* II-II, 19, 11, ad 2.

Causality, Negation, and Eminence

Knowing the Immutable God Since the way we name or speak of God follows the way we know him,[388] we should first consider the different ways we know about divine immutability before looking at the appropriateness of the ways we talk about it. Both our knowledge and our language about God's changelessness spring from the three ways of causality, negation, and eminence, which lead us to knowledge of God from creatures and teach us how the names or predicates we use of creatures may also be said of God.[389] In this section, therefore, we will first consider what we know about divine immutability and then discuss the various ways we express our knowledge by predicating immutability of God according to the modes of causality, negation, and eminence.

Aquinas's arguments for divine immutability have taught us to see this attribute as a sign of God's perfection in being. The way of causality reveals God as the "immovable (*immobile*) and perfect" cause of "defectible and changeable creatures."[390] We discover more about this cause as we unpack the modes of causality. The "five ways" of showing God's existence in the *Summa theologiae* reveal God as the efficient, exemplar, and final cause of all things.[391] As the ultimate cause of motion, God must be immovable, above the motion and rest of creatures.[392] He is the source of both change and "changelessness" in them as they participate his perfect immutability.[393] On a more profound level, God is also the cause of their very act of existing—of their "is" (*esse*). As the source of "is" in creatures, God is himself pure "is," *ipsum esse subsistens*, and his immutability takes on corresponding significance. The ways of eminence and negation remind us God must contain all creaturely perfection in a surpassing way and exclude all imperfection. Since his very essence is to-be (*esse*), God is pure dynamic actuality, with no potency, which implies limitation and is the mark of all changeable things. Since in

---

388. *ST* I, 13, 1, co.

389. *Super ad rom.* I, lect. 6 (§115); *In de div. nom.* I, lect. 3 (§§83, 85, 102).

390. *Super ad rom.* I, lect. 6 (§115). 391. *ST* I, 2, 3, co.

392. *In de div. nom.* IV, lect. 6 (§367).

393. *SCG* III, c.62.11 (§2374); c.72.4 (§2482); *ST* I, 10, 2, ad 1; a.3, co.; *De malo* Q.16, 2, ad 6; *De ver.* Q.5, 4, co.; *In de caelo*, II, lect. 18.6; *In de div. nom.* VII, lect. 4 (§733).

him essence and to-be (*esse*) are one, he is absolutely simple, transcending all composition required for change. Since he enjoys the boundless perfection of pure to-be (*esse*), there is no further perfection he could acquire or present perfection he might lose through change. In this way our knowledge of God's immutability springs from our recognition of his transcendent perfection in being.

Knowledge of other divine attributes may in turn be deduced from our recognition of God's immutability.[394] God must be eternal since he is not subject to motion and so is not bound by time, which is the measure of motion.[395] In virtue of his immutability, we deny of him passive potency,[396] matter,[397] composition,[398] passion,[399] and "whatever is violent or unnatural."[400] At the same time, we affirm goodness,[401] truth,[402] intelligence,[403] happiness,[404] and unending life.[405] Immutability also implies the necessity and surpassing perfection of divine being (*esse*).[406]

Naming the Immutable God As the three modes of causality, negation, and eminence direct our knowledge of God's immutability, they also guide our

394. *In meta.* XII, lect. 7–8; *Comp.* I, c.4, ff.; *SCG* c.14, ff.

395. *SCG* I, c.15.2–3 (§121–22); II, c.35.6 (§1116); *ST* I, 9, 1, *prologus;* Q.10, 1, co.; a.2, co.; a.3, co.; Q.79, 8, ad 2; *De malo* Q.16, 2, ad 6; *De aeter. mundi,* lines 278–96 (Leonine); *Comp.* I, c.5; c.7–8; *In de caelo* I, lect. 21.9; *Super de causis* Prop. 2 (Saffrey, p.11, line 25 to p.12, line 22); Prop. 30 (Saffrey, p.139, lines 12–24); *In de div. nom.* X, lect. 3 (§871). For a review and refutation of contemporary arguments against the notion of divine eternity, see John C. Yates, *The Timelessness of God* (Lanham, Md.: University Press of America, 1990), 301; Eleonore Stump and Norman Kretzmann, "Eternity," *Journal of Philosophy* 78 (1981): 429–58; John L. Tomkinson, "Divine Sempiternity and Atemporality," *Religious Studies* 18 (1982): 177–89.

396. *SCG* I, c.16.6 (§132).

397. *SCG* I, c.17.5 (§138); c.20.4 (§156); 20.8 (§160); 20.34 (§186); *ST* I, 3, 1, co.; *Comp.* I, c.16–17; *In phys.* VIII, lect. 21.1 (§1141).

398. *Comp.* I, c.9; *In meta.* V, lect. 6.14 (§840).

399. *SCG* I, c.89.4 (§738).

400. *SCG* I, c.19.5 (§152); *In meta.* V, lect. 6.15 (§841).

401. *SCG* I, c.37.3 (§305); *De pot.* Q.6, 6, co.; *De sub. sep.* c.2, lines 34–40 (Leonine).

402. *Sent.* I, 19, 5, 3, co.; III, 39, 1, 2, qc.1, ad 3; *ST* I, 16, 8, co.

403. *SCG* I, c.44.2–3 (§373–74).

404. *ST* I-II, 32, 2, co.; *In eth.* VII, lect. 14, line 267 c. (Leonine).

405. *SCG* I, c.99.5 (§826); *In de div. nom.* VII, lect. 1 (§697); *In meta.* XII, lect. 8 (§2544); *Super de causis* Prop. 18 (Saffrey, p. 102, line 11, to p. 103, line 23).

406. "Est autem ponere unum ens, quod est perfectissimum et verissimum ens: quod ex hoc probatur, quia est aliquid movens omnino immobile et perfectissimum, ut a philosophis est probatum" (*De pot.* Q.3, 5, co.). Cf.: *Comp.* I, c.6, c.21; *In de div. nom.* VIII, lect. 3 (§769).

language.[407] While all three modes are involved in anything we say about divine immutability, some of our statements may be more closely tied to one than another. To discern the meaning of our statements, therefore, we need to discover the particular significance of divine immutability according to each of the three ways of causality, negation, and eminence.

In saying God is immutable according to the way of causality, we do not intend to assert anything about his substance, but only about "his relationship to something else, or rather, the relationship of something else to him." Our statements "in no way signify his substance."[408] They simply describe the relationship of creatures to God and signify that God, as the source of motion and immovability in creatures, is immutable. If we want to do more than simply affirm God as the source of change and changelessness in creatures, we will have to go beyond the way of causality to find the meaning of divine immutability in the ways of negation and eminence.

The insight behind the way of negation is that, even though creatures are in some way like God who causes them, God is in no way like them.[409] Through the way of negation we know and speak of God in terms of his absolute distinction from creatures, denying of him every aspect of creatures that implies limitation or imperfection. Since motion as found in creatures implies limitation in its very definition ("the act of a being in potency"), it must be denied of God.[410] When we say God is immutable according to the way of negation, we mean simply that motion, insofar as it implies limitation and imperfection, does not belong to God.

But if creaturely motion can imply imperfection, so can creaturely immutability. The creature's motion implies a present lack of that fullness of perfection it is currently attaining through its motion. Its immutability, however, may suggest not only a lack of such future perfection but also the absence of any progress toward it. In this sense, immutability may imply a greater imperfection than changeableness.[411] Such immutability must be denied of God.

407. *ST* I, 13, 1, co.   408. *ST* I, 13, 2, co.
409. *ST* I, 4, 3, ad 4; *SCG* I, c.29.
410. "Ipse enim solus perfecte incorruptibilis est, qui est omnino immutabilis; omnis enim mutatio quaedam corruptio est" (*Super ad rom.* I, lect. 7 [§134]).
411. *Sent.* IV, 48, 2, 2, ad sed contra 5.

According to the way of negation, therefore, both motion and immutability are in some sense to be denied of God. In each case, however, our statement that "God is not movable" or that "God is not immovable" implies only that the motion or immutability characteristic of the creature must be denied of God. Even when the first statement is phrased as an affirmation ("God is immovable"), it is in no way intended as a positive description of the divine nature. For in the *via negationis,* names are not predicated of God "absolutely and affirmatively." They are rather said "negatively" and signify only the "remotion of something" from God: "In no way do they signify his substance."[412] According to the way of negation, therefore, the statement "God is immovable" means simply that motion as found in creatures is not found in God. Similarly, the statement "God is not immovable" means only that immovability, as found in creatures, is not found in God.

Unfortunately divine immutability, as predicated in the way of negation, is sometimes mistaken for a positive description of the divine nature.[413] The mistake is compounded if one also thinks it is the imperfect and limiting (stagnating) immutability of the creatures that is being predicated positively of God. We have already seen that creaturely immutability may imply insensitivity, apathy, inertness, stagnation, and a whole host of unhappy traits. Contemporary theologians who interpret divine immutability in this way are eager to add to the list. The unchanging God is "as cold and hard and unfeeling as cement."[414] He is "unconcerned" and "indifferent," a "loveless beloved" "ever unaffected in his Olympian immutability."[415] He possesses the "rigid immutability" of a "loveless monster."[416] He is "cold, static, immobile,

---

412. *ST* I, 13, 2, co.

413. "The very negative grammatical form of 'immutability' directly intends denying of God the imperfectness attending finite mutation, but unfortunately and unjustifiably it has been expanded into a positive idea of Divinity itself" (Hill, *Knowing,* 190). See also Thomas G. Weinandy, "Does God Suffer?" *First Things* no. 117 (November 2001) 38; Paul S. Fiddes, *The Creative Suffering of God* (Oxford: Clarendon Press, 1988), 51.

414. Jürgen Moltmann, *History and the Triune God: Contributions to Trinitarian Theology* (New York: Crossroad, 1992), 123.

415. Joseph Donceel, "Second Thoughts on the Nature of God," *Thought* 46 (1971): 347. Cf.: Moltmann, *Crucified,* 222; Wilhelm Maas, *Unveränderlichkeit,* 118.

416. Oeing-Hanhoff, "Krise," 291; K. J. Woolcombe, "The Pain of God," *Scottish Journal of Theology* 20 (1967): 130.

passionless," and "totally devoid of life and love."[417] He is, in a word, whatever repellent image of immutability human fantasy and eloquence can create.

Aquinas implicitly realizes such unfortunate interpretations are possible. He knows the predication of such undesirable aspects of immutability may yield a satanical image or metaphor.[418] In predicating immutability of God according to the *via negationis,* however, he certainly does not intend to create such an image. Far from attributing the imperfect immutability of creatures to God in a positive way, he proposes no positive statement at all. He wishes to make only a negative statement, and he makes that statement precisely to deny that creaturely imperfection may be found in God. And, lest anyone misunderstand his intention, he states it in the clearest possible fashion: "Regarding names which are said of God negatively, . . . it is evident that they in no way signify his substance."[419]

In his negative statement, Thomas denies both motion and immutability of God. To the extent that motion implies potency and imperfection, it is denied of God: "God is completely immovable."[420] To the extent that immutability may also imply imperfection, it is likewise rejected.[421] The immobility of material creatures is called "rest (*quies*)." Rest implies imperfection in its very definition since it is "the privation of motion in that which is susceptible of motion."[422] Although rest may also indicate perfection to the extent that it involves the completion of some motion and the attainment of a certain actuality, it always implies imperfection insofar as it implies a "lack of motion" (and thus a lack of actuality and a lack of advance toward further perfection) "in that which is susceptible of motion" (i.e., in that which is not yet entirely perfect). This immutability that is proper to creatures must therefore, like creaturely motion, be denied of God.[423]

---

417. Stokes, "Whitehead's," 7; Woolcombe, "Pain," 139. Similarly unhappy analogies may be found in Nicholas Wolterstorff, "Does God Suffer?" in *Questions about God: Today's Philosophers Ponder the Divine,* ed. Steven M. Cahn and David Shatz (New York: Oxford University Press, 2002), 127; Charles Hartshorne, *Reality as Social Process* (New York: Hafner, 1971), 137; *The Divine Relativity* (New Haven: Yale University Press, 1964), 42–43; John B. Cobb, Jr. and David Ray Griffin, *Process Theology: An Introductory Exposition* (Philadelphia: Westminster Press, 1976), 47.

418. *Super iob* XL, v.13, lines 371–85.
419. *ST* I, 13, 2, co.
420. *ST* I, 9, 1, co.
421. *In de div. nom.* V, lect. 3 (§673).
422. *In phys.* V, lect. 1.6 (§683).
423. *In phys.* VIII, lect. 5.2 (§1005). Since rest is attributed to God in Scripture (Gen 2:2), Thomas

A number of contemporary authors who reject divine immutability still seem in agreement with Aquinas that creaturely imperfection must be denied of God. As Marcel Sarot does here, they deny of God any aspects of creaturely motion that imply imperfection:

> God is a moved Mover rather than an unmoved Mover. In this I support the contemporary rejection of the traditional doctrine of divine impassibility. But when we reject the traditional position, we should see to it that we do not go from one extreme to the other. God may not be an unmoved Mover, but neither is God moved without being a Mover. God is not a passive victim of God's own emotions and therewith of our actions; God primarily is a Mover, an Actor, taking initiatives and keeping control, even though choosing to have feelings and to be vulnerable.[424]

Theologians who wrongly interpret the doctrine of immutability as positively attributing creaturely immutability or impassibility to God are nonetheless right in rejecting the attribution of imperfection to God. More worrisome are those thinkers, classical or contemporary, who interpret the doctrine of immutability as attributing creaturely imperfection to God yet persist in that affirmation. For they then seem to assert that God is indeed that compassionless entity that one envisions if one assumes that divine immutability is like the imperfect immutability of creatures. This is what the fourteenth-century Dominican mystic Meister Eckhart seems to imply when he says, "As the Son in the Godhead willed to and became man and suffered torture, that affected the immovable separateness of God as little as if he had never become man."[425] Similarly the twentieth-century Dominican Heinrich Maria

is careful to find ways it may be understood positively. See *Sent.* I, 8, 2, 1, ad 6; II, 15, 3, 2; *ST* I, 73, 2; *SCG* II, c.84.4 (§1690); *De ver.* Q.8, 17, ad 5. See David B. Burrell, *Aquinas God and Action* (Notre Dame, Ind.: University of Notre Dame Press, 1979), 36–37; Joseph Owens, "Aquinas—Existential Permanence and the Flux," *MS* 31 (1969): 85.

424. Marcel Sarot, "A Moved Mover? The (Im)passibility of God," in *Understanding the Attributes of God*, ed. Gijsbert van den Brink and Marcel Sarot (Frankfurt: Peter Lang, 1999), 133. See also Jürgen Moltmann, "The Crucified God: A Trinitarian Theology of the Cross," *Interpretation* 26 (1972): 287; Maas, *Unveränderlichkeit*, 21, 27; Charles Hartshorne, *Aquinas to Whitehead: Seven Centuries of Metaphysics of Religion* (Milwaukee, Wisc.: Marquette University Publications, 1976), 25.

425. "Als der Sohn in der Gottheit Mensch werden wollte und ward und die Marter erlitt, ging das die unbewegliche Abgeschiedenheit Gottes so wenig an, wie wenn er nie mensch geworden wäre" ("Traktate 3," in Meister Eckhart, *Die deutschen Werke*, ed. J. Quint. Stuttgart [Stuttgart: W. Kohlhammer, 1963], 542).

Christmann defends divine immutability even when it seems to imply "that God may be as little moved by the good fortunes as by the bad fortunes of nations and of humankind; as little moved by our prayers and liturgical services as by our offenses."[426] Lest we think Dominicans have a monopoly on such musings, however, we can consider Soren Kierkegaard's frightening description of the immovable God who seems to lie in wait for hapless human beings:

Is not this other sight still more terrifying: one infinitely powerful, who—eternally unchanged—sits quite still and sees everything, without altering a feature, almost as if he did not exist. . . . Why, do you think, is he so quiet? Because he knows with himself that he is eternally unchangeable. . . . Only one who is eternally immutable can be in this manner so still. He gives men time, and he can afford to give them time, since he has eternity and is eternally unchangeable. He gives time, and that with premeditation. And then there comes an accounting in eternity, where nothing is forgotten, not even a single one of the improper words that were spoken; and he is eternally unchanged.[427]

It can only be lamented that such assertions are sometimes taken to be the official teaching of the Church or of "classical theism." Their widespread rejection is not only understandable, but laudable.[428] It is unfortunate, however, that in rejecting such erroneous interpretations, some theologians think

426. Heinrich Maria Christmann, "Kommentar: *ST* I, 9, 1," in Thomas von Aquin, *Die Deutsche Thomas-Ausgabe* (Salzburg: A. Pustet, 1933), 1:500.

427. Soren Kierkegaard, "The Unchangeableness of God," in *Edifying Discourses: A Selection*, ed. Paul L. Holmer (New York: Harper and Bros., 1958), 258–59.

428. Johannes B. Brantschen rightly criticizes Heinrich M. Christmann's interpretation of divine immutability in "Die Macht," 225, 232. William Hill remarks, "This dissatisfaction with and desire to go beyond the traditional conception [of divine immutability] cannot but enlist sympathy" (*Knowing*, 189). Jacques Maritain criticizes theologians for retaining words and expressions that tend to make God look like an apathetic "potentate"; "Quelques réflexions sur le savoir théologique," *Revue thomiste* 69 (1969): 5–27. W. Norris Clarke avers, "Religion can and should have the right to challenge metaphysics to adapt, if need be, to make the fit closer between thought and life. I will also candidly admit that St. Thomas and Thomists in general—with some contemporary exceptions—have not said enough to make clear how this is possible in their metaphysical conception of God as Pure Act and absolutely immutable, with no 'real relation' to the world" ("Charles Hartshorne's Philosophy of God: A Thomistic Critique," in *Charles Hartshorne's Concept of God: Philosophical and Theological Responses*, ed. Santiago Sia (Dordrecht: Kluwer Academic Publishers, 1990), 111. See also W. Norris Clarke, "A New Look at the Immutability of God," in *God Knowable and Unknowable*, ed. R. J. Roth (New York: Fordham University Press, 1973), 44; Martin D'Arcy, "The Immutability of God," PACPA 41 (1967): 22, 25.

it necessary to deny divine immutability altogether. Here, the nuances of Aquinas's theology may be helpful.

If the imperfect motionlessness of creatures is not to be attributed to God, is there any way immutability can be affirmed as a positive divine attribute? To do this, we must turn from the way of negation to the way of eminence to see whether immutability can be viewed as a creaturely perfection to be attributed in an eminent way to God. Through the way of eminence, we recognize that since God is the cause of creatures and since the perfection of the effect must be in the cause in some eminent way, those qualities or perfections of creatures, which in themselves imply no imperfection, may be predicated of God in a surpassing way. To the extent, therefore, that immutability implies no imperfection, it may be predicated of God according to the way of eminence. But so may motion insofar as it also implies no imperfection.

Names predicated of God in the way of eminence are said of him not simply in terms of his relationship to creatures (as in the way of causality), nor negatively (as in the way of negation), but "properly (*proprie*)" and "substantially (*substantialiter*)."[429] In predicating such names of God, however, we do not know the perfections signified by these names as they actually are in God. We know them only as they are found in creatures and according to our limited mode of knowing. We affirm them of God, however, in a way that they do not exist in creatures and in a way that goes beyond our finite understanding.[430]

If we are to predicate immutability properly of God in the *via eminentiae*, we must find some sense in which the term "immutable" implies no imperfection. For names which inherently imply imperfection cannot be said of God "properly," but only metaphorically.[431] It might seem that the term "immutable" always implies imperfection. In our world change suggests life and activity while immovability is associated with the static and lifeless. Especially in our age, change exercises a particular fascination. "Progress," "newness," "development," and "growth" are all commonly accepted values. Through change, we move toward perfection. We delight not just in the achievement of some goal, but in our movement toward it.[432]

---

429. *ST* I, 13, aa.2–3.
431. *ST* I, 13, 3, ad 1.

430. *SCG* I, c.30.4 (§278); *Sent.* I, 35, 1, 1, ad 5.
432. *ST* I-II, 32, 2, co.; ad 1.

Aware of the delight we find in change, we might well ask with Lactantius, "How can God be blessed if he is in a state of torpor, at rest and without motion?"[433] An immovable God seems particularly alien to the spirit of our age. The "immovable eternity" of the heavenly kingdom appears not only uninteresting but repellent.[434]

But even in our age, some aspects of immutability still seem desirable. We no longer ponder the imperishable heavenly spheres, but do find modes of admirable immutability in such personal traits as integrity of character, steadfastness in virtue, loyalty in friendship and fidelity in marriage. Each suggests a kind of changelessness that may be predicated eminently of God. Even theologians who argue for a changeable God often find some predication of immutability appropriate.[435] And praising God's changelessness continues to be an instinct of Christian worship. Liturgical hymns still laud the "Almighty, Invisible, God only wise," celebrating that "naught changeth thee."[436] Sacramental prayers affirm, "You remain unchanged, but you watch over all creation and make it new through your Son, Jesus Christ our Lord."[437]

433. Lactantius, *De ira Dei* III, 5, in *Laktanz, Vom Zorne Gottes*, ed. H. Kraft and A. Wlosok (Darmstadt: Wissenschaftliche Buchgesellschaft, 1974), 8.

434. "Unchanging eternity, the more one imagines it, is not fascinating, even if based on happiness and love. The phantasm of boredom erases all its seduction" (Varillon, *Souffrance*, 60). "[I]n the end, incorruptibility and immortality do not appear to be especially desirable, but rather seem to be terrifying and boring" (Moltmann, *Crucified*, 230). See also Whitehead, *Process and Reality*, 347; Douglas Erlandson, "Timelessness, Immutability, and Eschatology," *International Journal for Philosophy of Religion* 9 (1978): 139.

435. Karl Barth, for instance, affirms God's unchanging faithfulness, but prefers the word "constancy (*Beständigkeit*)" to "the questionable negative word 'immutability (*Unveränderlichkeit*)'" (*Kirchliche*, II/1, 557). Process philosophers predicate immutability of God's "primordial nature" and motion of his "consequent nature." See Whitehead, *Process and Reality*, 105, 345–47; Hartshorne, *Divine*, 82–83, 156–57; "Reflections on the Strength and Weakness of Thomism," *Ethics* 54 (1943–44): 55. For other examples, see Pannenberg, "Aufnahme," 329; Moltmann, *Crucified*, 229–30; John Mahoney, *Charles Hartshorne's Dipolar Conception of God* (Grand Prairie, Tex.: Scholars Guild, 1974); J. Norman King and Barry Whitney, "Rahner and Hartshorne on Divine Immutability," *IPQ* 22 (1982): 209.

436. See *Lutheran Book of Worship* (Minneapolis: Augsburg Publishing House, 1978). A similar theme is expressed in Martin Luther's hymn "A Mighty Fortress Is Our God."

437. From the Rite for the Ordination of Deacons in *Ordination of Deacons, Priests and Bishops* (Washington, D.C.: United States Catholic Conference Publications Office, 1979). Similarly, the opening prayer for the Second Sunday of Lent begins, "Father of light, in you is found no shadow of change but only the fullness of life and limitless truth" (*The Sacramentary* [New York: Catholic Book Publishing, 1974]). The official Prayer of the Church includes the hymn, "Lord God and Maker of all Things . . . you are unchanging always new" (Friday Daytime Prayer, Week III), the poetry of Teresa of Avila, "Let nothing disturb

In the prayer life of the Christian community, it seems the unshakable "rock of ages" has not yet been replaced with "rolling stones."

If immutability, conceived as a perfection, may properly be predicated of God in the *via eminentiae,* so can motion. We have seen two sorts of motion that imply no imperfection.[438] One is the immanent motion of knowing and willing. Unlike transient motion, it is not the act of a being in potency, but the act of a being in act. It involves no imperfection, but is a sign of highest perfection and surpassing life. It is therefore predicated of God in an eminent way.[439] The second is transient motion, considered as the act not of the receiver but of the agent. As the act of the recipient, transient motion is the act of a being in potency. As the act of the agent, it is the "act of the actual," and does not imply imperfection. To the extent that this sort of motion resembles divine causality, it may be predicated of God.[440] Divine causality in creation and providence may then be understood as "a kind of motion (*quandam motionem*)."[441]

When we predicate motion of God in the way of eminence, the full significance of our words exceeds our understanding. We do not know what God is and so cannot comprehend divine motion. Still, we do know that our affirmation truly points to God as the supreme reality who surpasses the motion and the immutability of creatures. As Edward Schillebeeckx puts it, "I know that the word 'newness' always implies becoming for us, and we have to deny that in God. The eternal newness of an absolutely subsisting freedom exceeds our understanding. And yet this negative knowledge, though not comprehensible in words, is supported by an implicit, positive moment of knowledge—by a consciousness in which we, while affirming the 'move-

---

thee . . . God never changeth" (Tuesday Night Prayer), and the poetry of H. F. Lyte, "Abide with me . . . O Thou who changest not, abide with me" (Sunday Night Prayer), in *Christian Prayer: The Liturgy of the Hours* (Boston: St Paul Editions, 1976).

438. *Sent.* I, 4, 1, 1, ad 1; *SCG* II, c.1; *ST* I, 14, 1, *prologus;* Q.23, 2, ad 1; Q.27, 1; Q.34, 3, ad 2; *Super de trin.* Q.5, 4, ad 2; *In de div. nom.* V, lect. 3 (§672); *De pot.* Q.10, 1, co.

439. *Sent.* I, 8, 3, 1, ad 2; II, 11, 2, 1, co.; d.12, 1, 5, exp. *text; ST* I, 9, 1, ad 1; Q.18, 3, ad 1; *De ver.* Q.24, 1, ad 14; *In de caelo* II, lect. 4.5; *In phys.* VIII, lect. 2.16 (§986); lect. 12.3 (§1071); *In eth.* VII, lect. 14, lines 265–79 (Leonine); *De pot.* Q.3, 15 co.

440. *Sent.* I, 8, 3, 1, ad 1; ad 2; *ST* I, 9, 1, ad 2; *In de div. nom.* V, lect. 3 (§672); *Resp. ad venet.,* a.11, line 227 c.

441. *SCG* IV, c.20.4 (§3572); *ST* I-II, 112, 3, ad 1; *In de div. nom.* IX, lect. 4 (§839–42).

ability' (*Beweglichkeit*) of the divine essence, do not know *how* this moveability applies to God."[442]

God as Moving or Unmoving

We have seen that in the ways of causality, negation, and eminence, motion and immutability may be attributed to but also denied of God. The way of causality teaches that God as the first cause is wholly immovable, but also that his causality itself may be seen as a kind of motion. The way of negation shows that the imperfect motion of creatures must be denied of God, but so must their deficient immutability. The way of eminence indicates that immutability may be attributed surpassingly to God to the extent that it implies no imperfection, but so may movability insofar as it implies no defect. Since both motion and immutability may be said of God, we can ask which predication is more appropriate.

A Moving God

In the context of our own age, it may seem motion is the more appropriate predicate. Our world is in love with progress and growth, and averse to all that seems static or frozen. It might therefore seem better, at least *quoad nos*, to think of God as moving rather than immobile. In calling God immovable, we seem to place implicit limits on his freedom, as if we were "telling God" what he can or cannot do according to our own ideas of what is "fitting" or "not fitting" to his immutable nature. As Karl Barth remarks, "If there is a wretched anthropomorphism, it is the illusion of the immutability of God which rules out the possibility that he could let himself be determined in one way or another by his creation!"[443] Perhaps it is better, then, to predicate motion of God, concluding with Paul Claudel that "God is not expressed by motion, but even less by immobility."[444]

442. E. Schillebeeckx, "Die Heiligung des Namens Gottes durch die Menschenliebe Jesu des Christus," in *Gott in Welt*, ed. Herbert Vogrimler et al. (Freiburg: Herder, 1964), 2:51.

443. Barth, *Kirchliche*, III/4, 119–20. See also Kelly James Clark, "Hold Not Thy Peace at My Tears: Methodological Reflections on Divine Impassibility," in *Our Knowledge of God*, ed. Kelly James Clark (Dordrecht: Kluwer Academic Publishers, 1992), 187; Brantschen, "Macht," 231; Maas, *Unveränderlichkeit*, 102; S. Paul Schilling, *God and Human Anguish* (Nashville: Abingdon, 1977), 252.

444. Paul Claudel, *Journal*, ed. François Varillon and Jacques Petit (Paris: Editions Gallimard, 1969), 2:14.

Even in our mobile age, however, some modes of changelessness are still attractive. Why is it then that, when we speak of divine immutability, our assertion often dredges up repellent images of inertness and stagnation rather than positive ones of fidelity and steadfastness? Two reasons might be mentioned. One has to do with the role of the imagination in theology; the second, with the inadequacy of human concepts to represent divine realities.

All human knowledge begins in sense and imagination and is ever accompanied by one image or other, but it does not always end there. Our knowledge of divine things terminates in the intellect alone.[445] Since theological knowledge does not terminate in the imagination, mistakes can be made when it is not used properly—when we interpret statements about God in terms of "what is apprehended by imagination."[446] If the imperfect immutability of creatures is most prominent in our imagination and we use this to understand God's changelessness, we form rather monstrous images of the unchanging God. To correct this tendency, we do not have to reject the imagination entirely, since we still need and prize the vivid images and metaphors we find in Scripture and other theological writing. We must not, however, confuse those images with the divine reality itself, which ever exceeds all we can know or imagine.

If the misuse of the imagination can lead to error, so can a mistaken idea of how adequately our concepts represent God. We have already seen that human concepts fail to comprehend even created *esse*. How much less should we expect them to grasp divine *esse*. To some philosophers and theologians, however, human ideas not only are adequate for representing divine things, but are the very measure of reality.

Any philosophy that has lost touch with being—with the concrete reality of existing things—tends to look to human concepts and experience as the measure of the real. In such a philosophy, or in a theology based on such a philosophy, there is a tendency to reduce God to human terms.[447] On the human level, however, immutability often implies lack of progress while change

---

445. *Super de trin.* Q.6, 2, co.
446. *Super de trin.* Q.6, 2, ad 2.
447. On this tendency in modern theology, see William C. Placher, *The Domestication of Transcendence: How Modern Thinking about God Went Wrong* (Louisville, Ky.: Westminster John Knox Press, 1996).

suggests dynamic growth in perfection. If this is the case with humans, "why should it be otherwise with God?"[448] Why indeed, if God is to be understood according to the measure of our human concepts? And this is precisely what tends to happen in the philosophies of idealism, existentialism, and process. In idealism, where the real is rational and the rational is real, the human concept is evidently the measure of all things.[449] In existentialism, it is human existence with all its particular structures and limits that becomes the measure of reality. In process philosophy, there is an inevitable tendency to move toward some form of idealism in order to attain some assurance of stability and truth in a world of constant change and becoming.[450]

A theology based on idealism tends to treat of God "rationalistically," understanding him somehow within the limits of our human concepts.[451] Since it has lost contact with being—with "the radical newness of each concrete event"—a theology of this sort "finds itself enclosed within the limitations of whatever scheme of concepts it is that the individual has adopted as his own."[452] A theology based on existentialism is able to accept only a God who is himself subject to that particular sort of existence which is characteristic of human beings: "If one opts for the existentialist definition of being and attempts to construct a philosophical theology on such a base, one does more than merely restrict the name of being to *existing* things. In effect one draws an opaque curtain between beings and God which can only be parted by identifying God with the mere inner manifestation of human con-

448. This is the seductive question posed by John Stacer: "For us excellence of life involves both our developing actual potentialities and our ongoing activities. Why should it be otherwise with God? . . . Should not the divine total capability be pure act and thus developing rather than immutable?" ("Integrating Thomistic and Whiteheadian Perspectives on God," *IPQ* 21 [1981]: 359). Charles Hartshorne poses a similar question: "Does it not make God more real to us to think of him as subject to change, as like us in having purpose for the future, memories of the past, and the power to receive addition to his happiness?" ("The Three Ideas of God," *Journal of Liberal Religion* 1, no. 3 [1940]: 15).

449. E. Gilson describes such philosophy pointedly and accurately as "the eternal noeticism which puts knowledge ahead of being and does not hold anything as real except those things whose existence the understanding is able to justify from its own proper principles. One could say the philosopher gives things their permits to exist" ("L'être et Dieu," 406).

450. This tendency is pointed out by Guy Boissard, "Etre ou devenir? Une angoissante question de tous les temps," *Nova et vetera* 58 (1983): 119, 130.

451. W. Hill, "Seeking Foundations for Faith: Symbolism of Person or Metaphysics of Being?" *Thomist* 45 (1981): 221.

452. O'Neill, *Sacramental*, 145. Cf.: "Analogy," 48.

sciousness and by simultaneously subjecting him to the process of human history."[453] God must be like us, for otherwise he will be "indistinguishable from nothingness."[454] Only a theology that is rooted in being (*esse*) rather than in human "existence" can affirm the reality of a God who, as pure *esse*, is in no way like our limited sort of existence (though our limited existence is nonetheless like him).[455]

In process theology, there is again a tendency to try to contain God within the limits of human concepts.[456] The divine essence, as Charles Hartshorne explains, is "philosophically explicable and knowable."[457] Since God is knowable, the *via negationis* must be denounced as "scandalously illogical and arbitrary," for it interferes with "the consistent use of the way of eminence."[458] When the way of eminence is used consistently, no categories (such as passion or corporeality) are excluded from God as "unfitting."[459] Rather, all creaturely attributes are predicated eminently of God until God becomes the sort of giant creature that process philosophy considers him to be—a creature that is "eminently" mutable, passive, relative, composite, and so on.[460] When God is understood in this way, he is of course "philosophi-

---

453. Reichmann, "Immanently," 363–64.

454. "Analogy in an existentialist climate . . . means conceiving God as taking time within himself; otherwise he is indistinguishable from nothingness" (W. Hill, review of *God-Talk: An Examination of the Language and Logic of Theology*, by John Macquarrie, *Thomist* 32 [1968]: 125).

455. Ibid., and "Seeking," 236. See also W. Norris Clarke, "What Is Most and Least Relevant in the Metaphysics of St. Thomas Today?" *IPQ* 14 (1974): 417, 432.

456. Alfred North Whitehead, for instance, sees philosophy as "the endeavor to frame a coherent, logical, necessary system of general ideas in terms of which every element of our experience can be interpreted" (*Process and Reality*, 3). As Eric Mascall notices, in *Process and Reality* Whitehead "is not really concerned with *explanation* at all, but rather with logical arrangement. . . . His final ambition is to make everything fit into a niche that he has provided for it" (*The Openness of Being: Natural Theology Today* [London: Darton, Longman, and Todd, 1971], 170). The same tendency is evident in Hartshorne, *Divine*, xv–xvi. For critiques of these views, see Mahoney, *Charles*, 25–26, 120–24; John Wild, review of *The Divine Relativity*, by Charles Hartshorne, *Review of Metaphysics* 2 (1948): 71–72; "The Divine Existence: An Answer to Mr. Hartshorne," *Review of Metaphysics* 4 (1950): 63–66, 68, 70, 81; David Schindler, "Creativity as Ultimate: Reflections on Actuality in Whitehead, Aristotle, and Aquinas," *IPQ* 13 (1973): 161–71; "Whitehead's Challenge to Thomism on the Problem of God: The Metaphysical Issues," *IPQ* 19 (1979): 285–300; James Keller, "Basic Differences between Classical and Process Metaphysics and Their Implications for the Concept of God," *IPQ* 22 (1982): 3–20.

457. Hartshorne, *Divine*, xiii; "Redefining God," *New Humanist* 7, no. 4 (July, 1934): 13; "Two Levels of Faith and Reason," *Journal of Bible and Religion* 16 (1948): 32–33, 35.

458. Hartshorne, *Divine*, 78. Cf.: 34–36, 120.

459. Hartshorne, "Theological," 166.

460. Hartshorne, *Divine*, 120. Lewis Ford likewise praises the "rigors of univocal predication of

cally knowable"—perhaps too knowable, as John Wild muses: "One thing
that rather worries me about the surrelative deity is the fact that Mr. Hartshorne seems to be able to understand him so well."[461] Knowable perhaps,
but no longer the transcendent God whose dynamic "is" (*esse*) surpasses our
limited human understanding, and no longer the immanent God who, as the
cause of being in creatures, "is in all things and innermostly."[462] That God is
an inevitable casualty in a philosophy that substitutes becoming for being:

> God has died in the minds of many of our contemporary philosophers, one might
> suggest, because these same philosophers have made a concerted effort to substitute
> process or becoming for being. The modern experiment, begun by Descartes, devel-
> oped by Locke and Hume, and brought to maturity by Kant and Hegel, has seemingly
> run its predictable course, and now finds itself wandering in alien terrain quite in-
> hospitable to the theistic turn. Process philosophers, in announcing the death of the
> philosophy of being, now seem expressly aware that this announcement presages the
> death of God as well.[463]

An Unmoving God

All names we say of God designate the One who calls himself "He who
is" (Ex 3:14). This name indicates God's boundless perfection as dynamic "is"
(*esse*) itself.[464] Because God is "is" (*esse*) itself, he lies completely beyond our
powers of thought. We cannot know what God is, only what he is not. Since
God's being (*esse*) surpasses all other beings and all human knowledge, it is
best signified by those names that designate it precisely as exceeding all else
that is and all we can think.

Although both motion and immutability may be predicated of God, immutability seems to signify divine being (*esse*) more appropriately since it

---

metaphysical properties both to God and the world" in "Thomas Aquinas and Contemporary Philosophical Options," *Listening* 14 (1979): 246. John Wild indicates the image of God to which Hartshorne's
theology leads: "The picture he leaves in one's mind is that of a finite being, something very much like
a man on a vastly magnified scale, hemmed in by external obstructions and necessities, and struggling
with heroic intensity for an unattainable and non-existent goal" ("Existence," 78).

461. Wild, "Existence," 70.

462. *ST* I, 8, 1, co.

463. Reichmann, "Aquinas," 427. Cf.: Leo Scheffczyk, "Prozesstheismus und christlicher Gottesglaube," *Münchener theologische Zeitschrift* 35 (1984): 103.

464. *ST* I, 13, 11.

more clearly indicates its distinction from all other things and its transcendence of all human thought and language. Immutability implies distinction from creatures since all creatures are subject to motion and limited by potency. In all of them, essence is a principle of potency with respect to existence (*esse*), and in all that are corporeal, matter is again a principle of potency and change with respect to form. Immutability also indicates God's transcendence of human knowledge. Since all we know of being is derived from changeable creatures, we cannot comprehend the absolutely unchangeable. Consequently, we designate it most appropriately when we speak negatively, denying of it all the limited and changeable modes of being familiar to us. This use of the *via negationis* keeps us from imprisoning God within the confines of our conceptual understanding.[465] So we guard God's transcendence from our all-too-human tendency of thinking we know more than we do.[466] By predicating immutability of God, we admit the surpassing perfection of divine *esse* and the inherent limitations of our knowledge.

In our time, there are many philosophers and theologians who tend to think in one way or another that reality should somehow conform to their particular concepts. They do not acknowledge that reality is in fact greater than our concepts and that our ideas should, within the limits possible to them, conform to it.[467] Given these contemporary tendencies, it is much more appropriate *quoad nos* that we continue to affirm the immutability of God and so admit both the limits of human knowledge and the transcendence of God.[468]

The confession of divine immutability also safeguards God's sovereign freedom in theological discussions. Far from inclining us to place limits on God's freedom, it rather invites us to acknowledge our own limits as we profess a truth beyond the bounds of human understanding. Only by mistaking divine immutability for the creaturely brand could we be guiled into think-

465. "What is apt to be forgotten is that 'immutability' is only a negative designation of a perfection that lies beyond our positive conceptualizing powers" (Hill, *Knowing*, 268n58).

466. "There are some who have such a presumptuous opinion of their own ability that they deem themselves able to measure the nature of everything" (*SCG* I, c.5.4 [§31]).

467. See Jacques Maritain, *Réflexions sur l'intelligence et sur sa vie propre* (Paris: Desclée de Brouwer, 1930), 27–28.

468. See Anthony Kelly, "God: How Near a Relation?" *Thomist* 34 (1970): 215–16.

ing we really understood God's changelessness and, on the basis of that supposed understanding, attempt to "tell God" what he can and cannot do. But
this kind of mistake, as we have seen, is most likely to occur in a philosophy
where human concepts or human existence is somehow taken as the measure of reality. A philosophy of this sort (or a theology based on it) will often
tell God not only what he can and cannot do, but also what he can and cannot be—all based upon the particular concepts of the individual philosopher
or theologian. One of the first things such a philosophy or theology often
tells God that he must be is changeable. By predicating immutability of God,
we guard ourselves against just these tendencies by implicitly acknowledg-
ing our human limitations.

The true appropriateness of predicating immutability of God, however,
is seen not in what it guards us from, but in what it leads us to: the surpassing perfection of God as subsistent *esse*. The true significance of divine immutability in Aquinas's theology consists not in asserting the invariable self-
identity of God but in affirming the dynamic and boundless perfection of
God as *ipsum esse subsistens*.[469] But it is precisely the immutable God who enjoys this unbounded actuality:

When being is said to be proper to God, we are not to understand that there is no
other act of being than the uncreated one, but only that that act of being is properly
said to be, inasmuch as by reason of its immutability, it admits of no *has been* or *will
be*. But the act of being of the creature is said to be by a certain likeness to that first
being although it has in it an admixture of *will be* or *has been* by reason of the mutability of the creature.[470]

Far from implying, therefore, that God is somehow static or inert, immutability directly signifies that God, as subsistent *esse*, is pure dynamic actuality.[471] And while we may still rightly predicate motion of God in virtue of his

---

469. *ST* I, 4, 2, ad 3.

470. "Cum dicitur: esse est proprium Deo; non est intelligendum quod nullum aliud esse sit nisi
increatum; sed quod solum illud esse proprie dicitur esse, in quantum ratione suae immutabilitatis non
novit fuisse vel futurum esse. Esse autem creaturae dicitur esse per quamdam similitudinem ad illud primum esse, cum habeat permixtionem eius quod est futurum esse vel fuisse, ratione mutabilitatis creaturae" (*De ver.* Q.21, 4, ad 7).

471. A number of contemporary theologians misrepresent pure act by taking it to imply a static
condition, for example: Norman Pittenger, *Catholic Faith in a Process Perspective* (Maryknoll, N.Y.: Orbis,

immanent activity of knowing and willing and in virtue of his causative act
of creation and providence, we best designate the dynamic actuality of God
who exercises or, better, *is* this act when we speak not of a changing God,
who would possess only the limited actuality of a creature, but of the immutable God who is the boundless actuality of subsistent *esse* itself.[472]

1981), 77; Shubert M. Ogden, *The Reality of God and Other Essays* (New York: Harper and Row, 1966), 17–
18; Lee, *Suffering*, 112–13. For a correct understanding of the dynamic perfection of pure act in relation to
divine immutability, see Brito, "Dieu," 112–13; Barry Miller, *A Most Unlikely God: A Philosophical Enquiry into
the Nature of God* (Notre Dame, Ind.: University of Notre Dame Press, 1996), 164; Jean-Hervé Nicolas,
"L'acte pur de saint Thomas et le Dieu vivant de l'évangile," *Angelicum* 51 (1974): 531; Hill, *Knowing*, 191;
"The Historicity of God," *Theological Studies* 45 (1984): 328; Illtyd Trethowan, "God's Changelessness,"
Clergy Review 64 (1979): 19; John Wright, "The Method of Process Theology: An Evaluation," *Communio*
6 (1979): 51; Owens, "Immobility," 221.

472. See Thomas Weinandy, "Aquinas and the Incarnational Act: 'Become' as a Mixed Relation,"
Doctor Communis 22 (1979): 16; William Hill, *The Three-Personed God* (Washington, D.C.: The Catholic
University of America Press, 1982), 260; *Knowing*, 191; "Does the World Make a Difference to God?"
Thomist 38 (1974): 156.

CHAPTER THREE

The Motion of the Motionless God

✵

Can we attribute motion to God? Aquinas gives his answer in the *Commentary on Dionysius's On the Divine Names:* "Not only do theologians attribute motion to God, but it is also granted us that we may fittingly praise the motion of the immovable God."[1] He finds two fundamental ways for predicating motion of God:

There are two sorts of operation, as Aristotle teaches in *Metaphysics:* one that remains in the agent and is a perfection of it, as the acts of sensing, understanding, and willing; another that passes over into an external thing, and is a perfection of the thing made as a result of that operation, the acts of heating, cutting and building, for example. Now both kinds of operation belong to God: the former, in that he understands, wills, rejoices, and loves; the latter, in that he brings things into being, preserves them, and governs them.[2]

The first sort of divine motion leads us into the mystery of the Trinity, God's triune life of wisdom and love.[3] The second directs us to God's providential action in the world. Our discussion of divine motion will concern the dynamic life of the unchanging God and his steadfast love for the creatures he has made and redeemed.

---

1. *In de div. nom.* IX. lect. 4 (§841).
2. *SCG* II, c.1.2–3 (§853–54). Cf.: *De pot.* Q.10, 1, co.
3. *De pot.* Q.10, 1, co.

TRINITY

Aquinas uses the immanent motions of knowing and willing to pene-
trate the mystery of God's triune life. These actions do not imply imperfection, but the highest perfection in being.[4] He compares the procession of the
Son (the Word) from the Father to the procession of the mental word in the
immanent action of knowing. As the procession of the mental word in itself
implies neither potency nor transient motion, neither does the procession
of the Son.[5] As the word proceeds from, yet remains in, the knower, the Son
proceeds from, yet remains in, the Father.[6] As the intellect, "by its very act of
understanding is made one with the object understood," the Son is one with
the Father.[7] The procession of the Holy Spirit is compared to the immanent
motion of love. As love implies an "impulse toward an object," the action of
the Holy Spirit suggests a similar vitality.[8]

The difference between the immanent motions of knowing and willing
allows us to distinguish the processions of Son and Holy Spirit. In the activity of knowing, "the object understood is in the intellect according to its likeness." In the act of willing, however, the one loved is in the will not through a
likeness but as a "certain inclination" of the will toward the beloved.[9] As the
"concept of the intellect is a likeness of the object conceived," the Son is the
likeness of the Father, and his procession may be called "generation" since
generation implies a similitude of parent and offspring.[10] Because the procession of the will is not by similitude, it is not called generation. It is rather
a procession by way of inclination, "by way of impelling and moving toward
something." In the Trinity, therefore, the divine person who proceeds by way
of love is called spirit: "Therefore what proceeds in God by way of love does
not proceed as begotten (*genitum*) or as son, but proceeds rather as spirit;
which name expresses a certain vital movement and impulse (*quaedam vitalis*

4. *SCG* I, c.97.3 (§813); *ST* I, 18, 3; *De pot.* Q.10, 1, co.

5. *SCG* IV, c.14.2 (§3498); *Sent.* I, 13, 1, 1, ad 1; *ST* I, 27, 1, ad 1.

6. *ST* I, 42, 5, co.; *Sent.* I, 5, 3, *exp. text* (ITOO: line 100 c.); *Cat. aur. in joann.* XIV, lect. 3 (ITOO: lines 99–104).

7. *ST* I, 27, 1, ad 2.   8. *ST* I, 27, 4.

9. *ST* I, 27, 4, co.

10. *ST* I, 27, 2, co.; Q.41, 3, ad 4; *Sent.* I, 4, 1, 1, ad 1; *SCG* IV, c.3.16 (§3436); c.10.2 (§3447); c.14.2 (§3498).

motio et impulsio), according as anyone is said to be moved or impelled by love to perform some action."[11]

Viewed in terms of immanent motion, the three divine persons are not a static triad but a dynamic life, a never-ceasing yet ever-unchanging activity of knowledge and love. The Trinity involves the perfect reflection of the divine knowledge of the Father in the procession of the Son, the impulse of divine love of Father and Son in the procession of the Spirit, and the complete and continuous self-communication and interpenetration of Father, Son and Spirit.[12] The Christian God proclaimed by Aquinas is no stagnant, solitary self-contemplator, but a most blessed Trinity of unbounded wisdom, love, and life.[13]

CREATION

The Father, Son, and Holy Spirit freely will to communicate their being and life with creatures in the works of creation, redemption, and sanctification. Aquinas is careful to show the Trinitarian character of these works by linking them to the Trinitarian life of God.[14] He employs the idea of transient motion to maintain divine immutability while affirming the most intimate involvement of the Trinity in creation.[15]

11. *ST* I, 27, 4, co. Cf.: *SCG* IV, c.19.10 (§3566).

12. *ST* I, 42, 5.

13. Thomas remarks that to deny the processions of the Trinity in God is to render God "lifeless (*mortuus*)" and "without intellect (*sine mente*)" (*De pot.* Q.10, 1, co.). See John J. O'Donnell, *The Mystery of the Triune God* (London: Sheed and Ward, 1988), 168, 170.

14. Aquinas is sometimes accused of divorcing God's action in human history (economic Trinity) from God's inner life (immanent Trinity). See, for example, Karl Rahner, *The Trinity* (New York: Crossroad, 1997), 16–17; Catherine Mowry LaCugna, *God for Us: The Trinity and Christian Life* (San Francisco: Harper, 1992), 145–69. A careful reading of his theology, however, reveals how closely he links the immanent life of the Trinity with the creative and redemptive actions of the divine persons in the economy of salvation. See *ST* I, 32, 1, ad 3; 33, 3 ad 1; 34, 3; 37, 2 ad 3; 43, 7 ad 3; 45, 6. See Gilles Emery, *La Trinité creatrice: Trinité et création dans les commentaires aux Sentences de Thomas d'Aquin et de ses precurseurs Albert le Grand et Bonaventure* (Paris: J. Vrin, 1995); *Trinity in Aquinas* (Ypsilanti, Mich.: Sapientia Press, 2003); David B. Burrell, "Act of Creation with Its Theological Consequences," in *Aquinas on Doctrine: A Critical Introduction*, ed. Thomas Weinandy et al. (London: T and T Clark, 2004), 27–44; Wayne Hankey, "Aquinas and the Passion of God," in *Being and Truth: Essays in Honour of John Macquarrie*, ed. A. Kee and E. Long (London: SCM Press, 1986), 320.

15. In this he is unlike contemporary theologians who maintain that God's Trinitarian involvement in history must imply temporality or change in God. Roland Faber argues, for instance: "The God who

While immanent motion remains in the agent and is the perfection of the agent, transient motion passes in some way from a doer to a receiver.[16] As the act of the receiver, it is the act of a being in potency and implies imperfection. As the act of the doer, however, it is the act of a being in act and does not necessarily imply imperfection.[17] In this sense, it may be said of God. In predicating transient motion of God, Aquinas is speaking neither metaphorically (*metaphorice*) nor properly (*proprie*), but by a certain similitude (*similitudinarie*).[18]

Transient motion is applied to God in two ways. First, it is predicated of him insofar as he "brings things into being, preserves them, and governs them."[19] Thomas affirms with Dionysius that in virtue of such activity, "God is said to be moved (*moveri*)" and "to proceed toward all things." He also "remains in himself (*manet in seipso*)" since this motion implies no change or potency in him. He is described as "standing immutably (*stans*) insofar as he is not changed" and as "moved (*motus*) in that he imparts his similitude to others." In this sense Thomas speaks of God's "productive stillness (*statum generativum*)" and "stable procession (*processus stabilis*)."[20]

Transient motion is also predicated of God in the sending of a divine person to be present to creatures in a new way. This occurs in the missions of the Son and of the Holy Spirit. The Son is sent in the "visible mission" of the In-

---

shows himself trinitarian in historical action must (as always) be a historical God in himself. His being is communicated in a trinitarian way in that it is historically communicated" (*Der Selbsteinsatz Gottes: Grundlegung einer Theologie des Leidens und der Veränderlichkeit Gottes* [Würzburg: Echter Verlag, 1995], 252). Norbert Hoffman contends: "[I]n the mission of the Son and of the Spirit, God does not stand in a relation of 'Olympian' detachment from the world and the world's evil, but in a relation of unheard-of intimacy. If one avoids this . . . out of excessive respect for a notion of God that is more Greek than authentically Christian, and out of excessive respect for an understanding of the axiom of unchangeability and a-patheia derived from this Greek notion, one risks depriving the *specificum christianum* of its effective reality in the *oikonomia* and closing it in an inner sanctum of *theologia* wrongly understood as a simple beyond" ("The Crucified Christ and the World's Evil: Reflections on Theodicy in the Light of Atonement," *Communio* 17 (1990): 56.

16. *De pot.* Q.10, 1, co.

17. In creatures, transient motion always implies some imperfection, even when it is considered as the act of the agent. For through its motion, the creature is always in some way changed and perfected. See *Sent.* I, 13, 1, 1, ad 1; *SCG* IV, c.8.16 (§3436); *ST* I, 44, 4, co.

18. *ST* I, 9, 1, ad 2; ad 3.

19. *SCG* II, c.1.3 (§854).

20. *In de div. nom.* V, lect. 3 (§672); IX, lect. 4 (§840–42); XI, lect. 2 (§895).

carnation. Both Son and Spirit are sent invisibly in the divine indwelling of grace.[21] Aquinas uses transient motion as an analogy for these missions, but is careful to explain they imply change not in God, but only in the creature.[22]

Creation and Intimacy

In the act of creation, God wills to share his being and goodness with the creatures he makes.[23] Though this act exceeds our understanding, we can think of it as a sort of transient motion since the transient motion of creatures is in some ways like it.[24] There are fundamental differences, however, between how a natural agent is related to its effects and how God is related to creatures.

The notion of relation is a complex topic we cannot discuss in detail here.[25] For our purposes, it is sufficient to know that a relation always involves two terms or extremes and consists in a reference of one to the other.[26] There are three fundamental kinds of relation. In one, the relation exists in idea only in both terms. An example is the relationship of identity, where a thing is said to be the same as itself. If I say, for instance, "a rose is a rose," I take one object and treat it as two (as subject and predicate) and affirm that the two are identical. Since the rose is really one, the two terms and their relationship exist only in my mind. The relation is of reason only in both terms. Another kind of relation really exists in each term. Relations of this sort, such as "great and small" or "double and half," are based on some reality, such as quantity or action and passion, that really belongs to both terms. These are called real relationships. Finally, a relation may be real in one term but of idea only in the other. This occurs when the two extremes do not belong to the same order. For instance, the relationship between human

21. *Sent.* I, 15, 1, 1, ad 1; ad 4; d.16, 1, 1, ad 1; *ST* I, 43, 1, co.; a.2, co.; a.3, co.; a.5, co.; *Contra. err. graec.* I, c.14; *SCG* IV, c. 23.4 (§3594).

22. *ST* I, 43, 2, ad 2; *Sent.* I, 14, 1, 1, ad 2; 15, 4, 1, co.

23. *ST* I, 19, 4.

24. *ST* I, 14, 1, *prologus*; Q.45, 2, ad 2; *De pot.* Q.3, 2, co.

25. For an extensive study of the subject of relation, see A. Krempel, *La doctrine de la relation chez saint Thomas* (Paris: J. Vrin, 1952). See also Michael J. Dodds, "Ultimacy and Intimacy: Aquinas on the Relation between God and the World," in *Ordo Sapientiae et Amoris: Hommage au Professeur Jean-Pierre Torrell, O.P.,* ed. Carlos-Josaphat Pinto de Oliveira (Fribourg, Suisse: Editions Universitaires, 1993), 211–27.

26. *ST* I, 13, 7; Q.32, 2; *Sent.* I, 2, 1, 5. Cf.: Krempel, *Doctrine,* 39–53.

knowledge and the object known is real with respect to knowledge, since it arises from and truly depends on that object. But the object, as a reality existing in nature outside the intentional order, does not depend in any way on the knower and has no real relation to knowledge.[27] Our knowledge depends on the object, but the object in no way depends on our knowledge. Its relation to knowledge is therefore in idea only, insofar as the intellect apprehends it as the term of the relationship of knowledge. It has become customary to call relationships of this sort "mixed relations."[28]

Among creaturely agents, there is a real relation between cause and effect. The transient causal motion produced by a creaturely agent is an act distinct from the form of the agent. It is called a "second act" or "second perfection" of the agent in distinction from the agent's form or "first perfection." Through this action, the agent in some way imparts actuality to its effect and so produces some likeness of itself. The action of the agent, understood as passing from the agent to the effect, is seen as a sort of "intermediate action (actio media)" belonging to both the agent that causes it and the effect that receives it.[29] When the gas flame heats the frying pan, for instance, the act of heating belongs to both the flame as agent and the pan as receiver. By reason of this common act, the agent and its effect belong in some way to the same order—at least with respect to the particular action that belongs to both. Since the created agent and its effect are two distinct realities belonging to the same order, there can be a real relationship between them.[30]

God's creative action is in some ways similar to the transient action of the created agent since God imparts a share in his goodness and actuality to the creature. But while the act of the created agent is distinct from its form, the divine act is the divine substance itself.[31] For this reason, the divine cre-

27. ST I, 13, 7, co.

28. The three sorts of relation are explained in ST I, 13, 7, co., and Sent. I, 30, 1, 3, ad 3. For Aquinas's own terminology for "mixed relations," see In meta. X, lect. 8.13–14 (§2087–88) and Krempel, Doctrine, 458.

29. De pot. Q.7, 10, co. Thomas is speaking here according to the order of substantial change and so refers to the form as the first perfection of the substance. This presupposes the order of existence, where the ultimate act or perfection of the substance—that which is "formal" with respect to everything else— is the act of existence (esse). See De pot. Q.7, 2, ad 9.

30. De pot. Q.7, 10, co.; ad 1.

31. SCG II, c.9.4 (§901). Because the divine essence is the divine intellect and will, in acting by essence God acts by intellect and will. ST I, 19, 2, ad 1; a.4, ad 2.

ative act, unlike that of the created agent (which is in some way common to agent and effect), is in no way common to God and creatures. It is of an entirely different order from that of created being since God, as we have seen, "is above being (*ens*) insofar as he is infinite to-be itself (*ipsum esse infinitum*)."[32]

Since the creative act is in no way common to God and creatures, there is no common order of motion between them. For this reason the relationship between them, unlike the relationship between a natural agent and its effect, cannot be a real relationship with respect to both extremes. It is real in the creature (which really depends upon God as the cause of its being) and a relation of reason only in God (who is not of the same order as the creature).[33] In the creature, creation signifies a real relationship to God as the principle of its existence.[34] In God, it signifies the divine action that is God's substance along with a relationship of reason to the creature.[35]

The terms "real relation" and "relation of reason" may be easily misunderstood. According to William Hill, "Few tenets of classical Theism have been perhaps as commonly misunderstood as that which maintains that God is unchanged by his acting upon the world; that he bears no real relation to that world. This is frequently misread to mean that God is at an ontological remove from and without concern for the world he sustains in existence."[36] Some philosophers, such as Charles Hartshorne, believe that if God is "wholly absolute," without real relations to creatures, it would follow "that God does not know or love or will us, his creatures."[37] To avoid such misunderstandings, it is important to comprehend correctly what is and is not meant in saying God has no real relation to creatures. As Brian Shanley explains:

---

32. *Super de causis* Prop. 6 (Saffrey, p. 47, lines 8–12), cf: *Sent.* I, 7, 1, 1, ad 3.

33. *De pot.* Q.7, 10, co.; *De sp. cr.* a.4, ad 6; *Sent.* I, 30, 1, 3, ad 3.

34. *ST* I, 45, 3, co.

35. *ST* I, 45, 3, ad 1; *De pot.* Q.3, 3, co.; ad 2; Q.7, 9; *Sent.* I, 30, 1, 3, co.

36. Hill, *Knowing*, 177.

37. Hartshorne, *Divine*, 16. Similar views may be found in Burton Z. Cooper, *The Idea of God: A Whiteheadian Critique of St. Thomas Aquinas's Concept of God* (The Hague: M. Nijhoff, 1974), 35–36; Michael, *Comparison*, 189; Walter Stokes, "Is God Really Related to This World?" *PACPA* 39 (1965): 145–51; "God for Today and Tomorrow," *NS* 43 (1969): 351–78. Critiques of such views may be found in John Knasas, "Aquinas and Finite Gods," *PACPA* 53 (1979): 90.

Aquinas clearly thinks that God is "related" to the world in the sense that he creates, loves, knows, wills, governs, and redeems the world. The denial that God is "really related" to the world does not undermine any of those claims. It simply denies that God's causal activity, and any relational terms thereby ascribed to him, implies any alteration in his being. When God acts so as to bring creatures into relationship with him, all of the "happening" is located in creation rather than in God.[38]

When we say God has no real relation to creatures, we do not imply that he is remote or that there is no relationship at all between him and creatures. We rather designate the special kind of relation that exists between God and creatures, which allows both for God's complete distinction from creation and for the utter intimacy of his presence to each creature as the source of its very to-be (*esse*). In creating, God acts in virtue of no other act than his own substance. Because this act, unlike the act involved in the transient motion of the created agent, is in no way common to agent and effect, it establishes no common order between creator and creature. Since there is no common order between them, there can be no mutually real relation. Rather, the relation is real in the creature, but of reason only in God.

There is a relation between God and creature, and it is precisely the sort of relation proper to beings that are not of the same order. We may call it a "mixed relation." It is the sort of relation that exists "whenever two things are related to each other in such a way that one depends upon the other, but the other does not depend upon it." In the dependent member, the relation is real, but "in the independent member, the relation is merely one of reason—

---

38. Shanley, *Thomist*, 59. Cf.: William Hill, "The Implicate World: God's Oneness with Mankind as a Mediated Immediacy," in *Beyond Mechanism: The Universe in Recent Physics and Catholic Thought*, ed. David L. Schindler (Lanham, Md.: University Press of America, 1986), 87. A number of theologians, recognizing the difficulties implicit in the traditional terminology, have offered clarifications or possible alternatives. See Earl Muller, "Real Relations and the Divine: Issues in Thomas's Understanding of God's Relation to the World," *Theological Studies* 56 (1995) 673–95; Catherine LaCugna, "The Relational God: Aquinas and Beyond," *Theological Studies* 46 (1985): 661; Anthony Kelly, "Trinity and Process: Relevance of the Basic Christian Confession of God," *Theological Studies* 31 (1970): 412–13. Some argue that the term "real" should be affirmed in some way in describing God's relation to creatures. See John Wright, "Divine Knowledge and Human Freedcm: The God Who Dialogues," *Theological Studies* 38 (1977) 460; Hill, *Knowing*, 179; "Does the World," 163; "Historicity," 331–32; Stokes, "Really," 149; Clarke, "New," 59; "Relevant," 433; "Christian Theism and Whiteheadian Process Philosophy: Are they Compatible?" in W. Norris Clarke, *The Philosophical Approach to God*, ed. William E. Ray (Winston-Salem, N.C.: Wake Forest University Press, 1979), 90–91.

simply because one thing cannot be understood as being related to another without that other being understood as being related to it."[39] Because God is the highest cause, the cause of the very to-be (*esse*) of the creature, this sort of relationship pertains most especially to him.[40]

In virtue of this relation we name God as "Creator" and "Lord."[41] Names of this sort signify something not merely with respect to our way of thinking about God, but in regard to the very reality of God and creatures.[42] In predicating such names, we recognize that God truly is the cause of creatures, that he transcends all created being, and that creatures are really related to him as the source of their being.

As the source of created being, God is most intimately present to each thing. His presence is far more intimate than what is possible between the terms of a mutually real relation among creatures. In a mutually real relation of cause and effect, the created agent is related to the effect through the medium of the motion that it produces and that is distinct from its essence. God, however, as the cause of *esse* in creatures, is present to each one by his very essence.[43] And because *esse* is the innermost actuality of the creature, God is most intimately present to each thing.[44]

For these reasons, we come to the seemingly paradoxical affirmation that God can be most intimately present to all creatures only if he has no real relationship with any of them. For he is much more intimately involved with each of them than would be possible in a real relationship of transient causal motion.[45] His creative act may be likened to the transient motion of crea-

39. *De ver.* Q.4, 5, co.

40. *De pot.* Q.7, 8, co. Cf.: *SCG* I, c.11–12; *De ver.* Q.4, 5, co.

41. *ST* I, 13, 7, ad 2; *SCG* II, c.12.5 (§916). It is also in terms of this sort of relationship that God is said to "become our refuge" (*ST* I, 13, 7, ad 2; *De pot.* Q.7, 8, ad 5). Thomas points out that while "to become (*fieri*)" may be applied to God in reason but not in reality, "change (*mutatio*)" may be said of God neither in reason nor in reality (*Sent.* I, 30, 1, 1, ad 1; III, 7, 2, 1, ad 1).

42. The reality that these names signify directly is not the divine essence (*SCG* II, c.12.2 [§913]; c.13.5 [§920]). They signify rather the reality of the relation of the creature to God who is truly the cause of the being of the creature and who is thus called "Creator" and "Lord" not in idea only, but in reality. *ST* I, 13, 7, ad 5; *De pot.* Q.7, a.11, ad 3. Cf.: Hill, "Does the World," 154; Weinandy, "Aquinas," 25, 28.

43. *ST* I, 8, 3, ad 1.

44. *ST* I, 8, 1, co.

45. We remain, for the moment, with the intimacy possible between cause and effect since we are concerned with the causality of the creator, conceived as quasi-transient motion. We will see below that

tures, but in reality it occurs "without motion (*sine motu*)."[46] For the act by which the creature receives its very existence (*esse*) from God is infinitely more dynamic than any act of motion.[47] In virtue of this act, it may be said that the unchanging God, who alone in his supreme transcendence and total immanence is capable of such an act, "proceeds causatively toward all things" and "is placed outside himself by his providence for all existing things."[48]

Creation and Freedom

We understand creation as a free and gratuitous act of divine love. Can we affirm both God's freedom in creation and God's immutability in being? This double affirmation may seem problematic for two reasons. First, the very notion of freedom may seem to imply changeability of will. What is freedom if not, minimally, the ability to change one's mind? Second, the notion of creation may appear to imply some change in God. If God's will is the cause of creatures, how could there first be no creatures and then existing creatures except through a change in that will?

Immutability as Contradiction to Creative Freedom

The Creative Act Does the freedom of the divine creative act require that God's will be changeable? If creation is a free act, God can either will it or not. Must not God's will therefore be changeable, since whatever is able "to

---

God's loving, personal intimacy with creatures also infinitely surpasses the intimacy possible between creatures. See Dodds, "Ultimacy," 225–26; Weinandy, "Aquinas," 26–27; Mascall, *Openness*, 168.

46. "Unde Deus, creando, producit res sine motu" (*ST* I, 45, 3, co.). Cf.: I, 45, 2, ad 2; ad 3; *Sent.* I, 7, 1, 1, ad 3; *De pot.* Q.3, 2, co. As Brian Davies explains, "If we think of God as Creator of the universe, we have no option but to think of him as unchanging" (*Thinking about God* [London: Geoffrey Chapman, 1985], 163). Also see his article "The Action of God," 76–84.

47. "The great paradox here is that what appears at first hearing to be a philosophical theology of static immobility, turns out in the end to be the only view that guarantees the dynamism essential to the authentically creative act. Such a view has been made possible by Aquinas's dynamic vision of *esse*" (Reichmann, "Aquinas," 434). Cf.: Weinandy, "Aquinas," 25–27. Here we can see also the error in William Lane Craig's argument that the causality involved in sustaining the world must involve a real relationship of God to the creature. He fails to see that the causality of creation, the imparting of *esse*, is possible only if the cause is of a wholly other order than the effect and so has no real relation to the effect, while the effect is really related to the cause. See William Lane Craig, *Time and Eternity: Exploring God's Relationship to Time* (Wheaton, Ill.: Crossway Books, 2001), 88–89.

48. "[P]rocedit ad omnia causative" (*In de div. nom.* V, lect. 3 (§672); "extra seipsum fit ad omnia existentia providentiis" (*ST* I, 20, 2, ad 1).

incline to either of two opposites is mutable"[49] and since God can do other things than what he does?[50] Our freedom involves change anytime we stop willing one thing and begin to will another. Is this also the case with God? To answer these questions, we must first ask why the human will is changeable.

Aquinas thinks that since our will is directed to the good, there are two reasons it might change. First, something might become good for us through some change in our disposition (as medicine is good if we get sick). Second, we might realize something is good for us through some change in our knowledge (as we might learn the benefits of high-fiber foods). Since God is unchanging in both disposition (substance) and knowledge, his will must be unchangeable: "The substance of God and his knowledge are entirely unchangeable (*omnino immutabilis*). Therefore his will must be entirely unchangeable (*omnino immutabilem*)."[51]

Among human beings, an "unchangeable" will is not necessarily a good thing. It might signify the virtue of steadfastness but could also indicate the vices of stubbornness or indifference. We must be careful not to project the ambiguities of our will onto God. Our changeable will, though suited to our nature, is a sign of our limited mode of being and knowing. God's unchanging will is a sign not of imperfection, but of unbounded perfection. In one abiding act of wisdom and love, God freely and eternally wills to share his abundant goodness with creatures. Aquinas believes this is a gift God does not revoke since whatever God freely wills, he wills eternally and unchangeably.[52]

God's freedom regarding creation has given rise to a good deal of speculation about what God "might do" or "might have done" in the created realm. Some contemporary theologians have concluded that since God chose to create this world rather than some other, he must now be "different" from what he "might have been" had he chosen otherwise. But if choice entails a

49. *ST* I, 19, 7, obj.4. Cf.: Q.19, 3, obj.4.
50. *ST* I, 25, 5, ad 3; a.6, ad 3; *SCG* III, c.98.3 (§2744); *De pot.* Q.1, 5, co.
51. *ST* I, 19, 7, co.
52. "Et quia eius voluntas immutabilis est, si ponitur aliquando eum aliquid velle, necessarium est ex suppositione illud eum semper velle" (*De pot.* Q.5, 4, co.). "Similiter autem, cum Deus sit omnino immutabilis, impossibile est quod aliquid velit cum prius noluerit" (*SCG* III, c.98.3 [§2743]). Cf.: *ST* I, 19, 3, co.; a.7, ad 4; *Sent.* I, 8, 3, 2, co.; *De ver.* Q.24, 3, ad 3; *SCG* I, 91.16 (§766).

difference in God, God must be changeable. To evaluate such arguments, we might begin with two questions. First, can God will things other than those he wills? Second, if God were to will other things, would he then be different from what he is presently?

The first question arises because God's creative will is not subject to absolute necessity. Since it is not necessary that God will this particular world or these particular creatures, is it possible for God to will other things? The question may be answered using Aquinas's distinction between absolute necessity (*necessitas absoluta*) and conditional necessity (*necessitas ex suppositione*). Absolute necessity concerns what belongs to the essence of a thing, as that a triangle have three sides or that God exist.[53] Conditional necessity involves what belongs to a thing when a certain supposition is made.[54] If we suppose that something exists, for instance, our supposition has a certain necessity since we cannot simultaneously suppose it does not exist. In this way, the necessity of supposition is directly related to the principle of non-contradiction and tells us that "everything which is, necessarily is when it is" since "it is impossible both to be and not be at the same time."[55]

Both absolute necessity and the necessity of supposition may be concerned either with the logical order (the necessity of propositions) or the ontological order (the necessity of actually existing things).[56] It is absolutely necessary logically that a triangle have three sides since this is part of its definition, and it is absolutely necessary ontologically that God exist since existence (*esse*) is his very nature. It is conditionally necessary logically that Socrates cannot not be sitting if we grant the suppositional premise that he is sitting. It is conditionally necessary ontologically that Socrates cannot not be sitting in those moments when he is in fact sitting.

Absolute necessity may be applied to God only with respect to those things that belong to his nature. So it is absolutely necessary that God will his own goodness, but not that he will the existence of creatures.[57] For the

53. *Sent.* I, 6, 1, 1, co.; IV, 7, 1, 1, qc.2, co.
54. *Sent.* I, 6, 1, 1, co.; IV, 7, 1, 1, qc.2, co.; *ST* III, 1, 2.
55. *In peri herm.* I, lect. 15.2.
56. On the logical and ontological application of the necessity of supposition, see the word "*necessitas*" in Schütz, *Thomas-Lexikon*, 520–22.
57. *Sent.* III, 20, 1, 1, qc.3, co.; *ST* I, 19, 3, co.

existence of creatures does not contribute to God's goodness and so is not required for willing his goodness. In creating, therefore, God "does not act from necessity of nature but from freedom of will."[58]

When we speak in terms of conditional necessity (the necessity of supposition), however, there is a sense in which God's willing the existence of creatures is necessary. For when we say God wills the existence of creatures, we cannot also say he does not will them since this would imply a contradiction. Insofar as an agent is willing one thing, he cannot also not be willing that same thing. Insofar as Socrates is freely willing to sit, for example, he cannot also not be willing to sit. He must (by necessity of supposition) be (freely) willing to sit. So we can say also that God, insofar as he freely wills to create this world, cannot also not be willing to create it. He must (by necessity of supposition) be (freely) willing to create it. This sort of necessity, unlike absolute necessity, does not remove or diminish freedom of will. If anything, it increases it.[59]

When we talk of conditional necessity with respect to the divine will, we must remember God's will is not like ours. We choose the end by one act of will and the means by another. (Socrates wants to be comfortable and so decides to sit down.) We can therefore speak of individual acts of the human will, each of which (by necessity of supposition) cannot not be when it is. In God, however, there is only one act of will—the act by which God wills his own goodness and which is his very essence. We therefore cannot speak of God's will to create as if it were a separate and discrete act (like Socrates's will to sit down).

In predicating conditional necessity of God, we do not pretend to understand his will. Rather, we intend to indicate that, in the order of logic, if we suppose that God wills the existence of creatures, our conclusion that God cannot also not will their creation is necessary by supposition. In the ontological order, we cannot speak of God's will to create as if it were an actuality other than God's essence. We can recognize, however, that it is not absolutely necessary that God's willing of his own goodness terminate in the exis-

---

58. *Sent.* III, 20, 1, 1, qc.3, co.

59. "The necessity which is from the supposition of the will as immutably willing something does not diminish the aspect of voluntariness, but rather increases it insofar as it is considered more firmly holding to the thing willed so that it may not be moved" (*Sent.* III, 20, 1, 1, qc.3, ad 2).

tence of creatures. And we can see that since creatures are actually brought into being by God's act of willing his own goodness, they cannot also not be brought into being. It is opposed to the very nature of being that a creature, as existing, also not exist, and God cannot will something to be which is "opposed to the very nature of being."[60] In this way, we know it is impossible that God, in willing the existence of a creature, also not will its existence. In willing one thing, God cannot (by necessity of supposition) also not will that thing, and whatever God wills he must always will since his will is immutable. Because the necessity of supposition as applied to the divine will is so closely tied to divine immutability, it is sometimes called the "necessity of immutability (*necessitas immutabilitatis*)."[61]

We can now consider our original question (whether God can will things other than those that he wills) in terms of absolute and conditional necessity. In terms of absolute necessity (the necessity of God's willing his own goodness), it is possible to say God can will other things than those he wills, that God could have created a different world from the one that he created, and so on, since no created reality is required for God's willing his own goodness. We can make such statements, however, only by abstracting from the reality of what God in fact wills. When we remain within the realm of reality, we realize that God wills *this* world and therefore cannot (by necessity of supposition and because of the immutability of his will) not will it.

Our second question was whether God would be different from what he is presently if he were to will other things than he does. Contemporary theologians answer this question in various ways. Some, wishing at all cost to defend the absolute immutability of God, respond with a resounding "No!": "The immutability of God means just what it seems to mean: that there is not and cannot be in God any kind of change whatever. God as creator is exactly the same as he would have been if he had freely chosen not to create."[62]

---

60. *SCG* I, c.84.3 (§708). Cf.: *ST* I, 7, 2, ad 1; Q.25, 4; *De pot.*. Q.1, 5, co. Here we are not so much putting "logical restrictions" on divine power as admitting that when we ourselves speak in violation of the principle of non-contradiction, we are not really saying anything at all. See *ST* I, 25, 3.

61. *Sent.* III, 20, 1, 1, qc.3, co. Cf.: *Sent.* I, 39, 1, 1, co.; *ST* I, 19, 3, co.; *SCG* I, c.83.2 (§702); *De ver.* Q.2, 13, co.; Q.23, 4, ad 1.

62. Thomas Gornall, *A Philosophy of God* (London: Darton, Longman, and Todd, 1962), 74. Joseph Rickaby also believes "we may faintly surmise" how "an almighty agent would act without being in the

This negative response seems to imply a contradiction. For how can God insofar as he is willing the world be precisely the same as God insofar as he is not willing the world, unless his willing the world is the same thing as his not willing the world? But if it is the same thing, then God, insofar as he is willing the world, may also be not willing the world. This, however, implies a direct contradiction and therefore cannot be admitted as possible.[63]

Other authors, recognizing the contradiction implied in such a negative answer, give a qualified affirmative response. In some way God would be different if he were willing other creatures from those he in fact wills: "Still, somehow or other God with a creation and God without it are not entirely the same thing, and it appears overly facile to dismiss this as exclusively on the side of the creature. There remains the possibility of intrinsic difference in God's knowing and loving; difference which need not bespeak any transmutation of his being."[64] A number of these authors then go on, sometimes by way of a clever grammatical turn of phrase, from allowing that God *might be different* from what he is (if he were willing other things) to asserting God *is in fact different* presently from what he might have been (had he willed other things). Thus it is argued that because God has willed and is willing this particular world, "there occurs a determination within God as knowing and loving, on which basis he is other, relatively speaking, than he would be had he determined himself in some other way."[65] One can then assert that there

---

least altered by his action from the being that he would have been, had he remained at rest" (*Of God and His Creatures* [London: Burns and Oates, 1905; reprint, Westminster, Md.: Carroll Press, 1950], 63).

63. "Thus the divine will which, considered in itself, can will something and its opposite, as to save Peter or not, cannot will not to save Peter while it wills to save Peter" (*De pot.* Q.5, 4, co.).

64. Hill, "Does the World," 157. "It would be ridiculous to suppose that 'God willing to create' and 'God not willing to create' are in all aspects identical" (Fernand Van Steenberghen, "Connaissance divine et liberté humaine," *Revue théologique de Louvain* 2 (1979): 61. Cf.: Wright, "Divine," 458.

65. Hill, "Does the World," 157. "Thus, God the creator is different from what he would have been had he chosen not to create; the difference is neither just a fiction of the human mind and a matter of extrinsic denomination nor is it an increase or modification of the divine reality in itself, but it is an objective difference in intentionality, in objectively intelligible relations" (Wright, "Divine," 458). "God as the one revealing himself is different and intends to be different than if he had not revealed himself" (Walter Simonis, "Über das 'Werden' Gottes: Gedanken zum Begriff der ökonomischen Trinität," *Münchener theologische Zeitschrift* 33 [1982]: 134). Walter Stokes argues that in loving this particular world, God is "other than he could have been" ("Really," 150). W. Norris Clarke affirms that "it makes a *distinct difference* in the divine consciousness whether He creates or not" ("Relevant," 433). See also Clarke, "Charles Hartshorne's Philosophy," 112; Hartshorne, *Divine*, 11–12.

is a real difference in God presently because of the fact that he has not willed anything other than what he wills. Once this assertion finds acceptance, there remains only the troublesome problem of finding some dimension of God's being in which this difference may be located without endangering either God's ontological immutability or his absolute simplicity.

Fernand Van Steenberghen argues that there must be a domain in God for his free initiatives that is distinct from, and that does not change, his eternal perfection.[66] William Norris Clarke locates the "actual difference" in "the order of the divine knowledge and love, which is the order of intentionality (*esse intentionale* as opposed to *esse naturale*, in St. Thomas's words)."[67] John Wright and William Hill agree with this suggestion.[68] These views received encouragement from Lewis Ford, though Ford himself later asked how Clarke could make such a sharp distinction between divine intentionality and divine being "without jeopardizing pure [divine] simplicity."[69] Theodore Kondoleon critiques these views, but also concedes, as Clarke notes, "that the consciousness of God would have to be *different*—though not thereby changing—because He decided to create this world rather than some other or none at all."[70] Clarke himself is willing to admit that a change in divine intentionality must constitute a change in divine being:

I think it closer to the truth to say that God's inner being is indeed affected by His "extroverted" life of consciousness with respect to creatures. In consequence I would have to qualify again, a little more precisely, the immutability of God. I think that one can certainly say, and should definitely say, at least this much: there is an *absolute* (non-relative) dimension of the divine being that is indeed affected but not in any *absolute* way, by His relations to His creatures because it is by nature prior to and independent of any particular creation. . . . This eternal inner plenitude of power and life is not affected in any *absolute* way by the relations to His creatures, but is affected

66. See Van Steenberghen, "Connaissance," 61–65.

67. Clarke, "Relevant," 433. Cf.: "New," 67–68.

68. Wright, "Divine," 458; Hill, "Does the World," 157; *Three*, 182, 211, 288; "Historicity," 332–33.

69. Lewis Ford, "The Immutable God and Father Clarke," *NS* 49 (1975): 189–99; "Process and Thomist Views concerning Divine Perfection," in *Universe as Journey: Conversations with W. Norris Clarke, S.J.*, ed. Gerald A. McCool (New York: Fordham, 1988), 118.

70. W. Norris Clarke, "Comment on Professor Ford's Paper," in *Universe as Journey: Conversations with W. Norris Clarke, S.J.*, ed. Gerald A. McCool (New York: Fordham, 1988), 160; Theodore Kondoleon, "The Immutability of God: Some Recent Challenges," *NS* 58 (1984): 293–315.

precisely in the relative way proper to extroverted consciousness, to personal being's relations to its *other*. So God's whole being, including His absolute being, is indeed affected by all of His conscious life (both knowledge and love), but in some respects both absolutely and relatively (i.e., the eternal inner perfection of His nature independent of creatures plus the eternal interpersonal relations between the three Divine Persons), in other respects absolutely and not relatively (i.e., the eternal inner perfection of the divine nature in itself), and in other respects relatively and not absolutely (i.e., His extroverted knowledge and love relations with creatures).[71]

Clarke then attempt to explain that "the absolute nature of God being affected relatively to His creatures" would not imply some "real accidental change in God, some real composition of substance and accident that would contradict the divine simplicity." He suggests that in "Aristotelian-Thomistic, real accidental change there is always a change in the *absolute* (non-relative) being of the substance or subject of change," but that in the "present case of the relation of the absolute being of God to His relations with respect to creatures, nothing new in the absolute order is added or affected in the inner being of God" since what God knows with respect to creatures "neither augments nor raises to a higher absolute level the absolute perfection already there" in God. "In a word, there is a relative enrichment, if you will, but not an absolute one." But how a relative enrichment is possible in an absolutely simple being he does not explain. He does comment, "If this brings me somewhat closer to Whitehead's own distinction between the primordial and the consequent nature of God, reinterpreted as absolute and relative, so much the better."[72]

Rather than try to find some dimension in the absolute simplicity of God in which to locate a "real difference" in God resulting from God's not having willed anything other than what God has in fact willed, we would simply point out that the series of arguments leading to the assertion that there is presently some "real difference" in God is based upon the rather ephemeral foundation of a counter-to-fact supposition about a world that God might have created, but didn't.

In response to our second question, we can say two things. The first is simply a reminder that the premise of the question ("If God were to will

71. Clarke, "Comment on Professor Ford's Paper," 160–62.
72. Ibid.

other things than those that he is willing . . .") involves a supposition that, though admissible as an abstract possibility in that God's creative will is not subject to absolute necessity, is not admissible in reality since God is in fact willing certain things and therefore cannot, by necessity of supposition and because of the immutability of his will, not be willing them. If we maintain the quite reasonable practice of considering only "what in fact is" rather than "what might be," we seem justified in rejecting the question itself because it assumes something that is in fact (not absolutely but conditionally [*ex suppositione*]) impossible.

If however we agree to entertain the question insofar as it does not assume something that is absolutely impossible, we can still offer a response. Our response, however, will consist primarily in a confession of our human ignorance regarding the operation of the divine will. First, we have to admit that if God were not willing the things that he wills, he would be in some way different. If we do not admit this, we cannot avoid contradiction. For if God were *in no way* different, then in *not* willing the things that he wills, he would also *be* willing the things that he wills. Secondly, we can specify that in this case God's act of will is what would be different. Thomas explains that even under the supposition that God create some world other than this one, no difference is implied as such in God's knowledge. For his knowledge "pertains equally to beings and non-beings. If there were any change (*variatio*) in God, it would be in his will, which would be determining his knowledge to something to which it had not previously determined it." Thomas then goes on to reject the possibility of change in God's will because (by necessity of supposition) God cannot also not will what he is in fact willing, and (because his will is immutable) he cannot first will one thing and then not will that thing. Thomas allows, however, that "if we are speaking of absolute necessity, it is not necessary for him to wish what he wishes. Therefore, absolutely (*absolute*) speaking, it is possible for him not to wish it."[73]

On the level of absolute necessity, therefore, we are free to say God could create a different world and would then have a correspondingly different act of will. In saying this, however, we would also have to confess our own ignorance. For what is the act by which God wills any creatures and how could it

73. *De ver.* Q.2, 13, co.

be different? We have seen that in God there is only one act of will—the act by which God wills his own goodness, an act that is one with God's very being (*esse*). In that one act (in a way we don't understand), God wills both his goodness and the participation of his goodness by creatures.[74] It is possible, however, to distinguish in that one act a relation (*habitudo*) of the divine will to itself and to other things. Its relation to itself is natural, but its relation to other things is free: "Its relation to itself is necessary and natural, whereas its relation to other things is according to a certain befittingness, not indeed necessary and natural, nor violent and unnatural, but freely voluntary (*voluntaria*) for the freely voluntary need be neither natural nor violent."[75]

We cannot understand how, in the one act by which God necessarily wills his own goodness, he also freely wills the existence of creatures. We recognize, nonetheless, that this one act, insofar as it is one with the divine essence, is a necessary act that in no way requires the existence of creatures. This same act, insofar as it results in the existence of creatures, is not necessary but free, and would imply no difference with respect to the divine essence by its absence. For the absence of this act, when it is considered precisely and strictly insofar as it is directed toward or terminates in the existence of creatures, would imply no difference in the divine essence, but only in that toward which it is directed or terminated. If the act by which God wills his own goodness were not directed toward or terminated in the existence of a given creature, there would be no difference in the act with regard to the divine essence, but only with regard to that creature in which the act is terminated. For if it were not terminated in that creature, that creature would never exist. The existence or non-existence of the relationship between the divine will and the creature implies no difference in the divine will itself since it is a mixed relation, real in the creature but of reason only in God.[76] As Eleonore

74. "Voluntas namque sua uno et eodem actu vult se et alia" (*SCG* I, c.82.9 [§700]). Cf.: *SCG* I, c.76.1 (§647).

75. "Voluntas namque sua uno et eodem actu vult se et alia: sed habitudo eius ad se est necessaria et naturalis; habitudo autem eius ad alia est secundum convenientiam quandam, non quidem necessaria et naturalis, neque violenta aut innaturalis, sed voluntaria; quod enim voluntarium est, neque naturale neque violentum necesse est esse" (*SCG* I, c.82.9 [§700]). See also Dominicus Bañes, *Scholastica commentaria in primam partem Summae Theologicae S. Thomae Aquinatis* (Madrid: Hijo de F. Vives Mora, 1934), Pars I, Q.XIX, a.3, *Commentarium*, 414.

76. *ST* I, 45, 3, ad 1.

Stump explains, "The difference between the relationship of the divine will to the divine nature and the relationship of the divine will to creatures stems not from a difference in the divine will itself but from logical differences among the diverse objects of that will."[77] Whether God's act of willing his own goodness terminates in the existence of a particular creature or not implies no difference in that act insofar as that act is the divine essence. For that act is the divine essence insofar as it is the act of God's willing his own goodness, and the termination of that act in the existence of the creature is not necessary to it insofar as it is the act of God's willing his own goodness.

Our remarks regarding the act of the divine will are necessarily halting and inadequate since the operation of God's will infinitely exceeds the capacity of our thought and language. In what we say, we do not seek to explain the mystery of God's will, but only to preserve it from our all-too-human tendency to reduce God to something we can understand.[78] At the same time, in answering the hypothetical question that we have posed regarding what God "might do" or how God "might be," we refuse to abandon the actual truth that we have discovered about what God is: that God is pure actuality, *ipsum esse subsistens*, and that as such he is (unlike us) absolutely simple and unchanging. It is of course tempting to deny our ignorance and to pretend instead that God's will is like our own, with a multitude of acts, some of which would be different or changed if God did not will the creation of the world. But if we yield to that temptation, the God of whom we speak will be only a human God, made in our own image. He will be only a "pretend" God who "might be this" or "could be that." He will no longer be the God of transcendent mystery who has made us in his own image and likeness and who reveals himself as "He who is" (Ex 3:14).

The Beginning of the World It might seem difficult to reconcile the immutability of the divine will with the teaching of Scripture that the world has a beginning, an initial instantiation from nothing.[79] Since the world has a beginning, must not God's will to create it also have a beginning and so

---

77. Eleonore Stump, *Aquinas* (New York: Routledge, 2003), 125–26.

78. See *SCG* I, c.5.3–4 (§30–31).

79. Gen 1:1 and 2 Macc 7:28; Jn 17:5 and Prov 8:22. Aquinas cites the latter two references in *ST* I, 46, 1, sc.

be changeable? William L. Craig assumes this and argues that God's "time-less free decision to create a temporal world with a beginning is a decision on God's part to abandon timelessness and to take on a temporal mode of existence."[80] To address this argument we must remember God creates the world not by necessity of nature, but by freedom of will. If God acted by ne-cessity of nature, either the world would exist from all eternity or there would have to be some change in the divine nature to account for the fact that the world, which did not exist "before," began to exist at some point. Because God creates through his intellect and will, however, the world begins to be according to the ordination of his will.[81] In this way, it is possible for God, without changing his will, to will that certain things be changed. Without change of will, even we can will that one thing be done first and another af-terward, as I might decide to go the movies not now but later this evening. Without changing his will, God may will that the world exist not eternally, but "after" not existing.[82] The fact that God eternally wills the existence of the world does not require God will the world to exist eternally. Similarly, the fact that God wills that the world have a beginning does not imply a be-ginning in God's will to will the beginning of the world: "Since God's will is unchangeable (*immutabilis*), if it be supposed that he wills a certain thing at some time, on that supposition it is necessary that he will it always, although it is not necessary if he will a thing to last for a time, that he also will it to last for ever."[83]

Immutability as Confirmation of Creative Freedom

Seeing God's creative act in relation to divine immutability allows us to recognize God's freedom in creating. We can explore the freedom of any act

---

80. Craig, *Time and Eternity*, 97, 241.

81. See *ST* I, 19, 4; Q.46, 1, ad 6; ad 9; ad 10; Q.104, 3, co.; *Sent.* III, 20, 1, 1, qc.3, co.; *In phys.* VIII, lect. 2.18 (§988); *Comp.* I, c.96–97; *De pot.* Q.3, 14, ad.2; ad 5, ad 10; a.6, ad 22; *SCG* II, c.32–33; c.79.3 (§669); *De sub sep.* c.9, line 244 c. (Leonine); *Super de causis* Prop. 11 (Saffrey, p. 75, line 3–p. 76, line 17).

82. *ST* I, 19, 7, co.; Q.104, 3, co.; *SCG* II, c.35.3(§1113). The same argument may be applied not only to the act of creation, but to anything that God wills with regard to creatures. See *ST* I, 19, 7, co.; *SCG* II, c.36.4 (§1123); *Sent.* IV, 4, 2, 2, qc.1, ad 2; d.48, 2, 1, ad 2; *De virt.* Q.1, 11, ad 9. See Horst Seidl, "De l'immutabilité de Dieu dans l'acte de la création et dans la relation avec les hommes," *Revue thomiste* 87 (1987): 615–29.

83. *De pot.* Q.5, 4, co.

in terms of how it is ordered to its end. The end for which God acts in the work of creation is his own goodness, the proper object of his will. God wills this with absolute necessity and all other things as they are ordered to it.[84]

It is important to remember we are not speaking of two acts of the divine will, one directed toward God's goodness and another toward creatures. In God there is only one act of will, the act by which God loves his own goodness and which is one with his being. In that one act, God wills his own goodness not only in itself, but also as participated by creatures. We cannot understand the mode of operation of God's will, but we do know it is different from our own. Our will operates by a multiplicity of acts, willing the end by one act and the means to that end by another. We get some analogous idea of the action of the divine will if we think of God as willing both the end and the "means" (i.e., that which is ordered to the end) in a single act. In that one act, he wills both his own goodness (as the end) and creatures ordered to that end.[85] To decide whether or not God freely wills the existence of creatures, we must determine whether his willing their existence is necessary for his willing his own goodness.

There are two ways an agent may will things ordered to an end. If the end is not attainable without them, the agent wills them necessarily in willing the end. If I choose the "end" of going on a cruise, for instance, I must necessarily will myself a ship since that "end" (a cruise) is not attainable without that "means" (a boat). If the end is attainable without certain things that might be ordered to it, however, those things are willed not necessarily, but freely. If I want to go for a drive, for instance, I don't necessarily will myself a BMW when some humbler vehicle will do.

God wills the existence of creatures as ordered to the end that is his goodness. That end, however, is not something God has yet to attain, but something God, as *esse subsistens*, enjoys in unbounded and unchanging perfection: "Because his goodness is eternal and immutable (*immutabilis*), noth-

---

84. *Sent.* II, 1, 2, 1, co.; *ST* I, 19, 3, co. While allowing that the divine will has an end, Thomas is careful to note that "in no way (*nullo modo*) does the divine will have a cause" (*ST* I, 19, 7, co.). Because divine goodness is the proper object of the divine will, however, it may be said to move it: "The will of God in no way has a cause. . . . Nevertheless some reason (*ratio*) may be assigned for it . . . on the part of the one willing, and thus [God's] goodness is a certain reason for the divine will and moves it" (*Super ad eph.* I, lect. 1 [§12]).

85. *ST* I, 19, 5, co.

ing is able to be added to it."[86] There is no greater degree of goodness for God to attain since there is no good he does not already possess. The end for which God acts, therefore, is not something he seeks to attain, but something he possesses and loves in eternal and infinite fullness.[87] God necessarily wills this end that is his own goodness. It is not necessary, however, that in willing this end he will the existence of creatures ordered to it, since they in no way contribute to it and so are not necessary to its possession. It is in this roundabout way, therefore, not by pretending to understand the nature of the divine will, but by recognizing the indigency of creatures whose being depends wholly on God and who can in no way contribute to God's being, that we recognize God's creative act as proceeding not from necessity, but from unbounded freedom.[88] The freedom of this act is seen more clearly when the "transient motion" of the act of creation is viewed in the context of the immanent motion of knowing and loving that are understood to constitute God's Trinitarian life:

[Our] knowledge of the divine persons . . . was necessary for [our having] the right idea of creation. The fact of saying that God made all things by his Word excludes the error of those who say that God produced things by necessity. When we say that in him there is a procession of love, we show that God produced creatures not because he needed them, nor because of any other extrinsic reason, but on account of the love of his own goodness.[89]

PROVIDENCE

God's providential care for his creatures, like the act of creation, may be considered as transient motion.[90] Aquinas distinguishes the general notion of providence into the stricter idea of providence as God's plan for creation and the concept of divine governance. In the narrower sense, providence is

86. *SCG* II, c.35.7 (§1117).
87. "Deo competit agere propter amorem finis, cujus bonitati nihil addi potest" (*Sent.* II, 1, 2, 1, co.).
88. See *ST* I, 19, 3, co.; a.4, co.; Q.104, 3, ad 2; *De pot.* Q.1, 5, ad 3; ad 13; Q.3, 15, ad 7; Q.7, 10, ad 6; *De ver.* Q.23, 1, ad 7; a.4, co.; ad 12; *SCG* I, c.81.2 (§683); c.82.8 (§696); c.88; II, c.29.20 (§1062); c.35.7 (§1117); *Sent.* I, 43, 2, 2, ad 3; d.45, 1, 1, ad 3; III, 20, 1, 1, qc.3, co.
89. *ST* I, 32, 1, ad 3. Cf.: *SCG* IV, c.20.2–3 (§3570–71).
90. *De ver.* Q.2, 2, ad 2.

God's plan (*ratio*) of the order of things to their end. It is understood as an immanent act of knowing that remains in God. Governance is the execution of this plan. It can be conceptualized as transient motion that passes into creatures,[91] but is really a continuation of the act of creation, which is "without motion and time."[92]

In discussing the mystery of providence, we must preserve both God's immutability and the changeability of creatures. To some contemporary theologians, this seems an impossible task. How can God act in time, or know what is happening in time, or even know what time it is, unless he is himself somehow temporal or changeable? Does not the willing of any free act require some change in God's volition? How can God be truly involved in the life of his people unless he is somehow affected by their actions? Could an unchanging God act on changeable creatures without imposing necessity on them, depriving them of their contingency and freedom? We will address these questions by indicating certain principles in the theology of Aquinas that, while they by no means "solve" the mystery of divine providence, may help us avoid some pitfalls.

Providence and Divine Immutability

Aquinas believes God's providential care embraces all creation.[93] He does not think, however, that the changeableness of creatures requires any change in God's knowledge and love. Nor does he believe God's providential action deprives creatures of their contingency and freedom.

Divine Knowledge

If God's knowledge were like ours, it would be subject to change. Our knowledge varies continuously as the things we know change. For instance, my knowledge of a duck differs when it wades or waddles. If my knowledge did not change, it would cease to be true.[94] Many contemporary theologians

---

91. *ST* I, 22, 1, co.; ad 2; Q.23, 2, co.; ad 1; *SCG* IV, c.20.4 (§3572); *In de div. nom.* IX, lect. 4 (§840–41).

92. "[C]onservatio rerum a Deo non est per aliquam novam actionem; sed per continuationem actionis qua dat esse, quae quidem actio est sine motu et tempore" (*ST* I, 104, 1, ad 4). Cf.: *De pot.* Q.5, 1, ad 2; a.2, co.; *SCG* III, c.98.3 (§2744); c.64.4 (§2387); c.94.9 (§2694); *ST* I, 22, 4, ad 2; ad 3; *De ver.* Q.2. 2, ad 2; Q.5, 1, ad 3; ad 5; *Comp.* I, c.123; *De sub. sep.* c.15, lines 20–34.

93. *ST* I, 14, aa.5–6, 10–13; Q.19, aa.2–4; Q.20, 2; *ST* I, 22, 2, co.; a.3; Q.103, 1; a.5; a.6.

94. *ST* I, 16, 8, co.

take God's knowledge to be like ours and therefore changeable. Richard E. Creel maintains, for instance, that God's knowledge of "what is happening is determined by what is happening. . . . It cannot be an illusion that change is occurring in this world, and change cannot be known adequately except by an awareness that undergoes a corresponding change caused by the thing of which one is aware. This is a metaphysical principle to which there can be no exception."[95] Grace Jantzen argues that an immutable God "could not think or perceive or have any conscious processes, because these would involve changes in God."[96] William L. Craig believes that as the world "is in constant flux, so also must God's knowledge of what is happening be in constant flux."[97] Paul Helm thinks that the exercise of creaturely choices "will change God by increasing his knowledge."[98] William Hasker agrees: "When I do something wrong, God comes to be in a state of knowing that I am doing something wrong, and this a change in God."[99]

Thomas was aware of "certain ones" in his own time who came to similar conclusions based on the premise that God's knowledge is like ours.[100] He saw their mistaken assumption as jeopardizing both God's changelessness and providence.[101] He argued that, precisely because God's knowledge is not like ours, God can know changeable things without changing.

Aquinas thinks both faith and reason attest to God's changeless knowledge.[102] Since God's understanding (*intelligere*) is his to-be (*esse*), it is "sim-

95. Richard E. Creel, *Divine Impassibility: An Essay in Philosophical Theology* (Cambridge: Cambridge University Press, 1986), 205.

96. Grace Jantzen, *God's World, God's Body* (Philadelphia: Westminster, 1984), 55.

97. William L. Craig, *Time and Eternity*, 97, 241. Also see his *God, Time, and Eternity* (Dordrecht: Kluwer, 2001), 283–84.

98. Paul Helm, *Eternal God: A Study of God without Time* (New York: Oxford University Press, 1988), 92.

99. William Hasker, "Does God Change?" in *Questions about God: Today's Philosophers Ponder the Divine*, ed. Steven M. Cahn and David Shatz (Oxford: Oxford University Press, 2002), 143. See also William Hasker, *God, Time, and Knowledge* (Ithaca, N.Y.: Cornell University Press, 1989), 184, 198; Richard M. Gale, *On the Nature and Existence of God* (Cambridge: Cambridge University Press, 1991), 58, 91, 93, 95; Lewis S. Ford, "Temporality and Transcendence," in *Hartshorne, Process Philosophy and Theology*, ed. Robert Kane and Stephen H. Phillips (Albany: State University of New York Press, 1989), 151.

100. *De ver.* Q.2, 5, co.; Q.2, 12, co.; *SCG* III, c.98.6 (§2745).

101. *De ver.* Q.2, 12, co.

102. "[E]t hunc [intellectum divinum] quidem esse omnino immobilem, et fides tenet, et ratio demonstrat" (*Sent.* II, 17, 1, 1, co.). Cf.: *De ver.* Q.2, 13; *ST* I, 14, 15.

ple, eternal, and unchangeable (*invariabile*)."[103] As the first cause of all motion, "the divine intellect must be an absolutely unmoved mover (*movens non
motum*)."[104] Unlike our knowledge, which is caused by and depends on the
things it knows, God's knowledge creates the things he knows.[105] Unlike our
limited knowledge, God's is complete and perfect, a knowledge of all things
that have existed, will exist, or could possibly exist.[106] Any change in his
knowledge would imply a lessening of its perfection.[107]

How is it God can know changeable things without changing? We get
some clue if we remember that, in any act of knowing, the thing known is
in the knower not according to its own mode, but "according to the mode
of the knower."[108] This principle explains the permanence that characterizes
even our human knowledge of changeable things. Since our intellect is immaterial, it receives the species or intelligibility of movable things immaterially and "immovably (*immobiliter*)."[109] (So my knowledge of a soap bubble
doesn't disappear when the bubble pops.) This same principle is analogously
true of God's knowledge, which is not derived from things, but is rather their
cause.[110] We have seen that God is subsistent *esse* and therefore immutable
and eternal. His knowledge, which is one with his *esse*, is in him according to
the immutable and eternal mode of his being.[111] Because he is eternal, he sees
past, present, and future in a single intuition. Regardless of how things may
change in time, therefore, his knowledge of them does not change.[112]

Because all time is present to God in his eternity, and because he knows
things according to this eternal mode of his being, he can know even future
contingent events with a certain, infallible, and unchanging knowledge. Such

103. "Si autem divinum intelligere est eius esse, necesse est quod intelligere eius sit simplex, aeternum et invariabile" (*SCG* I, c.45.7 [§388]). Cf.: *ST* I, 14, 15, co.; Q.16, 8, co.; *De ver.* Q.2, 13; *De sub. sep.* c.14,
lines 31–39.

104. *SCG* I, c.57.7 (§479). Cf.: *De ver.* Q.2, 13, sc 2; *In* XII, lect. 11.8 (§2607);*De sub. sep.* c.14, lines
148–58.

105. *ST* I, 14, 8, co.; *De pot.* Q.7, 10, ad 5; *Sent.* I, 38, 1, 5, co.; d.39, 1, 2, ad 2; *De ver.* Q.12, 11, sc.3.

106. *ST* I, 14, aa.5–6, 9–14; *De ver.* Q.2, 13, co.

107. *In meta.* XII, lect. 11.8 (§2607). Cf.: *De sub. sep.* c.14, lines 152–58.

108. *ST* I, 14, 1, ad 3. Cf.: *ST* I, 50, 2, co.; Q.84, 1, co.

109. *Quodl.* III, Q.9, a.1 [21], co.

110. *De ver.* Q.2, 13, ad 3.

111. *SCG* I, c.45.7 (§388); cf: *ST* I, 14, 15, ad 1; *De ver.* Q.2, 13, ad 10.

112. *De ver.* Q.2, 5, ad 11.

events, though happening contingently (in that they happen through contingent causes) are nonetheless subject to a certain necessity (the necessity of supposition) in their instantiation. That Socrates is sitting, for example, is a contingent event. But, granted that he is in fact sitting, he must necessarily be sitting while he sits since "what is must be when it is." God knows contingent events eternally both in their causes (as contingent) and in their actual occurrence (as determined or necessary by supposition).[113] His knowledge of them is therefore unchanging.[114]

The eternal mode of divine knowing, of course, escapes our powers of thought. We can describe it "only after the manner of our own knowledge," but must ever deny the limits of our mode of knowing as we do so. In our halting way, however, we can still see that God's knowledge of contingent things need imply no change in God.[115]

Divine Will

If God's will were like human volition, it would also have to be changeable. What we will follows our knowledge or disposition as we respond to our surroundings.[116] Some contemporary theologians think God's will must act similarly as he responds to the changing behavior of his people. Edward Collins Vacek argues that "God loves *us*, and that means that who we are and what we do make a *difference* to God. God's being and action are modified by us and our actions."[117] Robert Brown agrees that "if knowing affects the one who knows, especially one who acts in a specific way in response to what is known, contingent events in the creation, in particular the free choices made

113. *SCG* I, c.67.3 (§558); *De ver.* 2, 12, ad 2.

114. *De ver.* Q.12, 3, co. Cf.: *ST* I, 14, 13; *SCG* I, c.67; *Super is.* III, v. 26, lines 520–45.

115. *De ver.* Q.2, 12, co. On God's eternal knowledge of contingent events, see Thomas D. Sullivan, "Omniscience, Immutability and the Divine Mode of Knowing," *Faith and Philosophy* 8 (1991): 21–35; Christopher Hughes, *On a Complex Theory of a Simple God: An Investigation in Aquinas's Philosophical Theology* (Ithaca, N.Y.: Cornell University Press, 1989), 120–27; William Lane Craig, *The Only Wise God: The Compatibility of Divine Foreknowledge and Human Freedom* (Grand Rapids, Mich.: Baker Book House, 1987); idem, "Divine Foreknowledge and Future Contingency," in *Process Theology*, ed. Ronald Nash (Grand Rapids, MI: Baker Book House, 1987), 91–115; William Hill, "Does God Know the Future? Aquinas and Some Moderns," *Theological Studies* 36 (1975): 7.

116. *ST* I, 19, 7, co.

117. Edward Collins Vacek, *Love, Human and Divine: The Heart of Christian Ethics* (Washington, D.C.: Georgetown University Press, 1994), 124.

by creatures, affect God and hence God cannot be strictly self-determined"[118] Richard Swinburne maintains that if God had "fixed intentions 'from all eternity' he would be a very lifeless thing; not a person who reacts to men with sympathy or anger, pardon or chastening because he chooses to there and then."[119]

Aquinas believes God is intimately involved in creation, but does not think this requires any change in God's will. If anything, it demands God be unchanged.[120] God's actions on behalf of his chosen ones may change without any variation in his will since without changing his will God may will that things be changed.[121] Nor must God change his will in order to answer the prayers of his people. To think so is to fundamentally misunderstand the nature of prayer.

It is often thought that the aim of prayer is to effect some change in God's will and that unless God's will is changeable, prayer is useless. Aquinas found such ideas among the Egyptians, Epicureans, and Stoics.[122] A number of contemporary theologians think the same. Garrett DeWeese maintains that anyone who "desires to retain a strong sense of God's sovereignty, let alone of strong immutability or impassibility, must confess mystification as to how petitionary prayer can be efficacious." Jean Galot argues that prayers "are able to obtain a modification of the divine plan in a particular domain."[123]

To solve such dilemmas, we must deny that prayer is intended to change

118. Robert Brown, "Divine Omniscience, Immutability, Aseity and Human Free Will," *Religious Studies* 27 (1991): 287.

119. Swinburne, *The Coherence of Theism*, 214. Cf.: Jay Wesley Richards, *The Untamed God: A Philosophical Exploration of Divine Perfection, Simplicity and Immutability* (Downers Grove, Ill.: InterVarsity Press, 2003), 200–202; Joshua Hoffman and Gary S. Rosenkrantz, *The Divine Attributes* (Oxford: Blackwell, 2002), 103–4; Colin E. Gunton, *Act and Being: Towards a Theology of the Divine Attributes* (Grand Rapids, Mich.: Eerdmans, 2003), 57; Jantzen, *God's World*, 55; Thomas F. Tracy, "The Moral Perfections of God," *Thomist* 47 (1983): 484; Jung Young Lee, "Can," 768–69; O'Donnell, *The Mystery of the Triune God*, 172.

120. See our discussion of the intimacy of divine friendship and compassion in chapter 4, below.

121. *ST* I, 19, 7, ad 1; ad 3. See our discussion of divine repentance in the section on Scripture as a source of Aquinas's teaching on divine immutability in chapter 2, above.

122. Thomas mentions the Egyptians as an example of those who believed that "the divine disposition is capable of being changed (*vertibilem*) by prayers" (*SCG* III, c.95–96.10 [§2717]). Cf.: *ST* I, 23, 8, co.; Q.116, 3, co. He names the Epicureans, Stoics, and "some Peripetetics" as examples of those who conclude that because the divine will is unchanging, prayer is ineffective. *SCG* III, c.95–96.9–14 (§2717–21); *In de div. nom.* III, lect. un. (§241).

123. Garrett DeWeese, *God and the Nature of Time* (Burlington, Vt.: Ashgate, 2004), 275; Galot, "Réalité," 232.

the divine will and see it rather as a secondary cause ordained by God's un-changing will. As the ultimate cause of all actuality, God freely chooses to act through secondary causes in accomplishing his will.[124] As food and nourish-ment are secondary causes through which God's will to sustain our life is ac-complished, so prayer is a secondary cause through which God's will for his creatures is achieved.[125] In recognizing prayer as a sort of secondary causal-ity, we discover its true nature. Prayer is not meant to change God's will, but rather to cooperate with God in the accomplishment of his eternal and un-changing will.[126] The efficacy of prayer does not depend on God's changing his will, but rather on the unchanging steadfastness of his will, manifested in his abiding love for his creatures.[127] Through prayer, it is not we who change God's will, but God who transforms us. Aquinas explains this, using Diony-sius's image of a "chain of abundant light hanging from the highest heaven and descending to the earth":

If we take hold of this chain and move ourselves hand over hand toward the top, we will seem to pull the chain downward, but really we will not bring it down. . . . Rather we ourselves will be raised into the greater splendor of that luminous chain. . . . Be-fore all acts, but most especially before theological work, it is beneficial for us to begin with prayer, not as if we were to draw down divine power which is everywhere present and nowhere contained, but as drawing and uniting ourselves to him through recol-lection and supplication.[128]

Providence and Creaturely Freedom

A number of contemporary theologians believe that an unchanging di-vine providence would impose necessity on creatures, depriving them of

---

124. *ST* I, 19, 5; Q.103, 6; Q.104, 2, *SCG* III, c.77.

125. *SCG* III, c.95.8 (§2716).

126. *ST* II-II, 83, 2, ad 2; *ST* I, 23, 8; *SCG* III, c.95.1 (§2702); c.96.14 (§2721); *Comp.* II, c.2; *Super ev. matt.* VI, lect. 3 (§584); *De ver.* Q.6, 6. On prayer and secondary causality, see also Richard Kocher, *Her-ausgeforderter Vorsehungsglaube. Die Lehre von der Vorsehung im Horizont der gegenwärtigen Theologie* (St. Ottil-ien: EOS Verlag, 1993), 296–301; Joseph Bobik, *Veritas Divina: Aquinas on Divine Truth* (South Bend, Ind.: St. Augustine's Press, 2001), 62–64. Alois Van Hove, "De immutabilitate Dei," *Collectanea Mechliniensia* 7 (1933): 45.

127. *SCG* III, c.95.2 (§2703); 95.5 (§2706). On the cogency of prayer to the unchanging God, see Mary Rousseau, "Process Thought and Traditional Theism: A Critique," *Modern Schoolman* 62 (1985): 53–54; John Knasas, "Aquinas: Prayer to an Immutable God," NS 57 (1983): 196–221.

128. *In de div. nom.* III, lect. un. (§239, 243–44). Cf.: *SCG* III, c.119.4 (§2911).

contingency and freedom. Leonard Eslick argues that the divine causality envisioned by Aquinas "eliminates from the divine effects any real contingency and freedom, any creaturely share (however modest) in divine causality."[129] Paul Helm thinks that divine foreknowledge "is logically incompatible with human (indeterministic) freedom."[130] Charles Hartshorne believes, "It simply cannot be that everything in God is necessary, including his knowledge that this world exists, unless the world is in the same sense necessary and there is no contingency whatever."[131] Those who share such views sometimes try to preserve creaturely contingency by denying divine providence altogether, removing contingent events from the sway of providence, or viewing providence as changeable.[132] Others, such as Arthur Peacocke, believe God can create a world of freedom and contingency only by imposing limits on his knowledge and power:

Considerations . . . on the role of "chance" in creation impel us also to recognize, more emphatically than ever before, the constraints which we must regard God as imposing upon himself in creation and to suggest that *God has a "self-limited" omnipotence and omniscience.* For, in order to achieve his purposes, he has allowed his inherent omnipotence and omniscience to be modified, restricted and curtailed by the very open-endedness that he has bestowed upon creation.[133]

129. Leonard Eslick, "From the World to God: The Cosmological Argument," *Modern Schoolman* 60 (1983): 153.
130. Helm, *Eternal God,* 98. Cf.: Stephen M. Cahn, "Does God Know the Future?" in *Questions about God: Today's Philosophers Ponder the Divine,* ed. Steven M. Cahn and David Shatz (Oxford: Oxford University Press, 2002), 149. Cf.: Michael D. Robinson, *Eternity and Freedom: A Critical Analysis of Divine Timelessness as a Solution to the Foreknowledge/Free Will Debate* (Lanham, Md.: University Press of America, 1995).
131. Hartshorne, *Divine,* 14. See also Pannenberg, "Aufnahme," 329.
132. We have already noted Thomas's awareness of the Epicureans, who denied divine providence altogether, of "some Peripatetics," who removed contingent events from the domain of providence, and of the Egyptians, who asserted that providence itself was changeable. See *SCG* III, c.98.4–6 (§2745); *In meta.* VI, lect. 3.13–14 (§1203–4); *Sent.* I, 38, 1, 5, co. Contemporary thinkers sharing such approaches would include Hartshorne, *Divine,* 137, and Jörg Jeremias, *Die Reue Gottes* (Neukirchen-Vluyn: Neukirchener Verlag, 1975), 123.
133. Peacocke, *Theology,* 121. Clark H. Pinnock agrees that the creation of the world "involved a self-limitation on God's part" (*Most Moved Mover: A Theology of God's Openness* [Grand Rapids, Mich.: Baker Books, 2001], 56). Cf.: Gloria L. Schaab, "A Procreative Paradigm of the Creative Suffering of the Triune God: Implications of Arthur Peacocke's Evolutionary Theology," *Theological Studies* 67 (2006): 544, 553, 555; Terrence E. Fretheim, *The Suffering God: An Old Testament Perspective* (Philadelphia: Fortress Press, 1984), 36–37. Such views are refuted by Henri Blocher, "Divine Immutability," in *The Power and Weakness of God: Impassibility and Orthodoxy,* ed. Nigel M. de S. Cameron (Edinburgh: Rutherford House Books, 1990), 14–15.

Thomas affirms both the immutability of divine providence and the changeability and contingency of creatures. To understand these affirmations, we will consider first the nature of God's providential knowledge and action in regard to changeable creatures and then how mutable creatures imitate the unchanging creator.

We have already discussed the eternal character of God's knowledge and how God may have an unchangeable knowledge of changeable creatures. God's eternity may also help us see why immutable divine knowledge does not impose necessity on the contingent actions of creatures. In his eternity, God knows the acts of creatures both in their causes (as contingent) and in their actual occurrence. In their actual occurrence, however, even contingent events are marked by a certain necessity—the necessity of supposition. Given, for example, that Socrates is (freely) sitting, he must (necessarily) be sitting as long as he continues to sit. In their actual occurrence, therefore, contingent events are marked by a kind of necessity that also stamps our knowledge of them. (I know for sure Socrates is sitting.) Such necessity, however, does not deprive events of their contingent character. As we can know such events in their actual occurrence with a certain necessity, God, who in his eternity sees all events in their actual occurrence, can have a knowledge of them that is certain, necessary, and unchangeable. As the necessity of our knowledge does not impose necessity on such events as they occur, neither does the necessity and immutability of God's knowledge deprive them of their contingent character.[134]

As God's immutable knowledge of changeable things does not impose necessity upon them, neither does his unchanging will. We will understand something of how God's unchanging will acts in changeable creatures only

134. De malo Q.16, 7, ad 15; Sent. I, 38, 1, 5, ad 4; In peri herm. I, lect. 14.21; ST I, 14, 13. On how God's knowledge is compatible with creaturely freedom, see Harm J. M. J. Goris, Free Creatures of an Eternal God: Thomas Aquinas on God's Infallible Foreknowledge and Irresistible Will (Leuven: Peeters, 1996); Eleonore Stump and Norman Kretzmann, "God's Knowledge and Its Causal Efficacy," in The Rationality of Belief and the Plurality of Faith: Essays in Honor of William P. Alston, ed. Thomas D. Senor (Ithaca: Cornell University Press, 1995), 94–124; Davies, Introduction to the Philosophy of Religion, 164–67; David Burrell, "Divine Practical Knowing: How an Eternal God Acts in Time," in Divine Action: Studies Inspired by the Philosophical Theology of Austin Farrer, ed. Brian Hebblethwaite (Edinburgh: T and T Clark, 1990), 93–102; and Charles E. Gutenson, "Does God Change?" in God under Fire: Modern Scholarship Reinvents God, ed. Douglas S. Huffman and Eric L. Johnson (Grand Rapids, Mich.: Zondervan, 2002), 231–52.

if we keep in mind that God, as *esse subsistens,* transcends all created beings. As subsistent to-be (*esse*), God "must be understood as existing (*existens*) beyond the order of beings (*entium*) as a certain cause pouring forth all being (*ens*) and all its differences." Because God is beyond all differences of being, he is also beyond the difference of "contingent" and "necessary." He belongs to neither of these classes of beings but is rather the source or origin of both, acting sometimes through necessary causes that produce necessary effects and sometimes through contingent causes that bring forth contingent effects. In this way, both necessary and contingent effects proceed from the unchanging God.[135]

In his providential activity, God acts in each creature according to its particular nature. His providence does not corrupt the creature, but preserves it.[136] He moves necessary causes so they produce necessary effects, and contingent causes to originate contingent effects.[137] One of those contingent causes is our human free will. Because God acts in us in accordance with the nature he has given us, and because free will belongs to us by nature, his causal action, far from destroying or diminishing our freedom, is rather its very source.[138]

The mystery of God's unchanging knowledge and will with respect to our human freedom is most profoundly evoked in the doctrine of predestination. Predestination is that part of divine providence according to which

---

135. "Nam voluntas divina est intelligenda ut extra ordinem entium existens, velut causa quaedam profundens totum ens et omnes eius differentias. Sunt autem differentiae entis possibile et necessarium; et ideo ex ipsa voluntate divina originantur necessitas et contingentia in rebus et distinctio utriusque secundum rationem proximarum causarum: ad effectus enim, quos voluit necessarios esse, disposuit causas necessarias; ad effectus autem, quos voluit esse contingentes, ordinavit causas contingenter agentes, idest potentes deficere. Et secundum harum conditionem causarum, effectus dicuntur vel necessarii vel contingentes, quamvis omnes dependeant a voluntate divina, sicut a prima causa, quae transcendit ordinem necessitatis et contingentiae" (*In peri herm.* I, lect. 14.22). Cf.: *De sub. sep.,* c.16, lines 138–50; *In meta.* VI, lect. 3.18–32 (§1208–22); *ST* I, 14, 13, ad 1; Q.19, 8, co.; Q.22, 4, ad 3; Q.67, 6; Q.103, 7, ad 3; *De ver.* Q.12, 11, co.; Q.23, 5, co.; *De malo* Q.6, art. unicus, ad 3; Q.16, 7, ad 15; *Comp.* I, c.140; *Sent.* I, 38, 1, 5, co.; d.47, 1, 1, ad 2; *Super iob* XIV, v.5, lines 8–27; *SCG* I, c.67.6 (§561); c.85; III, c.75.

136. *Sent.* II, 23, 1, 2, co. See Thomas S. Hibbs, *Dialectic and Narrative in Aquinas: An Interpretation of the Summa Contra Gentiles* (Notre Dame: University of Notre Dame Press, 1995), 117–22.

137. *De ver.* Q.23, 1, ad 2; *ST* I-II, 10, 4, co.; *Sent.* I, 45, 1, 3, ad 3.

138. *Comp.* I, c.129; *SCG* III, c. 67.4 (§2418); c.91.3–4 (§2663–64); c. 159.2 (§3313); *ST* I, 105, 4, co.; I-II, 9, 6; Q.10, 4; Q.79, 2; *De pot.* Q.3, 7, ad 13; ad 14; ad 15; *De malo* Q.3, 2, co.; Q.6, art. unicus, ad 3; ad 20; *Quodl.* I, Q.4, a.2 [7], ad 2.

God directs a rational creature to the end of eternal life. As part of God's providential knowledge and will, predestination is unchangeable.[139] Yet predestination does not impede or diminish the creature's freedom.[140] We cannot understand how this is possible since we do not comprehend God's transcendent causality. If we overlook it, however, predestination becomes an inscrutable conundrum. John C. Moskop, for instance, rejects Aquinas's account of divine transcendence and so concludes that his "doctrine of the divine will as ordering all things would, even if it is conceived as a timeless will, conflict with the doctrine of human freedom."[141] William Lane Craig misunderstands Aquinas's account of the relation of God's transcendent causality to secondary causes and so argues that "it is futile for him to contend that God's knowledge does not necessitate an effect because the effect may be impeded by its secondary cause, for this secondary cause is itself determined causally by God."[142] Even when we admit God's transcendence, predestination remains unknowable, not as a nasty conundrum but as a mystery of love. The abyss of God's love was manifested on the cross, and it is in the depths of the cross according to Aquinas that the mystery of God's providential plan lies hidden: "The cross is braced by its depth which lies concealed beneath the ground. It is not seen because the depth of divine love which sustains us is not visible insofar as the plan of predestination . . . is beyond our intelligence."[143]

---

139. *ST* I, 23, 6, ad 3; *De ver.* Q.6, 3; a.6.

140. "Unde et id quod est per liberum arbitrium, est ex praedestinatione" (*ST* 1, 23, 5, co.). Cf.: *Super II ad tim.* II, lect. 3 (§71).

141. John C. Moskop, *Divine Omniscience and Human Freedom: Thomas Aquinas and Charles Hartshorne* (Macon, Ga.: Mercer University Press, 1984), 98–99. Cf.: Antonie Vos, "Always on Time: On God's Immutability," in *Understanding the Attributes of God*, ed. Gijsbert van den Brink and Marcel Sarot (Frankfurt: Peter Lang, 1999), 59, 61.

142. William Lane Craig, *The Problem of Divine Foreknowledge and Future Contingents from Aristotle to Suarez* (Leiden: Brill, 1988), 125–26. Aquinas, of course, specifically rejects the idea that the contingency of an effect might be attributed solely to the contingency of a secondary cause since "no defect of a secondary cause can hinder God's will from producing its effect." An effect is contingent because God, as the ultimate cause, who transcends the orders of both contingency and necessity, wills that the effect occur contingently, and so orders contingent causes to its production: "Hence it is not because the proximate causes are contingent that the effects willed by God happen contingently, but because God has prepared contingent causes for them, it being his will that they should happen contingently" (*ST* I, 19, 8, co.).

143. *Super ad eph.* III, lect. 5 (§180). Cf.: *ST* I, 23, 4, co.; *De ver.* Q.6, 1.

Providence and Creaturely Perfection

Some contemporary theologians believe that imitating an immutable creator must render creatures apathetic. So Jürgen Moltmann, taking immutability as a synonym for indifference, argues, "To speak of an indifferent God would condemn men to indifference."[144] Charles Hartshorne asserts, "To attribute to God immunity in every sense to misfortune is merely to degrade God to the status of an abstraction from the total actuality. It also serves, most evilly, to reinforce our own tendency to deny our solidarity with the weal and woe of others, by making deity the model of such aloofness."[145]

Aquinas believes that every creature is in some way like the creator.[146] He argues, however, that creatures imitate the creator not by immobility, much less indifference, but through motion. To discover how a changeable creature resembles its unchanging creator, we have to know something about the nature of the creature since each imitates God in accordance with its particular nature. The rational creature, for instance, resembles God more perfectly than the irrational creature and so is called not only the "likeness" but also the "image" of God.[147] Each creature imitates God, however, not merely in its nature but also through its actions. By acting, the creature attains its proper perfection, which is a participation in the perfection of the creator.[148]

Through their actions, creatures share God's causal activity. Though God exercises his causality without motion, creatures share in it through their motion. The world governed by the immutable God is no static realm, nor are creatures deprived of their proper causality.[149] Rather, each creature imitates the immutable perfection of God and achieves its own perfection by exercis-

144. Moltmann, *Crucified*, 274.

145. C. Hartshorne, *Creative Synthesis and Philosophic Method* (London: SCM Press, 1970), 17. The falsity of such arguments has long been recognized. See Otto Zimmermann, *Der immergleiche Gott* (Freiburg: Herder, 1920), 130.

146. *ST* I, 4, 3.

147. Gen 1:26. Cf.: *ST* I, 98. 2.

148. "Ex hoc ipso quod aliquid actu est, activum est" (*SCG* I, c.43.2 [§357]). Cf.: *ST* I, 19, 2, co.; *SCG* III, c.24.8 (§2053).

149. *SCG* III, c.69.14 (§2444). On Aquinas's understanding of the causality proper to creatures, see William A. Wallace, "Aquinas and Newton on the Causality of Nature and of God: The Medieval and Modern Problematic," in *Philosophy and the God of Abraham: Essays in Memory of James A. Weisheipl, O.P.*, ed. R. James Long (Toronto: Pontifical Institute of Medieval Studies, 1991), 255–79; Etienne Gilson, *The Spirit of Thomism* (New York: P. J. Kenedy and Sons, 1964), 90–91; "Existence and Philosophy," *PACPA*

ing the motion proper to its nature. Necessary agents produce their effects necessarily, and contingent agents, contingently. God is present to them all, exercising his transcendent causality in each one according to its nature. And each one, by acting according to its nature, imitates the unchanging perfection of God.[150]

The world created and governed by the unchanging God is a dynamic place of causality, motion, and change. It is not, however, a realm where motion exists for its own sake. For each creature, through its motion, is seeking the fulfillment proper to its nature. We can therefore discover a certain order in the world that implies neither that the world is wholly determined nor that it is without surprises. For contingent and spontaneous causes are themselves part of this order. The order of the universe arises from the fact that it has one source and one end or goal, who is God himself. As the goal of the universe, God is sought and desired by all creatures that have not yet attained him, and possessed and enjoyed by those who have. Those of the first sort explain why our present world is marked by change, and those of the second sort manifest its changeless fulfillment. Each creature, through its motion, seeks to share God's goodness according to the capacity of its particular nature.[151] Aquinas, in accordance with the physics of his day, could see the presence of this desire in every sort of motion—from the "desire" or inclination of the stone to move toward its proper place in the universe, to the eschatological aim of the heavenly bodies to continue in their invariable motion until the ultimate purpose of creation is achieved, to the deepest desires of the human heart in its search for God: "Nothing in this life can fulfill man's desire, nor can any creature satisfy his longing. For God alone can satisfy and infinitely surpass his desire. And thus it is that he does not rest unless in God. [As] Augustine [says]: 'You have made us, Lord, for yourself, and our heart is restless until may rest in you.'"[152] In contemporary physics, it is not so easy to pinpoint the expression of each particular creature's desire

---

21 (1946): 12; *Being*, 183–85; Clarke, "Christian," 84–85; Finance, *Etre*, 228; J-P. Jossua, "L'axiome 'bonum diffusivum sui' chez s. Thomas d'Aquin," *Revue des sciences religieuses* 40 (1966): 151; Henri-Rousseau, "L'être," 272.

150. *De ver.* Q.9, 2, co.

151. *ST* I, 44, 4, ad 3; Q.6, 1, ad 2; *Sent.* II, 1, 2, 2, co.; IV, 49, 1, 2, qc.2; *De ver.* Q.21, 2, co.; *Super ad hebr.* XI, lect. 2 (§575).

152. *Super sym. apos.* ar.12, "vitam aeternam."

for the divine goal, but we continue to confess in faith that the world seeks its ultimate fulfillment in God: "Creation waits with eager longing for the revealing of the sons of God" (Rom 8:19).

A world of unending progress (and even more, a world where God himself is subject to ceaseless advance) is antithetical to the Christian vision of reality.[153] A realm where God and creature endlessly pursue "more and more" of nothing else but "more and more" is ultimately a place of endless frustration and lack of fulfillment. The God who governs such a world, ceaselessly seeking his own advancement and pleasure, but never ultimately attaining it, becomes a sort of Sisyphean figure, condemned to roll the stone of his creation up the unending incline of time but never able to reach the nonexistent summit.[154] Ironically, a world of this sort, though proclaiming itself a domain of endless progress, is ultimately a world bereft of progress. For if the world has no final goal by which to judge what truly constitutes "advancement" or "regression," the alleged "more and more" it is supposedly achieving will ultimately be only "more of the same." In such a world, there can be no discernable advancement—"nothing new under the sun."[155]

Nor is there any promise, in such a world, of final victory of good over evil. On the contrary, the struggle between them continues interminably, without hope of surcease.[156] In some versions of that world, human be-

---

153. P. Schoonenberg, "Process or History in God?" *Louvain Studies* 4 (1973): 313–14.

154. See John Wild's comparison of Charles Hartshorne's God to an "immortal Sisyphus, condemned to the constant climbing of a steep ascent which has no final summit" (Wild, "Existence," 78). Alfred North Whitehead also seems to picture God as a prisoner of "process": "Neither God, nor the World, reaches static completion. Both are in the grip of the ultimate metaphysical ground, the creative advance into novelty" (*Process and Reality*, 349).

155. Eccles 1:9. "Aquinas is firmly convinced that there can be no history without a transhistorical ground of history. To view God as intrinsically related to and thus dependent upon the world which proceeds from him, is simply to destroy God as the 'Lord of history', and to render process itself aimless and inexplicable" (Reichmann, "Aquinas," 433). Cf.: Scheffczyk, "Frage," 201; "Prozesstheismus," 88.

156. Some find a promise of eschatological fulfillment in Whitehead's statement that "the perfected actuality passes back into the temporal world, and qualifies this world so that each temporal actuality includes it as an immediate fact of relevant experience. For the kingdom of heaven is with us today" (*Process and Reality*, 351). David L. Wheeler argues that process theology can accommodate a form of realized eschatology regarding what has already been achieved in the world, but an eschatology envisioned as "the end of all things as *finis* . . . must appear mythological to many moderns and contradictory to Whiteheadians" ("Toward a Process-Relational Christian Eschatology," *Process Studies* 22 [1993]: 231). Marjorie Hewitt Suchocki argues for a sort of culmination or "end of evil," and posits this in the "continuous transformation" of evil "in God beyond all history." But there is no end to history in process thought

ings are mercifully spared from immortality, and so may drop into a sort of blessed oblivion at death.[157] But for their poor God, there is no such respite. He must continue to exist forever, without power or hope of vanquishing evil completely. Indeed, he has no guarantee that he himself will not one day be overcome by evil. So he lives on, sharing in the ephemeral joys of his passing creatures, but carrying as well the ever more oppressive memory of every tear-stained face, of every cry of fear or pain, of every fallen sparrow. He is perhaps the "fellow sufferer who understands," but has precious little hope to offer his unhappy friends.[158]

The Christian view of reality is quite different. There is a beginning and an end—a moment of creation and an unending moment of ultimate fulfillment. This view of the world demands a God who is both source and end of all things. He is the transcendent efficient, exemplar, and final cause of all creatures, calling them into existence through his free act of love and leading each to share his goodness according to its capacity of nature and grace.[159] He is not merely one being among others, but the principle of all

since this very transformation of evil in turn "provides possibilities for particular transformations in time" and "within the finitude of time, there can be neither full nor final perfection" (*The End of Evil: Process Eschatology in Historical Context* [New York: State University of New York Press, 1989], 155). As Joseph A. Bracken explains, God is "always in process of concrescence through interaction with creaturely actual occasions originating in space and time" ("The End of Evil," in *World without End: Christian Eschatology from a Process Perspective* (Grand Rapids, Mich.: Eerdmans, 2005), 11. For a cogent critique of the process theology account of eschatology, see David Basinger, *Divine Power in Process Theism: A Philosophical Critique* (Albany: State University of New York Press, 1988), 69–84.

157. Consider Charles Hartshorne's unhappy picture of personal immortality: "There may be personal immortality in the traditional sense—Whitehead's philosophy seems to leave the question open—but even so we would still really have suffered, and furthermore we would presumably suffer throughout our endless future, if it be true that tragedy arises from freedom" ("Is Whitehead's God the God of Religion?" *Ethics* 53 [1942–43]: 226). Small wonder he prefers to think there is no personal immortality; *Divine*, 132–34. Marjorie Suchocki attempts to find some room for personal immortality in Whitehead's philosophy, but admits "we are discussing a metaphysics whereby occasions of experience, not substantial persons, are resurrected into the life of God" (*The End of Evil*, 107).

158. The phrase is Whitehead's. *Process and Reality*, 351. If our view of process philosophy seems rather bleak, consider the remarks of one of its own spokespersons: "Classical theism . . . can be serene in the confidence that some day God will wipe out all evil. . . . Process theism . . . cannot have this traditional assurance about the future. . . . The world could possibly generate into near chaos. . . . There can be no metaphysical guarantee against such a catastrophe. . . . The forces of evil could conceivably overwhelm God" (L. Ford, *The Lure of God* [Philadelphia: Fortress, 1978], 119–20). Marjorie Suchocki also admits that although God proposes rich possibilities to the world, "whether these possibilities are actualized in time depends upon the free response of the world" (*The End of Evil*, 154).

159. *ST* I, 6, 4, co.

being (*principium totius esse*), who transcends the whole order of being.[160] In his boundless and unchanging perfection, he is not subject to progress, but is rather the ultimate source and goal of whatever progress is found among creatures.[161] The attainment of this ultimate goal does not imply a sort of "static completion."[162] Nor does it suggest that the creature's hopes for further progress have somehow been frustrated. It rather represents the dynamic fulfillment not only of all that the creature was seeking to attain through its progress, but also of all that its finite nature is capable of achieving. For human creatures, the attainment of this goal involves not only the superabundant fulfillment of all the potential of our human nature, but also the realization of those unfathomable possibilities that have been opened to us through grace (1 Cor 2:9). In this enduring and unalterable fulfillment, there is no hint of stagnation or inertia. There is only the dynamic stillness of abiding love—the unutterable joy of unending union with God in the warmth and light of his unchanging love.

INCARNATION

We have seen how God's abundant goodness flows out to creatures in the free act by which he calls the world into existence, and we have discussed how that act is continued in God's providential care for each of the things he has made. We now consider the event that is the highest expression of God's will to share his goodness with creatures: the incarnational sending of his Son.[163] This mission or sending of the Son may, like the act of creation, be understood as a sort of motion. In reality, however, the Incarnation (again, like the act of creation) involves neither motion nor change on God's part. For God who, in his abundant goodness, is the source of "every good gift and

---

160. *ST* I, 3, 5, co.; Q.12, 8, ad 4; *SCG* I, c.68.3 (§569); *Quodl.* I, Q.4, a.3 [8], ad 1; XII, Q:3, a.1 [3], ad 1; *In phys.* VIII, lect. 2.5 (§975).

161. "Through his own original and unique disclosure of *esse* as the 'act of acts and the perfection of perfections,' Aquinas at one stroke provides meaning to process in the world and to a world in process, and indicates why a world in process simply cannot be a world merely of process" (Reichmann, "Aquinas," 436). Cf.: Reichmann, "Immanently," 368–69; Hill, *Three*, 260.

162. The phrase is Whitehead's. See *Process and Reality*, 349. It is possible to characterize ultimate fulfillment as "static" only in a philosophy that values progress for progress's sake alone, and not for the sake of some goal toward which that progress is leading.

163. See *ST* III, 1, 1; *Sent.* III, 1, 1, 1, ad 2.

blessing," is himself subject to "no variation or shadow due to change" (Jas 1:17). But if there can be no change in God, how are we to understand the scriptural affirmation that "the Word became flesh" (Jn 1:14)?

If we were to accept this affirmation according to our usual way of speaking, we would probably think it implies some change in God. Normally "to become" implies "to change." Thomas was aware of various theologians who taught that the Incarnation implies change in God. Eutyches believed that the Word became flesh in the same way air might be changed into fire, or wheat into bread.[164] Apollinaris thought that something of the Word was converted into flesh as the water at Cana was miraculously converted into wine.[165]

In our own time, a number of theologians argue that the reality of the Incarnation can be preserved only by admitting some kind of change in God. Hans Urs von Balthasar, for example, contends that if the *kenosis* of the Son is to be correctly understood, the immutability of God must not be overly insisted upon: "It implied coming through a narrow pass: not so to guard the immutability of God that in the pre-existent Logos who prepares himself to become man nothing real happens and on the other hand not to let this real happening degenerate into divine suffering. . . . One has to say that P. Althaus is right: 'On this realization, the old concept of the immutability of God is clearly shattered. Christology must take seriously that God himself really entered into suffering in the Son and therein is and remains completely God.'"[166] Karl Rahner has his own mysterious phrase for the becoming of God in the Incarnation: "God who is not subject to change in himself can change in something else. . . . [H]e *himself* can become something in another."[167]

164. On Eutyches's teaching, see Leo the Great, *Epist. XXVIII ad Flavianum*, cap.6 (*PL* 45, 777); Boethius, *De duabus nat.*, cap.5–7 (*PL* 64, 1347–52). In Thomas, see *Super ad rom.* I, lect. 2 (§37); *Super ev. jo.* I, lect. 7 (§66).

165. On Apollinaris's teaching, see Augustine, *De haeresibus*, 55 (*PL* 42, 40). In Thomas, see *SCG* IV, c.31.1–2 (§3670); *De unione verbi*, a.1, co.

166. Hans Urs von Balthasar, "Mysterium Paschale," in *Mysterium Salutis*, ed. J. Feiner and Magnus Löhrer (Einsiedeln: Benziger, 1969), 3/2:144, 151–52. For an extensive review von Balthasar's notion of immutability, see Gerard F. O'Hanlon, *The Immutability of God in the Theology of Hans Urs von Balthasar* (Cambridge: Cambridge University Press, 1990).

167. Karl Rahner, *Foundations of Christian Faith*, trans. W. Dych (New York: Seabury, 1978), 219, 221. See also his "Selbstmitteilung Gottes," in *Sacramentum Mundi*, ed. K. Rahner and A. Darlap (Freiburg:

The danger must certainly be recognized that, in the interest of maintaining the absolute immutability of God, one might deny the reality of the Incarnation. Thomas notes, for instance, that "certain ones," in order to maintain the absolute immutability of the Logos, taught that the Incarnation consists merely in some sort of accidental addition of a human nature to the nature of the Logos. In becoming human, the Logos put on a human nature only in an accidental way, as one might put on clothes.[168] This interpretation certainly preserves the immutability of the Logos, but also makes it impossible to affirm that the Logos is truly human. For, in this interpretation, the Logos would not truly subsist in a human nature. But if the Logos does not subsist in a human nature, such things as birth, suffering, and death, which belong to the human nature, do not truly belong to the Logos. Thomas, while recognizing that such dangers may be involved in maintaining the immutability of the Logos, does not think that divine immutability must be sacrificed in the interest of preserving the doctrine of the Incarnation. On the contrary, in his theology the doctrine of the Incarnation may be preserved only by maintaining God's absolute immutability.

The words of John's Gospel that "the Word became flesh" must not be interpreted in a way that makes the Incarnation a mere fantasy.[169] God truly becomes human. But in doing so, he does not cease to be the unchangeable God. When properly understood, the Incarnation, far from denying the immutability of God, rather requires it. For if God changed in becoming human, he would no longer be truly God, and Jesus Christ would not be truly God and human.[170]

In discussing whether the statement "God was made man" implies change in God, Thomas alludes to the mixed relation between God and

Herder, 1969), vol. 4, col. 522–24; "Probleme der Christologie von Heute," *Schriften zur Theologie* (Einsiedeln: Benziger, 1958), 1:196; "Zur Theologie der Menschwerdung," *Schriften zur Theologie* (Einsiedeln: Benziger, 1960),4:145–49; "Bemerkungen zur Gotteslehre in der katholischen Dogmatik" *Schriften zur Theologie* (Einsiedeln: Benziger, 1967), 8:184; "Theologische Bemerkungen zum Zeitbegriff," *Schriften zur Theologie* (Einsiedeln: Benziger, 1970), 9:321. See also Varillon, *Souffrance,* 46; Maas, *Unveränderlichkeit,* 186–87. For a critique of Rahner's position, see Horst Seidl, "De l'immutabilité de Dieu."

168. *SCG* IV, c.37.1 (§3749). Cf.: *ST* III, 2, 6.

169. Jn 1:14. *SCG* IV, c.29.2 (§3647); c.37.

170. "Ostensum est enim supra quod Deus omnino immutabilis est. Omne autem quod in aliud convertitur, manifestum est mutari. Cum igitur Verbum Dei sit verus Deus, ut ostensum est, impossibile est quod Verbum Dei fuerit in carnem mutatum" (*SCG* IV, c.31.2 [§3671]). Cf.: 31.3 (§3672).

creatures, which allows "becoming" to be predicated of God without implying change in him.[171] In his providential activity, God is said to "become
our refuge" (Ps 89:1), not because of some change in God, but because of a
change that God effects in the welfare of his people. Similarly, God is said
to "become" the creator not because of any change in him, but because of
a "change" in the creature that, through God's creative act, begins to exist.
So also in the Incarnation, God becomes human, not because God changes,
but because human nature is changed by being united to him.[172] This is not
simply an accidental union. It is a true union of divine and human nature in
the person of the Son of God, but it is accomplished without alteration or
confusion of the two natures.[173] By reason of this union, those things that
are proper to the human nature truly belong to the Son of God and may be
predicated of God.[174] In this sense, we may say that, by assuming a human
nature, God "empties himself" (Phil 2:7) and "becomes flesh" (Jn 1:14).[175] In
all of this, however, it is not God who changes, but the human nature that
God assumes.[176]

Thomas believes the abiding immutability of God in the Incarnation is
confirmed by the authority of Scripture, the councils of the Church, and arguments from reason.[177] Only if the divine and human natures of the Son

171. *ST* III, 16, 6, ad 2. Overlooking the notion of mixed relation, Tersur Akuma Aben insists that
Aquinas must affirm "a real relational change" in God in the Incarnation. He suggests a "soft immutabil-
ity" with respect to God's "relational properties" as distinct from his essence. Tersur Akuma Aben, "The
Doctrine of Divine Immutability as God's Constancy" (Ph.D. diss., Calvin Theological Seminary, Grand
Rapids, Mich., 2000), 91–92. We would point out that such a predication violates divine simplicity.

172. *Super ad rom.* I, lect. 2 (§37). Cf.: *SCG* IV, c.31.6 (§3675); *ST* III, 16, 6, ad 2.

173. "[N]aturae quidem unitae sunt in Christo, non tamen in natura, sed in persona; quod apparet
ex hoc ipso quod dicuntur inconvertibiliter et inalterabiliter naturae esse unitae" (*De unione verbi* a.1, ad
3). Cf.: *Sent.* III, 1, 1, 2, ad 1.

174. *ST* III, 16, 1; a.4; *SCG* IV, c.39.2 (§3772).

175. "Sicut enim descendit de caelo, non quod desineret esse in caelo, sed quia incepit esse novo
modo in terris, sic etiam se exinanivit, non deponendo divinam naturam, sed assumendo naturam humanam. . . . Dicit ergo exinanivit, quia naturam humanam assumpsit" (*Super ad phil.* II, lect. 2 [§57]).
Cf.: *Super ad hebr.* II, lect. 2 (§109).

176. "[E]t ideo esse hominem praedicatur de novo de Deo absque eius mutatione, per mutationem
humanae naturae, quae assumitur in divinam personam. Et ideo, cum dicitur, 'Deus factus est homo,'
non intelligitur aliqua mutatio ex parte Dei, sed solum ex parte humanae naturae" (*ST* III, 16, 6, ad 2).
Cf.: *ST* III, 1, 1, ad 1; *Sent.* III, 1, 1, 1, ad 1; d.7, 2, 1, ad 1; *SCG* IV, c.49.3 (§3838); c.55.3 (§3934); *Super ad rom.* I,
lect. 2 (§37); *De rat. fid.* c.6, line 6 c.

177. For Thomas's scriptural arguments, see *Super ad rom.* I, lect. 2 (§37); *Super ev. jo.* I, lect. 7.1
(§166). Thomas refers to the Council of Constantinople against Apollinaris, and to the Council of

of God are truly distinct yet truly united in his person can he be called true
God and true man. If his divine nature changes in becoming man, he can no
longer be called God. If his human nature is not an integral human nature
like our own, he cannot truly be called man. But if he assumes a human nature while remaining the immutable and transcendent God, then he is truly
God and truly man. He is "like his brethren in every respect" (Heb 2:17), for
he, like all other human beings, is human by the fact that he has a human nature.[178]

In the Word made flesh we find the greatest sign of God's love for us. It
is he who reveals to us the motion of the immovable God. He teaches us of
the dynamic inner life of love that is the Triune God. It was through him that
God created the world in love.[179] It was through his free act of love (Jn 15:13)
that God redeemed his sinful creatures. It is he who promises to send the
Spirit (Jn 15:26; 16:7) and who assures us that the Trinity dwells in us (Jn
14:17, 23). Finally, it is through him that we shall be led to our ultimate fulfillment in an unending union of love with the Triune God.[180] Through the
manifestation of God's goodness and love in the Incarnation, desire for that
ultimate union with God is awakened in us:

Since man's perfect beatitude consists in the enjoyment of divinity, man's love had to
be disposed toward a desire of beatitude. But the desire to enjoy anything is caused

Chalcedon against Eutyches. See *De unione verbi* a. 1, co. Commenting on the decrees of Lateran IV, Thomas rejects the error that there is but one nature in Christ, whether that nature be said to be passible (The-
odosius) or impassible (Galanus). See *Super decret.* I, line 607 c. Reference is made to philosophical arguments for divine immutability in regard to the Incarnation in *SCG* IV, c. 31.2 (§3671); IV, c.35.8 (§3732);
and *ST* III, 2, 1, co.

178. "Si vero quaeris quomodo Verbum est homo, dicendum quod eo modo est homo quo
quocumque alius est homo, scilicet habens humanam naturam. . . . Hoc autem quod dicitur 'Verbum
caro factum est,' non aliquam mutationem in Verbo, sed solum in natura assumpta de novo in unitatem
personae divinae dicit. 'Et Verbum caro factum est,' per unionem ad carnem. Unio autem relatio quaedam est. Relationes autem de novo dictae de Deo in respectu ad creaturas, non important mutationem
ex parte Dei, sed ex parte creaturae novo modo se habentis ad Deum" (*Super ev. jo.* I, lect. 7.1 [§172]). Cf.:
SCG IV, c.55.14 (§3944).

179. Jn 1:10. Cf.: *ST* I, 32, 1, ad 3; Q.34, 1, ad 3; a.3; *De ver.* Q.4, 4; *Comp.* I, c.215; *Super ev. jo.* III, lect.
6.4 (§544).

180. See *Sent.* I, *prologus,* where Thomas explains the structure of the four books of the *Sentences* by
saying that it is through Christ, as the wisdom of God, that the hidden things of God are manifested
(Book I) and that the work of creation is accomplished (Book II), restored (Book III), and brought to
perfection (Book IV).

by love of that thing. Therefore, man, tending to perfect beatitude, needed inducement to the divine love. Nothing, of course, so induces us to love one as the experience of his love for us. But God's love for men could be demonstrated to man in no way more effective than this: He willed to be united to man in person, for it is proper to love to unite the lover with the beloved so far as possible. Therefore, it was necessary for man tending to perfect beatitude that God become man.[181]

181. *SCG* IV, c.54.5 (§3926). Cf.: *ST* III, 1, 2, co.; Q.46, 3, co.

CHAPTER FOUR

The Unchanging God of Love

In asking, "Whether there is love in God," Aquinas finds an initial response in the simple but eloquent words of St. John: "God is love."[1] These words evoke the whole spirit and teaching of the New Testament and accord with the philosophical conclusion that divine love "is the principle of all things."[2] But these simple words raise a profound question when considered in relation to the teaching that God is immutable, a teaching Thomas sees as common to the Old and New Testaments, the doctrinal statements of the Church, and the conclusions of human reason. How is love compatible with immutability? How can the God who is love also be the God "in whom there is no variation or shadow due to change" (Jas 1:17)? Human love is often associated with motion—the restlessness of desire, the impulse of passion, the steady unfolding of affection and commitment. If we tend to associate love with movement, how is it possible for us to attribute love to a Being in whom there is no movement or change? Must we agree with theologians such as Nicholas Wolterstorff that the notion of divine impassibility can be maintained only "by paying the price of removing from God all knowledge of, and love for, the particular things of this world"?[3] By employ-

---

1. Jn 4:16. See *ST* I, 20, 1, sc.
2. *SCG* I, c.91.14 (§765).
3. Wolterstorff, "Suffering Love," 223. See also Daniel A. Dombrowski, "Must a Perfect Being Be Immutable?" in *Hartshorne, Process Philosophy and Theology*, ed. Robert Kane and Stephen H. Phillips

ing Aquinas's account of how even human love involves both dynamism and stillness and his analogous description of divine love, we may begin answer such questions and come to a better understanding of the unchanging love of God.

HUMAN LOVE AS MOVING AND MOTIONLESS

To Aquinas, human love involves both motion and immutability. Love itself is a kind of motion, an immanent activity. At its inception, love always implies some change in our will. It originates in our recognition of the goodness of some object. We see an object (whether a person or thing) as good since it is in some way "akin and proportionate (*connaturale et proportionatum*)" to ourselves.[4] The goodness we recognize in the object awakens our love since it "moves the appetite, introducing itself as it were into its intention."[5] Love is this "first change (*prima immutatio*) wrought in the appetite by the appetible object."[6] It involves a "transformation (*transformatio*) of the affection into the thing loved."[7] It is "the first movement (*primus motus*) of the will and of any appetitive faculty."[8]

But this very motion of love possesses a certain immovable character. For, "when the affection or appetite is completely imbued with the form of the good which is its object, it is pleased with it and adheres to it as though fixed (*fixum*) in it, and then it is said to love it."[9] In this sense, love is not only a kind of motion but also a "stabilizing (*stabilimentum*) of the will in the good willed," and a "quieting of the affection (*quietatio affectus*)."[10] Love consists in a "union of affection" by which the lover is united to the beloved and is made in some way "one with the beloved."[11] This initial union of affection involves a resting of the lover in the beloved, but it is not yet that ultimate compan-

---

(Albany: State University of New York Press, 1989), 97: "To deny God the ability to change does avoid fickleness, but at the expense of the ability to react lovingly to the sufferings of others."

4. *ST* I-II, 27, 1, co.   5. *ST* I-II, 26, 2, co.
6. *ST* I-II, 26, 2, co. Cf.: *In de div. nom.* IV, lect. 10 (§427).
7. *Sent.* III, 27, 1, 1, co.
8. *ST* I, 20, 1, co. Cf.: *Sent.* III, 27, 2, 1, co.   9. *Sent.* III, 27, 1, 1, co.
10. *De pot.* Q.9, 9, co.; *Sent.* III, 27, 1, 1, ad 2; *Sent.* III, 27, 2, 1, co.
11. *ST* I-II, 28, 1, ad 2. Cf.: *Sent.* III, 27, 1, 1, co.; *ST* I-II, 25, 2, ad 2; Q.28, 1, co.

ionship the lover is seeking. That is found only in the real union of lover and beloved that flowers in the stillness of joy.[12]

Love is thus characterized by both motion and immovability. It arises through a change in the will brought about by the recognition of the goodness of some object. It consists in a union of affection with the object by which the will is fixed or stabilized in it. This fixing or stabilizing of the will, however, itself involves a sort of motion—the immanent activity or motion of willing that object. The union of affection, which is love itself, persists whether the beloved is actually present or not. When the beloved is present, it gives rise to delight in the beloved. When absent, it excites a restless desire for the beloved, which may induce the lover to initiate a series of actions aimed at achieving the joy of real union with the beloved.[13] So love is the source and principle of all movement toward that real union of lover and beloved that is the culmination of love. As the source of such movement, however, love is immovable:

> Among the various affections of the soul, love has priority. For love is called the perfection (*terminationem*) of the faculty of desire in that through love the faculty of desire is informed by its object. In all things, however, one finds that motion proceeds from an immovable first principle (*primo immobili quieto*). This is evident in natural things because the first mover in any genus is not moved by that genus of motion. For instance, the first cause of alteration is not itself subject to alteration. It is also evident in intellectual things. For the motion of discursive reason proceeds from the principles and quiddities of things by which the informed intellect is perfected. Therefore, since the faculty of desire is informed and perfected by love, as the intellect is by the principles and quiddities of things, as has been said, it is necessary that every motion of the faculty of desire proceed from the quiet and perfection of love.[14]

12. *ST* I-II, 25, 2, ad 2; Q.26, 2, co.; Q.28, 1, co.; ad 2. In tracing the development of Aquinas's theory of love, Michael Sherwin points out how love involves both motion and motionlessness: "Importantly, Aquinas recognizes that although love is the terminus of a motion, it is also the principle of a further motion." He notes that in Aquinas's later thought, he "seems to recognize more clearly that the 'rest' proper to love is not inactivity, but full actuality. . . . The will is said to rest in the beloved when it engages in the activity of delighting in the beloved" (*By Knowledge and by Love: Charity and Knowledge in the Moral Theology of St. Thomas Aquinas* [Washington, D.C.: The Catholic University of America Press, 2005], 66, 77).

13. *ST* I-II, 25, 2, ad 2; Q.26, 2, co.; Q.28, 1, ad 1; *SCG* IV, c.19.3 (§3559).

14. *Sent.* III, 27, 1, 3, co. Cf.: *SCG* IV, c.19.3 (§3559); *ST* I-II, 26, 1, co.; Q.28, 6, co.; *In de div. nom.* IV, lect. 9 (§408). On the unchanging character of love as the source of all the actions that may be involved

DIVINE LOVE AS DYNAMIC STILLNESS

Because God's love also involves aspects of motion and immutability, it may be characterized as dynamic stillness.[15] In its motion and immutability, however, God's love is by no means the same as ours. By considering God's love in terms of motion and motionlessness, we can come to see its dynamic character, gratuity, and intimacy.

The Dynamism of Unchanging Love

God's love may be seen as an immanent motion of the divine will.[16] Such motion opens into the mystery of the Trinity, where the procession of the Son may be considered according to the immanent motion of knowing and the procession of the Holy Spirit, according to that of love. In this eternal and unchanging activity God both loves himself in his own goodness and loves all creatures as they participate him.[17] In this way, the Trinitarian love of God embraces all of creation:

The Father loves not only the Son but also himself and us by the Holy Spirit. . . . As the Father speaks himself and every creature by his begotten Word, inasmuch as the Word begotten adequately represents the Father and every creature; so he loves himself and every creature by the Holy Spirit, inasmuch as the Holy Spirit proceeds as the love of the primal goodness whereby the Father loves himself and every creature. Thus it is evident that relation to the creature is implied both in the Word and in the proceeding Love, as it were in a secondary way, inasmuch as the divine truth and goodness are a principle of understanding and loving all creatures.[18]

Unlike our love, which is awakened by the goodness perceived in the beloved, God's love is not caused by the goodness of its object. His love for himself is not caused by his own goodness since it is one with his good-

---

in attaining real union, see William Rossner, "Towards an Analysis of 'God is Love,'" *Thomist* 38 (1973): 637, 642.

15. Or, in Aquinas's expression, "productive stillness *(statum generativum)*" *(In de div. nom.* IX, lect. 4 [§842]).

16. "Deus dicitur amor et amabilis quia 'Ipse' amat motu 'sui ipsius' et adducit se ad seipsum; velle enim est quidam motus" *(In de div. nom.* IV, lect. 11 [§444]).

17. *SCG* I, c.75.4 (§642); *Sent.* III, 32, 1, 1, co.; *ST* I, 20, 1, ad 3.

18. *ST* I, 37, 2, ad 3.

ness, and "a thing cannot be its own cause."[19] Nor is his love for creatures
caused by his love for his own goodness since it is by one and the same act
that God wills both his own goodness as his proper object and the existence
of creatures as ordered to his goodness, and again, a thing cannot be its own
cause.[20] And certainly his love for creatures is not caused by the goodness of
creatures since it is the very source of whatever goodness is found in them.[21]
God's love is in no way caused. No change in his will is brought about by the
goodness of the beloved. While our love has the character of both change
and immovability in its inception, God's eternal and abiding love has only
the character of immutability.[22]

As our love is the unchanging source of our deeds, God's love is the immutable source of his creative and providential action. But while our love
gives rise to various desires and passions as it seeks to attain union with
the beloved, God's love involves only the boundless joy of eternal possession
and complete union with his own goodness.[23] All passions implying imperfect possession of goodness are therefore said of God only metaphorically.[24]

The Gratuity of Creative Love

Our consideration of divine immutability has led us to see creation as a free
act. We shall now recognize it also as an act of gratuitous love. First, however, it
will be useful to consider some features of human love. Love consists in "will-

---

19. *ST* I, 19, 5, co.

20. Ibid.

21. *ST* I, 19, 5, co.; Q.20, 2, co.; *Sent.* III, 32, 1, 1, ad 4; *In de div. nom.* IV, lect. 10 (§439).

22. "Dilectio autem Dei, quantum est ex parte actus divini, est aeterna et immutabilis" (*ST* I-II, 113, 2, co.).

23. *Sent.* III, 32, 1, 1, ad 1. Cf.: *SCG* I, c. 90; c.91.12 (§763); 91.17 (§766); *ST* I, 20, 1, ad 1.

24. "[P]assiones quaedam important in sui ratione aliquam materialem transmutationem, et ideo non possunt transferri in Deum, nisi per similitudinem" (*Sent.* III, 32, 1, 1, ad 1). Cf.: *ST* I, 3, 2, ad 2; Q.20, 1, ad 1; ad 2. In denying passion of God, we must be careful not to confuse impassibility (*impassibilitas*), which is a sign of divine perfection, with insensibility (*insensibilitas*), which is a human vice. Such confusion is evident in Jean Galot, who makes divine impassibility look like insensibility: "Through a strange reversal of the situation, a radical insensibility has frequently been attributed to God, in opposition to human sensibility" (*Dieu souffre-t-il?* [Paris: Lethielleux, 1976], 131). François Varillon likewise tends to identify "impassible" with "insensible": "Impassible, that is to say insensible, thus indifferent, if one ignores or refuses the subtle play of '*distinguo*'" (*Souffrance*, 14). The same is true of Joseph M. Hallman: "Because God [in Aquinas's thought] has no potentiality, there simply cannot be a divine emotive life, even for a loving deity" ("The Mistake of Thomas Aquinas and the Trinity of A. N. Whitehead," *Journal of Religion* 70 (1990): 36.

ing some good to someone."[25] The person to whom I wish that good is loved with "the love of friendship." The good I wish that person is loved with "the love of concupiscence." The "someone" to whom I will that good may be either myself or another person. When the "someone" is myself, the love of concupiscence with which I will that good is directed toward my own benefit, pleasure, or utility, and I view that good as something to be acquired or attained.[26]

But the "someone" to whom I will that good need not (and should not) always be myself. It may also be another person in whom I see some quality that awakens my love. In virtue of that quality (which could be anything from our common humanity, to our shared interest in literature, to our peculiar partiality for Parcheesi) I view that person at first perhaps as a kindred spirit, but ultimately as another self.[27] I come to identify myself with that person and work for that person's good as I do for my own.[28] I view the quality or goodness I discover in the person not as something to be acquired from him or her, but as something to be cherished for its own sake. In this way, I affirm the goodness the person already possesses and wish for him or her whatever additional good I judge appropriate or beneficial. The love of concupiscence with which I love the good I wish for that person is directed not toward myself but toward that person and may be considered as an aspect or dimension of my friendship for the person.[29]

The love of concupiscence with which I love the good I wish to "someone" may therefore be either self-directed (when the "someone" to whom I wish that good is myself) or other-oriented (when the "someone" to whom I wish that good is a friend whom I regard as a "second self"). It is possible for me at times, however, while wishing some good to another person (and thus loving that person to some extent with the love of friendship), simultaneously to refer the very good of that person to myself. I might, for example, wish a fellow student to do well in a class so that she can better help me with my own classwork. In such cases, my love for that person is ultimately directed to my own good (to my own pleasure or utility). This sort of love must ul-

25. "[A]mare est velle alicui bonum." ST I-II, 26, 4, co. Cf.: I, 20, 2, co.
26. ST I-II, 27, 3, co.; Q.28, 1, co.; ad 2; In de div. nom. IV, lect. 9 (§404–6).
27. STI I-II, 27, 3, co.; Q.28, 1, co.; ad 2; In de div. nom. IV, lect. 2 (§404–6).
28. Sent. III, 27, 1, 1, co. Cf.: ST I-II, 26, 2, ad 2; Q.27, 3, co.; Q.28, 1, co.; a.2, ad 2.
29. ST II-II, 25, 3, co. Cf.: a.2, co.

timately be characterized as a self-directed love of concupiscence and not as a true love of friendship.[30]

The love characteristic of creatures is always colored to some extent by a self-directed love of concupiscence. Creatures always refer their actions in some way back to their own good. Each creature is perfectible and seeks to achieve its perfection through its actions. It acts not for an end it already possesses but for one it still desires. In loving another, the creature is always in some way seeking its own good. Its love always involves the self-directed love of concupiscence that seeks the good of the lover.[31] This fact does not render all human love "selfish" but does indicate the indigence of our human nature, which, even in its noblest actions, is always in some way seeking its own fulfillment.

In light of our discussion of human love, we can see that God's act of creation is an act of love of the purest sort. Since love consists in "willing some good to some being" and since God, in his creative activity, wills to share his own goodness with creatures to the extent that this is possible according to their various natures, God's creative act is evidently an act of love.[32] Unlike creatures, however, who are always in some way seeking their own perfection in each of their actions and whose love always involves the self-directed love of concupiscence, God is in no way seeking to enhance or augment his goodness through his creative activity. He wills only to share his goodness with creatures according to their capacities of nature and grace.[33]

If God were seeking his own advancement or acting to attain an end not yet possessed, his action would, like that of creatures, involve the self-directed love of concupiscence. We would then have to characterize God's love as *"eros"* rather than *"agape."* This is precisely the kind of love a number of contemporary thinkers attribute to God. According to Paul S. Fiddes, "God does not 'need' the world in the sense that there is some intrinsic necessity in his nature, . . . but he does need the world in the sense that he has freely chosen to be in need."[34] Vincent Brümmer maintains: "God can bestow value

30. *ST* I-II, 26, 4, ad 3. Cf.: *In de div. nom.* IV, lect. 9 (§404).
31. *SCG* I, c.93.7 (§785); *ST* I, 60, 3, co.
32. *ST* I, 20, 2, co. Cf.: *SCG* I, c.91.2 (§756).
33. *ST* I, 19, 2, co.; *Super ad eph.* I, lect. 1 (§13).
34. Paul S. Fiddes, *The Creative Suffering of God* (Oxford: Clarendon Press, 1988), 74.

on us and on our love only if he needs us to bestow value on him."[35] Alfred
North Whitehead explicitly identifies divine love as *eros* in describing the
God of process philosophy: "We must conceive the Divine Eros as the active
entertainment of all ideals, with the urge to their finite realization, each in its
due season. Thus a process must be inherent in God's nature, whereby his
infinity is acquiring realization."[36] But a God in need, as William Hill points
out in reference to Whitehead's philosophy, will always be somewhat selfish:
"God's love for the world . . . is *Eros* and not *Agape*. The motive for the love
in the final analysis is the self-fulfillment of the Divine Lover. . . . God acts
upon the world precisely to derive values from it, values which perdure only
in himself. The initiatives of God cannot, in this account, be seen as purely
altruistic, benefiting the beloved for the latter's own sake."[37] As Katherin A.
Rogers puts it, the idea of a God who "needs us to be fulfilled" is "a rather de-
pressing conception of divinity."[38]

In Aquinas's theology, God acts not out of desire for an end he has yet
to attain, but out of love for an end he eternally and unchangingly possesses
in infinite fullness—the end of his own unbounded goodness.[39] In this, he
is different from every created agent: "It does not belong to the First Agent,
who is agent only, to act for the acquisition of some end; he intends only to
communicate his perfection, which is his goodness; while every creature intends to acquire its own perfection, which is the likeness of the divine perfection and goodness."[40] Since God does not act for his own benefit, his love
for creatures in no way involves the self-directed love of concupiscence that

35. Vincent Brümmer, "Bestowed Fellowship: The Love of God," in *Understanding the Attributes of God*, ed. Gijsbert van den Brink and Marcel Sarot (Frankfurt: Peter Lang, 1999), 52.

36. Alfred North Whitehead, *Adventures of Ideas* (New York: Free Press, 1967), 277. Cf.: *Process*, 105 [161]. See also Charles Hartshorne: "For either God loves the creatures or he does not. If he does, then their interests contribute to his interests, for love means nothing more than this" (*Man's Vision of God and the Logic of Theism* [Chicago: Willet, Clark, 1941], 164). Cf.: Hartshorne, "Whitehead's," 222–23; "Three," 9–10.

37. W. Hill, "Does the World," 150. Cf.: William Hill, "Two Gods of Love: Aquinas and Whitehead," *Listening* 14 (1979): 249–65; John Quinn, "Triune Self-giving: One Key to the Problem of Suffering," *Thomist* 44 (1980): 188; Mahoney, *Charles*, 137; Knasas, "Finite," 90; Wright, "Method," 52, Pegis, *Greeks*, 50–56.

38. Katherin A. Rogers, *Perfect Being Theology* (Edinburgh: Edinburgh University Press, 2000), 52.

39. *SCG* I, c.76.6 (§652); II, c.19.6 (§960); c.35.7 (§1117); *ST* I, 19, 3, co.; Q.44, 4, ad 1; *De pot.* Q.5, 3, co.; *De ver.* Q.23, 1, ad 3; *In eth.* IX, lect. 4, lines 124–28 (Leonine).

40. *ST* I, 44, 4, co. Cf.: *Sent.* II, 1, 2, 1, co.; *De pot.* Q.3, 15, ad 14.

seeks the benefit of the lover. It is rather a love of friendship. With respect to rational creatures who are themselves capable of such love, his love is the purest kind of friendship since it in no way seeks his own benefit, but only the good of the friend. With respect to irrational creatures, which are incapable of being loved with the love of friendship,[41] his love is like that other-oriented love of concupiscence, which wills some good not for oneself, but for one's friend. For God wills the existence of irrational creatures not because of any need on his part or any benefit that could accrue to him, but for the sake of rational creatures to whom such beings are ordered.[42]

We can say that God loves some creatures with the love of concupiscence in that he orders them to the good of other creatures, but we must add that God loves each creature in itself insofar as he wills to each one the good of its own being.[43] Since all that God creates is ordered ultimately to his own goodness, we may say God wills all creatures for the sake of his goodness. We do not thereby imply, however, that his goodness is enhanced by their existence. We simply indicate that all things participate God's goodness insofar as they exist and are ordered to it as their end. There is therefore no contradiction between saying God wills creatures for their own sake, in that he wills to each its proper existence and perfection, and saying he wills them for the sake of his goodness, insofar as they participate in, and are ordered to it.[44]

We can recognize God's creative act as supremely free if we acknowledge that creatures are ordered to God's goodness but not necessary to it. Similarly, we can see it as a supremely gratuitous act of love if we recognize that God derives no benefit from it.[45] Thomas describes this gratuitous love as a "key" that unlocks the power of God in the act of creation: "Regarding the hand of his power, it is said in Ps 103:28: 'When you open your hand, all things will

---

41. *ST* I, 20, 2, ad 3; II-II, 23, 1, co.; Q.25, 3, co.
42. *ST* I, 20, 2, ad 3; II-II, 25, 3, co.
43. *SCG* I, c.21.3 (§757). Cf.: *ST* I, 20, 2.
44. "Deus autem creaturarum universitatem vult propter se ipsam, licet et propter se ipsum eam vult esse; haec enim duo non repugnant. Vult enim Deus ut creaturae sint propter eius bonitatem, ut eam scilicet suo modo imitentur et repraesentent; quod quidem faciunt in quantum ab ea esse habent, et in suis naturis subsistunt. Unde idem est dictu, quod Deus omnia propter se ipsum fecit . . . , et quod creaturas fecerit propter earum esse" (*De pot.* Q.5, 4, co.).
45. *SCG* I, c.93.7 (§785).

be filled with goodness.' For in his hand were all the ends of the earth which from eternity were in his power alone. But when his hand was opened by the key of love, creatures were produced."[46] As the font of creation, divine love may be seen as the "driving force (*vim impulsivam*)" in God's creative act:

Divine love did "not" allow "him to remain in himself without fruit," that is, without the production of creatures, but love "moved him to operate (*amor movit ipsum ad operandum*) according" to a most excellent mode of operation as he produced all things in being (*esse*). For from love of his goodness it proceeded that he willed to pour out and communicate his goodness to others, insofar as it was possible, namely by way of similitude, and that his goodness did not remain in him, but flowed out into others.[47]

The Intimacy of Divine Friendship

Reference to the immutability of divine goodness has shown us that God's love is not a self-seeking love of concupiscence but the absolutely gratuitous love of friendship. As we now consider the intimacy of God's love, we will need to distinguish between mere good will and actual love, and consider the particular qualities of friendship.

Thomas accepts and often employs Aristotle's definition that to love is "to wish good to someone."[48] He is aware, however, that love involves more than simply well-wishing.[49] To such benevolence, love adds "a resting (*quietationem*) of the appetite in the beloved."[50] This resting of the lover in the beloved implies a "certain union of affection between the lover and the beloved,

---

46. *Sent.* II, *prologus*.

47. *In de div. nom.* IV, lect. 9 (§409). Cf.: *SCG* IV; c.20.3 (§3571). Recognizing the freedom of God's creative act, we must disagree with Jürgen Moltmann's characterization of God as needing a creation. Jürgen Moltmann, *The Trinity and the Kingdom* (San Francisco: Harper and Row, 1981), 58–59. We agree rather with Frans Jozef van Beeck's argument that, properly understood, "apatheia safeguards God's transcendent freedom to be God-in-self-manifestation—that is, to communicate the divine Self to the world in wholly self-initiated love and mercy, regardless of humanity's or the cosmos' readiness and response" (*God Encountered: A Contemporary Catholic Systematic Theology* (Collegeville, Minn.: Liturgical Press, 1994), 2/2, 162–64. As C. S. Lewis points out: "In God there is no hunger that needs to be filled, only plenteousness that desires to give. The doctrine that God was under no necessity to create is not a piece of dry scholastic speculation. It is essential" (*The Four Loves* [New York: Harcourt, Brace, Jovanovich, 1960], 175).

48. See, for example, *ST* I-II, 26, 4, co.; I, 20, 2, co.

49. *ST* II-II; 27, 2, ad 1.

50. *Sent.* III, 27, 2, 1, co.

inasmuch as the lover deems the beloved as somehow one with himself or as belonging to himself and so tends toward it."[51] Both in the love of friendship where the beloved is regarded as one with the lover and in the love of concupiscence where the beloved is seen as belonging to the lover, there is a union of affection not implied by mere benevolence.

We say of God that he not merely wishes creatures well, but loves them. The object of his love is his own unchanging goodness. As creatures participate his goodness, however, he truly loves them in the same act by which he loves his own goodness.[52] We cannot therefore view his love for creatures as a kind of detached well-wishing. We will come closer to the truth if we, like Thomas, "boldly assert" with Dionysius that God's loving care for his creatures is best characterized as a kind of ecstasy:

> [Dionysius] says that "this" must be boldly asserted "for the sake of the truth" . . . "that he" who is "the cause of all things" through his good and beautiful love by which he loves all things according to the abundance of his goodness, by which he loves things, "is made [to be] outside himself (*extra seipsum*)" insofar as he provides for all existing things through his goodness and love. And in some way "he is drawn forth (*trahitur*) and somehow taken down (*deponitur*)" from his prominence according to which he exists (*existit*) "above all things and is set apart from all things," so that he may be "in all things" through the effects of his goodness "according to" a certain "ecstasy (*exstasim*)" which nevertheless so makes him to be in all lower things that his supersubstantial power does not depart from him.[53]

Even in attributing to God this ecstasy of love, we have not made bold enough to assert the whole truth of divine love. For we do not begin to appreciate its true character until we see it as the highest form of love, actual friendship. We have found that love (whether belonging to the sense appetite [*amor*] or to the will [*dilectio*]) may be divided into the "love of concupiscence," which regards the good we wish to someone, and the "love of friendship," which regards the person to whom we wish that good.[54] This "love of friendship,"

51. *ST* II-II, 27, 2, co.

52. *Sent.* III, 32, 1, 1, co. Cf.: *ST* I, 19, 5, co.; *In de div. nom.* IV, lect. 9 (§409).

53. *In de div. nom.* IV, lect. 10 (§437). Cf.: IV, lect. 10 (§430); *Sent.* III, 32, 1, 1, ad 3; *ST* I, 20, 2, ad 1. Regarding God's care for his creatures, see *In de div. nom.* III, lect. un. (§242); *SCG* III, c.95.2 (§2703); *ST* I-II, 21, 4, co.; *Super iob* XXXV, v.8, line 81.

54. *Sent.* III, 27, 2.

however, must be distinguished from actual friendship itself. For this reason, Aquinas distinguishes love not into friendship and concupiscence, but into "love of friendship and love of concupiscence."[55] The terminology is admittedly open to confusion since actual friendship is of course also a form of love. It is important, however, that we understand the distinction between actual friendship and "the love of friendship" if we are to appreciate the true character of divine love. Actual friendship, as we shall see, implies more than "the love of friendship" just as "the love of friendship" implies more than mere well-wishing. We will want to characterize God's love for humankind as the most perfect sort of love, and the most perfect sort of love is actual friendship.

We have seen that "the love of friendship" adds to mere well-wishing the element of a certain bond of affection—a "resting of the beloved in the one loved." Beyond this bond of affection, however, there is a special sort of devotion Thomas calls *amatio. Amatio* is understood as adding to the "love of friendship" a "certain intensity of love as a certain fervor."[56] *Amatio*, however, while it entails more than the "love of friendship," is not yet actual friendship. For *amatio* does not in itself imply a true mutuality or sharing of love. In addition to the intensity or fervor of love implied by *amatio*, therefore, actual friendship also requires a "mutual affection (*mutua amatio*)" or "fellowship (*societas*)" between lover and beloved that proceeds "from free choice (*ex electione*)" and that is founded on "some kind of sharing (*aliqua communicatione*)."[57] Actual friendship, the most perfect sort of love, is the kind found between God and human beings: "Friendship is the most perfect among those things which belong to love. . . . Therefore it is in this class that we must place charity, which is a certain friendship of man for God through which man loves God and God loves man."[58]

By our affirmation of divine friendship, we recognize that God's love implies both ardor and fellowship. In speaking of the ardor of divine love, we in

---

55. "Amor non dividitur per amicitiam et concupiscentiam, sed per amorem amicitiae et concupiscentiae" (*ST* I-II, 26, 4, ad 1).

56. "Amatio enim addit super amorem intensionem quandam amoris, quasi fervorem quemdam" (*Sent.* III, 27, 2, 1, co.).

57. *Sent.* III, 27, 2, 1, co. Cf.: d.32, 1, 2, co. "Sed nec benevolentia sufficit ad rationem amicitiae, sed requiritur quaedam mutua amatio: quia amicus est amico amicus. Talis autem mutua benevolentia fundatur super aliqua communicatione" (*ST* II-II, 23, 1, co.).

58. *Sent.* III, 27, 2, 1, co.

no way assert any passion in God, which might entail imperfection or limitation.[59] We refer rather to the vigor (*vigorem*) or power (*virtutem*) of his act of
love. For according to the vigor of one's act, one may be said to love more fer-
vently (*ferventius*). Since "every divine act is of one and the same power," the
fervor of God's love is ever infinite and unwavering.[60]

In addition to fervor, friendship demands a mutual fellowship of lover
and beloved founded on a certain communion or sharing. Because there is
such a communion between human beings and God in that God shares his
happiness with us, there is also a kind of friendship between humans and
God based on that communion. We call this friendship "charity."[61] In this
friendship, God wishes to us an infinitely greater good than to other creatures since he wills for us the same good he wills to himself—the eternal
good that is his very self:

> Every love of God is followed at some time by a good caused in the creature, but not
> co-eternal with the eternal love. And according to the difference of this good, the love
> of God for the creature is looked at differently. For one [love] is common, whereby he
> loves "all things that are" (Wis 11:25), and thereby gives things their natural being.
> But the second [love] is a special love, whereby he draws the rational creature above
> the condition of its nature to a participation of the divine good. And according to this
> love, he is said to love someone simply, since it is by this love that God simply wishes
> the eternal good, which is himself, for the creature.[62]

In communicating any sort of goodness to the creature, God is somehow present in it.[63] Because God shares with us the goodness that is his very
self, he is present to us in a special way and is said "to dwell" in us "as in his
own temple."[64] It is in virtue of such mutual communion and indwelling of
lover and beloved that love is called "intimate (*intimus*)."[65] We have already
seen that this intimate mode of divine presence involves a particular sort of
divine "motion"—the invisible mission or sending of a divine person by way
of grace.[66] By this motion of divine friendship, we are made lovers of God

59. *ST* I, 82, 5, ad 1; *ST* I, 20, 1, ad 1; ad 2; *Sent.* III, 32, 1, 1, ad 1.
60. *SCG* I, c.91.10–11 (§763).
61. *ST* II-II, 23, 1, co. Cf.: *Sent.* III, 27, 2, 1, co.; 32, 1, 1, ad 2; *ST* II-II, 23, 1, co.
62. *ST* I-II, 110, 1, co. Cf.: *Sent.* III, 32, 1, 2, co.   63. See *Sent.* III, 32, 1, 1, obj. 3; ad 3.
64. *ST* I, 43, 3, co.   65. *ST* I-II, 28, 2, co.
66. *ST* I, 43, 2, ad.2.

and raised up into the mystery of God's own Trinitarian life.[67] We enjoy an intimate fellowship with God consisting in "a certain familiar colloquy" that begins in this life but achieves its perfection only in the next:

Charity signifies not only the love of God, but also a certain friendship with him; which implies, besides love, a mutual return of love, together with a certain mutual communion. . . . That this belongs to charity is evident from 1 Jn 4:16: "He who abides in love abides in God, and God abides in him," and from 1 Cor 1:9, where it is written: "God is faithful, by whom you are called into the fellowship of his Son." Now this fellowship of man with God, which consists in a certain familiar colloquy with him, is begun here, in this life, by grace, but will be perfected in the future life, by glory.[68]

The Tenderness of Divine Compassion

We have seen there is a true friendship between the unchanging God and human beings. In every such friendship, however, the lover looks upon the joys and sorrows of the beloved as his own.[69] Because our joy is in some way a participation in God's own happiness, we can say God rejoices in the joys of his creatures.[70] Can we also say God suffers in their sufferings? To answer this question, we must consider the nature of divine compassion and the supreme manifestation of divine love and compassion in the sufferings and death of the Son. We will find God's love for creation is too intimate for us to say merely that God suffers in response to the distress of his creatures. We will rather have to affirm that the suffering of the creature is itself in some way the suffering of God.

When we are united to another person by the love of friendship, we see that person as "another self (*alterum se*)," and we will that person's good as we do our own.[71] Through the bond of love, the joys and sorrows of our friend become in some way our own. We can "rejoice with those who rejoice and

---

67. *SCG* IV, c 23.11 (§3601). Cf.: *Sent.* I, 14, 1, 1, ad 2; *ST* I, 37, 2, co.; ad 3. See also J-H. Nicolas, O.P., "La souffrance de Dieu?" *Nova et vetera* 53 (1978): 59: "But the love regarding which God loves [creation] is not contingent, since nothing of the contingent can enter into the necessary *esse*; there is only one love in God, the eternal love, the infinite love which unites the three Persons and which, through a marvelous condescendence, is extended freely to humans and angels."

68. *ST* I-II, 65, 5, co. Cf.: *ST* II-II, 23, 1, ad 1; Q.25, 2, ad 2.

69. *ST* I-II, 28, 2, co. Cf.: *ST* I, 20, 1, ad 3.

70. *SCG* I, c.90.6–7 (§753–54). Cf.: *In eth.* X, lect. 13, lines 116–21.

71. *ST* I-II, 28, 1, co.

weep with those who weep."[72] When we find our friend in pain or tears, our love prompts us both to share her tears and try, as best we can, to dry them by alleviating their cause.[73] Compassion is that twofold movement of the human person in which we both share in the suffering of our friend and seek to relieve that suffering. It is both a sign and a risk of love. Our love opens us to the risk of compassionate suffering, and our suffering manifests a love that was willing to take that risk. As C. S. Lewis explains, in this life all love involves some attendant risk of suffering:

> To love at all is to be vulnerable. Love anything and your heart will certainly be wrung and possibly be broken. If you want to make sure of keeping it intact, you must give your heart to no one. . . . Wrap it carefully round with hobbies and little luxuries; avoid all entanglements; lock it up safe in the casket or coffin of your selfishness. But in that casket—safe, dark, motionless, airless—it will change. It will not be broken; it will become unbreakable, impenetrable, irredeemable. The alternative to tragedy, or at least to the risk of tragedy, is damnation. The only place outside Heaven where you can be perfectly safe from all the dangers and perturbations of love is Hell.[74]

Because God loves his creatures with a love of friendship, his love must involve compassion. Scripture calls God compassionate and commands us to imitate his compassion: "Be merciful even as your Father is merciful."[75] As human compassion springs from love, we understand divine compassion as rooted in love: "God does not have mercy on us except on account of love, inasmuch as he loves us as something of himself."[76] To "have mercy (*misereri*)" is a "characteristic quality (*proprium*) of God."[77] Compassion belongs properly to God and is the source of all his works.[78]

---

72. Rom. 12:15. Cf.: *ST* I-II, 32, 5, co.; II-II, 28, 1, co.; Q.30, 2, co.

73. *ST* I, 21, 3, co.; *Sent*. IV, 46, 2, 1, qc.1, co. We may also be prompted to act out of pity toward others because of a realization that we are liable to suffer the same misfortune as they. This sort of compassion is in no way predicable of God and will therefore not enter into our considerations here. See *ST* II-II, 30, 2, co.

74. Lewis, *The Four Loves*, 169.

75. Lk 6:36. Cf.: Ex 34:6; Jer 3:12; 31:20; Is 49:14–15; Hos 11:8; Dt 4:31; 2 Chron 30:9; Neh 9:17, 31; Ps 103:8; 116:5; Joel 2:13; Jon 4:2.

76. "Deus non miseretur nisi propter amorem, inquantum amat nos tanquam aliquid sui" (*ST* II-II, 30, 2, ad 1).

77. *ST* II-II, 30, 4, co. Cf.: *ST* I, 21, 3; *Super iob* XL, v.14, lines 395–97. See also Louis-B. Gillon, "Tristesse et miséricorde du Père," *Angelicum* 55 (1978): 5.

78. "Compassion is most proper to God" (*Super ev. matt*. c.15, lect. 3 [line 131 c]). Cf.: *ST* I, 23, 3, co.;

In predicating compassion of God, we realize God's compassion cannot be precisely the same as ours. For we speak of God only by analogy, denying qualities that imply imperfection and affirming in an eminent way those that do not. Any aspects of human compassion that imply imperfection must therefore be denied of God, or if applied, must be understood metaphorically. Human compassion involves both a sharing in the suffering of one's friend and a response that seeks to alleviate that suffering. Sometimes we share another's suffering through a grief or distress in ourselves arising from, but distinct from, the suffering of the other person. We generally call this "sympathy." Visiting a friend who has cancer, for instance, I may feel a deep sadness in myself at her illness. In the most intimate instances of human love, however, we move beyond "sympathy" to "empathy." Here, we experience no distinct distress in ourselves at another's pain, but simply identify with the other person and regard their pain as our own. As Aquinas explains: "Just as, properly speaking, it is not 'compassion' but 'suffering' that describes our condition when we ourselves experience some cruel treatment, so also, if there are some persons so united to us as to be, in a way, something of ourselves (*quasi aliquid nostri*), such as children or parents, we do not have compassion at their distress but rather we suffer as in our own wounds."[79] In considering divine compassion, we will need to ask whether and how we should predicate of God the various dimensions of human compassion: sympathetic sadness, empathetic identification with the sufferer, and effective action to alleviate suffering.[80]

Sympathetic Suffering

Sympathetic suffering, like any human quality, may be said of God "only in the way that it is praiseworthy in us."[81] No form of human suffering or sadness, however, is desirable or admirable in itself.[82] Suffering is not a good

---

II-II, 21, 2, co.; Q.30, 4, co.; *Super 2 ad cor.*, c.1, lect. 2 (line 60 c.); *Super iob*, c.40, lines 395–97; *De veritate*, Q.28, 3, ad 15. "The effect of divine compassion is the foundation of all divine works" (*ST* I, 25, 3, ad 3). Cf.: *ST* I, 21, 4, co.

79. *ST* II-II, 30, 1, ad 2.

80. On the different dimensions of divine compassion, see Michael J. Dodds, "Thomas Aquinas, Human Suffering, and the Unchanging God of Love," *Theological Studies* 52 (1991): 330–44.

81. *Sent.* IV, 46, 2, 1, qc.1, ad 2.

82. "Tristitia ergo nulla, per se loquendo, est bona ut per se appetibilis; . . . omnis tristitia procedit

but an evil.[83] Since sadness and suffering are evils in themselves, they cannot properly be predicated of God: "It is impossible that God should be sad because he is not subject to evil of any kind."[84] The sadness that characterizes sympathetic suffering, however, though it must be recognized as an evil insofar as it is itself a form of suffering, may also be seen as good insofar as it is a loving response to the suffering of another: "Sadness is not praiseworthy except on the supposition of some existing evil. For when unhappiness (*miseria*) is presupposed, compassion (*misericordia*) is praiseworthy."[85] Indeed, when something saddening is presupposed, it would be an evil for a human being *not* to feel some sort of pain or sorrow.[86] Thomas does not follow the Stoics who reject all suffering as evil, but recognizes that some suffering may be good and praiseworthy, not in itself, but "on the supposition of something else."[87] Human sympathetic suffering is at once an evil (insofar as it is itself a form of suffering) and a good (insofar as it is a laudable response to the suffering of another).[88]

Because human sympathetic suffering has both good and evil aspects, it is difficult to decide whether and how such suffering should be attributed to God. If the lack of such suffering would imply a kind of divine indifference (as the lack of sympathetic suffering in a human being implies indiffer-

---

ex aliquo inconvenienti; habere autem aliquod inconveniens non potest esse per se appetibile" (*Sent.* IV, 49, 3, 4, qc.2, co.). Cf.: *ST* III, 39, 1, co.

83. "Talis autem est tristitia vel dolor: nam eius obiectum est malum iam inhaerens, sicut gaudii obiectum est bonum praesens et habitum. Tristitia igitur et dolor ex ipsa sui ratione in Deo esse non possunt" (*SCG* I, c.89.8–9 [§742]). Friedrich von Hügel points out that whenever suffering is attributed to God, there is an inherent tendency to deny the real evil of suffering: "Suffering is intrinsically an Evil. It is impossible to read much of the literature which insists upon the presence of Suffering in God, without being struck with the trend—I believe the inevitable trend, once Suffering has been admitted into God—to treat that Suffering as but a seeming Evil" (*Essays and Addresses on the Philosophy of Religion*, Second series [London: John Dent and Sons, 1951], 199). Jean Galot might serve as an example of this tendency: "In stimulating love, [suffering] is, despite appearances, a good and not an evil" (*Dieu*, 186). Elizabeth Johnson reaches a similar conclusion: "As a summation of compassionate love, the symbol of divine suffering appears not as an imperfection but as the highest excellence" (*She Who Is*, 266). See also Charles Taliaferro, "The Passibility of God," *Religious Studies* 25 (1989): 221.

84. *In meta.* I, lect. 3.12 (§63). Cf.: *Sent.* II, 11, 1, 5, co.; d.19, 1, 3, co.; *ST* I, 25, 1, co.

85. *Sent.* IV, 49, 3, 4, qc.2, ad 2. Cf.: *ST* I, 29, 1, co.

86. *ST* I-II, 39, 1, co.

87. *ST* I-II, 39, 1, co. Cf.: *ST* III, 46, 6, ad 2; I-II, 85, 5, ad 2; III, 69, 3, co.; *Super ad rom.* VIII, lect. 3 (§651).

88. See *ST* I-II, 39, 1, co.

ence), then such suffering could not be denied of God without detriment to
his perfection in love. But to the extent that such suffering in itself entails
imperfection, it cannot be applied to God without detriment to his perfection in being.

A number of theologians and philosophers, recognizing that human
compassionate suffering is in some way laudable and good and seeing that
the lack of such suffering in the face of human misery can imply indifference,
argue that divine love and compassion must also involve suffering. Elizabeth
Johnson believes that if God is thought of as personal and relational, "suffering can be conceived of ontologically as an expression of divine being insofar as it is an *act* freely engaged as a consequence of care for others."[89] John
Macquarrie asserts, "A God of love is inevitably vulnerable, for there is no
love that does not suffer."[90] To Jürgen Moltmann, "a God who cannot suffer
cannot love either."[91] Jean Galot argues, "The negation of suffering in God
implies the negation of compassion."[92] Some of these authors are careful to
point out that God's suffering is not imposed by another, but is the result
of God's own free decision to make himself vulnerable through his love.[93]

89. Johnson, *She Who Is*, 265.

90. John Macquarrie, *The Humility of God* (Philadelphia: Westminster, 1978), 69.

91. Moltmann, *Trinity*, 38. Cf.: Ibid., 23; Moltmann, *Crucified*, 222, 230. For a critique of Moltmann's argument that divine love is incompatible with immutability, see Henry Jansen, "Moltmann's View of God's (Im)mutability: The God of the Philosophers and the God of the Bible," *Neue Zeitschrift für system-atische Theologie und Religionsphilosophie* 36 (1994): 293, and Blocher, "Divine Immutability," 9–10.

92. Galot, "Réalité," 236. Many theologians share similar sentiments. "A God who cannot suffer cannot be close to the suffering creature" (Ulrich Eibach, "Die Sprache leidender Menschen und der Wandel des Gottesbildes," *Theologische Zeitschrift* [Basel] 40 [1984]: 57–58). "If God cannot feel anguish, he cannot love" (Schilling, *God*, 252–53). "An invulnerable Father would be a Father without tenderness" (Varillon, *Souffrance*, 21). "There can be no love without suffering" (Daniel Day Williams, *The Spirit and the Forms of Love* [New York: Harper and Row, 1968], 117). "The one who cannot suffer cannot love. The ability to suffer and to love go together" (J. Brantschen, "Leiden: theologische Perspektiven," in *Christ-licher Glaube in moderner Gesellschaft*, vol. 10 of *Enzyklopädische Bibliothek*, ed. Franz Böckle et al. [Freiburg: Herder, 1980], 45). "[T]he conclusion seems inescapable that a loving God must be a sympathetic and therefore suffering God" (Fiddes, *The Creative Suffering of God*, 17). See also Warren McWilliams, *The Pas-sion of God: Divine Suffering in Contemporary Protestant Theology* (Macon, GA: Mercer University Press, 1985); Piet Schoonenberg, "God as Relating and (Be)coming: A Meta-Thomistic Consideration," *Listening* 14 (1979): 275; Gisbert Greshake, *Der Preis der Liebe* (Freiburg: Herder, 1978) 52.

93. "God is not changeable as creatures are changeable. . . . If God is not passively changeable by other things like other creatures, this does not mean that he is not free to change himself, or even free to allow himself to be changed by others of his own free will" (Moltmann, *Crucified*, 229). Cf.: Clark H. Pin-nock, "Systematic Theology," and William Hasker, "A Philosophical Perspective," in *The Openness of God:*

They maintain that God suffers only in some particular aspect of his being and remains otherwise undiminished and unaltered.[94] Others argue that if suffering is predicated of God at all, it must be coextensive with divine being itself. So Christopher Mooney argues that God "suffers universally with the suffering of creation."[95] And Duncan Reid contends that "with the coming to be of a created order, God allows pain to find a place within God for all eternity."[96]

In all these arguments, there is an underlying supposition that, with regard to sympathetic suffering, divine love must resemble human love. Among humans, the evil that sympathetic suffering implies in itself and the good it represents as a response to another's misfortune are inseparable. Must this be the case with God? Human sympathy is a perfection, but an inherently limited one. It is good and laudable insofar as it implies solidarity with another in suffering, but an evil insofar as it is itself a sort of suffering. Must God's compassion be subject to the same limitation? Or could it be that specifically the suffering of human sympathy, though praiseworthy in the limited human creature, does not belong to the perfection of divine compassion? Are there not some inherently limited perfections that, though proper and praiseworthy in the creature, are not attributed to the creator?

God, as the transcendent source of all being, must contain all perfections of being.[97] But, by reason of God's very transcendence, "it is not necessary that whatever is of the excellence of the creature must be of the excellence of the creator, which exceeds it beyond all proportion (*improportionaliter*), as

---

A Biblical Challenge to the Traditional Understanding of God, ed. Clark Pinnock et al. (Downers Grove, Ill.: InterVarsity Press, 1999), 101–25, 126–54; Marcel Sarot, *God, Passibility and Corporeality* (Kampen: Kok Pharos Publishing House, 1992), 49–57, 67; Hans Urs von Balthasar, *Theodramatik*, vol. 4, *Das Endspiel* (Einsiedeln: Johannes, 1983), 200.

94. Richard Creel, for instance, admits that God is "possible in his knowledge of what is going on in the world," but does not suffer in himself because of worldly evils as if he were "possible in feeling" (*Divine Impassibility*, 206). Jean Galot argues that God's sufferings and joys that result from his dealings with humankind are taken on only in virtue of a "sovereignly free relationship," and that they "neither add nor detract anything from the perfection of divine being" ("Réalité," 241).

95. Christopher F. Mooney, *Theology and Scientific Knowledge: Changing Models of God's Presence in the World* (Notre Dame, Ind.: University of Notre Dame Press, 1995), 175.

96. Duncan Reid, "Without Parts or Passions? The Suffering God in Anglican Thought," *Pacifica: Australian Theological Studies* 4 (1991): 270. Cf.: Varillon, *Souffrance*, 12; Kazoh Kitamori, *Theology of the Pain of God* (Richmond, Va.: John Knox Press, 1965), 123.

97. *De pot.* Q.7, 3, co.; *In de div. nom.* XIII, lect. 1; *Sent.* I, 43, 1, 2, ad 1; *SCG* I, c.31; *ST* I, 4, 2; Q.61, 3, ad 2.

something is of the excellence of a dog such as to be ferocious which may be to the discredit (*ignobilitatem*) of a man."[98] In a similar way, sympathetic suffering, though recognized as good in a human being insofar as it is a response to the misfortune of another, is nonetheless seen as an evil insofar as it is in itself a sort of unhappiness. It is therefore not predicated of God. Similarly, the absence of sympathetic suffering, though indicative of some evil or lack of love in the human being, is indicative of the perfection of love and goodness in God:

> But it must be taken into consideration that sometimes one and the same thing is able to be good and evil to diverse natures. Thus [to be] irascible is good for a dog, but bad for a man. No one of sound mind, however, forms this into a doubt as to whether God does anything out of malice. For in the highest good there cannot be anything evil. But it may happen that something which belongs to divine goodness is evil in man. Thus not to have compassion according as compassion signifies suffering (*passionem*) indeed incurs censure in a man, but divine goodness nonetheless requires this on account of its perfection.[99]

In denying that compassion, insofar as it is itself an evil (i.e., insofar as it is itself a sort of suffering), is attributable to God, we do not imply that compassion is in no way attributable to God. For, insofar as compassion is a good (i.e., insofar as it involves and manifests love of another and insofar as it implies action to relieve the suffering of the beloved), it certainly belongs to God. But it might be argued, when we deny compassion of God insofar as compassion implies suffering, are we not denying of him the very essence of compassion? Is our qualified affirmation of divine compassion in reality no more than a subtle form of equivocation? We can answer these questions by considering more specifically the suffering of human compassion and by asking more precisely what it is about that suffering that makes it praiseworthy. Through such considerations, we may find that the essence of compassion is more truly embodied in the love from which it springs and in the will to alleviate the distress of the beloved than in the sadness that accompanies our loving response.

98. *Sent.* I, 2, 1, 1, ad 2.
99. *Super iob* X, v.3, lines 79–90.

The suffering of the compassionate person involves and manifests an undeniable nobility, tenderness, and grandeur of spirit.[100] But is it that suffering as such that we admire in the compassionate person, or is it not rather the greatness of love manifested in that suffering? Do we praise a compassionate person because of the magnitude of their sympathetic suffering, or because of the abundance of love that gives rise to it? In humans, these two are not separable, but are distinguishable. We can bring out the distinction through the example of a mother's compassionate love for her child amidst the myriad little heartaches that are part and parcel of the child's world. A mother who remained totally indifferent to the tears of her child might be judged as anything from insensitive to inhuman. A mother who wiped away those tears without becoming visibly saddened herself, however, might well be considered loving and compassionate. Finally, a mother who experienced her child's every bump and bee sting at practically the same emotional pitch as the child herself would hardly be deemed unloving, but her genuine sympathetic suffering, for all its intensity, might well be characterized more as a form of oversensitivity than of laudable compassion. It is not the degree of suffering as such we admire in the compassionate person, but the degree of love that suffering manifests. When Jesus wept at the death of Lazarus, the crowd did not say, "See how he suffers," but "See how he loved him" (Jn 11:35–36).

There is an undeniable power in the suffering of the compassionate person that can act to relieve and comfort the one to whom such compassion is directed. But again, we may ask whether it is compassionate suffering itself that consoles the beloved, or whether it is not rather the love that shines through such suffering. If it were my friend's compassionate suffering itself that brought me consolation, then I would be in the peculiar situation of reacting in quite the opposite way to my friend's suffering from the way he reacts to mine. For I would be taking some sort of joy in his suffering while he reacts rather with sadness at my own.[101]

Compassionate suffering is both a consequence and a sign of love. But it is love rather than suffering that we truly admire in the compassionate per-

---

100. See Maritain, "Quelques," 23.
101. *ST* I-II, 38, 3, ad 2. Cf.: obj.2, co., ad 1.

son, and it is love rather than suffering that brings healing and comfort to the person for whom we have compassion. The suffering of human compassion is a good, but a limited good, and whatever goodness it has springs from the love that informs it. As Richard Creel argues, "It is love that makes suffering admirable. Suffering in and of itself is odious."[102] In speaking of divine compassion, therefore, we should not apply to it that inherently limited good that we find in the compassion of the creature (however noble that good may be as found in the creature who is likewise limited). We attribute to God rather the unlimited goodness of compassionate love—a love that is in no way subjected to evil, but rather overcomes evil, bringing unending comfort, healing, peace, and joy.

Were we to attribute suffering to God, we would in fact diminish the abundance of his love. We have seen that a wholly gratuitous divine love stands at the heart of the creation, governance, and redemption of the world. Would a God who is subject to the evil of suffering be capable of such love? Would he not rather himself be somehow in need of redemption, and so act not simply for the good of his creatures, but to increase his own good and diminish his own pain?[103] Would God be capable of ensuring the ultimate triumph of good over evil and of joy over suffering if he were himself subject to evil and suffering? Will God, who is love, ever be able to overcome suffering if love itself is conceived as implying suffering by its very nature? Will we be forced to admit, in stoical fashion, that only the absence of love can ensure absence of suffering—that the *only* place "to be perfectly safe from all the dangers and perturbations of love is Hell"?[104] Or shall we not rather recognize that "an unhappy God would mean a bankrupt universe, a demonstrated pessimism, a doomed faith"?[105] Shall we not seek a love that is not subject to evil and suffering, but rather overcomes them—a love that "casts out fear" (1 Jn 4:18) and that will one day "wipe away every tear" (Rev 21:4)?

---

102. Creel, *Divine Impassibility*, 123.

103. This is the position of Moltmann, to whom the "redemption of the world is bound up with the self-deliverance of God from his sufferings." In this view, "not only does God suffer with and for the world; liberated men and women suffer with God and for him" (Moltmann, *Trinity*, 60). Similarly, Edward Collins Vacek asserts God has a real relation to the world that is "mutually perfecting," so that "God's love for creation also brings about an enrichment in God" (*Love*, 89–90, 96).

104. Cf.: Lewis, *The Four Loves*, 169.

105. Robert Mackintosh, *Historic Theories of Atonement* (London: Hodder and Stroughton, 1920), 254.

Empathetic Identification with the Sufferer

Compassion that takes the form of sympathetic suffering (implying a re-action of suffering in the sympathizer distinct from the suffering of the be-loved) must be denied of God since such suffering is always, in itself, an evil. But even apart from that argument, sympathy is inappropriate for God since it does not represent the highest form of love. Beyond sympathy, compas-sionate empathy (which does not imply a distinct suffering in the compas-sionate person but a simple identity with another in their distress) repre-sents a more profound union of love. Is it appropriate to attribute empathetic compassion to God? Is it possible to say the suffering of an afflicted person is itself the very suffering of God? It would be quite an audacious claim for a theologian were it not the profession of Christ himself: "I was hungry and you gave me food; I was thirsty and you gave me drink; I was a stranger . . . ; I was naked . . . ; I was sick . . . ; I was in prison . . . ; As you did it to one of the least of these, . . . you did it to me" (Mt 25:35–40). St. Paul, recounting the story of his conversion, witnesses the same solidarity of Christ with his suffering people: "I heard a voice saying to me, 'Saul, Saul, why do you perse-cute me?' . . . 'I am Jesus of Nazareth whom you are persecuting.'"[106] In these passages, Jesus does not refer to a distinct pain or grief in himself caused by the suffering of his people, but simply identifies their suffering as his own. He does not say, "You were hungry, and it troubled me; you were thirsty and I grieved for you," but "*I* was hungry . . . ; *I* was thirsty." Here we are faced with the mystery of God, the wholly other, speaking not only as intimately present, but as somehow identified, somehow *one* with his suffering people.

Because Jesus is God, we can say his human suffering is the suffering of God. But how are we to understand his claim that *our* sufferings are also God's? The key to understanding the suffering of Jesus as God's suffering lies in the unity of his personal identity (in the union of the human and divine natures in the single person, Jesus of Nazareth). Analogously, the key to un-derstanding our suffering as God's lies in the unity of love. Even the love of

---

106. Acts 22:6–8. There are also instances of God's identity with the poor and suffering in the Old Testament (Prov 14:31; 17:4; 19:17). Aquinas is not unaware of such passages. See *Super ev. matt.* c.25, lect. 3 (line 565 c.).

concupiscence involves a kind of unity. There, the lover is united to the one loved "as to something belonging to himself or herself (*ut ad aliquid sui*)."[107] A deeper unity is found in the love of friendship, where "the lover is related to the beloved . . . as to his very self (*ut ad seipsum*)"[108] and sees the beloved "as another self (*ut alterum se*)"[109] in a love that "makes two persons one."[110] Here the lover is "afflicted with sorrow at the distress of another as though it were his own," and "seeks to dispel the other's distress as if it were his own."[111]

This account of divine compassion denies any reaction of suffering in God distinct from the suffering of God's creatures, but does not for that reason imply any lessening of God's love.[112] We have already seen that it is not the denial of such reactive suffering in God but its attribution that would diminish God's love by making it less than purely gratuitous. In fact, the absence of such suffering points to the perfection of divine love. Even in human love, at its deepest level, there is not so much a reaction of suffering in the lover distinct from the suffering of the beloved as an identity of the lover with the beloved in his or her own suffering. To put it another way, the most profound human love is characterized not by an awareness of one's own sadness at the affliction of another, but by a simple identity of oneself with the other in their distress. One suffers not so much "with" the other through a kind of sympathetic response as "in" the other by a sort of empathetic union. To illustrate this, we might consider the difference between the reaction of an audience to a sad movie and that of a loving mother to the suffering of her child. While the audience are aware of and identify with the plight of the tragic victim in the film, they are also acutely conscious of their own particular feelings of sadness as they watch the show. The mother, on the other hand, may be hardly aware of her own feeling of sadness, conscious only of

107. *ST* I-II, 28, 1, ad 2.

108. "[A]mans se habet ad amatum, in amorem quidem amicitiae, ut ad seipsum"; *ST* I-II, 28, 1, ad 2. Cf.: *ST* I-II, 20, 1, ad 3.

109. *ST* I-II, 28, 1, co.

110. *SCG* III, c.158.7. "[T]hrough love, the lover is made one with the beloved" (*Sent.* III, 27, 1, 1, co.). "[T]he power of love . . . makes one consider one's friend the same as oneself" (*ST*, I-II, 32, 5, co.). Cf.: *ST* I-II, 25, 2, ad 2; 28, 1, co.; *SCG* I, c.91.4–7.

111. *ST* I, 21, 3, co. Cf.: *ST* II-II, 30, 1, ad 2; 2, co.; *Sent.* IV, d.46, Q.2, a.1, qc.2, co.

112. *Sent.* II, d.11, Q.1, a.5, co., and ad 2. *"Impassibilitas"* (absence of passions) is often taken to imply lack of love when it is confused with *"insensibilitas"* (the moral fault of apathy in human beings).

her child's pain, which she somehow experiences as her own. Here the lack of any reaction of sadness or suffering in her, distinct from that of her child, points not to apathy, but to the profundity of her love.

If human love can imply such an identity of lover and beloved, how much more will divine love? If, as C. S. Lewis says, "the intimacy between God and even the meanest creature is closer than any that creatures can attain with one another,"[113] how complete will be the intimacy between God and those creatures he names as friends? When we love someone most deeply—when we love a person not as a mere possession (love of concupiscence), nor even as another self (love of friendship), but as part of our very selves (*quasi aliquid nostri*)—we are not said to experience a suffering in ourselves distinct from the suffering of that person. Rather, we so identify ourselves with that person in their suffering as to suffer in them "as in our own wounds."[114] In a similar way, God in his love for us "does not have compassion on us except on account of love, insofar as he loves us as something of himself (*tanquam aliquid sui*)."[115] Just as we, seeing those whom we love most deeply "as something of ourselves," are identified with them in their suffering, so God, seeing us "as something of himself," makes us one with him in love and so calls our suffering his own.

Compassion in Action

Compassion is attributed to God not according to the limited mode of the suffering of human sympathy, but according to a divine mode that both identifies itself with the suffering person and acts to relieve that suffering:

If anything is said of God and of man, it is understood of each one according to his mode. Therefore, when compassion is said of God, it is taken according to the mode of God, and in man, according to the mode of man. Compassion is in man when he suffers (*compatitur*) at the distress of another. . . . But it is not in God in this way. For

---

113. Lewis, *The Problem of Pain,* 41. The phrase echoes the thought of Aquinas in *ST* I, 8, 1. See also Gerald Vann, *The Pain of Christ and the Sorrow of God* (New York: Alba House, 2000), 76–78, 91.

114. *ST* II-II, 30, 1, ad 2. Cf.: *Super ev. matt.* c.5, lect. 2 (line 543 c.); *Sent.* IV, 42, 2, 1, qc.1, co.

115. "Deus non miseretur nisi propter amorem, inquantum amat nos tanquam aliquid sui" (*ST* II-II 30, 2, ad 1). "And [the affliction] he views as his own, he ought to drive away as his own. Thus, God is called compassionate insofar as he drives away affliction" (*Super ev. matt.* c.15, lect. 3, [line 141 c.]). Thomas explains elsewhere that the human being is "something of God (*aliquid Dei*)," as God's "creature and image (*creatura et imago*)" (*ST* II-II, 59, 3, ad 2).

God is impassible (*impassibilis*) and does not suffer (*compatitur*). . . . Compassion is in God when he repels the distress of any particular thing.[116]

God is called compassionate not because of a suffering in him at the distress of another, but because of identity with the other and action to overcome the other's suffering.[117] In this, as in all things, God acts not for his own benefit, but for the good of the creature.[118] Broadly speaking, we may say all of the works by which God shares his goodness with his creatures are rooted in his compassion.[119] His compassion, like his goodness, is unfailing and "unchanging (*invariabili*)."[120]

The fact that divine compassion does not involve sympathetic suffering implies no defect in divine love.[121] It rather indicates the perfection of that love, which can overcome the defects of creatures. Nor does the absence of suffering in God reduce divine compassion to a sort of benevolence or beneficence that would accomplish good for others, but at a level less than love. For the compassionate action God initiates on behalf of the creature—like the caring deed a human being might undertake on behalf of an unfortunate friend—is an action springing from love.[122] As a friend regards the sufferings of the beloved as his own, so God is said to look upon our distress as his own in dispelling it.[123] The effect of removing our sufferings, the effect in vir-

116. *In psalmos*, XXIV.8.

117. *ST* I, 21, 3; *SCG* I, c.91.16 (§766); *Sent.* IV, 46, 2, 1, qc.1, co.

118. "Deus per sua beneficia repellens nostram miseriam non ordinat hoc ad suam utilitatem sed ad nostram" (*Sent.* IV, 46, 2, 1, qc.1, co.).

119. *ST* I, 21, 4; II-II, 21, 2, co.; *In psalmos*, XXIV.8; *De ver.* Q.28, 3, ad 15; *Super ad eph.* II, lect. 2 (§86).

120. "[I]pse [Deus] una et invariabili misericordia cum omnibus misericorditer agit" (*Sent.* IV, 46, 1, 2, qc.4, ad 2). Cf.: *Super ad rom.* X, lect. 2 (§834); *Super ad eph.* II, lect. 2 (§86–87).

121. *Sent.* II, 11, 1, 5, co.; ad 2. On how we may affirm divine compassion while denying divine suffering, see Weinandy, *Does God Suffer?* 159–68; Enrico Zoffoli, *Mistero della sofferenza di Dio? Il pensiero di S. Tommaso*, Studi Tomistici, 34 (Vatican City: Pontificia Accademia di S. Tommaso, 1988); Herbert McCabe, "The Involvement of God," *New Blackfriars* 66 (1985): 469–70; Nicolas, "Aimante," 277; William J. Hill, "Does Divine Love Entail Suffering in God?" in *God and Temporality*, ed. Bowman L. Clarke and Eugene T. Long (New York: Paragon, 1984), 64; and Gillon, "Tristesse," 9–11. On how we should conceive God's "responsiveness" to our human situation of distress, see Dodds, "Ultimacy," 218–19; Rousseau, "Process Thought," 53.

122. *ST* I, 21, 3, co.

123. "[S]ed ipse [Deus] hoc modo se habet in repellendo miserias aliorum, sicut se habet homo in repellendo miseriam suam [Parm: "eorum"]. Sicut homo enim in repellendo miseriam alicujus considerat hominis utilitatem cujus repellit miseriam; ita et Deus per sua beneficia repellens nostram miseriam, non ordinat hoc ad suam utilitatem, sed ad nostram; unde inquantum nostra miseria est quasi sua

tue of which we attribute compassion to God, itself springs from the affection of the divine will: "It is commonly said that in him [God] there is not compassion according to passion, but according to effect. Nevertheless, this effect proceeds from the affection (*affectu*) of the will, which is not a passion, but a simple act of the will."[124] This simple act of will is, of course, that one simple act of love which is one with the divine being: the act by which God loves himself and all things.[125] This simple act of will is identified as an act of love: "God does not have mercy (*miseretur*) except on account of love, insofar as he loves us as something of himself."[126]

Because God's compassionate love exceeds our understanding, we have but a stammering way of speaking about it. We know that suffering is an evil and that in God there can be no defect. But we also recognize that the suffering of human compassion is marked by a particular nobility in that it springs from and reveals a special depth of love. How, then, can we both affirm that depth of love in God and yet deny the presence of suffering? We do so only by recognizing the infinitude of the mystery of divine love and the limitations of our human knowledge, imagination, and language.

secundum reputationem quamdam ipsius qui eam repellit, sic dicitur misericors, et misereri" (*Sent.* IV, 46, 2, 1, qc.1, co.). Cf.: *Super ev. matt.* XV, lect. 3 (§1340).

124. "[U]nde inquantum nostra miseria est quasi sua secundum reputationem quamdam ipsius qui eam repellit, sic dicitur misericors, et misereri, et propter hoc communiter dicitur, quod non est in eo misericordia secundum passionem, sed secundum effectum; qui tamen effectus ex affectu voluntatis procedit; qui non est passio, sed simplex voluntatis actus" (*Sent.* IV, 46, 2, 1, qc.1, co.). Cf.: *ST* I, 21, 3; *In psalmos*, XXIV.8 (line 71 c.); 50.1 (line 130 c.).

125. "[B]y the same love, however, God loves both himself and others on account of his goodness" (*SCG* IV, c.23.11). Cf.: *Sent.* III, 32, 1, 1, co.; *ST* I, 19, 5, co.; Q.37, 2, co.; ad 3; *In de div. nom.*, IV, lect. 9 (§ 409).

126. "Deus non miseretur nisi propter amorem, inquantum amat nos tamquam aliquid sui" (*ST* II-II, 30, 2, ad 1). The phrase *"tamquam aliquid sui"* was used earlier to distinguish the love of concupiscence, in which the lover "is related to the beloved as to something of himself (*ut ad aliquid sui*)", from the love of friendship, in which the lover is related to the beloved "as to himself (*ut ad seipsum*)" (*ST* I-II, 28, 1, ad 2). Here the phrase does not imply that God loves us with a self-seeking love of concupiscence for, as we have already seen, God's love for creatures is not directed toward his own benefit. The phrase rather seems to indicate the transcendent nature of God in virtue of which he is able to act compassionately toward his creatures by removing their miseries. This is the sense in which the phrase was used in the *Commentary on Dionysius's On the Divine Names* to characterize the relationship that is present when "the lover is more perfect (*perfectius*)" than the beloved. In this case, "the love of the lover is carried into the beloved as into something of his [the lover's] own (*sicut in aliquid suum*)" (*In de div. nom.* IV, lect. 10 [§431]). In this sort of relationship, the lover seeks not his own benefit, but the good of the beloved: "The better, that is the superior things, love the lesser, that is the inferior things, providently, that is insofar as they provide for them, as containing [them] under themselves (*ut sub se contentis*)" (*In de div. nom.* IV, lect. 9 [§407]).

In the human person, the absence of compassionate suffering in the face of another's serious grief or distress is a sign of indifference or lack of love. Either one is saddened by such misfortune or one is indifferent. We have already seen, however, that God's infinite being transcends such "either/or" situations of limited creatures. For he "must be understood as existing beyond the order of beings (*entium*) as a certain cause pouring forth all being (*ens*) and all its differences."[127] An example of such transcendence is found in the case of motion and rest. The limited mobile creature is either in motion (which implies limitation and potency) or it is at rest (which may also imply limitation and lack of further progress). God is not in motion (since he is pure act) but neither is he said to be at rest. He transcends both categories.[128] In a similar way, we can see that the limited human creature either is saddened at the misfortune of another or is indifferent. God, however, is neither saddened nor indifferent. He transcends this dichotomy of the limited creature in the infinity of his love.

Recognizing the infinite depth of divine love, we make use of metaphorical images to evoke some sense of a love that exceeds all our ideas. These are the rich images Scripture uses for the God whose heart "recoils" within him and whose "compassion grows warm and tender" (Hos 11:9); who led his people "with cords of compassion and with bonds of love" (Hos 11:4); and who "was afflicted" in all their affliction (Is 63:9).[129] Through such images, we best indicate the profundity and intimacy of divine love.

In view of the limitations of human language and thought, however, we will not mistake these images for literal descriptions of divine love. We will rather see them as metaphors for a kind of love and compassion that infinitely surpasses our understanding.[130] We will not try to replace the richness of these metaphorical images with inadequate prosaic statements. But we will not hesitate to employ even the most prosaic of language to ensure that

127. *In peri herm.* I, lect. 14.22. Cf.: *Super de causis,* Prop. 6 (Saffrey, p. 47, lines 8–12).

128. *In de div. nom.* IV, lect. 6 (§367).

129. In commenting on Is 63:9, which, in the Latin text provided by the Leonine edition of *Super is.,* reads, "In omni tribulatione eorum non est tribulatus," Thomas writes: "Et quantum ad diligentem protectionem, in omni tribulatione et ipse [Deus] est tribulatus, per compassionem: vel non est, statim, sed distulit etiam nunc, ut quasi corrigerentur" (*Super is.* LXIII, v.9, lines 160–63).

130. *ST* I, 20, 1, ad 2; Q.113, 7, ad 1; *Sent.* II, 11, 1, 5, co; ad 1.

such metaphors are not mistaken for the reality they signify.[131] It is for this reason that we make our stammering assertion: the God of love is not a God who suffers, but a God who, in his tender and unceasing care for his people, casts out and triumphs over suffering.

Incarnate Love

Divine Love in the Suffering of Jesus

Although we find no word of human language to express the abyss of divine love, God himself reveals the depths of his love in the Word that he speaks and sends into the world. The Word is the incarnate expression of divine love (Jn 3:16). All we can know of divine love in this life is present in Christ, the Word made flesh (Jn 1:18). He manifests the mystery of God's love most especially through his Passion (Jn 15:13). Because Christ is truly God and human, Aquinas can rightly say that in Christ "the impassible God (*impassibilis Deus*) suffers and dies."[132] But we will rightly understand this statement only if we have correctly grasped the manner in which divinity and humanity are united in Christ. This cannot be an accidental union, for then what belongs to the human nature would not truly belong to God. It must rather be conceived as a union in the person or "hypostasis" of the Logos (hypostatic union). Because the union of the two natures takes place in the person, that which is proper to either nature may be predicated of the person. And since "the same hypostasis is designated by the name of either nature," that which is said of Christ "either according to his human nature or according to his divine nature may be said either of God or of man."[133]

When we say anything of Christ, however, we should distinguish between what we say and why we say it: "Things that belong to the divine nature are

131. Recognizing the poverty of our language for discussing divine things, Jacques Maritain asks whether there might not be some quality in God that corresponds to human compassion precisely in the nobility of its suffering, but for which we have no adequate word; "Quelques," 17, 26. François Varillon poses a similar question; *Souffrance*, 17, 65. To such questions and suggestions, we respond that there certainly is something in God much more profound and splendid than the grandeur of human compassion. That quality infinitely outstrips the limits of our language, and so we resort to metaphors to designate it. But when we speak of God properly and analogously, rather than metaphorically, we do better to call that quality "love" rather than "suffering."

132. "[I]mpassibilis Deus patiatur et moriatur" *Super I ad cor.* XV, lect. 1 (§896).

133. *ST* III, 16, 4, co.; Q.2, 2.

predicated of Christ according to his divine nature and things that belong to the human nature are predicated according to his human nature."[134] When we say, therefore, that Christ suffered, we may affirm that God suffered, since Christ is truly God. We can distinguish, however, that Christ suffered in his human nature and not in his divine nature: "In the mystery of the Incarnation, we may say that the Son of God suffered, yet we do not say that the divine nature suffered."[135] Similarly, because God is impassible, we may say that Christ is impassible, but to avoid error and misunderstanding, we must qualify our statement and say, "Christ was incorporeal and impassible (*impassibilis*) in his Godhead."[136]

Our distinction between what is proper to the divine and human natures of Christ and our insistence that the crucified Christ does not suffer in his divine nature do not require, as Jürgen Moltmann argues, that the cross "be evacuated of deity."[137] For on the cross it is truly the Son who suffers, but he suffers *as we do, as human*. In the one who is "like us in all things but sin," God does indeed suffer, but he suffers "by the fact that he has a human nature" and he suffers in that human nature.[138] As Paul Gavrilyuk eloquently affirms: "The Word made human experiences his very own by transforming them from within: that which was violent, involuntary, tragically purposeless, and fatal for an ordinary human being was made voluntary, soteriologically purposeful and life-giving in the ministry of the Word. The Word who is above suffering in his own nature suffered by appropriating human nature and obtained victory over suffering."[139]

Even if we were to suppose the impossible situation that in Christ God suffers as God in his divine nature, such suffering would have little to do with us, for we do not suffer *as God*, but *as humans*. If God is to redeem us and

134. *ST* III, 16, 4, co.

135. "Et similiter in mysterio incarnationis dicimus quod Filius Dei est passus, non autem dicimus quod natura divina sit passa" (*ST* III, 16, 5, ad 1). See also the discussion of how the terms "mutable" and "immutable (*immutabilis*)" may be respectively predicated of Christ according to his human and divine natures in *ST* III, 16, 4, obj. 1, and ad 1.

136. "Christus secundum deitatem est incorporeus et impassibilis" (*ST* III, 16, 8, ad 2). Cf.: *ST* III, 57, 1, ad 1; a.2, co.

137. Moltmann, *Crucified*, 214.

138. "God truly suffers, not (as Moltmann would have it) in his very deity, but in and through his humanity which is one with the humanity of all men and women" (Hill, "Does Divine," 68).

139. Gavrilyuk, *The Suffering*, 175.

manifest himself to us in Christ, he must reveal himself in a way we can understand, in a human way. If he is to redeem us and reveal himself to us especially through the suffering of Christ, then it is particularly appropriate that Christ suffer not as God (whatever that might mean if it were even possible), but as human, in the same way we also suffer. In this sense, "Christ was made a participant of our affliction."[140] As John Paul II notes, because Christ is God, he experiences our human sufferings in his human nature with "a unique and incomparable depth and intensity which only the man who is the only-begotten Son could experience."[141] Aquinas finds this experience of Christ most especially in the Passion: "Compassion (*miseratio*) is said as a heart is sorrowful (*miserum*) at the miseries (*miseria*) of another. This may happen in two ways. One way is through understanding alone. And thus God, without any passion, understands our misery. For he knows our frame as it is said in Ps 102:14. Another way is through experience. And thus Christ has experienced our misery, especially in [his] Passion."[142]

To affirm that Christ experienced *our* miseries and suffered as we do, we must maintain not that he suffered in his divinity, but that he, like us, suffered humanly.[143] Since he is God, he can reveal God to us (Jn 1:18). Since he is human, he reveals God in a way appropriate to us (Jn 14:9). It is especially in his suffering and death (Jn 15:13) that he reveals God's love, and it is because he suffers as we do—as human—that we can understand that revelation. We cannot understand God, but we can know something of human suffering and how love may be manifested in it. So we can know something about God to the extent that he reveals himself to us in the human suffering of Christ.

A number of contemporary authors argue that Christ's sufferings reveal a suffering in God himself. Jean Galot maintains that the "compassion of the

---

140. "Christus autem factus est particeps miseriae nostrae" (*In psalmos*, 40.7 [line 5 c.]).

141. John Paul II, *On the Christian Meaning of Human Suffering* (*Salvifici Doloris*), Apostolic Letter, Feb. 11, 1984 (Washington, D.C.: U.S. Catholic Conference), 18.

142. "Miseratio dicitur quasi miserum cor super aliena miseria, et hoc est dupliciter. Uno modo per solam apprehensionem, et sic Deus sine passione nostram miseriam apprehendit. Ipse enim cognovit figmentum nostrum, ut dicitur in Ps 102:14. Alio modo per experientiam, et sic Christus potissime in passione expertus est miseriam nostram" (*Super ad hebr*. II, lect. 4 [§153]).

143. "Pertinet ergo passio Christi ad suppisitum divinae naturae ratione naturae passibilis assumptae, non autem ratione divinae naturae impassibilis" (*ST* III, 46, 12, co.). Cf.: ad 2; I-II, 102, 5, ad 7; *SCG* IV, c.55.17 (§3947); *Sent*. III, 6, 2, 1, ad 5.

Father is essential to the revelation which Jesus gives us of God: if Christ crucified did not represent a God who suffers, his revelatory mission would be seriously deficient."[144] Such arguments are often aimed against the immutable
"God of philosophy," devotion to whom has supposedly caused the Church to
overlook the true meaning of Christ's suffering for twenty centuries.[145] The affirmation of suffering in God is presented as a return to the purity of scriptural revelation.[146] None of the arguments presented for the contention that
the suffering of Christ reveals a sympathetic grief or sadness in the Father or
in the Holy Spirit, however, enjoys any firm scriptural foundation.[147]

We have already seen that suffering cannot be predicated of God without both diminishing the gratuity and perfection of God's love and jeopardizing the possibility of an ultimate victory over evil and suffering. We must
say therefore that Christ's Passion reveals not suffering in the divine nature,
but infinite love:

Among means to an end, that one is the more suitable whereby more things coin-
cide which are themselves helpful to that end. But in this, that man was delivered by
Christ's passion, many other things which pertain to man's salvation occurred in addition to deliverance from sin. In the first place, man knows thereby how much God
loves him and is thereby stirred to love him in return, and herein lies the perfection
of human salvation; hence the Apostle says (Rom 5:8): "God shows his love for us in
that while we were yet sinners Christ died for us."[148]

---

144. Galot, *Dieu*, 111. Cf.: Moltmann, *Crucified*, 192, 207, 216, 227, 243; *Trinity*, 22; Varillon, *Souffrance*, 38,
74, 106; Hartshorne, "Two," 35; Kitamori, *Theology*, 45, 123; Eberhard Jüngel, *The Doctrine of the Trinity* (Grand
Rapids, Mich.: Eerdmans, 1976), 87. For a critique of contemporary views of divine immutability and the
Incarnation, see Frank Meessen, *Unveränderlichkeit und Menschwerdung Gottes: Eine theologiegeschichtlich-systematische Untersuchung* (Freiburg: Herder, 1989); Mark-Robin Hoogland, *God, Passion and Power: Thomas Aquinas
on Christ Crucified and the Almightiness of God* (Leuven: Peeters, 2003), 288–89; Thomas G. Weinandy, *Does
God Change? The Word's Becoming in the Incarnation* (Still River, Mass.: St. Bede's Publications, 1985).

145. "[T]he Platonic axiom of the essential *apatheia* of God sets up an intellectual barrier against the
recognition of the suffering of Christ, for a God who is subject to suffering like all other creatures cannot
be 'God'" (Moltmann, *Crucified*, 227–28). Cf.: Galot, *Dieu*, 170, 213–14.

146. Galot, *Dieu*, 90–91, 213–14.

147. The scriptural references that Jean Galot offers as evidence of the compassionate suffering or
grief of the Father at the death of the Son (e.g., Rom 8:32) require a good deal of tortuous interpretation
before they will say what he wants them to say. See Galot, *Dieu*, 92–97. As Jean-Hervé Nicolas points
out, "Scripture does not make the least allusion to a suffering of the Father" ("Aimante," 290n23).

148. *ST* III, 46, 3, co. Cf.: *ST* III, 1, 2, co.

The Passion of Christ reveals not a divine love subject to evil and suffering but one that overcomes suffering. Human compassion cannot overcome the evil of suffering without itself being touched by that evil. In a marvelous way, in human compassion, the very sadness that shows that we have been touched by that evil is also the medium revealing the depth of our love. But the power and the beauty of our compassion lie not in its sadness, but in its love. We cannot imagine a love so wonderful as to have all the warmth and depth and concern of human compassion and yet transcend the reach of sadness. For our human love, to the extent that it is genuine, must in this life be open to sorrow and suffering. Although we cannot comprehend such depth of love, we see and recognize it revealed to us in the suffering of Christ. As the suffering of any compassionate person demonstrates a love that has in it the power to overcome suffering, so that most profound human suffering, which we recognize in Christ, shows a love transcending all suffering and yet present and involved in every suffering creature. What Christ reveals in his suffering is not emptiness and pain at the heart of God, but infinite love strong enough to fill our emptiness and to transform our pain into the plenitude of joy. In Gerald Vann's phrase, "meditation on Calvary pulls back the curtain to show God not as suffering but as boundlessly caring, as illimitable will-to-share, as infinite love giving himself in the making and remaking of man."[149] Recognizing such love in the suffering of Christ, we find our own hope strengthened and our love enkindled to strive with our whole heart and mind and soul and strength toward complete and everlasting union with God: "It was not right for God to take flesh incapable of suffering and death ... but rather, capable of suffering and death. First, indeed, because it was necessary for men to know the beneficence of the Incarnation so as to be thereby inflamed in the divine love."[150]

Divine Love in the Mystical Body of Christ

The theme of God's oneness with his people is developed in the New Testament through the image of the Body of Christ, in which all Christians are united as members with Christ the head.[151] The image is in one sense a

---

149. Gerald Vann, *The Son's Course* (London, 1959), 139, as cited in Quinn, "Triune," 193.
150. *SCG* IV, c.55.14 (§3944). Cf.: c.54.5 (§3926); *ST* III, 1, 2, co.; Q.49, 1, co.
151. Eph 1:23; 4:12; 5:29–32. Rom 12:4–5; 1 Cor 12:12–27; Col 1:18, 24.

metaphor since we, unlike the human nature of Jesus of Nazareth, are not
hypostatically united to the Logos. In another sense, however, it is more than
a metaphor, since we are truly united with Christ and made truly one in the
Spirit.[152] Aquinas argues that if human love is able to "make two persons
one," Christ's love can make us somehow one person with him: "As a natural body is one, though made up of various members, so the whole Church,
which is the Mystical Body of Christ, is reckoned as one person with its
head, who is Christ."[153] Because we are one body with Christ, Christ loves
us "as something of himself (*sicut aliquid sui*)."[154] In this union of love, our
sufferings are in some way Christ's own. It is in this sense, as Thomas explains, that Christ suffers in us: "'I make up those things which are lacking
from the suffering of Christ' that is, [from the suffering] of the whole Church
whose head is Christ. . . . For this was lacking, that as Christ suffered in his
own body, so he would suffer in Paul, his member, and similarly in others."[155]
The sufferings of Paul were the sufferings of Christ since Paul was a member
of Christ. Our sufferings are also Christ's since we are members of him. In
this way Thomas explains how Jesus calls our sufferings his: "'Hence whatever you do to one of these least of my brothers, you do to me,' . . . because
the head and the members are one body."[156] Since Jesus is God, it is God
himself who is identified with us in our suffering. It is God himself who has

---

152. Aquinas sees the metaphorical nature of the image of the Body of Christ, but does not lose
sight of the reality it expresses. See *De ver.* 29, 4, co.; *ST* III, 8, 1, ad 1; *Super ev. matt.* c.24, lect. 3 (line 760
c.). On these themes, see also "The Dogmatic Constitution on the Church," no. 7–8, in *The Documents of
Vatican II; and Pius XII, "The Mystical Body of Christ," nos. 60–63, 86, in *Four Encyclicals of Pope Pius XII*
(New York: Paulist, 1961), 29–30, 39.

153. *ST* III, 49, 1, co.; cf: *ST* III, 48, 2, ad 1; *Sent.* 22, 3, 3, qc. 3, *exp.*, line 21 c.; *SCG* III, c.158.7.

154. "Thus he says, 'as Christ [loves] the Church.' He loves it, namely, as something of himself, because we are members of [his] body" (*Super ad eph.* 5, lect. 9 [line 105 c.]).

155. "'Adimpleo ea quae desunt passionum Christi,' id est totius ecclesiae, cuius caput est Christus.
'Adimpleo,' id est, addo mensuram meam. Et hoc 'in carne,' id est ego ipse patiens. . . . Hoc enim deerat,
quod sicut Christus passus erat in corpore suo, ita pateretur in Paulo membro suo, et similiter in aliis"
(*Super ad col.* 1, lect. 6 [line 55 c.]). It is also in this union that Christ's sufferings are ours and so have redemptive value for us: "Through baptism a person is incorporated into Christ, and is made a member
of him; and therefore the pain which Christ underwent is reputed to the person as satisfaction: 'because
if one member suffers, all the others suffer with that one,' as it is said in 1 Cor. 11 [*RSV:* 12:26]" (*Sent.* IV,
d.4, Q.2, a.1, qc.2, ad 1). Cf.: *ST* III, 49. 1, co.

156. "Unde quamdiu fecistis uni de his fratribus meis minimis, mihi fecistis . . . quia caput et mem-
bra sunt unum corpus" (*Super ev. matt.* 25, lect. 3 [line 450 c.]).

compassion on us "on account of love, insofar as he loves us as something of himself."[157]

ESCHATOLOGICAL UNION WITH THE
UNCHANGING GOD OF LOVE

Aquinas teaches that God's gratuitous love has called us from nothingness into being, creating us in his own image and likeness and gifting us by grace with a special love of friendship.[158] Since our being is from God, we seek him in every act, striving for our own perfection or fulfillment, which is a similitude of his being.[159] When we recognize the love of God manifested in creating us and more especially in redeeming us through the suffering and death of Christ, our own love is inflamed to seek that union with him that he has always willed for us.[160] Our union of friendship with God begins in this life as we taste the joy of divine friendship:

Joy is caused by love, either through the presence of the one loved, or because the proper good of the one loved exists and endures in it. . . . Now charity is love of God whose good is unchangeable (*immutabile*), since he is his goodness. And from the very fact that he is loved, he is in those who love him by his most excellent effect, according to 1 Jn 4:16: "He who abides in love abides in God and God in him." Therefore, spiritual joy is caused in us by charity.[161]

By charity, we rejoice principally in the divine good, loving God in friendship "for his own sake."[162] The principal source of our joy is simply the fact that the proper good of the God whom we love exists and endures in him.[163] Because this divine good is unchanging and incompatible with any admixture of evil, the joy that accompanies this love is abiding and "incompatible with any admixture of sorrow."[164]

Aquinas maintains that charity also causes us to rejoice in our participation in divine goodness. We find joy in God as we are one with him in a

---

157. *ST* II-II 30, 2, ad 1.   158. *SCG* III, c.151; *De car.* a.2, ad 15.
159. *ST* I, 6, 1, ad 2.
160. *SCG* I, c.91.4 (§758); 91.6 (§760); III, c.151.2–3 (§3235–36); *ST* III, 46, 3, co.
161. *ST* II-II, 28, 1, co.
162. *ST* II-II, 23, 5, ad 2; Q.26, 3, ad 3; Q.28, 2, co.; *Sent.* III, 29, 1, 3, co.
163. *ST* II-II, 28, 2, co.   164. Ibid.

union of love. In our present life, our joy remains incomplete and mixed with sorrow. For although God dwells within us already (1 Jn 4:16), our fellowship with him is not yet perfect. He is present to us by faith, but not yet by sight: "Beloved we are God's children now; it does not yet appear what we shall be, but we know that when he appears we shall be like him, for we shall see him as he is."[165] In this life, we grieve over whatever stands in the way of complete participation in God's goodness, hindered as we are by any evil, physical or moral.[166] We are saddened not only by what blocks our way to participation in God's goodness, but by all that impedes our neighbor, whom we see as ourselves in love. The same love of God that prompts us to overcome whatever evil stands in our way moves us also to dispel any evil that afflicts our neighbor, whose suffering we regard as our own.[167]

We, who have recognized in the suffering of Christ the revelation of an unfathomable love that transcends all suffering, refuse to accept the evil of suffering as part of the eternal way of things, much less as part of the eternal being of God. Rather, we find in God's unfailing love and unchanging goodness the resolution to combat evil and suffering, and the hope that evil shall one day be completely overcome—the hope that we and those we love will ultimately share completely and eternally the infinite joy of God himself.[168]

Since God alone is the source of ultimate joy, only in union with him do we find rest for the restless searching of our hearts.[169] The rest we find in God is neither the stillness of indifference nor the torpor of ennui that can sometimes ensnare and oppress our spirit in this life, rendering us stagnant. It is rather the rest of ultimate fulfillment, where we desire nothing more, simply because our every desire has been attained.[170] This rest, far from all stagnation, is a most perfect motion since it comprises the perfect immanent motions of knowing and loving.[171] It consists in a vision of the very essence

---

165. Jn 3:2. Cf.: *ST* II-II, 23, 1, ad 1; Q.28, 1, ad 1; ad 3; a.2, co.

166. *ST* II-II, 23, 2, ad 1; *Super ad rom.* VIII, lect. 5 (§692–93).

167. *ST* II-II, 28, 1, ad 2; a.2, co.; *ST* I, 21, 3, co.

168. St. Thomas explains that divine immutability may be seen as the foundation of our hope. Our hope is firm and certain since we rely "on God who is unchangeable (*incommutabilis*)" (*In psalmos*, XXX.1). Cf.: *In psalmos*, XLIII.2; *In jer.* XXXI, lect. 11.

169. *ST* I-II, 2, 8, co.   170. *ST* II-II, 28, 3, co.

171. *Sent.* III, 31, 2, 2, ad 4; IV, 49, 1, 2, qc.3, ad 2; *ST* I, 12, 1, co.; I-II, 1, 8, co.; Q.2, 7, co.; Q.3, 2, co.; ad 3; a.4, co.; a.8, co.

of God that love opens to us, filling our whole being with joy and delight.[172] In that vision we shall be joined to the unchanging God of love in unending union:

If this vision were to cease, bringing this union to an end, it would have to be done by a change in the divine substance, or in the intellect of the one who sees it. Both of these changes are impossible: for the divine substance is immutable (*immutabilis*) . . . and also the intellectual substance is raised above all change when it sees God's substance. Besides, the nearer a thing is to God, who is entirely immutable (*omnino immobilis*), the less mutable it is and the more lasting. . . . But no creature can come closer to God than the one who sees his substance. So the intellectual creature that sees God's substance attains the highest immutability (*summam immutabilitatem*). Therefore, it is not possible for it ever to lapse from this vision.[173]

The joy that will be ours in that union—in that ultimate rest which is at once an unending dynamism of knowing and loving—infinitely exceeds our every hope and desire:

Desire will be at rest, not only our desire for God, but all our desires: so that the joy of the blessed is full to perfection—indeed over-full, since they will obtain more than they were capable of desiring: "Nor has it entered into the heart of man what things God has prepared for those that love him" (1 Cor 2:9).[174]

172. *ST* I, 12, 6, co.; II-II, 3, 8, co.; a.4, co. For an imaginative representation of the dynamic character of the happiness of heaven, see C. S. Lewis, *The Chronicles of Narnia*, vol. 7, *The Last Battle* (New York: Collier Books, 1975).

173. *SCG* III, c.62.10–11 (§2373–74).

174. "Et ideo quiescet desiderium non solum quo desideramus Deum, sed etiam erit omnium desideriorum quies. Unde gaudium beatorum est perfecte plenum, et etiam superplenum: quia plus obtinebunt quam desiderare suffecerint; 'non enim in cor hominis ascendit quae praeparavit Deus diligantibus se,' ut dicitur *I ad cor.*2:9" (*ST* II-II, 28, 3, co.).

Conclusion

"To Praise the Motion of the Immovable God"

𝕯

Our examination of divine immutability in the thought of Thomas Aquinas has led us from the immobility of the lowest creatures to the unchanging
splendor of the Triune God. By considering the notion of immutability in
regard to creatures, we discovered its positive and negative connotations. To
the extent that a creature is considered as perfectible and achieving its perfection through motion, motion and change are good and desirable, and immutability may imply stagnation or lack of progress. To the extent, however, that the creature is viewed as having achieved some degree of perfection,
the immutability by which it retains that quality is good and desirable, while
change may imply loss of perfection.

Having seen the significance of immutability with regard to creatures, we
turned to the immutability of God. First, we examined in their approximate
chronological order the arguments by which Thomas establishes divine immutability in his various works. While we did not discover evidence of any
substantial development or change in his thought on divine immutability,
we did find his arguments to be modified considerably from one work to another. In his commentaries, the order of his arguments varies according to
the order of the work he is discussing. In his independent works, the order is
changed in accordance with the needs of the intended audience.

From his earliest works to those he left unfinished at his death, Aquinas consistently identifies divine immutability as a truth established by both

Scripture and rational argument. To him, divine immutability is a sign of perfection in being. He indicates the nature of that perfection most profoundly through his teaching that God is subsistent to-be itself—*ipsum esse subsistens*. As such, God is the transcendent efficient, exemplar, and final cause of all things. He is pure actuality, characterized by absolute simplicity and unbounded perfection. All of Thomas's major arguments for divine immutability spring from the premises of God's absolute simplicity, ultimate perfection, pure actuality, and primary transcendent causality. Since those premises are themselves founded in his understanding of God as *ipsum esse subsistens*, divine immutability in Thomas's theology indicates not simply the stability and constancy of God's being, but his dynamic perfection as *ipsum esse subsistens*—pure "is," unlimited by any potency.

The significance and appropriateness of predicating immutability of God were seen in greater detail by consideration of divine immutability in terms of the three ways of causality, negation, and eminence, by which we know and speak of God. Here our initial research on the immovability of creatures was instrumental in showing how immutability may appropriately be predicated of God. In seeing how immutability applies to God, however, we also found a number of ways that motion—to the extent that it implies no imperfection—may also be said of God.

Following Aquinas's lead, we considered ways we might attribute motion to God. We saw how the immanent motions of knowing and loving may lead us into the mystery of God's triune life. We also explored how transient motion may be attributed to God in view of his creative, providential, and redemptive activity. By distinguishing divine "transient motion" from the transient motion of creatures, we were able to appreciate God's uniquely intimate presence in all creation. This also allowed us to see that God's unchanging causality does not jeopardize, but is the very source of, the contingent actions of creatures. Here we could affirm the dynamic character of the created world, where creatures share God's own causal activity and through their proper motions imitate the unchanging creator.

Finally, we pondered divine immutability in relation to divine love. Far from being opposed to love, immutability was seen as essential to the absolute gratuity of God's love. Our affirmation of divine immutability did not force us to deny or diminish the compassionate character of God's love, but did induce us to admit the limitations of our knowledge and language, and so kept us from reducing God and his infinite compassionate love to the boundaries of that finite human love and compassion familiar to us. By affirming God's immutability, we could join Aquinas in "praising the motion of the immovable God"[1] and recognize God's abiding love, revealed in the redemptive act of Christ, as a love that surpasses our understanding but nonetheless inflames our hearts to seek our ultimate peace and joy in union with the unchanging God of love:

> May nothing disturb you,
> Nothing alarm you,
> All things are passing,
> God does not change,
> The practice of patience
> accomplishes all things;
> One who has God
> is lacking in nothing:
> Alone God suffices.
>
> —St. Teresa of Avila[2]

---

1. *In de div. nom.* IX, lect. 4 (§841).

2. "Nada te turbe, / Nada te espante, / Todo se pasa, / Dios no se muda, / La paciencia / Todo lo alcanza; / Quien a Dios tiene / Nada le falta: / Sólo Dios basta." (St. Teresa of Avila, "Nada te turbe," in *Obras Completas*, 511.

Bibliography

Works of Thomas Aquinas

Thomas Aquinas. *Breve principium de commendatione Sacrae Scripturae.* Vol. 4 of *Opuscula omnia.* Edited by P. Mandonnet. Paris: Lethielleux, 1927, 481–96.

———. *Catena aurea in Joannem.* Vol. 5 of *Opera omnia ut sunt in Indice Thomistico.* Stuttgart: Frommann-Holzboog, 1980, 367–441.

———. *Catena aurea in Matthaeum.* Vol. 5 of *Opera omnia ut sunt in Indice Thomistico.* Stuttgart: Frommann-Holzboog, 1980, 128–246.

———. *Commentarium in Aristotelis libros Peri hermeneias.* Turin and Rome: Marietti, 1955.

———. *Commentarium in libros Aristotelis De caelo et mundo.* Vol. 3 of *Opera omnia.* Rome: Typographia polyglotta, 1886.

———. *Compendium theologiae.* Vol. 42 of *Opera omnia.* Rome: Typographia polyglotta, 1979, 83–191.

———. *Contra doctrinam retrahentium a religione.* Vol. 41 of *Opera omnia.* Rome: Typographia polyglotta, 1970, 103–25.

———. *Contra errores graecorum.* Vol. 40A of *Opera omnia.* Rome: Typographia polyglotta, 1969.

———. *Contra impugnantes Dei cultum et religionem.* Vol. 41 of *Opera omnia.* Rome: Typographia polyglotta, 1970.

———. *De aeternitate mundi.* Vol. 43 of *Opera omnia.* Rome: Typographia polyglotta, 1976, 85–89.

———. *De articulis fidei et ecclesiae sacramentis.* Vol. 42 of *Opera omnia.* Rome: Typographia polyglotta, 1979, 245–57.

———. *De caritate.* Turin and Rome: Marietti, 1965.

———. *De duobus praeceptis caritatis.* Vol. 30 of *Opera omnia ut sunt in Indice Thomistico.* Stuttgart: Frommann-Holzboog, 1980.

———. *De ente et essentia.* Vol. 43 of *Opera omnia.* Rome: Typographia polyglotta, 1976, 369–81.

———. *De principiis naturae.* Vol. 43 of *Opera omnia.* Rome: Typographia polyglotta, 1976, 39–47.

———. *De rationibus fidei.* Vol. 40B of *Opera omnia.* Rome: Typographia polyglotta, 1969.

———. *De substantiis separatis.* Vol. 40D of *Opera omnia.* Rome: Typographia polyglotta, 1969.

———. *De unitate intellectus.* Vol. 43 of *Opera omnia.* Rome: Typographia polyglotta, 1976, 291–314. [English translation: *On the Unity of the Intellect against the Averroists.* Translated by B. Zedler. Milwaukee, Wisc.: Marquette University Press, 1968.]

———. *Epistola ad Bernardam abbatem Casinensem.* Vol. 42 of *Opera omnia.* Rome: Typographia polyglotta, 1979, 413–15.

————. *Expositio et lectura super epistolas Pauli apostoli.* 2 vols. Turin and Rome: Marietti, 1953.

————. *Expositio super Iob ad litteram.* Vol. 26 of *Opera omnia.* Rome: Typographia polyglotta, 1965.

————. *Expositio super Isaiam ad litteram.* Vol. 28 of *Opera omnia.* Rome: Typographia polyglotta, 1974.

————. *Expositio super librum Boethii De Trinitate.* Edited by B. Oecker. Leiden: E. J. Brill, 1959. [English translation of QQ.5–6: *The Division and Method of the Sciences.* Translated by A. Maurer. Toronto: Pontifical Institute of Mediaeval Studies, 1953.]

————. *Expositio super primam et secundam decretalem.* Vol. 40E of *Opera omnia.* Rome: Typographia polyglotta, 1969.

————. *Expositio super symbolo apostolorum.* Vol. 4 of *Opuscula omnia.* Edited by P. Mandonnet. Paris: Lethielleux, 1927.

————. *In Aristotelis librum De anima commentarium.* Vol. 45/1 of *Opera omnia.* Rome: Typographia polyglotta, 1984.

————. *In Jeremiam prophetam expositio.* Edited by S. Fretté. Vol. 19 of *Opera omnia.* Paris: Vivès, 1882.

————. *In librum beati Dionysii De divinis nominibus expositio.* Turin and Rome: Marietti, 1950.

————. *In librum De memoria et reminiscentia commentarium.* Turin and Rome: Marietti, 1928.

————. *In librum De sensu et sensato commentarium.* Turin and Rome: Marietti, 1928.

————. *In Metaphysicam Aristotelis commentaria.* Turin and Rome: Marietti, 1926. [English translation: *Commentary on the Metaphysics of Aristotle.* 2 vols. Translated by J. Rowan. Chicago: Regnery, 1961.]

————. *In octo libros Physicorum Aristotelis expositio.* Turin and Rome: Marietti, 1965. [English translation: *Commentary on Aristotle's Physics.* Translated by R. Blackwell et al. New Haven: Yale, 1963.]

————. *In psalmos Davidis expositio.* Edited by S. Fretté. Vol. 18 of *Opera omnia.* Paris: Vivès, 1889, 228–556.

————. *Opera omnia cum hypertextibus in CD-ROM.* 2nd ed. Edited by Robert Busa. Milano: Editoria Elettronica Editel, 1996.

————. *Opera omnia ut sunt in Indice Thomistico.* Edited by Robert Busa. Stuttgart: Frommann-Holzboog, 1980.

————. *Principium de commendatione et partitione sacrae Scripturae.* Vol. 4 of *Opuscula omnia.* Edited by P. Mandonnet. Paris: Lethielleux, 1927, 481–96.

————. *Quaestio disputata de anima.* Edited by J. Robb. Toronto: Pontifical Institute of Mediaeval Studies, 1968.

————. *Quaestio disputata de spiritualibus creaturis.* Edited by L. Keeler. Rome: Università Gregoriannae, 1937.

————. *Quaestiones disputatae de malo.* Vol. 23 of *Opera omnia.* Rome: Typographia polyglotta, 1982.

————. *Quaestiones disputatae de potentia.* Turin and Rome: Marietti, 1965. [English translation: *On the Power of God.* Translated by the English Dominican Fathers. Westminster, Md.: Newman Press, 1952.]

————. *Quaestiones disputatae de unione verbi incarnati.* In *Quaestiones disputatae.* Turin and Rome: Marietti, 1965, 2:421–435.

————. *Quaestiones disputatae de veritate.* Vol. 22/1–3 of *Opera omnia.* Rome: Typographia polyglotta. 1972–1976. [English translation: *Truth.* 3 vols. Translated by R. Mulligan et al. Chicago: Regnery, 1952–54.]

————. *Quaestiones disputatae de virtutibus in communi.* Turin and Rome: Marietti, 1965.

————. *Quaestiones quodlibetales.* Turin and Rome: Marietti, 1949.

————. *Responsio ad lectorem Venetum de 36 articulis.* Vol. 42 of *Opera omnia.* Rome: Typographia polyglotta, 1979, 321–24.

————. *Responsio ad magistrum Ioannem de Vercellis de 108 articulis.* Vol. 42 of *Opera omnia.* Rome: Typographia polyglotta, 1979, 279–94.

————. *Scriptum super libros Sententiarum.* Edited by S. E. Fretté and P. Maré. Vols. 7–11 of *Opera omnia.* Paris: Vivès, 1882–89.

————. *Sententia libri Ethicorum.* Vol. 47/1–2 of *Opera omnia.* Rome: Typographia polyglotta, 1969. [English translation: *Commentary on the Nicomachean Ethics.* Translated by C. Litzinger. Chicago: Regnery, 1964.]

————. *Sermo de omnibus sanctis: "Beati qui habitant."* Edited by T. Käppeli. In "Una raccolta di prediche attribuite a S. Tommaso d'Aquino," *Archivum Fratrum Praedicatorum* 13 (1943): 88–94.

————. *Summa contra gentiles.* 3 vols. Turin and Rome: Marietti, 1961. [English translation: *On the Truth of the Catholic Faith: Summa Contra Gentiles.* 4 vols. Translated by A. Pegis et al. Garden City, N.Y.: Image Books, 1955–57.]

————. *Summa theologiae.* Rome: Editiones Paulinae, 1962. [English translation: *Summa Theologica.* 3 vols. Translated by the Fathers of the English Dominican Province. New York: Benziger Bros., 1946.]

————. *Super evangelium S. Ioannis lectura.* Turin and Rome: Marietti, 1952.

————. *Super evangelium S. Matthaei lectura.* Turin and Rome: Marietti, 1951.

————. *Super librum De causis expositio.* Edited by H. D. Saffrey. Fribourg-Louvain: Société Philosophique, 1954. [English translation: *Commentary on the Book of Causes.* Translated by Vincent A. Guagliardo, Charles R. Hess, and Richard C. Taylor. Washington, D.C.: The Catholic University of America Press, 1996.]

Other Works

Aben, Tersur Akuma. "The Doctrine of Divine Immutability as God's Constancy." Ph.D. diss., Calvin Theological Seminary, Grand Rapids, Mich., 2000.

Anawati, Georges. "Théologie musulmane et théologie de S Thomas d'Aquin: quelques thèmes comparés." In *Fides quarens intellectum: Beiträge zur Fundamentaltheologie.* Edited by Michael Kessler, Wolfhart Pannenberg, and Hermann Josef Pottmeyer. Tübingen: Francke, 1992, 557–67.

Anderson, James F. *St. Augustine and Being.* The Hague: Martinus Nijhoff, 1965.

Arias Reyero, Maximo. *Thomas von Aquin als Exeget.* Einsiedeln: Johannes, 1971.

Aristotle. *The Basic Works of Aristotle.* Translated by R. McKeon. New York: Random House, 1941.

Augustine. *The Confessions of St. Augustine.* Translated by J. Ryan. Garden City, N.Y.: Doubleday, 1960.

Balthasar, Hans Urs von. "Mysterium Paschale." In *Mysterium Salutis.* Edited by J. Feiner and M. Löhrer. Einsiedeln: Benziger, 1969, vol. 3/ 2, 133–319.

————. *Theodramatik.* Vol. 4, *Das Endspiel.* Einsiedeln: Johannes, 1983.

Bañez, Dominicus. *Scholastica commentaria in primam partem Summae Theologicae S. Thomae Aquinatis.* Madrid: Hijo de F. Vives Mora, 1934.

Barbour, Ian. *Religion and Science: Historical and Contemporary Issues.* San Francisco: HarperSanfrancisco, 1997.

Barth, Karl. *Die Kirchliche Dogmatik.* 4 vols. Zollikon: Evangelischer Verlag, 1957–67.

Basinger, David. *Divine Power in Process Theism: A Philosophical Critique.* Albany: State University of New York Press, 1988.

Bauckham, Richard. "Only the Suffering God Can Help: Divine Passibility in Modern Theology." *Themelios* 9 (1984): 6–12.

Beeck, Frans Jozef van. *God Encountered: A Contemporary Catholic Systematic Theology*. Collegeville, Minn.: Liturgical Press, 1994.

Beek, A. van de. *Why? On Suffering Guilt and God*. Grand Rapids: Eerdmans, 1990.

Blocher, Henri. "Divine Immutability." In *The Power and Weakness of God: Impassibility and Orthodoxy*. Edited by Nigel M. de S. Cameron. Edinburgh: Rutherford House Books, 1990, 1–22.

Bobik, Joseph. *Veritas Divina: Aquinas on Divine Truth*. South Bend, Ind.: St. Augustine's Press, 2001.

Boff, Leonardo. *Passion of Christ, Passion of the World*. Maryknoll, N.Y.: Orbis, 1987.

Boissard, Guy. "Etre ou devenir? Une angoissante question de tous les temps." *Nova et vetera* 58 (1983): 113–31.

Bracken, Joseph A. "The End of Evil." In *World without End: Christian Eschatology from a Process Perspective*. Edited by Joseph A. Bracken. Grand Rapids, Mich.: Eerdmans, 2005, 1–11.

Brantschen, Johannes B. "Leiden: theologische Perspektiven." In *Christlicher Glaube in moderner Gesellschaft*. Vol. 10 of *Enzyklopädische Bibliothek*. Edited by Franz Böckle et al. Freiburg: Herder, 1980.

———. "Die Macht und Ohnmacht der Liebe." *Freiburger Zeitschrift für Philosophie und Theologie* 27 (1980): 224–46.

Brito, Emilio. "Dieu en mouvement: Thomas d'Aquin et Hegel." *Revue des sciences religieuses* 62 (1988): 111–36.

Brown, Robert. "Divine Omniscience, Immutability, Aseity and Human Free Will." *Religious Studies* 27 (1991): 285–95.

Brümmer, Vincent. "Bestowed Fellowship: The Love of God." In *Understanding the Attributes of God*. Edited by Gijsbert van den Brink and Marcel Sarot. Frankfurt: Peter Lang, 1999, 33–52.

Brunn, Émilie zum. "L'immutabilité de Dieu selon saint Augustin." *Nova et vetera* 41 (1966): 219–25.

Buckley, Michael. *Motion and Motion's God*. Princeton, N.J.: Princeton University Press, 1971.

Burrell, David B. "Act of Creation with its Theological Consequences." In *Aquinas on Doctrine: A Critical Introduction*. Edited by Thomas Weinandy et al. London: T and T Clark, 2004, 27–44.

———. *Aquinas God and Action*. Notre Dame, Ind.: University of Notre Dame Press, 1979.

———. "Distinguishing God from the World." In *Language, Meaning and God: Essays in Honour of Herbert McCabe, O.P.* Edited by Brian Davies. London: Geoffrey Chapman, 1987, 75–91.

———. "Divine Practical Knowing: How an Eternal God Acts in Time." In *Divine Action: Studies Inspired by the Philosophical Theology of Austin Farrer*. Edited by Brian Hebblethwaite. Edinburgh: T and T Clark, 1990, 93–102.

———. "Thomas Aquinas and Islam." *Modern Theology* 20 (2004): 71–89.

Busa, Robert, ed. *Index Thomisticus: Sancti Thomae Aquinatis Operum Omnium Indices et Concordantiae*. Stuttgart: Frommann-Holzboog, 1975.

———. *Thomae Aquinatis Operum Omnium cum hypertextibus in CD-ROM*. 2nd ed. Milano: Editoria Elettronica Editel, 1996.

Cahn, Stephen M. "Does God Know the Future?" In *Questions about God: Today's Philosophers Ponder the Divine*. Edited by Steven M. Cahn and David Shatz. Oxford: Oxford University Press, 2002, 147–52.

Chenu, Marie-Dominique. *Towards Understanding St. Thomas*. Translated by A. Landry and D. Hughes. Chicago: Regnery, 1964.

Chisholm, Robert B. "Does God 'Change His Mind'?" *Bibliotheca Sacra* 152 (1995): 387–99.

Christmann, Heinrich M. "Kommentar." In Thomas von Aquin, *Die Deutsche Thomas Ausgabe*. Salzburg: A. Pustet, 1933, 1:425–523.

Clark, Kelly James. "Hold Not Thy Peace at My Tears: Methodological Reflections on Divine Impassibility." In *Our Knowledge of God*. Edited by Kelly James Clark. Dordrecht: Kluwer Academic Publishers, 1992, 167–93.

Clark, Mary T. "Augustine on Immutability and Mutability." *American Catholic Philosohical Quarterly* 74 (2000): 7–27.

Clarke, W. Norris. "Charles Hartshorne's Philosophy of God: A Thomistic Critique." In *Charles Hartshorne's Concept of God: Philosophical and Theological Responses*. Edited by Santiago Sia. Dordrecht: Kluwer Academic Publishers, 1990, 103–23.

———. "Christian Theism and Whiteheadian Process Philosophy: Are They Compatible?" In *The Philosophical Approach to God: A Neo-Thomist Perspective*. Edited by William E. Ray. Winston-Salem, N.C.: Wake Forest University Press, 1979, 66–109.

———. "Comment on Professor Ford's Paper." In *Universe as Journey: Conversations with W. Norris Clarke, S.J.* Edited by Gerald A. McCool. New York: Fordham, 1988, 159–69.

———. "The Limitation of Act by Potency: Aristotelianism or Neoplatonism?" *New Scholasticism* 26 (1952): 167–94.

———. "A New Look at the Immutability of God." In *God Knowable and Unknowable*. Edited by R. J. Roth. New York: Fordham University Press, 1973, 43–72.

———. "What Is Most and Least Relevant in the Metaphysics of St. Thomas Today?" *IPQ* 14 (1974): 411–34.

Claudel, Paul. *Journal*. Edited by François Varillon and Jacques Petit. 2 vols. Paris: Editions Gallimard, 1969.

Clavell, Luis. "El nombre mas proprio de Dios y el acto de ser." In *Tomasso d'Aquino nel suo settimo centenario*. Atti del congresso internazionale (Roma-Napoli, 17–24 Aprile 1974). Vol. 3, *Dio e l'economia della salvezza*. Napoli: Edizione Domenicane Italiane, 1976, 269–74.

Cobb, John B., Jr., and David R. Griffin. *Process Theology: An Introductory Exposition*. Philadelphia: Westminster Press, 1976.

Colish, Marcia L. "Avicenna's Theory of Efficient Causation and Its Influence on St. Thomas Aquinas." In *Tomasso d'Aquino nel suo settimo centenario*. Vol. 1, *Tommaso d'Aquino: nella storia del pensiero*. Part 1, *Le fonti del pensiero di S. Tommaso*. Napoli: Edizione Domenicane Italiane, 1975, 296–306.

Congar, Yves. *The Meaning of Tradition*. New York: Hawthorn Books, 1964. Reprint, San Francisco: Ignatius, 2004.

Cooke, Bernard J. "The Mutability-Immutability Principle in St. Augustine's Metaphysics." *Modern Schoolman* 23 (1945): 175–93; 24 (1946): 37–49.

Cooper, Burton Z. *The Idea of God: A Whiteheadian Critique of St. Thomas Aquinas's Concept of God*. The Hague: M. Nijhoff, 1974.

Craig, William Lane. "Divine Foreknowledge and Future Contingency." In *Process Theology*. Edited by Ronald Nash. Grand Rapids, Mich.: Baker, 1987, 91–115.

———. *God, Time, and Eternity*. Dordrecht: Kluwer, 2001.

———. *The Only Wise God: The Compatibility of Divine Foreknowledge and Human Freedom*. Grand Rapids, Mich.: Baker Book House, 1987.

———. *The Problem of Divine Foreknowledge and Future Contingents from Aristotle to Suarez*. Leiden: Brill, 1988.

———. *Time and Eternity: Exploring God's Relationship to Time*. Wheaton, Ill.: Crossway Books, 2001.

Creel, Richard E. *Divine Impassibility: An Essay in Philosophical Theology*. Cambridge: Cambridge University Press, 1986.

Crouzel, Henri. "La passion de l'impassible: un essai apologétique et polémique du IIIe siècle." In *L'homme devant Dieu. Mélanges offerts au Père Henri de Lubac*. Paris: Aubier, 1963, 1:269–79.

D'Arcy, Martin. "The Immutability of God." *Proceedings of the American Catholic Philosophical Association* 41 (1967): 19–26.

Davies, Brian. "The Action of God." *New Blackfriars* 75 (1994): 76–84.

———. *An Introduction to the Philosophy of Religion*. Oxford: Oxford University Press, 1993.

———. *Thinking about God*. London: Geoffrey Chapman, 1985.

Denzinger, Heinrich, and Peter Hünermann. *Enchiridion symbolorum, definitionum et declarationum de rebus fidei et morum*. Freiburg: Herder, 2005.

Dewan, Lawrence. "St. Thomas and the Causality of God's Goodness." *Laval théologique et philosophique* 34 (1978): 291–304.

———. "St. Thomas and the Distinction between Form and *Esse* in Caused Things." *Gregorianum* 80 (1999): 353–70.

DeWeese, Garrett. *God and the Nature of Time*. Burlington, Vt.: Ashgate, 2004.

The Documents of Vatican II. Edited by Austin P. Flannery. New York: Pillar Books, 1975.

Dodds, Michael J. "Of Angels, Oysters and an Unchanging God: Aquinas on Divine Immutability." *Listening* 30 (1995): 35–49.

———. "St. Thomas Aquinas and the Motion of the Motionless God." *New Blackfriars* 68 (1987): 233–42.

———. "Thomas Aquinas, Human Suffering, and the Unchanging God of Love." *Theological Studies* 52 (1991): 330–44.

———. "Top Down, Bottom Up or Inside Out? Retrieving Aristotelian Causality in Contemporary Science." In *Science, Philosophy and Theology*. Edited by John O'Callaghan. South Bend, Ind.: St. Augustine's Press, (forthcoming).

———. "Ultimacy and Intimacy: Aquinas on the Relation between God and the World." In *Ordo Sapientiae et Amoris: Hommage au Professeur Jean-Pierre Torrell, O.P.* Edited by Carlos-Josaphat Pinto de Oliveira. Fribourg, Suisse: Editions Universitaires, 1993, 211–27.

Doig, James C. *Aquinas on Metaphysics: A Historico-Doctrinal Study of the Commentary on the Metaphysics*. The Hague: M. Nijhoff, 1972.

Dombrowski, Daniel A. "Must a Perfect Being Be Immutable?" In *Hartshorne, Process Philosophy and Theology*. Edited by Robert Kane and Stephen H. Phillips. Albany: State University of New York Press, 1989, 92–111.

Donceel, Joseph. "Second Thoughts on the Nature of God." *Thought* 46 (1971): 346–70.

Ducoin, Georges. "St. Thomas: commentateur d'Aristote." *Archives de philosophie* 20 (1957): 78–117, 240–71, 392–445.

Duhem, Pierre. *Le système du monde*. 10 vols. Paris: Hermann, 1959.

Eckhart, Meister. "Traktate 3." In *Die deutschen Werke*. Edited by J. Quint. Stuttgart: W. Kohlhammer, 1963, 5:539–47.

Edwards, Rem B. "The Pagan Dogma of the Absolute Unchangeableness of God." *Religious Studies* 14 (1978): 305–14.

Eibach, Ulrich. "Die Sprache leidender Menschen und der Wandel des Gottesbildes." *Theologische Zeitschrift* (Basel) 40 (1984): 34–65.

Elders, Léon. "Les cinq voies et leur place dans la philosophie de saint Thomas." In *Quinque sunt viae.* Studi Tomistici, no. 9. Edited by León Elders. Vatican City: Libreria Vaticana, 1980, 133–46.

———. "St. Thomas Aquinas's Commentary on the *Metaphysics* of Aristotle." *Divus Thomas* (Piacenza) 86 (1983): 307–26.

Elert, Werner. *Der Ausgang der altkirchlichen Christologie.* Berlin: Lutherisches Verlagshaus, 1957.

Elizabeth of the Trinity. *The Complete Works.* Translated by Aletheia Kane. 2 vols. Washington, D.C.: ICS Publications, 1984.

Emery, Gilles. *La Trinité creatrice: Trinité et création dans les commentaires aux Sentences de Thomas d'Aquin et de ses précurseurs Albert le Grand et Bonaventure.* Paris: J. Vrin, 1995.

———. *Trinity in Aquinas.* Ypsilanti, Mich.: Sapientia Press, 2003.

Erickson, Millard. "God and Change." *Southern Baptist Journal of Theology* 1, no. 2 (1997): 38–51.

Erlandson, Douglas. "Timelessness, Immutability, and Eschatology." *International Journal for Philosophy of Religion* 9 (1978): 129–45.

Eslick, Leonard. "From the World to God: The Cosmological Argument." *Modern Schoolman* 60 (1983): 145–69.

Ewbank, Michael B. "Diverse Orderings of Dionysius's triplex via by St. Thomas Aquinas." *Mediaeval Studies* 52 (1990): 82–109.

Faber, Roland. *Der Selbsteinsatz Gottes: Grundlegung einer Theologie des Leidens und der Veränderlichkeit Gottes.* Würzburg: Echter Verlag, 1995.

Fabro, Cornelio. *Participation et causalité selon s. Thomas d'Aquin.* Louvain: Université de Louvain, 1961.

———. "Platonism, Neoplatonism, Thomism." *New Scholasticism* 44 (1970): 69–100.

Feldman, Seymour. "Philosophy: Averroes, Maimonides, and Aquinas." In *Religious Foundations of Western Civilization: Judaism, Christianity, and Islam.* Edited by Jacob Neusner. Nashville: Abingdon, 2006, 209–44.

Fiddes, Paul S. *The Creative Suffering of God.* Oxford: Clarendon Press, 1988.

Finance, Joseph de. *Etre et agir dans la philosophie de saint Thomas.* 3rd ed. Rome: Université Grégorienne, 1965.

Fogelin, Robert. "A Reading of Aquinas's Five Ways." *American Philosophical Quarterly* 27 (1990): 305–14.

Ford, Lewis. "The Immutable God and Father Clarke." *New Scholasticism* 49 (1975): 189–99.

———. *The Lure of God.* Philadelphia: Fortress Press, 1978.

———. "Process and Thomist Views concerning Divine Perfection." In *Universe as Journey: Conversations with W. Norris Clarke, S.J.* Edited by Gerald A. McCool. New York: Fordham, 1988, 115–29.

———. "Temporality and Transcendence." In *Hartshorne, Process Philosophy and Theology.* Edited by Robert Kane and Stephen H. Phillips. Albany: State University of New York Press, 1989, 151–67.

———. "Thomas Aquinas and Contemporary Philosophical Options." *Listening* 14 (1979): 237–48.

Forgie, J. William. "The Cosmological and Ontological Arguments: How Saint Thomas Solved the Kantian Problem." *Religious Studies* 31 (1995): 89–100.

Fretheim, Terence E. *The Suffering God: An Old Testament Perspective.* Philadelphia: Fortress Press, 1984.

Frohnhofen, Herbert. *Apatheia tou Theou: Über die Affektlosigkeit Gottes in der griechischen Antike und bei den griechischsprachigen Kirchenvätern bis zu Gregorios Thaumaturgos.* Frankfurt am Main: Peter Lang, 1987.

Gale, Richard M. *On the Nature and Existence of God.* Cambridge: Cambridge University Press, 1991.

Galot, Jean. *Dieu souffre-t-il?* Paris: Lethielleux, 1976.

———. "La réalité de la souffrance de Dieu: Actualité du problème théologique." *Nouvelle revue théologique* 101 (1979): 224–45.

Gavrilyuk, Paul L. *The Suffering of the Impassible God: The Dialectics of Patristic Thought.* Oxford: Oxford University Press, 2004.

Geenen, Godefroid. "The Place of Tradition in the Theology of St. Thomas." *Thomist* 15 (1952): 110–35.

———. "Saint Thomas et les pères." In *Dictionnaire de théologie catholique.* Edited by A. Vacant et al. Paris: Librairie Letouzey et Ané, 1946, vol. 15/ 1, cols. 738–61.

Geffré, Claude. "Sens et non-sens d'une théologie non-métaphysique." *Concilium* 76 (1972): 89–98.

Geiger, Louis Bertrand. "Saint Thomas et la métaphysique d'Aristote." In *Aristote et saint Thomas d'Aquin.* Edited by P. Moraux et al. Louvain: Université de Louvain, 1957, 175–220.

Gersh, Stephen. *From Iamblichus to Eriugena: An Investigation of the Prehistory and Evolution of the Pseudo-Dionysian Tradition.* Studien zur Problemgeschichte der Antiken und Mittelalterlichen Philosophie, no. 8. Leiden: E. J. Brill, 1978.

Gerson, Lloyd P. "Aristotle's God of Motion." In *God and Greek Philosophy: Studies in the Early History of Natural Theology.* New York: Routledge, 1990, 82–141.

Gervais, Michel. "Incarnation et immutabilité divine." *Revue des sciences religieuses* 50 (1976): 215–43.

Gillon, Louis-B. "Dieu immobile et Dieu en mouvement." *Doctor Communis* 29 (1976): 135–45.

———. "Tristesse et miséricorde du Père." *Angelicum* 55 (1978): 3–11.

Gilson, Etienne. "Avicenne en occident au moyen âge." *Archives d'histoire doctrinale et littéraire du moyen âge* 36 (1969): 89–121.

———. *Being and Some Philosophers.* Toronto: Pontifical Institute of Mediaeval Studies, 1952.

———. *The Christian Philosophy of St. Thomas Aquinas.* New York: Random House, 1956.

———. *The Elements of Christian Philosophy.* New York: Mentor Books, 1963.

———. "L'être et Dieu." *Revue thomiste* 62 (1962): 181–202, 398–416.

———. *L'être et l'essence.* Paris: J. Vrin, 1948.

———. "Existence and Philosophy." *Proceedings of the American Catholic Philosophical Association* 21 (1946): 4–16.

———. *God and Philosophy.* New Haven: Yale University Press, 1946.

———. *Reason and Revelation in the Middle Ages.* New York: Charles Scribner's Sons, 1938.

———. *The Spirit of Medieval Philosophy.* New York: Charles Scribner's Sons, 1940.

———. *The Spirit of Thomism.* New York: P. J. Kenedy and Sons, 1964.

Goetz, Ronald. "The Suffering God: The Rise of a New Orthodoxy." *Christian Century* 103 (1986): 385–389.

Goris, Harm J. M. J. *Free Creatures of an Eternal God: Thomas Aquinas on God's Infallible Foreknowledge and Irresistible Will.* Leuven: Peeters, 1996.

Gornall, Thomas. *A Philosophy of God.* London: Darton, Longman, and Todd, 1962.

Grabmann, Martin. "Esencia y significacion del aristotelismo de santo Tomas de Aquino." *Ciencia Tomista* 67 (1944): 323–37.

Greshake, Gisbert. *Der Preis der Liebe: Besinnung über das Leid.* Freiburg: Herder, 1978.

Grillmeier, Alois. "Hellenisierung-Judaisierung des Christentums als Deuteprinzipien der Geschichte des kirchlichen Dogmas." *Scholastik* 33 (1958): 321–35, 528–58.

Gunton, Colin E. *Act and Being: Towards a Theology of the Divine Attributes.* Grand Rapids, Mich.: Eerdmans, 2003.

Gutenson, Charles E. "Does God Change?" In *God under Fire: Modern Scholarship Reinvents God.* Edited by Douglas S. Huffman and Eric L. Johnson. Grand Rapids, Mich.: Zondervan, 2002, 231–52.

Hallman, Joseph. *The Descent of God: Divine Suffering in History and Theology.* Minneapolis: Fortress Press, 1991.

———. "The Emotions of God in the Theology of St. Augustine." *Recherches de théologie ancienne et médiévale* 51 (1984): 5–19.

———. "The Mistake of Thomas Aquinas and the Trinity of A. N. Whitehead." *Journal of Religion* 70 (1990): 36–48.

———. "The Mutability of God: Tertullian to Lactantius." *Theological Studies* 42 (1981): 373–93.

Hankey, Wayne. "Aquinas and the Passion of God." In *Being and Truth: Essays in Honour of John Macquarrie.* Edited by A. Kee and E. Long. London: SCM Press, 1986, 318–33.

———. *God in Himself: Aquinas's Doctrine of God as Expounded in the Summa Theologiae.* New York: Oxford University Press, 1987.

———. "The Place of the Proof of God's Existence in the *Summa Theologiae* of Thomas Aquinas." *Thomist* 46 (1982): 370–93.

Harnack, Adolf von. *Lehrbuch der Dogmengeschichte.* 3 vols. Tübingen: Mohr, 1931.

Hartshorne, Charles. *Aquinas to Whitehead: Seven Centuries of Metaphysics of Religion.* Milwaukee, Wisc.: Marquette University Publications, 1976.

———. *Creative Synthesis and Philosophic Method.* London: SCM Press, 1970.

———. *The Divine Relativity.* New Haven: Yale University Press, 1964.

———. "Is Whitehead's God the God of Religion?" *Ethics* 53 (1942–43): 219–27.

———. *Man's Vision of God and the Logic of Theism.* Chicago: Willet, Clark, 1941.

———. *Reality as Social Process.* New York: Hafner, 1971.

———. "Redefining God." *New Humanist* 7, no. 4 (July 1934): 8–15.

———. "Reflections on the Strength and Weakness of Thomism." *Ethics* 54 (1943–44): 53–57.

———. "The Three Ideas of God." *Journal of Liberal Religion* 1, no. 3 (1940): 9–16.

———. "Two Levels of Faith and Reason." *Journal of Bible and Religion* 16 (1948): 30–38.

Hasker, William. "Does God Change?" In *Questions about God: Today's Philosophers Ponder the Divine.* Edited by Steven M. Cahn and David Shatz. Oxford: Oxford University Press, 2002, 137–45.

———. *God, Time, and Knowledge.* Ithaca, N.Y.: Cornell University Press, 1989.

———. "A Philosophical Perspective." In *The Openness of God: A Biblical Challenge to the Traditional Understanding of God.* Edited by Clark Pinnock et al. Downers Grove, Ill.: InterVarsity Press, 1999, 126–54.

Healy, Nicholas M. "Introduction." In *Aquinas on Scripture: An Introduction to His Biblical Commentaries.* Edited by Thomas G. Weinandy et al. London: T and T Clark, 2005, 1–20.

———. *Thomas Aquinas: Theologian of the Christian Life.* Burlington, Vt.: Ashgate, 2003.

Helm, Paul. *Eternal God: A Study of God without Time.* New York: Oxford University Press, 1988.

———. "The Impossibility of Divine Passibility." In *The Power and Weakness of God: Impassibility and Orthodoxy.* Edited by Nigel M. de S. Cameron. Edinburgh: Rutherford House Books, 1990, 119–40.

Henri-Rousseau, Jean-Marie. "L'être et l'agir." *Revue thomiste* 53 (1953): 488–531; 54 (1954): 267–97; 55 (1955): 85–118.

Hertog, Gerard. "The Prophetic Dimension of the Divine Name: On Exodus 3:14a and Its Context." *Catholic Biblical Quarterly* 64 (2002): 213–28.

Hibbs, Thomas S. *Dialectic and Narrative in Aquinas: An Interpretation of the Summa Contra Gentiles*. Notre Dame: University of Notre Dame Press, 1995.

Hill, William. "Does Divine Love Entail Suffering in God?" In *God and Temporality*. Edited by Bowman L. Clarke and Eugene T. Long. New York: Paragon, 1984, 55–71.

———. "Does God Know the Future? Aquinas and Some Moderns." *Theological Studies* 36 (1975): 3–18.

———. "Does the World Make a Difference to God?" *Thomist* 38 (1974): 146–64.

———. "The Historicity of God." *Theological Studies* 45 (1984): 320–33.

———. "The Implicate World: God's Oneness with Mankind as a Mediated Immediacy." In *Beyond Mechanism: The Universe in Recent Physics and Catholic Thought*. Edited by David L. Schindler. Lanham, Md.: University Press of America, 1986.

———. *Knowing the Unknown God*. New York: Philosophical Library, 1971.

———. Review of *God-Talk: An Examination of the Language and Logic of Theology*, by John Macquarrie. *Thomist* 32 (1968): 116–26.

———. "Seeking Foundations for Faith: Symbolism of Person or Metaphysics of Being?" *Thomist* 45 (1981): 219–42.

———. *The Three-Personed God: The Trinity as a Mystery of Salvation*. Washington, D.C.: The Catholic University of America Press, 1982.

———. "Two Gods of Love: Aquinas and Whitehead." *Listening* 14 (1979): 249–65.

Hoffman, Joshua, and Gary S. Rosenkrantz. *The Divine Attributes*. Oxford: Blackwell, 2002.

Hoffmann, Norbert. "The Crucified Christ and the World's Evil: Reflections on Theodicy in the Light of Atonement." *Communio* 17 (1990): 50–67.

Hoogland, Mark-Robin. *God, Passion and Power: Thomas Aquinas on Christ Crucified and the Almightiness of God*. Leuven: Peeters, 2003.

House, Francis. "The Barrier of Impassibility." *Theology* 83 (1980): 409–15.

Hübner, Reinhard M. *Der Gott der Kirchenväter und der Gott der Bibel: Zur Frage der Hellenisierung des Christentums*. Eichstätter Hochschulreden, no. 16. München: Minerva Publikation, 1979.

Huffman, Douglas S., and Eric L. Johnson. *God under Fire: Modern Scholarship Reinvents God*. Grand Rapids, Mich.: Zondervan, 2002.

Hügel, Baron Friedrich von. *Essays and Addresses on the Philosophy of Religion*. Second series. London: John Dent and Sons, 1951.

Hughes, Christopher. *On a Complex Theory of a Simple God: An Investigation in Aquinas's Philosophical Theology*. Ithaca, N.Y.: Cornell University Press, 1989.

Ivanka, Endre von. "S. Thomas platonisant." In *Tommaso d'Aquino nel suo settimo centenario*. Vol. 1, *Tommaso d'Aquino: nella storia del pensiero*. Part 1, *Le fonti del pensiero di S. Tommaso*. Napoli: Edizione Domenicane Italiane, 1975, 256–257.

Jansen, Henry. "Moltmann's View of God's (Im)mutability: The God of the Philosophers and the God of the Bible." *Neue Zeitschrift für systematische Theologie und Religionsphilosophie* 36 (1994): 284–301.

Jantzen, Grace. *God's World, God's Body*. Philadelphia: Westminster, 1984.

Jenkins, John. *Knowledge and Faith in Thomas Aquinas*. Cambridge: Cambridge University Press, 1997.

Jeremias, Jörg. *Die Reue Gottes: Aspekte alttestamentlicher Gottesvorstellung.* Biblische Studien, no. 65. Neukirchen-Vluyn: Neukirchener Verlag, 1975.

John Paul II. *Fides et Ratio: On the Relationship between Faith and Reason.* Encyclical Letter. Washington, D.C.: U.S. Catholic Conference, 1998.

———. *On the Christian Meaning of Human Suffering (Salvifici Doloris).* Apostolic Letter, Feb. 11, 1984. Washington, D.C.: U.S. Catholic Conference, 1984.

Johnson, Elizabeth A. *She Who Is: The Mystery of God in a Feminist Theological Discourse.* New York: Crossroad, 1992.

Jordan, Mark D. *Rewritten Theology: Aquinas after His Readers.* Oxford: Blackwell, 2006.

———. "Theology and Philosophy." In *The Cambridge Companion to Aquinas.* Edited by N. Kretzmann and E. Stump. Cambridge: Cambridge University Press, 1993, 232–51.

Jossua, Jean-Pierre. "L'axiome 'bonum diffusivum sui' chez s. Thomas d'Aquin." *Revue des sciences religieuses* 40 (1966): 127–53.

Judy, Albert. "Avicenna's *Metaphysics* in the *Summa Contra Gentiles.*" *Angelicum* 52 (1975): 340–84, 541–86; 53 (1976): 185–226.

Jüngel, Eberhard. *The Doctrine of the Trinity: God's Being Is in Becoming.* Translated by Scottish Academic Press, Ltd. Grand Rapids, Mich.: Eerdmans, 1976.

Kaiser, Walter C., Jr. *Malachi: God's Unchanging Love.* Grand Rapids, Mich.: Baker Book House, 1984.

Keller, James. "Basic Differences between Classical and Process Metaphysics and Their Implications for the Concept of God." *IPQ* 22 (1982): 3–20.

Kelly, Anthony. "God: How Near a Relation?" *Thomist* 34 (1970): 191–229.

———. "Trinity and Process: Relevance of the Basic Christian Confession of God." *Theological Studies* 31 (1970): 393–414.

Kerr, Fergus. *After Aquinas: Versions of Thomism.* Oxford: Blackwell, 2002.

———. "Theology in Philosophy: Revisiting the Five Ways." *International Journal for Philosophy of Religion* 50 (2001): 115–30.

Kierkegaard, Soren. "The Unchangeableness of God." In *Edifying Discourses: A Selection.* Edited by Paul L. Holmer. New York: Harper and Bros., 1958.

King, J. Norman, and Barry Whitney. "Rahner and Hartshorne on Divine Immutability." *IPQ* 22 (1982): 195–209.

Kitamori, Kazoh. *Theology of the Pain of God.* Richmond, Va.: John Knox Press, 1965.

Knasas, John. "Ad mentem Thomae: Does Natural Philosophy Prove God?" *Proceedings of the American Catholic Philosophical Association* 61 (1987): 209–20.

———. "Aquinas and Finite Gods." *Proceedings of the American Catholic Philosophical Association* 53 (1979): 88–97.

———. "Aquinas: Prayer to an Immutable God." *New Scholasticism* 57 (1983): 196–221.

Kocher, Richard. *Herausgeforderter Vorsehungsglaube. Die Lehre von der Vorsehung im Horizont der gegenwärtigen Theologie.* St. Ottilien: EOS Verlag, 1993.

Kondoleon, Theodore. "The Immutability of God: Some Recent Challenges." *New Scholasticism* 58 (1984): 293–315.

Krempel, A. *Le Doctrine de la relation chez saint Thomas.* Paris: J. Vrin, 1952.

Kretzmann, Norman. *The Metaphysics of Theism: Aquinas's Natural Theology in Summa contra gentiles I.* Oxford: Clarendon Press, 1997.

LaCugna, Catherine Mowry. *God for Us: The Trinitiy and Christian Life.* San Francisco: Harper, 1992.

———. "The Relational God: Aquinas and Beyond." *Theological Studies* 46 (1985): 647–63.

Laktanz. *Vom Zorne Gottes.* Edited by H. Kraft and A. Wlosok. Darmstadt: Wissenschaftliche Buchgesellschaft, 1974.

Lambert, Richard. "A Textual Study of Aquinas's Comparison of the Intellect to Primary Matter." *New Scholasticism* 56 (1982): 80–99.

Langevin, Giles. "L'action immanente d'après saint Thomas d'Aquin." *Laval théologique et philosophique* 30 (1974): 251–66.

Langslet, Lars Roar. "La conversion de Sigrid Undset." *Revue des sciences religieuses* 40 (1966): 240–57.

Laso Gonzales, José M. "La idea del motor inmovil a partir de las doctrinas fundamentales de Aristóteles." *Salmanticensis* 15 (1968): 351–78.

Lee, Chung Young. *The Suffering God: A Systematic Inquiry into a Concept of Divine Passibility.* Ann Arbor, Mich.: University Microfilms, 1968.

Lee, Jung Young. "Can God Be Change Itself?" *Journal of Ecumenical Studies* 10 (1973): 752–70.

Levering, Matthew. *Scripture and Metaphysics: Aquinas and the Renewal of Trinitarian Theology.* Oxford: Blackwell, 2004.

Lewis, C. S. *The Chronicles of Narnia.* Vol. 7, *The Last Battle.* New York: Collier Books, 1975.

———. *The Four Loves.* New York: Harcourt, Brace, Jovanovich, 1960.

Litt, Thomas. *Les corps célestes dans l'univers de saint Thomas d'Aquin.* Louvain: Publications Universitaires, 1963.

Loftus, J. V. "The God of Aristotle and St. Thomas." *Modern Schoolman* 11 (1934): 42–44.

Luyten, Norbert A. "Der Begriff der Materia Prima nach Thomas von Aquin." In *La philosophie de la nature de saint Thomas d'Aquin.* Studi Tomistici, no. 18. Edited by Léon Elders. Vatican City: Libreria Vaticana, 1982, 28–44.

———. "Der erste Weg: *Ex parte motus.*" In *Quinque sunt viae.* Studi Tomistici, no. 9. Edited by Léon Elders. Vatican City: Libreria Vaticana, 1980, 29–41.

———. "Matter as Potency." In *The Concept of Matter.* Edited by E. McMullin. Notre Dame, Ind.: University of Notre Dame Press, 1963, 122–33, 136–39.

Maas, Wilhelm. *Unveränderlichkeit Gottes: Zum Verhältnis von griechisch-philosophischer und christlicher Gotteslehre.* München: F. Schöningh, 1974.

MacDonald, Scott. "Aquinas's Parasitic Cosmological Argument." *Medieval Philosophy and Theology* 1 (1991): 119–55.

Mackintosh, Robert. *Historic Theories of Atonement.* London: Hodder and Stroughton, 1920.

Macquarrie, John. *The Humility of God.* Philadelphia: Westminster, 1978.

Mahoney, John. *Charles Hartshorne's Dipolar Conception of God.* Grand Prairie, Tex.: Scholars Guild, 1974.

Maritain, Jacques. "Quelques réflexions sur le savoir théologique." *Revue thomiste* 69 (1969): 5–27.

———. *Réflexions sur l'intelligence et sur sa vie propre.* Paris: Desclée de Brouwer, 1930.

Mascall, Eric L. *He Who Is: A Study in Traditional Theism.* London: Longmans, Green, 1945.

———. *The Openness of Being: Natural Theology Today.* London: Darton, Longman, and Todd, 1971.

Maurer, Armand. "St. Thomas on the Sacred Name 'Tetragrammaton' (Yahweh)." *Mediaeval Studies* 34 (1972): 275–86.

McCabe, Herbert. "The Involvement of God." *New Blackfriars* 66 (1985): 464–76.

McFague, Sallie. *Models of God: Theology for an Ecological, Nuclear Age.* Philadelphia: Fortress, 1987.

McInerny, Ralph. *Aquinas and Analogy.* Washington, D.C.: The Catholic University of America Press, 1996.

McNamara, Martin. "Process Thought and Some Biblical Evidence." In *Charles Hartshorne's Concept of God: Philosophical and Theological Responses.* Edited by Santiago Sia. Dordrecht: Kluwer, 1990, 197–218.

McNiff, James F. "Aristotle's Argument from Motion." *IPQ* 32 (1992): 313–23.

McWilliams, Warren. "Divine Suffering in Contemporary Theology." *Scottish Journal of Theology* 33 (1980): 35–53.

———. *The Passion of God: Divine Suffering in Contemporary Protestant Theology.* Macon, Ga.: Mercer University Press, 1985.

Meessen, Frank. *Unveränderlichkeit und Menschwerdung Gottes: Eine theologiegeschichtlich-systematische Untersuchung.* Freiburg: Herder, 1989.

Merlan, Philip. "Aristotle's Unmoved Movers." *Traditio* 4 (1946): 1–30.

Michael, Chester P. *A Comparison of the God-Talk of Thomas Aquinas and Charles Hartshorne.* Ann Arbor, Mich.: University Microfilms, 1975.

Milano, Andrea. "Il 'divenire di Dio' in Hegel, Kierkegaard, e san Tommaso d'Aquino." In *San Tommaso e il pensiero moderno.* Studi Tomistici, no. 3. Vatican City: Libreria Vaticana, 1976, 284–94.

Miller, Barry. *A Most Unlikely God: A Philosophical Enquiry into the Nature of God.* Notre Dame, Ind.: University of Notre Dame Press, 1996.

Moberly, R. W. L. "'God Is Not a Human That He Should Repent' (Numbers 23:19 and 1 Samuel 15:29)." In *God in the Fray: A Tribute to Walter Brueggemann.* Edited by Tod Linafelt and Timothy K. Beal. Minneapolis: Fortress, 1998, 112–23.

Moltmann, Jürgen. "The Crucified God: A Trinitarian Theology of the Cross." *Interpretation* 26 (1972): 278–99.

———. *The Crucified God.* Translated by R. Wilson and J. Bowden. New York: Harper and Row, 1974.

———. *History and the Triune God: Contributions to Trinitarian Theology.* New York: Crossroad, 1992.

———. *The Trinity and the Kingdom.* San Francisco: Harper and Row, 1981.

Mooney, Christopher F. *Theology and Scientific Knowledge: Changing Models of God's Presence in the World.* Notre Dame, Ind.: University of Notre Dame Press, 1995.

Moreno, Antonio. "Generation and Corruption: Prime Matter and Substantial Form." *Angelicum* 57 (1980): 54–76.

———. "The Law of Inertia and the Principle 'Quidquid movetur ab alio movetur.'" *Thomist* 38 (1974): 306–31.

Moskop, John C. *Divine Omniscience and Human Freedom: Thomas Aquinas and Charles Hartshorne.* Macon, Ga.: Mercer University Press, 1984.

Mozley, John K. *The Impassibility of God: A Survey of Christian Thought.* New York: Macmillan, 1927.

Mühlen, Heribert. *Die Veränderlichkeit Gottes als Horizont einer zukünftigen Christologie.* Münster: Verlag A. Schendorff, 1969.

Muller, Earl. "Real Relations and the Divine: Issues in Thomas's Understanding of God's Relation to the World." *Theological Studies* 56 (1995): 673–95.

Muller, Richard A. "Incarnation, Mutability, and the Case for Classical Theism." *Westminster Theological Journal* 45 (1983): 22–40.

Nichols, Aidan. *Discovering Aquinas: An Introduction to His Life, Work and Influence.* Grand Rapids, Mich.: Eerdmans, 2002.

Nicolas, Jean-Hervé. "L'acte pur de saint Thomas et le Dieu vivant de l'évangile." *Angelicum* 51 (1974): 511–32.

———. "Aimante et bienheureuse Trinité." *Revue thomiste* 78 (1978): 271–92.

———. "La souffrance de Dieu?" *Nova et vetera* 53 (1978): 56–64.

Nnamani, Amuluche Gregory. *The Paradox of a Suffering God: On the Classical, Modern-Western and Third World Struggles to Harmonize the Incompatible Attributes of the Trinitarian God.* New York: Peter Lang, 1995.

Noblesse-Rocher, Annie. "Le nom et l'être de Dieu (Exode 3, 14) selon Thomas d'Aquin et Martin Bucer." *Revue d'histoire et de philosophie religieuses* 81 (2001): 425–47.

Nugent, Francis. "Immanent Action in St. Thomas and Aristotle." *New Scholasticism* 37 (1963): 164–87.

O'Donnell, John J. *The Mystery of the Triune God.* London: Sheed and Ward, 1988.

Oeing-Hanhoff, Ludger. "Die Krise des Gottesbegriffs." *Theologische Quartalschrift* 159 (1979): 285–303.

Ogden, Shubert M. *The Reality of God and Other Essays.* New York: Harper and Row, 1966.

O'Hanlon, Gerard F. *The Immutability of God in the Theology of Hans Urs von Balthasar.* Cambridge: Cambridge University Press, 1990.

Oliver, Simon. *Philosophy, God and Motion.* New York: Routledge, 2005.

O'Meara, Thomas F. *Thomas Aquinas: Theologian.* Notre Dame, Ind.: University of Notre Dame Press, 1997.

O'Neill, Colman E. "Analogy, Dialectic, and Inter-confessional Theology." *Thomist* 47 (1983): 43–65.

———. "La prédication analogique: l'élément négatif." In *Analogie et dialectique: Essais de théologie fondamentale.* Edited by J. L. Marion et al. Geneva: Labor et Fides, 1982.

———. *Sacramental Realism: A General Theory of the Sacraments.* Wilmington, Del.: Michael Glazier, 1983.

O'Rourke, Fran. *Pseudo-Dionysius and the Metaphysics of Aquinas.* Leiden: E. J. Brill, 1992.

Owens, Joseph. "Aquinas and the Proof from the Physics." *Mediaeval Studies* 28 (1966): 119–50.

———. "Aquinas as Aristotelian Commentator." In *St. Thomas Aquinas 1274–1974: Commemorative Studies.* Edited by A. Maurer et al. Toronto: Pontifical Institute of Mediaeval Studies, 1974, 1:213–38.

———. "Aquinas—Existential Permanence and the Flux." *Mediaeval Studies* 31 (1969): 71–92.

———. *The Doctrine of Being in the Aristotelian Metaphysics.* Toronto: Pontifical Institute of Mediaeval Studies, 1951.

———. "Immobility and Existence for Aquinas." In *St. Thomas Aquinas on the Existence of God: The Collected Papers of Joseph Owens.* Edited by John Catan. Albany: State University of New York Press, 1980, 208–27.

Pannenberg, Wolfhart. "Die Aufnahme des philosophischen Gottesbegriffs als dogmatischer Problem der frühchristlichen Theologie." In *Grundfragen systematischer Theologie.* Göttingen: Vandenhoeck and Ruprecht, 1967, 296–346.

Paulus, Jean. "La théorie du premier moteur chez Aristote." *Revue de philosophie* 33 (1933): 259–94, 394–424.

Peacocke, Arthur. *Theology for a Scientific Age: Being and Becoming—Natural, Divine and Human.* Minneapolis: Fortress Press, 1993.

Pegis, Anton. "Penitus manet ignotum." *Mediaeval Studies* 27 (1965): 212–26.

———. *St. Thomas and Philosophy.* Milwaukee, Wisc.: Marquette University Press, 1964.

———. *St. Thomas and the Greeks.* Milwaukee, Wisc.: Marquette University Press, 1951.

Pelikan, Jaroslav. *The Christian Tradition.* Vol. 1, *The Emergence of the Catholic Tradition (100–600).* Chicago: University of Chicago Press, 1971.

———. *The Christian Tradition.* Vol. 3, *The Growth of Medieval Theology.* Chicago: University of Chicago Press, 1978.

Pfeil, Hans. "Die Frage nach der Veränderlichkeit und Geschichtlichkeit Gottes." *Münchener theologische Zeitschrift* 31 (1980): 1–23.

Phelan, Gerald Bernard. *Selected Papers.* Toronto: Pontifical Institute of Mediaeval Studies, 1967.

Phillips, Anthony, and Lucy Phillips. "The Origin of 'I Am' in Exodus 3:14." *Journal for the Study of the Old Testament* 78 (1998): 81–84.

Pieper, Josef. *Guide to Thomas Aquinas.* New York: Mentor Books, 1962.

Pinnock, Clark H. *Most Moved Mover: A Theology of God's Openness.* Grand Rapids, Mich.: Baker Books, 2001.

———. "Systematic Theology." In *The Openness of God: A Biblical Challenge to the Traditional Understanding of God.* Edited by Clark Pinnock et al. Downers Grove, Ill.: InterVarsity Press, 1999, 101–25.

Pittenger, Norman. *Catholic Faith in a Process Perspective.* Maryknoll, N.Y.: Orbis Books, 1981.

Placher, William C. *The Domestication of Transcendence: How Modern Thinking about God Went Wrong.* Louisville, Ky.: Westminster John Knox Press, 1996.

Quinn, John. "Triune Self-giving: One Key to the Problem of Suffering." *Thomist* 44 (1980): 173–218.

Rahner, Karl. "Bemerkungen zur Gotteslehre in der katholischen Dogmatik." In *Schriften zur Theologie.* Einsiedeln: Benziger, 1967, 8:165–86.

———. *Foundations of Christian Faith.* Translated by W. Dych. New York: Seabury, 1978.

———. "Probleme der Christologie von Heute." In *Schriften zur Theologie.* Einsiedeln: Benziger, 1958, 1:269–22.

———. "Selbstmitteilung Gottes." In *Sacramentum Mundi.* Edited by K. Rahner and A. Darlap. Freiburg: Herder, 1969, vol. 4, cols. 521–26.

———. "Theologische Bemerkungen zum Zeitbegriff." In *Schriften zur Theologie.* Einsiedeln: Benziger, 1970, 9:302–22.

———. *The Trinity.* New York: Crossroad, 1997.

———. "Zur Theologie der Menschwerdung." In *Schriften zur Theologie.* Einsiedeln: Benziger, 1960, 4:135–56.

Ratzinger, Joseph. "Foi, philosophie et théologie." In *Eglise et théologie.* Paris: Editions Mame, 1992, 15–36.

———. *Introduction to Christianity.* Translated by Michael J. Miller. San Francisco: Ignatius Press, 2004.

———. *The Nature and Mission of Theology: Essays to Orient Theology in Today's Debates.* Translated by Adrian Walker. San Francisco: Ignatius, 1995.

———. *Truth and Tolerance: Christian Belief and World Religions.* San Francisco: Ignatius Press, 2004.

Reichmann, James B. "Aquinas, God and Historical Process." In *Tommaso d'Aquino nel suo settimo centenario.* Vol. 9, *Il cosmo e la scienza.* Napoli: Edizioni Domenicane Italiane, 1978, 427–36.

———. "Immanently Transcendent and Subsistent *Esse:* A Comparison." *Thomist* 38 (1974): 332–69.

Reid, Duncan. "Without Parts or Passions? The Suffering God in Anglican Thought." *Pacifica: Australian Theological Studies* 4 (1991): 257–72.

Reitan, Eric A. "Aquinas and Weisheipl: Aristotle's Physics and the Existence of God." In *Philosophy and the God of Abraham: Essays in Memory of James A. Weisheipl, O.P.* Edited by R. James Long. Toronto: Pontifical Institute of Mediaeval Studies, 1991, 179–90.

Rice, Richard. "Biblical Support for a New Perspective." In *The Openness of God: A Biblical Challenge to the Traditional Understanding of God.* Edited by Clark Pinnock et al. Downers Grove, Ill.: InterVarsity Press, 1999, 11–58.

Richards, Jay Wesley. *The Untamed God: A Philosophical Exploration of Divine Perfection, Simplicity and Immutability.* Downers Grove, Ill.: InterVarsity Press, 2003.

Rickaby, Joseph. *Of God and His Creatures: An Annotated Translation (with Some Abridgement) of the Summa contra Gentiles of Saint Thomas Aquinas.* London: Burns and Oates, 1905. Reprint, Westminster, Md.: Carroll Press, 1950.

Robinson, Michael D. *Eternity and Freedom: A Critical Analysis of Divine Timelessness as a Solution to the Foreknowledge/Free Will Debate.* Lanham, Md.: University Press of America, 1995.

Rocca, Gregory. *Speaking the Incomprehensible God: Thomas Aquinas on the Interplay of Positive and Negative Theology.* Washington, D.C.: The Catholic University of America Press, 2004.

Rogers, Katherin A. *Perfect Being Theology.* Edinburgh: Edinburgh University Press, 2000.

Rossner, William. "Towards an Analysis of 'God Is Love.'" *Thomist* 38 (1973): 633–67.

Rousseau, Mary. "Process Thought and Traditional Theism: A Critique." *Modern Schoolman* 62 (1985): 45–64.

Rowe, William V. "Adolf von Harnack and the Concept of Hellenization." In *Hellenization Revisited: Shaping a Christian Response within the Greco-Roman World.* Edited by Wendy E. Helleman. Lanham, Md.: University Press of America, 1994, 69–98.

Sacchi, Mario Enrique. "El Dios inmutable de la filosofía perenne y de la fe Católica." *Doctor Communis* 42 (1989): 243–73.

Sarot, Marcel. *God, Passibility and Corporeality.* Kampen: Kok Pharos Publishing House, 1992.

———. "A Moved Mover? The (Im)passibility of God." In *Understanding the Attributes of God.* Edited by Gijsbert van den Brink and Marcel Sarot. Frankfurt: Peter Lang, 1999, 119–37.

Schaab, Gloria L. *The Creative Suffering of the Triune God: An Evolutionary Theology.* New York: Oxford University Press, 2007.

———. "The Creative Suffering of the Triune God: an Evolutionary Panentheistic Paradigm." *Theology and Science* 5 (2007): 289–305.

———. "A Procreative Paradigm of the Creative Suffering of the Triune God: Implications of Arthur Peacocke's Evolutionary Theology." *Theological Studies* 67 (2006): 542–66.

Scheffczyk, Leo. "Die Frage nach der Hellenisierung des Christentums unter modernem Problemaspekt." *Münchener theologische Zeitschrift* 33 (1982): 195–205.

———. "Prozesstheismus und christlicher Gottesglaube." *Münchener theologische Zeitschrift* 35 (1984): 81–104.

———. *Tendenzen und Brennpunkte der neueren Problematik um die Hellenisierung des Christentums.* München: Bayerische Akademie der Wissenschaften, 1982.

Schillebeeckx, Edward. "Die Heiligung des Namens Gottes durch die Menschenliebe Jesu des Christus." In *Gott in Welt.* Edited by H. Vorgrimler et al. Freiburg: Herder, 1964, 2:43–91.

———. *Jesus: An Experiment in Christology.* Translated by H. Hoskins. New York: Seabury, 1979.

Schilling, S. Paul. *God and Human Anguish.* Nashville: Abingdon, 1977.

Schindler, David. "Creativity as Ultimate: Reflections on Actuality in Whitehead, Aristotle and Aquinas." *IPQ* 13 (1973): 161–71.

———. "Whitehead's Challenge to Thomism on the Problem of God: The Metaphysical Issues." *IPQ* 19 (1979) 285–300.

Schönberger, Rolf. *Thomas von Aquins Summa Contra Gentiles.* Darmstadt: Wissenschaftliche Buchgesellschaft, 2001.

Schoonenberg, Piet. "God as Relating and (Be)coming: A Meta-Thomistic Consideration." *Listening* 14 (1979): 265–78.

———. "Process or History in God?" *Louvain Studies* 4 (1973) 303–19.

Schütz, Ludwig. *Thomas-Lexikon.* Paderborn: F. Schöningh, 1895.

Schulte, Raphael. "Unveränderlichkeit Gottes." In *Lexikon für Theologie und Kirche.* Edited by J. Höfer and K. Rahner. Freiburg: Herder, 1965, vol. 10, cols. 536–37.

Seidl, Horst. "De l'immutabilité de Dieu dans l'acte de la création et dans la relation avec les hommes." *Revue thomiste* 87 (1987): 615–29.

Shanley, Brian. "Commentary." In Thomas Aquinas, *The Treatise on the Divine Nature: Summa Theologiae I, 1–13.* Translated by Brian Shanley. Indianapolis: Hackett Publishing, 2006, 152–354.

———. *The Thomist Tradition.* Dordrecht: Kluwer Academic Publishers, 2002.

Sherwin, Michael S. *By Knowledge and by Love: Charity and Knowledge in the Moral Theology of St. Thomas Aquinas.* Washington, D.C.: The Catholic University of America Press, 2005.

Simon, Yves. *Introduction à l'ontologie du connaître.* Paris: Desclée de Brouwer, 1934.

Simonis, Walter. "Über das 'Werden' Gottes: Gedanken zum Begriff der ökonomischen Trinität." *Münchener theologische Zeitschrift* 33 (1982): 133–39.

Sobrino, Jon. *Jesus the Liberator: A Historical-Theological Reading of Jesus of Nazareth.* Maryknoll, N.Y.: Orbis Books, 1993.

Spicq, Ceslas. "Saint Thomas d'Aquin, exégète." *Dictionnaire de théologie catholique.* Edited by A. Vacant et al. Paris: Librairie Letouzey et Ané, 1946, vol. 15/ 1, cols. 694–738.

Stacer, John. "Integrating Thomistic and Whiteheadian Perspectives on God." *IPQ* 21 (1981): 355–77.

Stokes, Walter. "God for Today and Tomorrow." *New Scholasticism* 43 (1969): 351–78.

———. "Is God Really Related to This World?" *Proceedings of the American Catholic Philosophical Association* 39 (1965): 145–51.

———. "Whitehead's Challenge to Theistic Realism." *New Scholasticism* 38 (1964): 1–21.

Stump, Eleonore. *Aquinas.* New York: Routledge, 2003.

Stump, Eleonore, and Norman Kretzmann. "Eternity." *Journal of Philosophy* 78 (1981): 429–58.

———. "God's Knowledge and Its Causal Efficacy." In *The Rationality of Belief and the Plurality of Faith: Essays in Honor of William P. Alston.* Edited by Thomas D. Senor. Ithaca: Cornell University Press, 1995, 94–124.

Suchocki, Marjorie Hewitt. *The End of Evil: Process Eschatology in Historical Context.* New York: State University of New York Press, 1989.

Sullivan, Thomas D. "Omniscience, Immutability and the Divine Mode of Knowing." *Faith and Philosophy* 8 (1991): 21–35.

Swinburne, Richard. *The Coherence of Theism.* Oxford: Clarendon Press, 1986.

Taliaferro, Charles. "The Passibility of God." *Religious Studies* 25 (1989): 217–24.

Taylor, Richard C. "Faith and Reason, Religion and Philosophy: Four Views from Medieval Islam and Christianity." In *Philosophy and the God of Abraham.* Edited by R. James Long. Toronto: Pontifical Institute of Mediaeval Studies, 1991, 217–33.

Temple, William. *Christus Veritas.* London: Macmillan, 1924.

Teresa of Avila. *Obras Completas.* Edited by Efren de la Madre de Dios and Otger Steggink. Madrid: Biblioteca de Autores Cristianos, 1967.

Teske, Robert. "Divine Immutability in Saint Augustine." *Modern Schoolman* 63 (1986): 233–50.

Tomkinson, John L. "Divine Sempiternity and Atemporality." *Religious Studies* 18 (1982): 177–89.

Tonquédec, Joseph de. *Questions de cosmologie et de physique chez Aristote et saint Thomas.* Paris: J. Vrin, 1950.

Torrell, Jean-Pierre. *Aquinas's Summa: Background, Structure and Reception.* Translated by Benedict M. Guevin. Washington, D.C.: The Catholic University of America Press, 2005.

———. *Saint Thomas Aquinas.* Translated by Robert Royal. 2 vols. Washington, D.C.: The Catholic University of America Press, 1996, 2003.

Tracy, Thomas F. "The Moral Perfections of God." *Thomist* 47 (1983): 473–500.

Trethowan, Illtyd. "A Changing God." *Downside Review* 84 (1966): 247–61.

———. "God's Changelessness." *Clergy Review* 64 (1979): 15–21.

Tugwell, Simon. "Spirituality and Negative Theology." *New Blackfriars* 68 (1987): 257–63.

Turner, Denys. *Faith, Reason, and the Existence of God.* Oxford: Cambridge University Press, 2004.

———. "On Denying the Right God: Aquinas on Atheism and Idolatry." *Modern Theology* 20 (2004): 141–61.

Twetten, David. "Clearing a 'Way' for Aquinas: How the Proof from Motion Concludes to God." *Proceedings of the American Catholic Philosophical Association* 70 (1996): 259–78.

———. "Why Motion Requires a Cause: The Foundation for a Prime Mover in Aristotle and Aquinas." In *Philosophy and the God of Abraham: Essays in Memory of James A. Weisheipl, O.P.* Edited by R. James Long. Toronto: Pontifical Institute of Mediaeval Studies, 1991, 235–54.

Vacek, Edward Collins. *Love, Human and Divine: The Heart of Christian Ethics.* Washington, D.C.: Georgetown University Press, 1994.

Valkenberg, Wilhelmus. *Words of the Living God: Place and Function of Holy Scripture in the Theology of St. Thomas Aquinas.* Leuven: Peeters, 2000.

Van Hove, Alois. "De immutabilitate Dei." *Collectanea Mechliniensia* 7 (1933): 42–47.

Van Steenberghen, Fernand. *La philosophie au XIIIe siècle.* Philosophes médiévaux, no. 9. Louvain: Publications Universitaires, 1966.

———. "Connaissance divine et liberté humaine." *Revue théologique de Louvain* 2 (1979): 46–68.

———. *Le problème de l'existence de Dieu dans les écrits de s. Thomas d'Aquin.* Philosophes médiévaux, no. 23. Louvain: Editions de l'Institut Supérieur de Philosophie, 1980.

———. *Thomas Aquinas and Radical Aristotelianism.* Washington, D.C.: The Catholic University of America Press, 1980.

Vann, Gerald. *The Pain of Christ and the Sorrow of God.* Oxford: Blackfriars Publications, 1947. Reprint, New York: Alba House, 2000.

Varillon, François. *La souffrance de Dieu.* Paris: Seuil, 1975.

Vaux, Roland de. *Histoire ancienne d'Israel.* Paris: Librairie Lecoffre, 1971.

Velde, Rudi A. Te. *Participation and Substantiality in Thomas Aquinas.* New York: Brill, 1995.

Vos, Antonie. "Always on Time: On God's Immutability." In *Understanding the Attributes of God.* Edited by Gijsbert van den Brink and Marcel Sarot. Frankfurt: Peter Lang, 1999, 53–73.

Wallace, William. "Appendix 3: Ancient and Medieval Astronomy," and "Appendix 9: "Hexaemeron." In *Summa Theologiae.* Edited by T. Gilby. London: Eyre and Spottiswoode, 1967, 10:182–87, 219–24.

———. "Aquinas and Newton on the Causality of Nature and of God: The Medieval and Modern

Problematic." In *Philosophy and the God of Abraham: Essays in Memory of James A. Weisheipl, O.P.* Edited by R. James Long. Toronto: Pontifical Institute of Medieval Studies, 1991, 255–79.

———. "The Cosmological Argument: A Reappraisal." *Proceedings of the American Catholic Philosophical Association* 46 (1972): 3–57.

Weinandy, Thomas G. "Aquinas and the Incarnational Act: 'Become' as a Mixed Relation." *Doctor Communis* 22 (1979): 15–31.

———. *Does God Change? The Word's Becoming in the Incarnation.* Still River, Mass.: St. Bede's Publications, 1985.

———. *Does God Suffer?* Notre Dame, Ind.: University of Notre Dame Press, 2000.

———. "Does God Suffer?" *First Things* no. 117 (November 2001): 35–41.

Weisheipl, James A. "The Commentary of St. Thomas on the *De Caelo* of Aristotle." *Sapientia* 29 (1974): 11–34.

———. *Friar Thomas D'Aquino: His Life, Thought, and Works.* Oxford: Blackwell, 1975.

———. "Thomas's Evaluation of Plato and Aristotle." *New Scholasticism* 48 (1974): 100–124.

Wheeler, David L. "Toward a Process-Relational Christian Eschatology." *Process Studies* 22 (1993): 227–37.

Whitehead, Alfred North. *Adventures of Ideas.* New York: Free Press, 1967.

———. *Process and Reality.* Corrected Edition. Edited by D. Griffen and D. Sherburne. New York: Free Press, 1978.

Wild, John. "The Divine Existence: An Answer to Mr. Hartshorne." *Review of Metaphysics* 4 (1950): 61–84.

———. Review of *The Divine Relativity*, by Charles Hartshorne. *Review of Metaphysics* 2 (1948): 65–77.

Wilken, Robert Louis. *The Spirit of Early Christian Thought: Seeking the Face of God.* New Haven: Yale University Press, 2003.

Williams, Daniel Day. *The Spirit and the Forms of Love.* New York: Harper and Row, 1968.

Wippel, John F. *Metaphysical Themes in Thomas Aquinas II.* Washington, D.C.: The Catholic University of America Press, 2007.

———. *The Metaphysical Thought of Thomas Aquinas: From Finite Being to Uncreated Being.* Washington, D.C.: The Catholic University of America Press, 2000.

Wolterstorff, Nicholas. "Does God Suffer?" In *Questions about God: Today's Philosophers Ponder the Divine.* Edited by Steven M. Cahn and David Shatz. New York: Oxford University Press, 2002.

———. "Suffering Love." In *Philosophy and the Christian Faith.* Edited by Thomas V. Morris. Notre Dame, Ind.: University of Notre Dame Press, 1988, 196–237.

Woolcombe, K. J. "The Pain of God." *Scottish Journal of Theology* 20 (1967): 129–48.

Wright, John. "Divine Knowledge and Human Freedom: The God Who Dialogues." *Theological Studies* 38 (1977): 450–77.

———. "The Method of Process Theology: An Evaluation." *Communio* 6 (1979): 38–55.

Yates, John C. *The Timelessness of God.* Lanham, Md.: University Press of America, 1990.

Young, William W. "From Describing to Naming God: Correlating the Five Ways with Aquinas's Doctrine of the Trinity." *New Blackfriars* 85 (2004): 527–41.

Zimmermann, Otto. *Der immergleiche Gott.* Freiburg: Herder, 1920.

Zoffoli, Enrico. *Mistero della sofferenza di Dio? Il pensiero di S. Tommaso.* Studi Tomistici, no. 34. Vatican City: Pontificia Accademia di S. Tommaso, 1988.

Index of Texts of Thomas Aquinas on Divine Motion and Immutability

*Texts referring to the ways motion may be attributed
to God are marked with an asterisk (*).*

Index of Names

Aben, Tersur Akuma, 201n171, 247
Absolon of St. Victor, 123
Albert the Great, 20
Althaus, P., 199
Anawati, Georges, 133n340, 247
Anderson, James F., 117n246, 247
Apollinaris, 199, 201n177, 247
Arias Reyero, Maximo, 106n179, 110n211, 111n216
Aristotle, 9–10, 17, 19–21, 26, 31n174, 33, 47, 48n10, 59–62, 64, 66–69, 71–74, 82–90, 92–93, 113, 121, 123–32, 161, 213, 246, 247
Augustine, St., 1, 14, 47–48, 52, 76, 101, 112, 115, 119–21, 124, 195, 199n165, 247
Averroes, 48n10, 59
Avicenna, 59, 72–73, 82, 126–27, 131

Balthasar, Hans Urs von, 199, 222n93, 247
Bañez, Dominicus, 179n75, 247
Barbour, Ian, 4n12, 247
Barth, Karl, 114, 115n234, 151n435, 153, 247
Basil, St., 112
Basinger, David, 197n156, 247
Bauckham, Richard, 114n230, 248
Beeck, Frans Jozef van, 213n47, 248
Beek, A. van de, 109, 110n207, 248
Blocher, Henri, 190n133, 221n91, 248
Bobik, Joseph, 189n126, 248
Boff, Leonardo, 4n12, 248
Boissard, Guy, 155n450, 248
Bracken, Joseph A., 197n156, 248
Brantschen, Johannes B., 115n235, 124n283, 149n428, 153n443, 221n92, 248

Brito, Emilio, 2, 160n471, 248
Brown, Robert, 187, 118n118, 248
Brümmer, Vincent, 210, 211n35, 248
Brunn, Émilie zum, 119n259, 248
Buckley, Michael, 62n54, 248
Burrell, David B., 118n248, 133n340, 148n423, 163n14, 191n134, 248
Busa, Robert 3n9, 246, 248

Cahn, Stephen M., 147n417, 185n99, 190n130, 248, 253, 263
Chenu, Marie-Dominique, 51n16, 53n24, 68n74, 106n179, 107n195, 113n225, 123n275, 124n284, 131n322, 248
Chisholm, Robert, 109, 248
Christmann, Heinrich Maria, 149, 249
Clark, Kelly James, 153n443, 249
Clark, Mary T., 120n262, 249
Clarke, W. Norris, 127nn307–8, 129n315, 130n318, 149n428, 156n455, 168n38, 175n65, 176–77, 195n149, 249
Claudel, Paul, 153, 249
Clavell, Luis, 130n321, 249
Cobb, John B., 147n417, 249
Colish, Marcia L., 131n329, 249
Congar, Yves, 110n213, 249
Cooke, Bernard, 120n262, 122n267, 249
Cooper, Burton Z., 167n37, 249
Craig, William Lane, 170n47, 181, 185, 187n115, 193, 249
Creel, Richard E., 185, 222n94, 225, 250
Crouzel, Henri, 112n218, 250

The Unchanging God of Love: Thomas Aquinas and Contemporary Theology on Divine Immutability was designed and typeset in Vendetta by Kachergis Book Design of Pittsboro, North Carolina. It was printed on 50-pound Natural and bound by United Graphics of Mattoon, Illinois.